THE KEYS TO
AVALON

THE KEYS TO

AVALON

THE TRUE LOCATION OF
ARTHUR'S KINGDOM
REVEALED

STEVE BLAKE and SCOTT LLOYD
with John Baldock

ELEMENT

Shaftesbury, Dorset • Boston, Massachusetts • Melbourne, Victoria

© Element Books Limited 2000
Text © Steve Blake & Scott Lloyd 2000

First published in the UK in 2000 by
Element Books Limited
Shaftesbury, Dorset SP7 8BP

Published in the USA in 2000 by
Element Books, Inc.
160 North Washington Street,
Boston, MA 02114

Published in Australia in 2000 by
Element Books and distributed
by Penguin Books Australia Ltd
487 Maroondah Highway, Ringwood,
Victoria 3134

Cover illustration and design by The Bridgewater Book Company
Maps by Richard Constable
Designed and typeset by
THE BRIDGEWATER BOOK COMPANY
Printed and bound in Great Britain by Creative Print and Design, Ebbw Vale, Wales

British Library Cataloguing in Publication data available

Library of Congress Cataloging in Publication data available

HB ISBN 1 86204 735 9
PB ISBN 1 86204 723 5

This book is jointly dedicated to
the Reverend A. W. Wade-Evans and John Gwenogfryn Evans,
who asked the right questions and blazed the trail ahead.

This book is dedicated to my source of inspiration and love, my wife Dee,
without whose support, selflessness and belief, this present work
would never have seen the light of day.

Steve Blake

To my parents, for letting me go my own way.

Scott Lloyd

Contents

Acknowledgements *viii*
List of Illustrations *x*
Preface *xiii*

Part One
The Arthurian Enigma *1*
The Myth of Arthur *7*
The Keys to Arthur's Kingdom *21*
Britain Before Arthur *45*
Merlin and Uthyr Pendragon *71*
Arthur the Battle Leader *87*
King Arthur and Camlan *105*

Part Two
The Keys to Avalon *121*
Avalon, Annwn and the Celtic Otherworld *139*
The Politics of Arthur and Avalon *155*
In Search of Glaestingaburh *167*
Avalon: The World's End *183*
The Grail Land *199*

Epilogue
Appendix One: Arthur's Relatives *218*
Appendix Two: The Unknown Arthur *225*
Appendix Three: The 'Lost' Kingdoms of Northern Britain *237*
Appendix Four: Source Materials *243*
Select Bibliography *255*
Notes *257*
Glossary of Personal Names *277*
Gazetteer of Comparative Place Names *278*
Glossary Elements of Welsh Place Names *280*
About the Authors *282*
Useful Addresses *282*
Index *284*
Stop Press *302*

ACKNOWLEDGEMENTS

First and foremost our gratitude must go to our guiding light John Baldock, our editor and friend whose experience and craftsmanship gave this work form, may the force be ever with you. Our heartfelt thanks to all within the Element family who experienced the labour pains of this project with us and never lost sight of the magic, especially Julia McCutchen, Sarah Sutton and Sue Lascelles. We would also like to thank the chairman of Element Books, Michael Mann, for his faith in this project. To our friend and fellow musketeer Nigel Davies, for his faith, professionalism and support above and beyond the call of duty. James Crane for his help with drawing up the genealogical charts and all things technical. Sandra Thomas and John Noonan for their invaluable help in translating texts from Welsh and Latin respectively. The staff of the Flintshire Library Headquarters, who have given their time and assistance to this project, and also the staff of the Flintshire and Denbighshire County Record Offices. Richard Barber of Boydell and Brewer Ltd for permission to use the extract from the *Vera Historia de Morte Arthuri*, P.C. Bartrum for permission to quote from his *Welsh Classical Dictionary*, Mr J.B. Lawson for information on the Shrewsbury School manuscripts and Keith Nurse for providing his invaluable article at the last minute.

Steve Blake and Scott Lloyd

To my mother, whose love and support has always been an eternal light in the dark and John Shore for his never-ending patience and help. To my sisters and extended family for always being there. To Bill and Elsie for all their support. Special thanks to the brothers and sisters of my spiritual family, Skeeter and Sam, who forever restore my faith in humanity. To Andy and Sue, forever my companions on the greater journey, and to my spiritual grandmother Ashera, who awakened the Magpie. To my friends who have persevered with my seclusion during the creative process and who have supported and helped in many ways: Gemma and Abby, Ali the Wanderer, Graham and Debbie and Big Mark, true friends all. To my friends and fellow Eagle Owls, Ken, Simon, Rhys, Ceri, Emma, who have all been subjected to my indecipherable historical ramblings over the years, and to my friends of the Wolf Clan, Anna, Janet and Grandmother T. To our friends and fellow Pendragons, Charles Evans-Gunther and Fred Stedman-Jones, for sharing their enthusiasm of history with us. To Barry and family plus the many other friends who have joined us on this and other journeys. And last, but by no means least, to those of Ancient Names who have navigated us through many turbulent times on the long and winding road.

Steve Blake

To my parents for always being there when I needed them and making sure I didn't starve. John Eirwyn Williams for being a good friend, who has listened from the start, even when I must have been boring him to death! James Crane, a truly supersonic friend. Richard Holland, a true Antiquarian, for the many days out in obscure corners of Wales. My sister Fay, who always looks after her big brother, John Appleby, for nurturing my interest and love of the mountains, Arnold 'Yakman' Bantzer, a better travelling companion I couldn't ask for, Matthew Jones with whom I have shared many happy days on the rock and who will never let me forget powdered water! Simon Taylor, with whom I was fortunate to share many early adventures and will never forget, Stephen Whitaker, who showed me around the world of second-hand books and too many car-boot sales to mention! Jane Wolfe for many happy days discussing all matters historical in the Eloquent Page and letting me sleep on the floor. Mark Olly, who always seems to find things, Cathy Hughes for her encouragement, Richard Murray for some memorable hitching trips and Anne Robinson for making me smile. I would also like to thank the older members of the rural communities of Wales, whose memories hold the keys to the truth about our past. There are many others, too numerous to mention, who have helped me in many ways – you know who you are and I thank you.

Scott Lloyd

LIST OF ILLUSTRATIONS

Black and white plates

1   As this signpost shows, Arthur's lost court of Gelliwig still exists on the map. (© Scott Lloyd)

2   A view of Gelliwig. The grove of trees in the middle ground marks the site of Gelliwig. Within the grove sits the ancient manor house of Gelliwig itself. (© Scott Lloyd)

3   Nat Gwrtheyrn – Vortigern's Valley. Tradition states that Vortigern sought refuge in this wild and inaccessible valley on the coast of North Wales. The mound rising on the right-hand side against the backdrop of the sea is the location of Castell Gwrtheyrn, Vortigern's castle. In the late 18th century local villagers opened a burial chamber at the site and the bones of a tall male were found within a stone coffin. Was this the grave of Vortigern? (© Scott Lloyd)

4   The site of the of the Giants' Dance on Maes Mawr in Cymry (the Great Plain in Wales). Part of the area is named Cor Saeson (the Circle of the Saxons) and overlooks the village of Cerrigydrudion (the Stones of the Heroes). (© Scott Lloyd)

5   The authors resting upon one of the several large mounds of stones that surround Cor Saeson. These stones were located by following the clues given in the *Brut* in relation to the memorial constructed by Myrddin. The memorial was built to mark the site of the Treachery of the Long Knives, where many nobles of Ynys Prydein were killed. (© Dee Blake)

6   The high ground on which the stone mounds are situated is known as Mynydd Main (Maen) – the Mountain of Stones. The Welsh word *maen* was often used to designate sacred stones. (© Dee Blake)

7   The 300-metre-high cliffs of Lliwedd next to the summit of Snowdon, one of the many places where Arthur is supposed to sleep until his country needs him. The mountain pass on the right is called Bwlch y Saetheau (Pass of the Arrows) and is claimed to be the site of Camlan, Arthur's last battle. (© Scott Lloyd)

8   The summit of Snowdon, one of the sites where Arthur is said to have fought Rhita Gawr. (© Scott Lloyd)

9   Breidden Hill on the Shropshire border with Wales is the probable site of the Battle of Badon (© Scott Lloyd)

10 The parish church of Llangollen opposite the castle of Dinas Bran upon the sacred River Dee. (© Dee Blake)

11 (*Top and Bottom*) Eliseg's Pillar, dating from the ninth century, traces the lineage of the Princes of Powys back to Vortigern and stands near the site of the Valle Crucis Abbey. (© Scott Lloyd)

12 The remains of the Cistercian monastery of Valle Crucis. (© Dee Blake)

13 Do the remains of the original Glaestingaburh lie beneath these ancient walls? (© Dee Blake)

Colour plates

1   Dinas Bran, the original Castle of the Grail, sits high above the Abbey of Valle Crucis, dominating the skyline from the valley below. (© Dee Blake)

2   Another view of Valle Crucis. (© Dee Blake)

3   An early Christian/Celtic Wheel Cross from Valle Crucis Abbey. (© Dee Blake)

4   The natural fortress at World's End where Melwas took and abducted Gwenhwyfar. The rocks in view are Craig y Forwyn (the Cliff of the Maiden). (© Scott Lloyd)

5   Caer Drewyn, the fortress of Gwyn ap Nudd overlooking the River Dee near Corwen. (© Dee Blake)

6   Moel Arthur and Moel Famau viewed from Caer Afallach (the Fortress of Afallach). (© Dee Blake)

7   Caer Afallach. The Halls of Afallach whence, according to Welsh tradition, Arthur was taken following the Battle of Camlan. (© Dee Blake)

8   The Wirral peninsula viewed from Caer Afallach: this is the original Wirral referred to as the landing place of St Joseph of Arimathea in the Glastonbury texts. These traditions were corrupted and relocated in Somerset, resulting in the name Wearyall Hill. (© Dee Blake)
9   Castell Dinas Bran – the Castle Corbenic of the Grail Romances and home to the Holy Grail. (© Dee Blake)
10 Another view of Dinas Bran. (© Dee Blake)
11 Wat's Dyke, the wall spoken of by Procopius, which marks the boundary of the Land of the Dead where it passes over the slopes of Caer Afallach. (© Dee Blake)

Maps		Page
1	Tripartite division of England and Wales	23
2	The traditional locations of the three divisions	25
3	The three divisions of Ynys Prydein	26
4	Showing the three rivers, three towns and boundaries of the three divisions	35
5	Traditional location of Deira and Bernica, the two kingdoms that make up Northumbria	37
6	The true location of Deifyr and Bernica, which together form the Kingdom of Northumbria	38
7	Location of Kernyw	40
8	Traditional view of the geography of Dark Age Britain	41
9	Original location of Ynys Prydein and its place names	42
10	The three strongholds of Elen and the Roman roads that link them	48
11	Possible location of Caer Wynt	51
12	The Saxon invasion	61
13	The three walls	66
14	Sites associated with Merlin	74
15	Sites linked to the last days of Vortigern	78
16	The Giants' Dance	84
17	Sites linked to Arthur's early life	90
18	Possible sites of Dinas Verolam	94
19	Sites of Arthur's battles	100
20	Arthur's last campaign – Camlan	112
21	Ynys Afallach and the Three Perpetual Harmonies	129
22	The Land of the Dead	144
23	The sacred river and the myth of the Mabon	153
24	The sons of Cunedda in Wales	172
25	Glast and the Sow's Way	175
26	St Collen and Gwyn ap Nudd	180
27	Arthur and Gleastingaburh	185
28	The realm of Melwas	188
29	The abduction of Gwenhwyfar	192
30	The family of St Gildas	197
31	St Joseph's arrival in Britain	204
32	Geography of Arthur's relatives	218
33	Arthur's courts	230
34	The location of Rheged in North Wales	239

Charts		Page
1	A simplified view of the transmission of texts	19
2	Arthur's family from Llydaw	50
3	Arthur's immediate family	92
4	The descendants of Cunedda	170
5	Arthur's extended family tree	224

PREFACE

THE JOURNEY that led to this book began with a chance encounter many years ago in Chester, a historic city situated close to the border between England and Wales. The meeting took place on an otherwise unremarkable overcast day in October 1994, when the ancient sandstone walls of the city were still glistening from the most recent downpour of a very wet month.

My wife and I were on a mission. As bibliophiles, we had many friends in the book trade and while visiting their establishments we would often spend pleasurable hours drinking coffee, discussing history and putting the world to rights. There was one particular bookshop perched on the city walls that we had visited many times in the past. We hurried towards it now, anticipating interesting finds.

Upon entering the premises of the shop, we were immediately struck by the absence of the usual proprietor; in his place sat a stocky young man sporting a goatee beard. He was faintly tanned, suggesting that he had recently returned from foreign climes. After my wife and I had spent some time browsing through the shelves, the figure behind the counter chose to introduce himself. His name was Scott Lloyd and it transpired that he had indeed just returned from one of his many trips around the major historical sites of the world, this time to the landmarks of Tibet.

As we talked we discovered that Scott and I shared not only a fascination for antiquarian books but also a passion for a period of history popularly known as the Dark Ages or, more correctly, the Early Medieval period. My own fascination in all things historical stemmed from my father's influence in my childhood. However, I was only able to pursue my interest properly in adulthood when ill health obliged me to lead a more sedentary lifestyle. Then my passion re-emerged, taking me on a literary pilgrimage into the history, mythology, folklore and sacred landscape of our ancestors. Scott, on the other hand, journeyed more literally, dividing his time between travelling overseas and working in the book trade. Our mutual interests led to a long conversation and the beginnings of a shared venture into the past, which continues to this day.

Shortly after this first meeting Scott settled down to run a bookshop in Chester in partnership with a wonderful Canadian jazz singer/Saxon historian called Jane Wolfe. Subsequently Scott and I spent many entertaining afternoons and evenings in the Eloquent Page deliberating over the problems of Dark Age history.

We were exceedingly fortunate in that one of the world's premier Arthurian collections was housed in Flintshire County Library Headquarters in the historic market town of Mold, close to where we both live. This collection of Arthurian and Dark Age source material proved invaluable in our quest to make sense of history. The collection was started by Mr E.R. Harries, the county librarian, who donated it to the county in 1952. The county have cared for it and updated it on a regular basis ever since.

One evening, following a day spent looking through the library's archives together, Scott and I found ourselves returning again and again to the subject of Arthur and the origin of the early material relating to him. We were both well aware of the problems presented by the evidence, but little did we know that we had embarked upon a course that would have us reappraising accepted history and questioning the very origins of our nation...

Steve Blake
October 1999

PART ONE

CHAPTER ONE

THE ARTHURIAN ENIGMA

'How often it is still true – that what
we need is not fresh evidence, but fuller
understanding of what we have already.'
J.H.B. Masterman[1]

THE SPECTRE of the legendary King Arthur looms large not only over the British Isles but throughout the world. Arthur and his magical entourage have inspired countless books, plays, paintings and films, and their story has been translated into numerous languages. From the nursery room to Hollywood, Arthur has captured our hearts and our imaginations. And yet what do we really know about him?

It is commonly accepted today that Arthurian legend has its roots in reality, but the historical Arthur has remained an enigma, unfathomable yet haunting, as elusive as a will o' the wisp leading scholars on a merry dance around Britain. Indeed, so evasive is the historical Arthur that many have preferred to doubt his very existence, dismissing him as a mere figment of fairy-tale. But, as we will see, the truth about Arthur is locked into the landscape of Britain. He was once as real as the soil beneath our feet.

Over the years many have tried to establish the true historical context for this most enduring of the world's legends, Arthur the Once and Future King, ruler of Britain and embodiment of the British ideal. Barely a week goes by without somebody trying to wake him out of his mythical slumber with a fresh rendition of his legend or another account about where he once ruled. This tradition of reinventing Arthur to suit contemporary whims dates as far back as the pages of Geoffrey of Monmouth's work

Historia Regum Britanniae (The History of the Kings of Britain), written in the early 1130s. Geoffrey of Monmouth had his own agenda when he drew upon the tale of Arthur, and his work was instrumental in robbing Arthur of his true historical identity, obscuring it behind a fraudulent framework of connections. With the notable exception of this book, virtually all subsequent conjecture about Arthur has been based upon Geoffrey's earlier reworking of his story.

From the 12th century on, retellings of Arthur's story have been inextricably intertwined with political intrigue or tainted by the tourist dollar. Even Arthur's birthplace was conveniently relocated centuries ago. Modern legend has it that Arthur's magical conception took place at Tintagel Castle, which clings to the craggy coast of Cornwall in the southwest of England. However, Tintagel was only named as Arthur's birthplace in editions of *Historia Regum Britanniae* dating from the early 1140s, and was then only introduced in the work at the request of Robert, Earl of Gloucester – Geoffrey's patron. Significantly, Tintagel happened to belong to another of Henry I's illegitimate sons, Robert's brother Reginald, Earl of Cornwall. Before the erection of the castle, between the fifth and ninth centuries the site had been home to a sizeable Celtic religious centre, though this was certainly not the place referred to in Geoffrey's work.

Similarly, Winchester's association with Arthur's court fares no better. A dignified cathedral city with long-established royal connections, Winchester boasts a prestigious 'Arthurian' relic in its oak Round Table. However, scientific techniques such as dendrochronology, radiocarbon dating and examination of its construction suggest that in fact the table dates from no earlier than the reign of King Edward III.[2] Historical events support this date, as in 1344 Edward had attempted to evoke Arthurian myth by establishing his own chivalric Order of the Round Table. When this failed he founded the Order of the Garter in 1348, but was nevertheless famed for holding great feasts and jousts known as the Feasts of the Round Table: the Table would appear to be a relic of those days. Likewise, Winchester's connection to Arthur in Thomas Malory's work *Le Morte d'Arthur*, a prose collection of Arthurian legends translated from the French around 1470, is undermined within the work itself. Although Malory locates Camelot firmly at Winchester, in the introduction to the work the printer William Caxton reminds the reader that Camelot is in fact a town in Wales![3]

Other attempts to locate Camelot on the map of England have been equally bound to failure. Within the rural county of Somerset lies the hilltop earthworks of Cadbury Castle, which also claims to be the true site of Camelot, though this association only appears after 1542, when the antiquarian Leyland recorded a local legend to that effect; but he was completely at a loss in finding any other specific Arthurian tales connected to the site. All said and done, Camelot would appear to be the invention of 12th-century Continental writers.

Invention and commercial endeavour have, in equal measure, clouded Arthur's history from his conception to his death. The Somerset town of Glastonbury – Mecca of the New Age movement and all things mystical – promotes itself as the site of Arthur's burial, yet has no more claim to be Arthur's Avalon than has Winchester to be Camelot. In fact, the scheming of some very enterprising medieval monks lies behind the supposed discovery of Arthur's bones within the abbey at Glastonbury; the town's claims to be Avalon and its associations with the legend of St Joseph of Arimathea and the Holy Grail both have their origins in the same political reappropriation of another nation's culture and history. The popular version of the Glastonbury legend, including the celebrated Glastonbury Thorn, did not appear until after the 16th century; even the famous Wearyall Hill is nothing but 'a pleasant bit of folk-etymology'.[4] The final version of the Glastonbury legend as it has been handed down to us today in fact owes its origins to an 18th-century innkeeper's commercial acumen![5]

So if we cannot place our faith in the sites popularly associated with Arthur, where can we look for him? Where shall we find the keys to Avalon? Our answer lies within the source material from the Dark Ages that originally informed Geoffrey of Monmouth's work so many centuries ago. It still bears the imprint of the landscape that shaped them, and through it we shall discover the exact location of Arthur's kingdom. Avalon exists, although its identity has been shrouded by the passage of time. This book aims to lift the veil of the Dark Ages to reveal the boundaries of Arthur's domain.

The period known as the Dark Ages begins with the withdrawal of the Roman legions from the British Isles in the fourth century AD and ends with the Norman invasion of 1066. Unfortunately, as the name of the period would suggest, much Dark Age history appears to consist of hypothesis based upon hypothesis, as time and again the accepted theoretical understanding of the period does not agree with the details of the actual sources themselves, whether primary (written at the time) or secondary (written later, based upon earlier documents). In the course of our research for this book, we found that a disturbing amount of 'history' as it is taught in our schools and universities appears to be based on little more than assumption, and that if assumption is repeated often enough it will be accepted as established fact. This means that new findings – which may be the result of excellent work – are frequently distorted to fit the accepted theory, causing glaring anachronisms.

We need to listen to what the voices of the Dark Ages have to say about themselves, not what we would like to hear them say for the convenience of our modern theories. As A.W. Wade-Evans pointed out in 1959, 'inquirers into such a subject as this, baffled by obscure, unsifted, written sources, are tempted in their search to substitute archaeology, philology or what not for history, and even on the strength or supposed strength of such to pass history by'.[6] We took this to heart and, having no particular hypothesis to prove to ourselves, followed up as many leads from all the sources we could, whether they were in Latin, Saxon English, French or – most crucially – Welsh. Armed with textual evidence, traditions and place names preserved within these texts, we were able to establish a much clearer picture of the period in question.

As we studied the sources, it soon became obvious to us that the main problem with understanding Dark Age history and the Age of Arthur lay not with the texts but with the geography that had been used to interpret them. The surviving Welsh manuscripts contain possibly the most important clues to the Dark Age history of Britain, yet they have often been overlooked. To our amazement, time and again, the Welsh sources yielded place names that still exist today or that have been commemorated in local traditions. Bit by bit the ancient map of Dark Age Britain began to unfold before us.

In many instances the place names recorded in the old Welsh texts still survived but had been ignored as, according to the accepted modern version of history, the events in question could never have occurred there. However once we had uncovered the original location of sites it become possible to understand how events actually were connected to them. We had begun to redraw the map of Dark Age Britain.

As will become clear, one of our greatest discoveries came in the guise of a great Roman wall over 100 miles long that was mentioned in all of the earliest texts. In the standard account of Dark Age Britain, historians had misplaced this wall by several hundred miles, identifying it with Hadrian's Wall in the North. As if this monumental revelation wasn't enough, we also discovered that the present understanding of the Saxon invasion of Britain was based upon very little evidence and that it seems to have taken place in very different circumstances in an entirely different place! In the process of exploring the geography set out in the Dark Age texts, we came across many more intriguing items that have considerable implications for our understanding of British history. In searching for Arthur, we uncovered a lost kingdom that is the true heritage of the British. Whether considered in the light of hazy myth or harsh reality, Arthur is the embodiment of a forgotten people.

Modern British culture is diverse and reflects the comings and goings of various peoples and powers throughout history. But where now there is continuous movement, there was once relative stasis, with the local populations of many areas of Britain – usually on high ground such as the Highlands of Scotland or in the mountain regions of Wales – remaining reasonably stable until quite recent times. People lived out their whole lives in the region where they were born; there existed a particular sense of belonging and of strong cultural ties.

Sadly, wrapped up in its everyday business, modern life has tended to neglect and forget the stories and beliefs that once anchored whole communities. Hence, in the course of our research, we read time and again that there are only fragments of British tradition left. However, far more survives than might be supposed.

There is a British tradition that stretches back thousands of years. Originally oral in nature, it was passed down through the generations in stories and song. Despite the persecution of those who relayed the tradition, it eventually found its way through the British bards into numerous manuscripts. It is this tradition, accessed in the original source materials, that holds the key to a nation's forgotten identity. Often it has been dismissed out of hand, which must lead us to ask why we British are so willing to accept the authenticity of oral cultures in other traditions but remain so reluctant to accept our own. The references in this book show how descriptions of historical events and characters in bardic sources tally with other evidence. We hope that many readers will be prompted to rediscover these voices of our ancestors.

The last remnants of the bardic tradition maintain a foothold, although modern agricultural problems and new technologies threaten to eradicate what little is left of the way of life that supports the tradition. Within Britain there are still those who farm and care for lands that have been in the possession of their families for generation after generation. Sadly, many of the most recent generation have been forced by modern economics to abandon the ways of their forefathers. With the passing of their traditional way of life we suffer a greater loss: the loss of the story of the land.

In the course of our research for this book we enjoyed many conversations, over farm gates and field walls, with these keepers of tradition. From experience we can vouch that a certain paradigm shift takes place when you have been privileged to a conversation with someone who has little knowledge of Dark Age history, but who has lived on the land for decades and can recite stories known only to academics from ancient manuscripts and is able to identify landmarks named only in obscure historical records. In many instances we found that place names, folklore and mythology from a very early period have been handed down virtually unaltered. We found that historical material remains but that it is also being slowly consigned to oblivion because it does not conform to the standard theories of our time.

We believe that the time is right to reassess our traditional heritage. In this book we have taken the first step towards piecing together the jigsaw puzzle that is our history. We regret that the scope of this book makes it impossible for us to address every issue or point of evidence surrounding the material that we have presented as we have necessarily restricted our discussion to the story of Arthur and Avalon. We could not even hope to try to address every misplacement of Dark Age history within this work, but hope that it will at least inspire others to take up the challenge, to look at our history afresh.

History belongs to us all; the air we breathe is steeped in it; the ground we walk on was witness to it. We must learn to listen again to the voices of our ancestors. Only then can we sift fact from fiction, myth from reality. Only then can we access our past in the landscape of today and journey back to Avalon.

CHAPTER TWO

THE
MYTH OF
ARTHUR

O UR STORY begins in Wales in 1136. After many months travelling from monastery to monastery, Walter, Archdeacon of Oxford, is preparing for the long journey back to his home in England. Carefully stowed away in his baggage is a book acquired during his travels, chronicling the history of the British people from the arrival of Brutus the Trojan in about 1200 BC to the death of the last British king in the seventh century AD. It is a book that will alter, quite literally, the course of history.

The England to which Walter is about to return is in a state of near civil war following the death of the king, Henry I. Before dying, Henry had named his daughter Mathilda as his heir, but Henry's nephew Stephen had usurped the throne in her place. However, as Stephen had spent most of his life in Normandy in northern France, he was not a popular choice as king. Mathilda's campaign to reclaim the throne was led by her half-brother Robert, Earl of Gloucester, ably supported by his powerful neighbours, the lords and earls who governed the lands along the Welsh borders and in the southwest of England.

On his return to Oxford Walter gave the precious chronicle to his friend Geoffrey of Monmouth, who translated it into Latin under the title *Historia Regum Britanniae* (The History of the Kings of Britain) and dedicated it to his patron, Robert, Earl of Gloucester. In the introduction to his *Historia*, Geoffrey described the source of his work as 'a very ancient book in the

British tongue ... which Walter the archdeacon of Oxford brought from Britannia ... It is this book which I have been at such pains to turn into Latin.' As Oxford is itself in Britain, it seems odd that Geoffrey should state that the book he had translated had been 'brought from Britannia' by Walter. As Walter had brought the book back from his travels in Wales, was 'Britannia' simply another name for Wales?

Significantly for Robert, Geoffrey's *Historia* contained an account of the life of a sixth-century British king named Arthur, whose campaigns against the Saxon invaders provided an uncanny parallel with Robert's own fight against the usurper Stephen. In what now seems like a masterstroke of propaganda, Robert was to turn Arthur into a powerful ally in his attempt to regain the throne for Mathilda. As Geoffrey tells us in his introduction: 'I ask you, Robert, Earl of Gloucester, to do my little book this favour. Let it be so emended by your knowledge and your advice that it must no longer be considered as the product of Geoffrey of Monmouth's small talent.'[1] Whereas Geoffrey's source book had confined Arthur's activities to the ancient realm of Britannia, his translation was modified at Robert's instigation to include brief explanatory notes linking the obscure British place names of the original with locations that fell within the lands governed by Robert and his allies. In effect, Geoffrey's *Historia* now turned this once obscure King of Britannia into the powerful ruler of much of the British Isles. This portrayal of Arthur was further embellished by endowing him with qualities that epitomized the chivalric ideal that was to become so popular in 12th-century Europe. More importantly, as a result of Robert's 'corrections' the history of Britannia contained in the book that Walter brought back from 'Britannia' was incorporated into the history of England in such a way that ever since then 'Britain' has been little more than a synonym for the lands ruled over by the English.

Over 200 manuscript copies of Geoffrey's Latin text are now known to exist and although they contain slight variants, the same basic history is given in each. Uthyr Pendragon, with the aid of Merlin, changes his appearance to that of his enemy, Gorlois, and spends the night with Eigyr, the wife of his enemy, and from this union Arthur is conceived. Arthur is made leader on his 15th birthday and then spends many years fighting the Picts, Scots and Saxons, culminating in the Battle of Badon. Following his victory over his enemies, Arthur and his knights expand their kingdom by invading neighbouring realms and on returning home Arthur receives a special coronation in recognition of his efforts. At this ceremony messengers arrive from Rome with a letter from the Senate stating that by invading the other kingdoms Arthur has insulted the Senate, so he must come to Rome to receive his punishment; otherwise the Roman army will invade. Arthur and his army head off for the Continent and win many battles, but as they are about to reach Rome a messenger informs Arthur that his wife Guinevere has married his nephew Medrod (Mordred) and together they are ruling Britannia. Arthur returns home to fight Medrod and the two finally meet at the Battle of Camlan, where both are mortally wounded. Arthur requests to be taken to the Isle of Avalon for his wounds to be healed and thus passes from the pages of the book.

The story of Arthur caught the imagination of the people of the day. In the years following the publication of the *Historia*, Geoffrey's account of Arthur's exploits was embellished by poets and chroniclers across Western Europe. The first of these was the *Roman de Brut* by Robert Wace, from Jersey in the Channel Islands, who translated Geoffrey's Latin text into Norman French in 1155, introducing to it the concept of the Round Table, where everybody who sat at the table was considered equal as no one person was seated at the head and therefore in a dominant position. This idea spread with the retelling of Arthur's story at courts across Europe, and was adopted by many leaders who imagined themselves ruling in the mould of the chivalric ideal that Arthur had now become.

Geoffrey's original story was elaborated further by the French poet Chrétien de Troyes, who wrote four long romances relating the exploits of Arthur and his knights. In 1182, in his poem *Perceval*, which was left unfinished at his death, Chrétien introduced a significant new element to the story of Arthur: the Quest for the Holy Grail. The romances of the Quest worked on two levels: firstly to tell the story of Arthur and his knights in order to entertain the court; and secondly to use the Grail as the epitome of spiritual perfection, with the adventures of Arthur and his knights working in parallel with the winning of this goal. *Perceval* was the first of several long romances written on the theme of the Holy Grail, which was variously reported to be anything from the cup used by Jesus at the Last Supper to a stone from the heavens.

The story of Arthur took on the form most familiar to us in a series of romances known today as *The Vulgate Cycle*.[2] Written by Cistercian monks around 1220, these romances comprised several books that gave a complete history of Arthur, the Holy Grail, Merlin, Lancelot and the other knights of the Round Table. By the beginning of the 13th century the romances of Arthur and his knight had appeared in German in Wolfram von Eschenbach's *Parzifal*, and Norse translations of the romances had appeared in Scandinavia by 1250. Spanish, Portuguese, Dutch and Italian texts soon followed and the Crusaders in the Holy Land often compared themselves to the characters from the romances. Within 200 years of Geoffrey's book appearing, Arthur had become a byword for the chivalric Christian knight and was personified as such across Europe.

In 1485 the Tudor dynasty came to the throne of England and Wales and Henry VII wasted no time in using the Arthurian tales to his advantage by naming his oldest son and heir Arthur. The same year saw the publication of *Le Morte d'Arthur* by Sir Thomas Malory, one of the earliest works to be printed in the English language. Using the numerous romances then available, Malory not only wrote the first cohesive narrative for the story of Arthur and the Grail in the English language but also created one of the great classics of Arthurian literature, still widely read today.

Over the next 200 years the popular perception of Arthur as the epitome of the chivalric ideal merged with the image of a legendary British ruler who had led his conquering army across mainland Europe to the gates of Rome. Meanwhile, however, Arthur's original British roots were further blurred by the two Acts of Union of 1536 and 1707, the first of which united Wales with England, placing it under English rule and law, while the second saw the union of Scotland to England and Wales to create the Kingdom of Great Britain. Following the accession of the German House of Hanover to the throne in 1714, Arthur sank into relative obscurity as history was rewritten to support the ascendancy of the new dynasty. Even in Wales and southwest England, where the stories of Arthur had always been held dear, interest gave way in the face of the revised history of Britain. In the middle of the 19th century interest in Arthurian matters underwent a revival, with works such as Tennyson's poem *Idylls of the King*, the engravings of Gustave Doré (1832–83) and the illustrations of Aubrey Beardsley (1872–98) creating the romantic image of Arthur that has stayed with us to the present day.

The final years of the 19th century saw an increase in the study of the historical Arthur by scholars in both Europe and America. In 1927 the publication of *Arthur of Britain* by E.K. Chambers set the tone for the serious investigation into Arthur's origins that continues today. The rise in popularity of all things mythical and spiritual in the 1960s saw a further development in the popular image of Arthur as, along with Merlin, he became the focal point for the increasing interest in the indigenous Celtic religion and culture of the British Isles. For many, Arthur has become the epitome of Celtic spirituality and a figurehead for alternative ways of thinking, while the Grail Quest has evolved into the archetypal spiritual journey.

By the end of the 20th century the myth of Arthur has been immortalized in hundreds of publications and its popularity is stronger than ever. In the absence of any definitive facts concerning his origins, new and increasingly unlikely theories have been put forward on a regular basis. According to some Arthur was Welsh, to others he was Scottish, or Cornish or French; to yet others, he never existed but was simply a figment of one person's fertile imagination. That person was Geoffrey of Monmouth, who first created the stories of Arthur as we know them today, and so it was to Geoffrey we turned in our quest to uncover the truth about Arthur. As his work was the source for the Arthurian story we know today, we decided to look at the internal evidence of his text and try to find the answer to the age-old question: where did Geoffrey acquire his material?

GEOFFREY OF MONMOUTH AND
THE HISTORY OF THE KINGS OF BRITAIN

Apart from the personal information he included in his chronicle, there are only a handful of hard facts known regarding the life of Geoffrey of Monmouth. Of his early life we know nothing, but from the evidence of his name it has been presumed that he was born on the Welsh border at Monmouth. Geoffrey is known to have been at Oxford until 1139. He was then in South Wales, either at or closely connected to Llandaff Cathedral where, according to some authorities, he was one of the editors of *The Book of Llandaff*, which consisted of the lives of saints and supposedly ancient charters in an attempt to prove that the Norman invention of the see of Llandaff had an older history. In 1151 Geoffrey was made Bishop of St Asaph in North Wales and, according to an entry in the Welsh *Brut y Tywysogion* (Chronicle of the Princes), died in the year 1155. The rest of his life is open to conjecture.[3]

In the introduction to the *Historia* Geoffrey bemoans the lack of available information regarding the pre-Christian kings of Britain and the acts of Arthur in the works of the earlier historians Bede and Gildas.[4] He also mentions his source on several occasions, and what he says is very informative. He describes it as: '*Quemdam Britannici sermonis librum uetustissimum*' (A very ancient book in the British tongue)[5] and refers to '*librum istum Britannici sermonis quem Gualterus Oxenfordensis archidiaconus ex Britannia aduexit*' (The book in the British tongue which Walter the Archdeacon of Oxford[6] brought from Britannia.)[7] Geoffrey also tells us one more crucial thing concerning this book: 'At Walter's request I have taken the trouble to translate the book into Latin.'[8]

Our next step was to understand exactly what Geoffrey meant by the book being written 'in the British tongue' and 'from Britannia'. This point has been the cause of much heated debate between academics. Many scholars are of the opinion that Geoffrey's work was a complete fiction, and by taking this view they absolve themselves of any responsibility for addressing the questions surrounding the origins of this influential work. Those scholars who believe that Geoffrey did use an original source have argued as to whether it was a text, now lost, from Brittany or Wales, a debate that centres around the exact meaning of the word 'Britannia' and the reference to the work being written 'in the British tongue'. The fact that Geoffrey *translated* his work is often overlooked today, but his contemporaries were well aware of the fact. For example, when telling us of Geoffrey's death in 1152, Robert de Torigny, the Abbot of Mont St Michel, referred to 'Geoffrey of Monmouth who translated *The History of the Kings of Britain* from British into Latin, who is the bishop of Saint Asaph in North Wales.'[9]

One of the earliest mentions of the book dedicated to Robert of Gloucester is found in the poem *L'Estoire des Englies* (The History of the English) written by Geoffrey of Gaimar around 1140:

> *Robert li quens de Gloucestre*
> *Fist translater icele geste*
> *Solum les liveres as Waleis*
> *Kil aveient des Breton reis*

> (Robert, the Earl of Gloucester
> Had this history translated
> According to the books of the Welsh
> Which he had, about the British kings.)[10]

This reference led Professor E.K. Chambers to conclude in 1927 that: 'In any case the book done for Robert of Gloucester was probably the *Historia* itself, and Gaimar regarded it as taken from the Welsh.'[11] Here we find both Robert de Torigny and Geoffrey of Gaimar, two contemporaries from the courts of the Norman kings and nobility for which Geoffrey of Monmouth wrote, stating that he had translated his work from the 'books of the Welsh', confirming what Geoffrey himself tells us in his introduction: he had translated his *Historia* from a British (i.e. Welsh) text.

The next obvious question was: do any Welsh versions of the history told by Geoffrey still exist? The simple answer is yes. There are over 70 surviving manuscripts of a Welsh text known as *Brut y Brenhinedd* (*Chronicle of the Kings*), which tells the same history as Geoffrey, from the arrival of Brutus to the death of the last British king, Cadwaladr.[12] (*Brut* is the Welsh for chronicle; from here on the *Brut Y Brenhinedd* will be referred to simply as the *Brut.*) The earliest of these surviving manuscript copies of the *Brut* dates from around 1200 and therefore cannot itself be the original used by Geoffrey. However, prior to the Hanoverian ascent to the throne in the 18th century and the subsequent decline in popularity of Geoffrey's account of British history, many scholars and historians in Wales considered the Welsh *Brut* to be later copies of the original book that had been translated by Geoffrey in 1136.[13]

In more recent times, the long accepted opinion that the surviving manuscripts of the *Brut* were nothing more than mere translations of Geoffrey's Latin *Historia* was first questioned by the Reverend Acton Griscom in two articles published in the 1920s.[14] The major thrust of Griscom's argument was that the Welsh *Brut* contained material not found in the Latin *Historia*, which indicated to him a native origin for some of this material. This realization led Griscom to propose that the some of the remaining Welsh manuscripts of the *Brut* might be copies, either complete or in part, of the original book translated by Geoffrey. Despite the arguments put forward by Griscom, many historians today still consider all of the Welsh *Brut* texts simply to be copies of Geoffrey's Latin *Historia*, and until a complete correlation between all of the surviving Welsh manuscripts is undertaken a definitive answer to this question remains impossible.

It was Griscom who, in 1929, produced the first critical academic edition of the Latin text of Geoffrey's *Historia*, with a parallel English translation of the Welsh *Brut*. His lead was followed by other scholars, with the publication of a Welsh text with a parallel English translation in 1937, an edition of the earliest Welsh text in 1942 and an English translation of Griscom's 1929 Latin text in 1966, which has since become the standard version read by most people. Apart from a few articles in academic journals and a study of some extracts from one of the Welsh manuscripts nothing further was done until 1984, when Neil Wright edited an academic edition of the Latin *Historia* from an early manuscript kept in the Stadtbibliothek in Bern, Switzerland.[15] Geoffrey's text is viewed by many today as an interesting piece of literature and is studied accordingly, but what of Griscom's arguments from the 1920s?

The basic principles of Griscom's argument have not been disproved, and some of the Welsh *Brut* texts may well preserve a version similar to the original source translated by Geoffrey. By using the surviving Welsh manuscripts of the *Brut*, we wondered if we would be able to establish the original names of the people and places that Geoffrey had before him when he did his translation in Oxford in 1136. We were helped in this by the fact that within Geoffrey's translation there are numerous instances where the place name is still to be found in its original Welsh form alongside the 'corrected' location provided for the book's Norman audience:

Kaerreint id est cantuariam. (Caer Ceint that is Canterbury.)
Kaerguenit id est Guintoniam. (Caer Wynt that is Winchester.)
Kaerpenhuelgoit que exonia vocatur. (Caerpenhuelgoit now called Exeter.)[16]

These corrections – or 'explanations' – were absent from nearly all of the Welsh copies of the *Brut*, presumably because the latter were intended for a Welsh audience who would have known where these places were. As these were the very explanations that had corrupted the geographical locations mentioned in the *Historia*, we felt convinced that by locating the original Welsh-British names we would not only be able to define the region called 'Britannia', the home of Geoffrey's source for the *Historia*, but also discover the original location of Arthur's kingdom.

IN SEARCH OF BRITANNIA

We found the name Britannia mentioned on several occasions in manuscripts that survive from the 12th century and earlier. One of the first of these was *The Book of Llandaff* – written around 1150 and reputedly edited by Geoffrey of Monmouth – which contained a document entitled *The Privilege of St Teilio*. In the text of the *Privilege*, which was written in both Latin and Welsh, we found the following entry in Latin:

aregibus istis & principibus brittannie (the Kings and Princes of Britannia).[17]

In Welsh the text was given as:

Breenhined hinn hatouyssocion cymry (the Kings and Princes of Cymry).[18]

Here, in two different languages, were two different names – Britannia and Cymry – for the same geographical region. Cymry is the Welsh name for Wales – any reader who has driven across the border into Wales will have been greeted by signs saying *Croeso I Cymru* (Welcome to Wales), for Cymru is the modern Welsh spelling of Cymry. This implied that in the 12th century 'Britannia' did not denote the whole of Great Britain as we know it today but referred specifically to Wales. This raised a crucial question: if Britannia was the Latin name for Wales, what had been the original Latin name for England? We again found the answer to this in the 12th-century *Book of Llandaff*, where the name of the land that bordered Britannia was given on more than one occasion: 'The borders of Britannia and Anglia towards Hereford ... From both parts of Anglia and Britannia ... '[19]

Having discovered evidence that the land bordering Britannia was called Anglia – after its inhabitants the Angles, sometimes written as Engles – and later came to be known as England, our next step was to search for a geographical reference point for the border between these two regions. We found this in *The Life of King Alfred*, written by Asser, a Welsh monk, in 893. At the beginning of his work Asser gives a condensed version of Saxon history and describes the construction of a physical boundary to Britannia: 'There was of late in Mercia a certain strenuous king and a formidable one among all the kings about him and the neighbouring countries, Offa by name, who ordered to be made between Britannia and Mercia the great dyke from sea to sea.'[20]

Here was further evidence that Britannia was an old name for Wales, for Offa's Dyke – which separated the Saxon kingdom of Mercia from Britannia – which is still in existence today. It is an earthwork that runs from the Dee estuary in North Wales to the Severn estuary in the South. Our own conclusions concerning the identity of Britannia found confirmation in Hugh Williams's 1901 study of Gildas, a contemporary of Arthur, in which he stated succinctly: 'Britannia in the tenth century ... meant Wales.'[21]

THE REALM OF BRITAIN/YNYS PRIDEIN

How had the confusion over the geographical identity of Britannia/Britain arisen? The answer lay yet again in Geoffrey of Monmouth's translation of the Welsh *Brut* into Latin. Where the Latin text of the *Historia* reads Insula Britannia or Britannia, the Welsh text of the *Brut* reads Ynys Prydein or Prydein. The confusion created by Geoffrey stems from the meanings of the two words *ynys* and *insula*, and the key to understanding how this confusion arose lies in the original meaning of *ynys*.

In modern Welsh *ynys* means 'island' or refers to an area of land bordering water, whether this is a river estuary or a coast. Numerous examples of this use of the word *ynys* can be seen on a large-scale map of the North Wales coast between Porthmadog and Aberystwyth: Ynys Tachwedd, to the north of Borth, the hamlet of Ynys on the A496, north of Harlech, and Ynys y Gwely and Ynys Ceiliog, on the banks of the River Glaslyn north of Minffordd, near Porthmadog. In medieval Welsh the word *ynys* also meant 'realm' or 'kingdom'. An example of this particular meaning can be illustrated with the help of the poetry of two 15th-century Welsh bards. Guto'r Glyn refers to Gwenwynwyn – in the Welsh region of Powys – as Gwlad Wenwynwyn (the *land* of Wenwynwyn), whereas a poem from the same period by Gutun Owain names it as Ynys Gwenwynwyn (the *realm* of Wenwynwyn). *Ynys* is also used with the meaning of realm or kingdom on several occasions in the Welsh chronicle *Brenhinedd y Saesson* (c.1450), and this meaning was still in use in Wales as late as the 16th century.[22]

The source of the confusion lies in the fact that Geoffrey understood the word *ynys* to mean 'island' and translated it as *insula*.[23] As a result the

Welsh Ynys Prydein (the Realm of Prydein) became the Latin Insula Britannia (the Island of Britannia), which in turn became the island of Britain, or Great Britain as we know it today. As confirmation of this we found dozens of instances in the poetry of the Welsh bards where Prydein is used to describe Wales.[24] Finally, even the differences between the titles in Welsh and Latin seemed to proved the point. The Welsh title *Brut Y Brenhinedd* simply means *Chronicle of the Kings*. However, the Latin title translates as *The History of the Kings of Britannia*, not *The Kings of Anglia*. Having discovered that the Britannia of Geoffrey of Monmouth's *Historia* referred to a particular area of the British Isles originally called Ynys Prydein and known today as Wales, Geoffrey's references to Arthur having been King of Britannia took on a new light. If Arthur really had been a ruler in Wales, our next task was to discover exactly what the early Welsh source texts said about him.

THE SEARCH FOR THE HISTORICAL ARTHUR

The publication of Geoffrey of Monmouth's *The History of the Kings of Britannia* in 1136 is a pivotal point in the study of the historical Arthur for it divides the source materials into two groups: pre-1136 and post-1136. The sources that come after Geoffrey, many of which are familiar to anyone interested in the Arthurian legends, have been outlined above. But what of the sources that come before Geoffrey? How familiar are these early sources, and how informative are they?

For hundreds of years ancient tribal cultures the world over preserved their history and the genealogy of their ancestors by passing them on orally from one generation to the next. For example, the histories and legends of the Native American peoples have only been written down in the last hundred years or so, but nobody would deny that they go back many centuries. Similarly, the Welsh bards, who preserved the oral tradition of Wales through their poetry, enabled us to access some of the oldest references to Arthur and his companions. Written down for the first time in the 12th and 13th centuries, the poetry and histories of the bards preserve the original names of people and places connected with the historical Arthur. By using these earliest written sources, whose oral origins pre-date Geoffrey's *Historia*, we were able to begin to penetrate the confusion that has arisen around Arthur and his times.

Professor Thomas Jones of the University of Wales neatly summed up the situation regarding these early Arthurian sources in an excellent article called 'The Early Evolution of the Legend of Arthur', published in 1958.[25] 'The evidence for the existence of traditions and stories about Arthur in the period before 1136 is restricted to Welsh texts and a few Latin texts, which are for the most part the work of Welshmen.'[26] The texts 'written by Welshmen', mentioned by Professor Jones contain some of the earliest known references to Arthur in literature. The most famous of these Welsh sources is the collection of 11 tales known as *The Mabinogion*, preserved in two manuscripts dating from between 1300 and 1400. Arthur is mentioned in five of these 11 tales, with three of the five similar to the French romances of Chrétien de Troyes.[27] In our search for the origins of Arthur the remaining two tales were to prove the most important. The earliest and most valuable of these two tales is called *Culhwch and Olwen*, the composition of which, in its present form, has been dated to the tenth century, making it almost 200 years older than Geoffrey's *Historia*, although it may even contain material from a much older period.[28] The tale relates the accomplishment by Culhwch of many tasks set for him by the giant father of his true love Olwen. To help him complete the tasks, Culhwch enlists the aid of his cousin Arthur. The second of the two tales is *The Dream of Rhonabwy*, in which the eponymous hero falls asleep in the border region of North Wales and dreams about Arthur and the events before the Battle of Badon, known to the Welsh as Caer Faddon. *The Dream of Rhonabwy* also names the 42 counsellors of Arthur's court. The publication of these stories in English by Lady Charlotte Guest in 1839 was the first time that attention had been drawn to them outside Wales. Even in Wales their existence was not widely known.

We also consulted the *Triads*, another important early Welsh source, which owe their name to the fact that they group important things together in threes – for example, the Three Courts of Arthur or the Three Beautiful Women of Ynys Prydein. This three-part grouping may seem strange to us nowadays, but they were probably written in this way as a mnemonic device for the bards who memorized the Welsh oral tradition.[29] Arthur is mentioned by name in 13 of the *Triads* while others list people and places connected with Arthur.[30] Together with the information in *Culhwch and Olwen*, the material contained within these valuable sources preserves the old oral traditions of Wales and makes up the bulk of evidence we have for the earliest origins of Arthur, making it possible to build up a picture of his activities and companions.

One source sadly often neglected in the search for the historical Arthur is the bards collectively known as the *Gogynfeirdd* – literally 'not so early bards', also known as the Poets of the Princes – from the period between 1100 and 1300. Unfortunately for both Arthurian studies and the history of Wales, it is only in the last decade that the poetry of the Gogynfeirdd has begun to receive the same level of academic editorship as medieval poetry from elsewhere and the few translations that have been done are scattered through various works.[31] Within the poems of the Gogynfeirdd are references to many Arthurian characters and localities from the early pre-Norman Welsh tradition that are of vital importance in piecing together the Arthurian puzzle. These sources have rarely been used in previous studies,[32] and our purpose in drawing attention to them here is to make these otherwise little known texts more widely known to the general reader, perhaps stimulating interest in them among readers beyond Wales in the hope that this will lead to a higher profile and therefore further translations of these valuable poems.

The importance of the oral tradition in Wales is further shown in the Welsh obsession with genealogy. Writing in 1188, the cleric Giraldus Cambrensis states in his *Description of Wales* that 'even the common people know their family tree by heart and can readily recite from memory the list of their grandfathers, great-grandfathers, great-great-grandfathers, back to the sixth or seventh generation.'[33] Many important manuscripts have survived that preserve such genealogies and research into these has been carried out over the last 50 years by Professor P.C. Bartrum, culminating in his *Welsh Classical Dictionary*, which is priceless for research into early British history.[34]

In our search for the original Arthur we found the many *Lives of the Welsh Saints* that pre-date Geoffrey of Monmouth invaluable as they provided us with some of the earliest place names associated with Arthur in Wales. We also discovered that Arthur did not always live up to his image of the chivalric ideal, for these particular works often depict him as a tyrant and a tormentor of saints.[35]

Going further back in time, we found further mention of Arthur in the *Historia Brittonum*, commonly attributed to Nennius, a Welsh monk who lived around 800.[36] This early text is noted for its inclusion of a list of the 12 battles that Arthur fought against the Saxons (see Chapter 6) and is the earliest text to portray Arthur in a form that corresponds with the image we have of him today.

Finally the earliest text of relevance to the study of the historical Arthur was written by his contemporary Gildas, a Welsh monk. Much has been made of the fact that Gildas's work *De Excido Britannia* (The Ruin of Britannia), which was written around 540, makes no mention of Arthur, leading many to allege that Arthur did not exist, but in his *Description of Wales* Giraldus Cambrensis offers an explanation for this omission: 'The Britons maintain that, when Gildas criticized his own people so bitterly, he wrote as he did because he was so infuriated by the fact that King Arthur had killed his own brother, who was a chieftain of Alban. When he heard of his brother's death, or so the Britons say, he threw into the sea a number of outstanding books which he had written in their praise and about Arthur's achievements. As a result you will find no book which gives an authentic account of that prince.'[37]

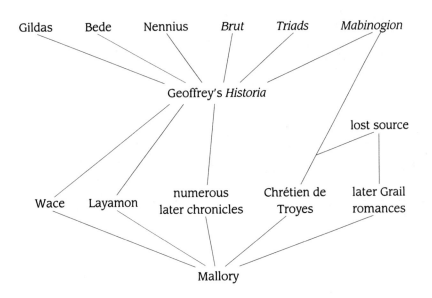

A simplified view of the transmission of texts

Armed with a knowledge of the texts that came before Geoffrey's *Historia*, our next step in the search for Arthur and the mythical Avalon was to take a closer look at the geography of events as described in the Welsh *Brut*. As we looked at the history of Arthur contained in the Welsh texts and compared it with that in the Latin ones, our conviction that the geographical areas and place names had become confused in translation was soon reinforced. This was the crux of the whole Arthurian problem. Once we had understood this, a closer study of the source material in its original Welsh-British language led us on a journey back into the hidden history of Britain. We began to uncover answers to perennial questions such as: 'Where was Arthur's court?'; 'Where did Arthur's battles take place?'; and 'Where is Avalon?' Having rescued this information from the historical oblivion to which it was heading, we can now begin to tell the story of the true land of Arthur – the original realm of Britain – and the sacred landscape within it.

CHAPTER THREE

THE KEYS TO ARTHUR'S KINGDOM

TO HELP us on our journey back through time in search of Arthur's Britain we need a map of the landscape. But not any map will do, because the maps presented in our atlases and history books merely perpetuate the misconception that Arthur's Britain corresponds to the British Isles. Instead we need a new map, or more correctly an ancient map, the map that belongs to those original texts from which our history is taken and where the sources speak for themselves.

OWAIN GLYNDWR AND THE TRIPARTITE INDENTURE

Having established that Britannia was a Latin word for that part of the British Isles we know today as Wales, our next question was: 'How far to the east did the boundaries of this kingdom extend?' We already knew from Asser's *Life of King Alfred* that the ninth-century border had been marked by Offa's Dyke, but what of the time of Arthur? Did his kingdom extend as far as the present border of the mountainous country of Wales or across into the fertile plains and river valleys of the border regions known as the Marches, which comprise the modern English counties of Cheshire, Shropshire and Herefordshire? This question caused us many sleepless nights until one day we came across the missing link on a map in *An Historical Atlas of Wales*.[1]

In the first decade of the 15th century the Welsh, under the leadership of a certain Owain Glyndwr, rebelled against English rule over their land and achieved a surprising amount of success. Owain Glyndwr went on to become one of the most powerful men in the country and, as the self-styled Prince of Wales, threatened to undermine the monarchy in Wales. In 1405 Glyndwr met two of the most powerful men in England – Lord Edmund Mortimer and Henry Percy, son of the Earl of Northumberland – in a room at the house of the Archdeacon of Bangor in North Wales. The three men had come together to draw up an agreement that would overthrow the Lancastrian usurper Henry IV and divide the realm into three parts. Had it succeeded, this agreement would have changed the history of the British Isles beyond recognition. The actual document, which still exists, became known as the Tripartite Indenture, but what interested us were the boundaries agreed upon for the three divisions.[2] Lord Edmund Mortimer was given all of England south of the Trent; Percy, the Earl of Northumberland, was given all of England north of the Trent; and Owain Glyndwr was given Wales. For us, the most interesting part of the actual document was the description of the eastern boundary of the lands to be given to Owain Glyndwr:

> The following borders, limits, and bounds: from the Severn estuary as the river Severn flows from the sea as far as the northern gate of the city of Worcester; from that gate directly to the ash trees known in the Cambrian or Welsh language as Onennau Meigion [the Ashtrees of Meigion] which grow on the high road leading from Bridgnorth to Kinver; then directly along the highway, popularly known as the old or ancient road, to the head or source of the river Trent; thence to the head or source of the river commonly known as the Mersey and so along that river to the sea.[3]

How had this boundary been arrived at? We found a clue in a Welsh poem entitled *A Conversation Between Merlin and his Sister Gwenddydd*, in which the Onennau Meigion are referred to as a boundary marker to the limits of the Kingdom of Ynys Prydein. This suggests that the bards at Owain Glyndwr's court, who would have advised him in such matters, used bardic knowledge drawn from a centuries-old oral tradition when redefining the boundaries of 15th-century Wales.[4]

The line of the Owain Glyndwr's boundary from 'the source of the Trent to the source of the Mersey' corresponds approximately with today's border between the counties of Cheshire and Staffordshire, and explains

Map 1 Tripartite division of England and Wales

why Cheshire has always had a narrow strip of land extending up into Longdendale in the Peak District, where the source of the Mersey is located. The border marks the watershed between the drainage basin of the Trent and the southern half of the drainage basin of the Mersey, a name that is derived from the same root as Mercia and means 'border' or 'boundary'. The Trent flows eastward towards the Humber estuary and thence into the North Sea, whereas the Mersey and the Severn flow westward into the Irish Sea, so the watershed of these three rivers forms a natural boundary.

A watershed is an unchangeable boundary. Even today, parochial and national boundaries often run along river channels or over the highest peaks forming the watershed between two adjoining drainage basins. Within Wales most of the smaller regional boundaries follow this rule, a fact that was to enable us to find the limits of the British-Welsh kingdoms and to understand why particular battles had taken place at certain river fords or on strategic passes over mountain tops.

KEY 1: THE THREE REALMS OF YNYS PRYDEIN

The ancient realm of Britain/Ynys Prydein had had its own tripartite division. Writing in 1188, Giraldus Cambrensis declared that these three divisions were already ancient in his time and gave their Latin names as Venedotia, Powisia and Sudwallia.[5] According to the Welsh *Chronicle of the Princes*, Rhodri Mawr, the Prince of Wales (c.870), divided his kingdom between his three sons, each of whom became king of their respective realm.[6] These three kingdoms were named as Gwynedd, Powys and Deheubarth – the original Welsh names for Giraldus's divisions. Within the Latin texts of Gildas and Nennius we found reference to *Tria Regne Britanniae* (the Three Kingdoms of Britain) while in the Welsh texts of the *Brut* the same phrase appears as *Teir Ynys Prydein* (the Three Realms of Prydein), with the three realms named as Cymry, Alban and Lloegyr. As Gildas was writing around 540, this tripartite division had evidently been established at least as far back as the early sixth century. In fact the three-fold division of Ynys Prydein is first mentioned in the Welsh *Brut* as having occurred around 1200 BC, in the time of Brutus. Whatever the historical significance of the Trojan occupation of Britain may be, this legend preserves the boundaries of the original threefold division under the names Cymru, Alban and Lloegyr. The three divisions met at only one point, near the modern town of Machynlleth in the Dyfi estuary, which led Owain Glyndwr to site his court and parliament at Machynlleth in the fifteenth century.

When Geoffrey of Monmouth translated the *Brut* into Latin the three regions of Ynys Prydein/Britannia were named as Cambria, Albania and Logres, which the English translation renders as Wales, Scotland and England. This has resulted not only in confusion over the location of many historical events, but also in Arthur being linked to sites as far apart as the Scilly Isles in the South and Scotland in the North. Historians agree that no single king of the sixth century could have ruled from Cornwall to Scotland, and for this reason Geoffrey's Latin text is often classed as fantasy. The real reason for Geoffrey's absurd geography was a misunderstanding in the translation of place names from Welsh to Latin.

THE THREE REALMS OF YNYS PRYDEIN/BRITANNIA

Source			
Brut (Welsh)	Cymru	Alban	Lloegyr
Geoffrey of Monmouth, 1136 (Latin)	Cambria	Albania	Logres
Geoffrey of Monmouth (English translation)	Wales	Scotland	England
Giraldus Cambrensis, 1180 (Latin)	Venedotia	Powisia	Sudwallia
Chronicle of the Princes (Welsh)	Gwynedd	Powys	Deheubarth
Present day	Gwynedd	Powys	South Wales

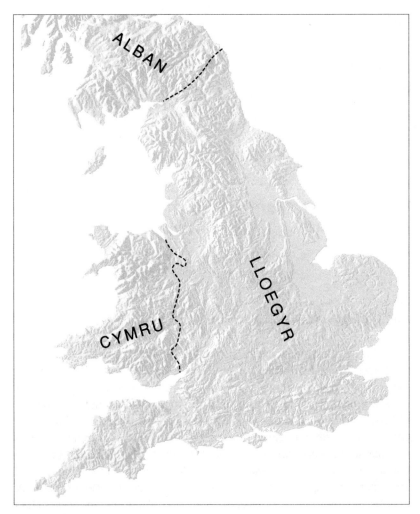

Map 2 The usual locations of the three divisions

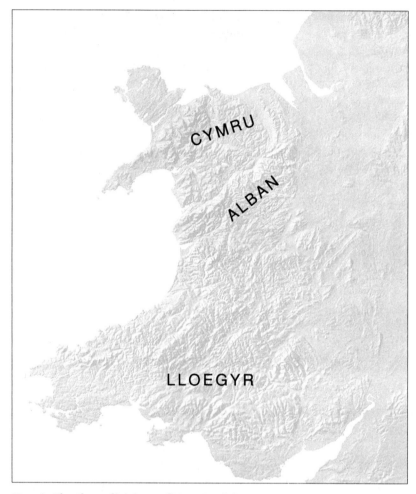

Map 3 The three divisions of Ynys Prydein

In effect, the location of events in the Welsh *Brut* had been stretched by Geoffrey's *Historia* to cover the whole of Great Britain, whereas in fact these events had only ever taken place in Prydein/Britannia. With our revised geography of ancient Britain, the previously confused location of historical events in the period known as the Dark Ages, including those connected to Arthur, began to make sense. Geoffrey of Monmouth's 'Kings of Alban and Loegria' were no longer the Kings of Scotland and England, but the Kings of Powys and South Wales. And yet this geographical misunderstanding had led to English kings quoting from Geoffrey's work in order to prove their claim over Scotland and Wales, and the *Historia* had even been used in the English parliament to settle political arguments![7]

CONFIRMATION FROM SCHOLARS OF THE PAST

When we uncovered this new map of the original Kingdom of Britain, a part of us hoped we were wrong. If we were right, and these three divisions were all in the western part of Britain, then all of the history we had been taught in school would be incorrect.

Thinking that we were alone in this discovery it was heartening to find that at least one well-respected academic from the past, the Reverend A.W. Wade-Evans, had spent over 60 years promoting his theory that Insula Britannia was a region in the west of Britain consisting of Wales and the southwestern peninsular counties of Devon and Cornwall. But for many people Wade-Evans's theory was too controversial. For the first edition of his last work, *The Emergence of England and Wales*, he found that he was forced to take it to Belgium for publication, as no British publisher was prepared to print a book that called into question so many long-held assumptions regarding this period of British history. That was as recent as 1956 and it wasn't until three years later, after the book had provoked discussion within academic circles, that it received a British publication.[8] At the tender age of 84 Wade-Evans finally saw his full theory regarding the original location of Britannia published in Britain. Today this work is considered essential reading by anybody interested in this period of history.

With the encouragement of the detailed works of Wade-Evans we read the *Brut* again, using wherever possible the other primary source materials of Gildas, Nennius and Bede, as well as *The Anglo-Saxon Chronicle*. Our new understanding of the three kingdoms of ancient Britain worked with a frightening degree of accuracy, and from the descriptions of events narrated in the *Brut* we were able to find the original locations of a majority of the sites linked to such famous characters of British history as Vortigern and Arthur.

It is interesting to note that the two 20th-century scholars who called the accepted ideas on this period into question were also the two people who made a greater contribution to the promotion and publication of source materials than anyone else. They therefore knew the sources better than most, agreed that the present ideas were wrong, and offered explanations of their own. The arguments of the Reverend Wade-Evans still stand today in many respects and his tireless efforts in editing and translating source texts are, in some cases, still the only versions available.[9] The other scholar was Dr John Gwenogfryn Evans, an expert on early Welsh manuscripts. His publications of the major Welsh source texts in diplomatic editions, which he produced virtually single-handed on his small hand-operated printing press between 1900 and 1927, made early

Welsh texts available to scholars the world over. Nearly 100 years later many of his publications have yet to be superseded. This part of Evans's career is well known, unlike his radical ideas on the chronology and geography of early Welsh poetry, which made him no friends and led to some remarkable attacks on his critics in academic journals. Today they are viewed as a glitch in an otherwise outstanding career.[10] In addition to his admittedly dubious ideas on the chronology of Welsh poetry, though, he raised doubts about the geography of this poetry, and it is this aspect of his work that interested us.

Evans's pioneering work on the poetry of the Gogynfeirdd bards of the 12th and 13th centuries included an index of personal and place names found in this body of poetry which, in his own words, is 'a shortcut to the evidence there is, and also saves from a fruitless search and haunting fears by its silence'.[11] Evans maintained the view that the traditional ideas regarding the geography of events were wrong and used many examples from the Gogynfeirdd poetry to prove his point. This part of his argument has long been ignored by historians, but by using some of his conclusions, along with his invaluable index of place names, we were able to locate many of the place names found in the *Brut*.

KEY 2: THE RIVERS AND TOWNS OF YNYS PRYDEIN

In order to gain a clearer understanding of the geography of Arthur's kingdom our next task was to locate the three regions of Ynys Prydein/Britannia on our new map. First, we found that the boundaries of these regions are determined by three rivers, named in the Welsh text *Enwau Ynys Prydein* (The Names of Ynys Prydein) as '*Teir Prif Avon Ynys Prydein: Temys, a Hafren, a Hwmyr*' (Three chief rivers of Ynys Prydein: the Temys, Hafren and Hwmyr).[12] These three rivers have been translated from the Latin text of Geoffrey of Monmouth's *Historia* as the Thames, the Severn and the Humber, but these identifications have been made on the misunderstanding that the Britannia (Ynys Prydein) of Geoffrey's text refers to the whole of Great Britain.

The names of the three principal towns of Ynys Prydein – one for each of the three regions – are given on several occasions in the story of Arthur told in the *Brut*, but they were also the subject of a particularly revealing entry concerning the bishops Dyfan and Ffagan, who came from Rome to establish Christianity in Britannia in the second century.[13] Referring to the three archbishoprics founded by Dyfan and Ffagan in 156 AD, the *Brut* tells us: 'And the three archbishop houses were in the three most noble cities of the realm, that is, Llundain, Caerlleon and Caer Efrog. And when the bishop houses were divided between them, to Caer Efrog belonged Deifyr and Bryneich and all the north [i.e. Alban], as the Hwmyr separates them from Lloegyr. And to the archbishop house of Llundain was partitioned Lloegyr and Kernyw. And to the archbishop house of Caerlleon, all Cymru was in its boundaries.'[14]

According to the original Welsh of the *Brut*, therefore, Llundain was the chief town of Lloegyr, Caerlleon the chief town of Cymru, and Caer Efrog the chief town of Alban. (*Caer* means 'city', and should be understood in the sense of a Dark Age settlement.) In the Latin of Geoffrey of Monmouth's *Historia*, however, these towns became Londinium, Urbes Legionis and Eboracum and subsequently, in English, London, Caerlleon and York. Before we unravel the geographical confusion created by Geoffrey's *Historia*, the following table shows how today's confusion surrounding the three rivers and towns of Ynys Prydein/Britannia arose:

THE THREE RIVERS AND REGIONAL TOWNS OF YNYS PRYDEIN/BRITANNIA

Welsh (source the *Brut*)

Region	Cymru	Alban	Lloegyr
Town	Caerlleon	Caer Efrog	Llundain
River	Hafren	Hwmyr	Temys

Latin (source the *Historia*)

Region	Cambria	Albania	Logres
Town	Urbes Legiones	Eboracum	Londinium
River	Sabrina	Humbrum	Tamensis

Modern English

Region	Wales	Scotland	England
Town	Caerlleon	York	London
River	Severn	Humber	Thames

CONFUSION 1: THE RIVER THAMES/TEMYS AND LONDON/LLUNDAIN

There is only one possible candidate for the River Temys in Wales and that is the River Teme, which flows from the mountains south of Newtown to join the River Severn near Worcester. The *Brut* relates that Brutus founded the city of Llundain on this river and this led us to look at early settlements there. The earliest settlement we found was the Roman fort of Brangoumine at Leintwardine, but we were guided towards the true location of Llundain when we read that it had been known originally as

Caer Lud. The 'Lud' element of the original name is preserved in the medieval walled town of Ludlow, the largest town on the Teme. With this in mind we examined the history of Ludlow and discovered that the huge castle situated on the bank of the Teme had been the major residence of the princes of Wales, where they kept law and order in Wales and the Marches. Prince Arthur, the oldest son of Henry VII, spent most of his adult life at Ludlow Castle and when he died in 1502 his body was displayed there for three weeks before being buried in Worcester Cathedral. The evidence convinced us that Ludlow was to all intents and purposes the capital of the Prince of Wales and in our opinion Ludlow, not London, was the original site of city of Llundain described in the *Brut*.

CONFUSION 2: THE RIVER SEVERN/
HAFREN AND CAERLEON/CAERLLEON

The task of locating the River Temys and the town of Llundain on our new map had been relatively straightforward. Our search to identify the other two rivers and towns of Ynys Prydein was to prove more complicated.

The River Hafren referred to in the *Brut* has been identified with the Sabrina (Severn), because of Geoffrey's Latin translation which told us that the river was 'called Habren in the British language, although by a corruption of speech it is called Sabrina in the other tongue'.[15] It is evident that this 'corruption of speech' has caused confusion ever since. We found a further reference to River Hafren in *Culhwch and Olwen*, the earliest Arthurian tale, where it was mentioned in connection with a city named 'Caer Loyw'. It was by locating this mysterious city that we were able to find the original identity of the River Hafren.

In the *Brut* we are told that Caer Loyw was founded by a Roman emperor called Gloyw (the Welsh name for Claudius) in honour of Gweirydd, a British king better known under his Latin name Arviragus. Arviragus also appears in the satires of Juvenal, the contemporary Roman author, where he is described as 'king of the Britons',[16] while the 16th-century poet Robert Chester refers to him as the 'King of Venedotia' (North Wales).[17] The fact that Arviragus's son Marius is traditionally held to have built the walls of Chester led us to consider the possibility that this important Roman city was the original site of Caer Loyw, even though it was on the River Dee in North Wales.[18] The traditional view locates Caer Loyw at the cathedral city of Gloucester on the River Severn, despite the fact that Nennius describes the original foundation of that city in his *Historia Brittonum* as the work of 'Glovi, who built a great city on the bank of the river Sabrina, which is called in the British tongue Cair Glovi, but in Saxon Gloecester'.[19] Glovi was the great-grandfather of Vortigern and lived 300 years later than the Roman Emperor Claudius (Welsh 'Gloyw'), who as we have just seen was the founder of Caer Loyw according to the *Brut*. Gloucester, or Caer Glovi, with the independent story of its foundation, was therefore not Caer Loyw.

We found further evidence to identify Chester as the location of the original Caer Loyw in the *Brut*, which states that the Roman legions wintered in Caer Loyw and went to conquer Iwerddon (Ireland). Many of the later chronicles regarding the history of Britain mention the fact that the Emperor Claudius, having succeeded where Julius Caeser had failed and conquered the Britons, wintered with his troops in Chester. The mounting evidence from the texts, combined with archaeological evidence for the early Roman origins of Chester, with its magnificent circuit of city walls, amphitheatre and other extensive remains, led us to conclude that Chester was indeed the site of Caer Loyw. As Chester is on the River Dee, this led us to ask ourselves whether the Dee had ever been known as the 'Hafren'. In a version of the *Brut* written by Gutyn Owain (c.1470) we found a reference to the Battle of Bangor, which had been fought on the River Dee in 601: 'And after they had been fighting thus for a long time, Brochwel had to retreat through the River Afren, because of the number of Saxons.'[20]

The above evidence led us to the conclusion that, contrary to the traditional view, the River Hafren referred to in the *Brut* is the River Dee, not the River Severn as stated in Geoffrey's translation of 1136.

Although we had earlier established that the town of Caer Loyw was indeed Chester, we still needed to identify the principal city and seat of one of the three archbishoprics that was associated with the River Hafren. In the *Brut* this city is named as Caerlleon ar Wysg, but in Geoffrey's *Historia* we find it called Urbs Legionum (City of the Legions), with the additional information 'situated as it is in Glamorganshire on the river Usk, not far from the Severn Sea'.[21] This addition is not in the Welsh *Brut*, for Caerlleon simply means 'City of the Legions', a name that also applied to Chester. The *Historia*'s identification of Caerlleon with the site of the Roman town of Isca on the River Usk – the modern town of Caerlleon on the Usk – is a prime example of how the geography of Ynys Prydein/Britannia has been corrupted through its translation into Latin. As far as we know, there is no record of there ever having been an archbishopric at Caerleon. However, Chester was made the centre of a palatine earldom in 1071 and has been the seat of a bishopric ever since. Was Chester in fact the archbishopric of Caerlleon ar Wysg? We needed to be absolutely certain that we were correct in this identification, for throughout the *Brut*, *The Mabinogion* and the romances Caerlleon is referred to as the major court of Arthur.

We turned back to the texts again and in a Welsh tract known as *The Twenty-Four Mightiest Kings* (c.1475), which describes the cities founded by noble kings of the past, we found accounts of the foundation of both Caerlleon and Caerlleon ar Wysg:

> He [Lleon Gawr] founded a city on the bank of the river Dee and called it Caerlleon from his own name. And so it is still called in Welsh and in English Chester.

> Beli founded a great city on the bank of the river Wysg, where Lleon Gawr had his castle. And that fortress was known as Caerlleon ar Wysg.[22]

Lleon Gawr founded Chester on the River Dee and Beli had founded Caerlleon ar Wysg on the same site, which suggested to us that Caerlleon ar Wysg was on the River Dee. We found confirmation of this in two different descriptions of the same event in Welsh and Saxon texts. Under the entry for the year 973, the Welsh *Brut Y Tywysogion* (Chronicle of the Princes) reads: 'And then Edward king of the Saxons gathered a huge fleet to Kaerllion ar wysc.'[23] In the *Anglo-Saxon Chronicle* the entry for the same event is given under the year 972 as: 'The king [Edward] led his whole raiding ship army to Chester.'[24]

Caerlleon ar Wysg was indeed Chester, so what did *Wysg* actually mean if it was not a Welsh name for the River Usk? We found the answer in a book called *Drych Y Prif Oesoedd* (Mirror of the Chief Ages) written by Theophilus Evans in 1710: 'Everyone knows that the Wysc is the name of a big river in Wales; and that the Con-wy, Tywi and Wy[e] are just separate names for the same meaning ... Nobody knows the meaning of the word but the Gwyddel of Ireland only have one other word for Dwfr (waters) which is visc.'[25]

What Evans is saying is that wysc means the same as dwfr (the Welsh word for 'waters') and uses *visc* (the Irish word for 'waters') to prove the point. This was very important as it meant that 'Caerlleon ar Wysg' could also mean 'Caerlleon ar Dwfr' (Caerlleon on the waters) and the Welsh name for the River Dee on which Caerlleon is situated is Dyfrdwy, meaning 'the Waters of the Goddess'. We therefore felt certain that Caerlleon ar Wysg had absolutely nothing to do with the Caerleon on the Usk in South Wales. Our identification of Caerlleon ar Wysg with Chester also made sense of the lands of Cymru said to be under the jurisdiction of this archbishopric in the *Brut*. As we have already seen, the region of Cymru corresponds with Gwynedd, and Chester was indeed the major city in the Kingdom of Gwynedd.

In conclusion, the River Hafren and town of Caerlleon referred to in Geoffrey's source, the Welsh *Brut*, are not the River Severn and Caerleon on the Usk as the traditional view would have us believe. They are the River Dee and the city of Chester.

CONFUSION 3: THE RIVER HUMBER/ HWMYR AND YORK/CAER EFROG

The *Historia* translated Hwmyr from the Welsh *Brut* into Latin as Humbrum and this river has since become identified with the River Humber in eastern England. In the Welsh *Brut* the Hwmyr is always used to to divide Ynys Prydein into north and south. The land to the north of the Hwmyr was simply called *Y Gogledd*, meaning 'the North', but through the misconception that the Hwmyr was the River Humber 'the North' became known as 'Northumbria' and was located in the northeast of England.

The one river that cuts right across Wales and provides a north–south division is the Severn, and it is our conclusion that although Hwmyr was the original name for the River Severn the name fell out of use within a few decades of Geoffrey's appropriation of the name Hafren for the Severn. This would seem to be confirmed by the fact that we were unable to find any references in Welsh texts to the River Hwmyr outside of the *Brut*, and all references to the River Severn *after* 1136 refer to it as the Hafren.

The major city and archbishopric of Alban was Caer Efrog, which is currently identified with the northern cathedral city of York. However, the true location for Caer Efrog was provided for us by a Welsh bard called Guto'r Glyn, who in a poem from 1450 writes: *'Yn Efrog yng Nglan Hafren'* (In Efrog on the banks of the Hafren).[26] By 1450 the Welsh had applied the name Hafren to the River Severn, so if Caer Efrog was on the River Severn it could not be York as is widely held. In the *Brut* Caer Efrog is also mentioned as the burial place of the Emperor Constantine, and this tradition survives on the banks of the River Severn, in the village of Eaton Constantine near a burial mound said to contain his remains. Within two miles of this village are the remains of the important Roman town of Viroconium near the village of Wroxeter on the River Severn. As this is the only major Roman town on the banks of the River Severn in the region of Alban, it is our conclusion that this is the original site of the Caer Efrog described in the *Brut* as one of 'the three most noble cities of the realm'.

In our search to make sense of the confusion created by Geoffrey of Monmouth's Latin translation of the Welsh *Brut*, the geography of our new map of Ynys Prydein/Britannia seems to have worked. In the following table our revised geography for the three rivers and towns of the ancient kingdom of Ynys Prydein is set alongside the traditional locations. With these new identifications in mind it should be possible to read the *Brut* and the Arthurian romances in a new light, and what was once deemed fictional may begin to take on a level of authenticity not previously supposed to exist.

THE THREE RIVERS AND REGIONAL TOWNS OF YNYS PRYDEIN/BRITANNIA

Welsh (source the *Brut*)

Region	Cymru	Alban	Lloegyr
Town	Caerlleon	Caer Efrog	Llundain
River	Hafren	Hwmyr	Temys

Latin (source the *Historia*)

Region	Cambria	Albania	Logres
Town	Urbs Legionum	Eboracum	Londinium
River	Sabrina	Humbrum	Tamensis

Traditional geography

Region	Wales	Scotland	England
Town	Caerleon	York	London
River	Severn	Humber	Thames

Revised geography

Region	Gwynedd	Powys	South Wales
Town	Chester	Wroxeter	Ludlow
River	Dee	Severn	Teme

CONFUSION 4: THE KINGDOM OF NORTHUMBRIA – DEIRA/DEIFYR AND BERNICA/BYRNEICH

Following our identification of the Hwmyr as the River Severn rather than the Humber, we had to reassess the location of the Saxon Kingdom of Northumbria in order to confirm our theory. The location of this kingdom in northeast England is so well established that we doubted whether we would find any evidence to support our theory, but we found the evidence we needed when we looked closely at the two smaller kingdoms of Northumbria known as Deira and Bernica. In Welsh these kingdoms were called Deifyr and Bryneich.

On the present maps of Dark Age Britain, Deira is located in the northeast of England, extending from Hadrian's Wall as far south as York. This area has been defined using the clues given in the texts from Saxon and Latin sources, but what of Welsh-British sources? Deira, or Deifyr, is mentioned many times by the Welsh bards as late as the fourteenth century. A poem by Gruffudd ap Maredudd called *I'r Grog o Gaer* (To the

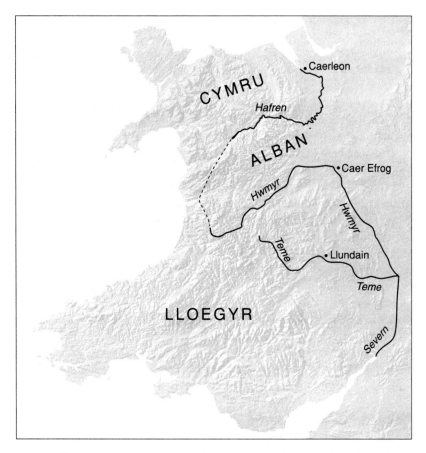

Map 4 Showing the three rivers, three towns and boundries of the three divisions of Ynys Prydein

Chester Cross) tells of a wooden cross that washed up in the land of Deifyr, at Chester:

> *Dylan natur fawrdeg eglur fordwy gogledd*
> *Delais arwain o ddwfr dwyrain I ddeifr diredd*
> *Dyddug mordon ar ei ddwyfron arwy dyfredd*
> *Dyfrdwy waedd greg arial gwaneg ar ael Gwynedd.*[27]

(The northern sea, vast and fair and bright, with its flowing nature, bore it and led it from eastern waters to the lands of Deifr; the sea wave brought it upon its breasts, as a chain of waters, into hoarse-sounding, violent-waved Dee on the border of Gwynedd.)

Drwy fordwy Dyfrdwy deifrdir eithaf.[28]

(He came through the seas into the Dee on the extremity of the land of Deifr.)[29]

In the words of Professor T. Gwynn Jones, who translated the above, 'It may be interesting to note that Deifyr seems to be used to denote a territory including Cheshire. It is the Welsh name for Deira.'

Another poem from the 12th century actually describes Deira as being in the vicinity of the River Dee: '*Lleudir y Deivrdir amgylch dyfvrdwy*' (An open land is the land of Deira about the river Dee).[30] Going yet further back in time, the old Roman name for Chester as given by Ptolemy in his *Geographia* of c.140 and later Roman sources is Deva, which is very close in pronunciation to Deifyr, indicating that this name is of some antiquity. There are over a dozen references to Deifyr as an area in or near Wales in the poetry of the Gogynfeirdd.[31] We wondered why this evidence had not been used by any historians since Dr John Gwenogfryn Evans first brought attention to it in the 1920s. We feel the answer lies in the fact that this poetry is not very well known to most people in Wales, let alone Saxon historians from outside of the country, so the connections have not previously been made.

On the Dark Age map Bernica is located to the north of Hadrian's Wall, running up to Edinburgh. Under the name of Bryneich there are over 30 references to it in the poetry of the Welsh bards. We found a clear clue to the true location of Bryneich when we read that Llywelyn ap Grufudd '*Bryneich a dreisyr dros glawdd Offa*' (Ravaged Bernica across Offa's Dyke).[32] The poem tells us that Bryneich was a region adjoining Offa's Dyke which, as we saw earlier, is an earthwork that runs the length of Wales from the Dee estuary in the north to the Severn estuary in the south. And, as far as we know, Llywelyn ap Grufudd, the last Prince of Wales (d.1282), never went to Scotland.

Another poem from the 12th century describes Owain Gwynedd, the ruler of North Wales, as the Braw Bryneich (Terror of Bernica).[33] Again, if Bernica was north of Hadrian's Wall, how could it have been terrorized by a Welsh prince who is not recorded as ever having left Wales?

Our proposed new location for the Kingdom of Northumbria is not as bizarre as it might first seem, for the counties of Cheshire and Shropshire contain a large number of churches and holy wells dedicated to such Northumbrian saints as St Chad and St Oswald. Writing in 731, the historian Bede tells us that Oswald was the first to set up a cross to Christ in the land of Bernica, at Hefenfelth, the site of his battle; that is, the town of Oswestry in Shropshire, which suggests that the latter was in the Kingdom of

Bernica. In a version of the *Historia Brittonum* compiled in 944 and kept in the Vatican, we found a reference to Caer Efrog being in Bernica,[34] which reveals the confusion underlying the traditionally accepted geography according to which Bernica is north of the Hadrian's Wall and Caer Efrog is York, far to the south. When we apply our new geography, which identifies Caer Efrog as Wroxeter and Bernica as northern Shropshire, the county where Wroxeter is located, this text makes perfect sense. For us this was further proof that the original sources are correct; it is our present framework that is wrong and it needs revising. When the kingdoms of Deira and Bernica, which are defined by Welsh sources as Cheshire and northern Shropshire, are resited in their original location many historical anomalies are resolved and a part of the history of the British Isles that has always posed problems for historians begins to make sense. (The Northern Kingdoms are dealt with in more detail in Appendix 3.)

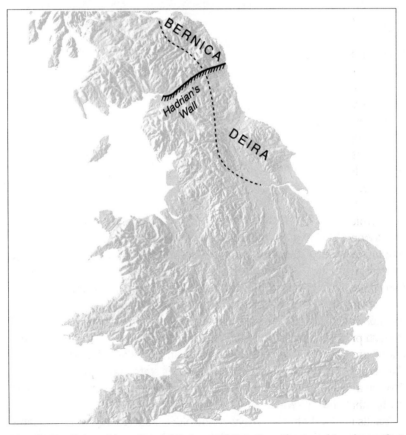

Map 5 Traditional location of Deira and Bernica, the two kingdoms that make up Northumbria

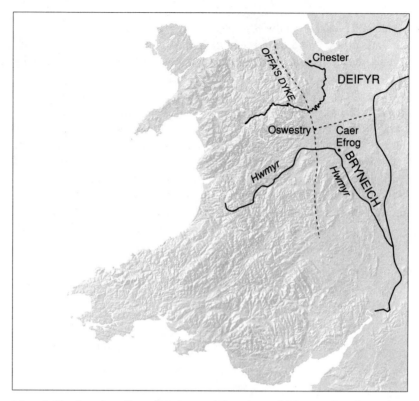

Map 6 The true location of Deira and Bernica, which together form the Kingdom of Northumbria

CONFUSION 5: CORNWALL/KERNYW

The lands of Cornwall have always played a large part in the legend of Arthur because of the reference in Geoffrey of Monmouth's *Historia* to events in his life taking place in a region called 'Cornubia'. When we looked for the Welsh name for this region in the *Brut* we found that it was originally called Kernyw. According to Welsh sources Kernyw is also the location for several major sites connected with Arthur, of which the most important are Dindagol, which was the place of his conception (better known as Tintagel), his court at Gelliwig, and the site of his final battle at Camlan. As the *Brut* and other Welsh sources state that Kernyw is in Ynys Prydein, this led us to look for the original site of this region, so central to the life of Arthur, in Wales.

Searching for Arthur's Kernyw in the oldest sources available, we came across a connection that narrowed down our hunt to one particular region of Wales. In the tale of *Culhwch and Olwen* we found a reference to a giant called Rhita Gawr, who was titled 'the Chief Elder of Kernyw'. In our hunt for further references to Rhita Gawr we came across an old manuscript concerning Welsh giants that described Rhita as 'the king of Gwynedd in the time of Arthur'.[35] As Gwynedd was the name for the ancient Kingdom of North Wales, it was evidently here that we needed to look for Kernyw. A closer look at Welsh folklore led us to a tale recounting how Rhita Gawr had fought with Arthur on a hilltop in the hope of defeating him, thereby adding his beard to the cloak he had made from the beards of other rulers he had beaten in combat. Two hilltop sites for this battle are recorded. The first is the summit of Snowdon, referred to in local tradition as Gwyddfa Rita (Rhita's Tumulus); the second is an exposed mountain pass called Bwlch Y Groes (Pass of the Cross), situated beneath the brooding Aran Mountains, high above Lake Bala at the headwaters of the River Dee. Realizing that both of these sites were also located in the ancient Kingdom of Gwynedd, we decided to take a closer look at the actual meaning of the word kernyw. In modern Welsh cern means 'the side of the head', implying that Kernyw might actually denote a headland or peninsula. If this were the case, there was only one option: the area known today as the Lleyn Peninsula, which stretches from North Wales into the Irish Sea. As if to confirm this, the name of most important hillfort in the area retains a link with Rhita Gawr, the giant who was Chief Elder of Kernyw. It is called Tre'r Ceiri (the Town of Giants).

The task of narrowing down the location of Kernyw was made easier by the reference to it in the Brut that we had found during our earlier search for 'the three most noble cities' of Ynys Prydein. There Kernyw, along with Lloegyr, was described as being under the authority of the bishop's house at Llundain. From this we concluded that Kernyw most probably shared a border with the realm of Lloegyr (South Wales). We also knew that Kernyw was in Gwynedd, and as the latter touches the border of Lloegyr at only one place, Machynlleth, this suggested that the original extent of Arthur's Kernyw was the coastal region of Gwynedd, north from Machynlleth to the Lleyn Peninsula.

KEY 3: THE THREE SEAS OF YNYS PRYDEIN

Having established on our new map the original locations for the ancient kingdoms, rivers and towns of Ynys Prydein/Britannia, there remained the confusion created by Geoffrey of Monmouth's Historia concerning the three seas that surround Ynys Prydein. In the Welsh Brut these three seas are named as Mor Caitness, Mor Iwerddon and Mor Ud – mor is Welsh for 'sea' – and the Historia identifies these as the Sea of Caithness off the

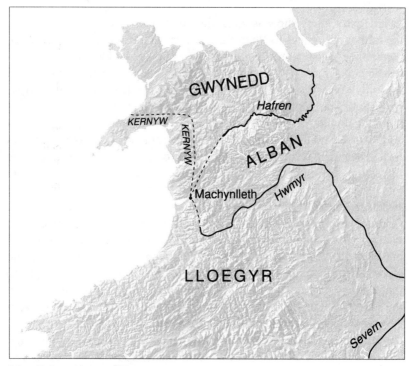

Map 7 Locations of Kernyw

northern coast of Scotland, the Irish Sea between Wales and Ireland and the English Channel.

The *Brut* relates a story that a certain King of Prydein called Beli built a road from Kernyw to the Sea of Caitness in the north.[36] This road equates with Sarn Elen, an old paved way that runs from Pennal near Machynlleth (in the southern part of Kernyw), through Dolgellau to the Conwy valley in the North. This suggested to us that the Sea of Caitness was off the coast of North Wales,[37] whereas the traditional argument insists that it is the sea off the coast of Caithness in the far north of Scotland. Admittedly, this is the only option available when the realm of Ynys Prydein/Britannia is understood to be the whole of Britain. Here, again, Geoffrey's *Historia* has confused the issue, for in translating the story of the building of Beli's road it has moved Kernyw south to Cornwall and the north coast of Prydein to the northernmost coast of mainland Britain.

Of the other two seas, the Sea of Iwerddon is easily identified with the Irish Sea, as Iwerddon is the Welsh name for Ireland, and we suggest that Mor Ud is the original name for the Severn estuary and the Bristol Channel, the area of sea between South Wales and the southwest peninsula of Devon and Cornwall.

THE THREE SEAS OF YNYS PRYDEIN

Welsh name	Traditional location	Revised location
Mor Catneis	Caithness (Scotland)	North Wales coast, Liverpool Bay and Dee estuary
Mor Iwerddon	Irish Sea	the sea channel between Ireland and Wales, from Anglesey to Pembroke
Mor Ud	English Channel	Bristol Channel and Severn estuary

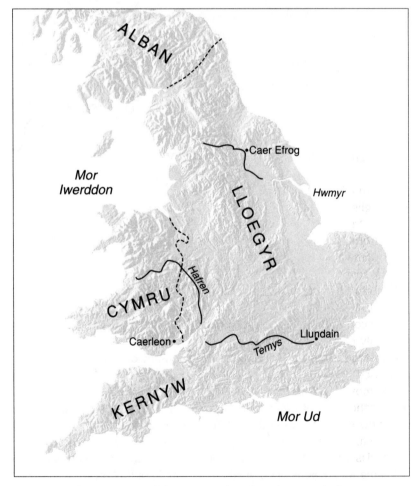

Map 8 Traditional view of the geography of Dark Age Britain

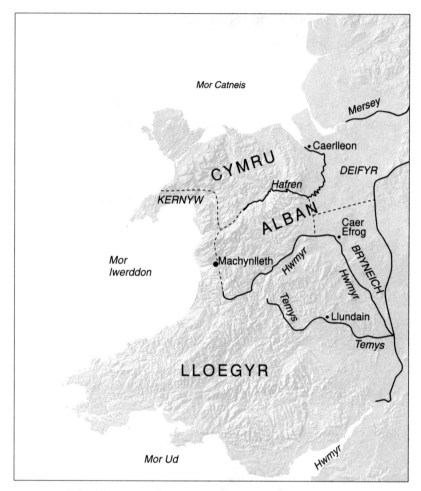

Map 9 Original location of Ynys Prydein and its place names

SUMMARY

In this chapter we have redefined the geography of Arthur's kingdom as follows:

- Arthur's realm of Britain – Ynys Prydein in Welsh – extended over the area known today as Wales and the Marches.
- The three regions of Arthur's Britain – Cymru, Alban and Lloegyr, traditionally identified as Wales, Scotland and England – correspond to the modern regions of Gwynedd, Powys and South Wales.

- The three chief towns of Arthur's Britain – Caerlleon, Caer Efrog and Llundain, traditionally identified as Caerleon, York and London – correspond to the modern towns of Chester, Wroxeter and Ludlow.
- The three rivers of Arthur's Britain – the Hafren, Hwmyr and Temys, traditionally identified as the Severn, Humber and Thames – were the Dee, Severn and Teme.
- The Saxon kingdoms of Deira and Bernica, traditionally located in the northeast of England astride the border with Scotland, correspond to the modern counties of Cheshire and Shropshire.
- The Arthurian realm of Kernyw, traditionally identified as Cornwall, extended over an area of northwestern Wales that included the Lleyn Peninsula and the southern coastal region of Gwynedd.
- The three seas bordering Arthur's Britain, traditionally identified as the Sea of Caithness, the Irish Sea and the English Channel, have been redefined as the seas along the southern, western and northern coasts of Wales.

As we have said before, our radical revision of the geography of Britain may at first appear odd. A close reading of the events related in the Welsh *Brut* shows that it works time and time again, though. With this new map in front of us we can now begin to understand some of the historical anomalies surrounding Arthur and his contemporaries. The next section of the *Brut* introduced us to such famous characters as Vortigern, Uthyr Pendragon and Merlin. By using our new geography we found that hidden amidst the mass of Welsh folklore and other manuscripts was information that had preserved the location of one of the most important events in British history.

CHAPTER FOUR

BRITAIN BEFORE ARTHUR

ALTHOUGH THE major events of Arthur's life – his magical conception at Tintagel, the sword in the stone, his final battle at Camlan and his journey to Avalon – may have a certain ring of familiarity, when invited to go into further detail most people will simply shrug their shoulders. For many, questions such as 'Who was Uthyr Pendragon, Arthur's father?', 'Did the magical characters of Merlin and Morgan Le Fay really exist?', 'Where was Avalon?' and even 'Who was Arthur?' remain shrouded in mystery. Their answers can only be understood when Arthur's life is put into its proper context. In other words, in order to make sense of Arthur and the legends that have sprung up around him we need to understand the events that took place before his lifetime, in that murky period of European history appropriately known as the Dark Ages.

This chapter examines the *Brut Y Brenhinedd*, the Welsh chronicle that Geoffrey of Monmouth translated into Latin as *Historia Regum Britanniae*, but with one very important difference. We shall be using the original Welsh place names of the *Brut* rather than the 'corrected' names that appeared in the *Historia*. This will enable us to take a look at the story in a form closer to the original source, and therefore closer to Arthur than ever before. The original Welsh personal names for the cast of characters involved will also be retained, along with their Anglicized renderings as these are better known. Many of the events related in the *Brut* are also found in other historical documents, and in such cases we have used these other sources to help us deepen our understanding of them. By using all of the available source materials in this way, we were able to build up a picture of the period before Arthur, from the end of Roman rule in Ynys Prydein, through the story of Vortigern and the Saxons and the appearance of Merlin, to the rise to power of Uthyr Pendragon and the coming of Arthur. Our journey back into history begins with the end of Roman rule in Prydein and the arrival of Custennin, grandfather of Arthur.

At the end of the fourth century the Roman Empire was in a state of decline and the island situated at the northwestern limits of its empire was becoming too troublesome to hold on to. The natives were continually fighting against the Romans and, with Rome itself under threat from the Visigoths, it was decided to leave the island to its own devices. The Welsh *Brut* gives a brief account of the end of Roman rule in Prydein, but more detail is found in *The Dream of Macsen Wledig*, an independent story from *The Mabinogion*. Written down in its present form around 1100, the story describes a Roman emperor called Macsen Wledig – better known to the history books as Magnus Maximus – and a dream he had while sleeping during a hunting trip near Rome. In his dream Maximus travels across the sea to a distant land where he sees the most beautiful woman in the world. On waking from the dream he describes his journey to his messengers, who set off in search of the mysterious land. When they arrive there they inform the woman of the emperor's desire to marry her.

The tale describes the locations to which the messengers journey. First they arrive in Ynys Prydein, which as we saw in the previous chapter is the area covered by Wales and the Marches, where they travel across the high mountains of Eryri (the Welsh name for the mountains of Snowdonia) until they see Mon (Anglesey) and the land of Arfon (literally, the land opposite Mon). As they look out over the land of Arfon from the mountains they see the harbour and boats described to them by Maximus. The story names this place as Aber Seint (the mouth of the River Seint) and describes an actual site in North Wales that still exists today: the walled town of Caernarfon, dominated by a huge castle where Prince Charles was invested with the title Prince of Wales in 1969, on the River Seint overlooking the Menai Straits to Anglesey. Known in Roman times as Segontium, the ruins of which still remain, it was a powerful Roman centre known to have been occupied in the closing years of the fourth century, the time in which this tale is set.[1] The messengers inform Maximus that they have found the city and the woman he saw in his dreams and he comes to Caernarfon to marry her. The tale details the people present on his arrival and we are introduced to four early ancestors of Arthur: Eudaf

Hen, his two sons Cynan and Gadeon and his daughter Elen, the beautiful woman of Maximus's dream.

When Maximus marries Elen, she asks – as her maiden's fee – that her father be given the Kingdom of Prydein 'from Mor Ud [Bristol Channel] to Mor Iwerddon [the Irish Sea] and the three adjacent islands'.[2] She also asked that three strongholds be made for her, the most exalted at Arfon (Caernarfon) and two others at Caerlleon (Chester) and Caer Fyrddin (Carmarthen). Here we have our first example of our new geography making sense of the material. If Ynys Prydein meant Great Britain as we know it today, why would the three strongholds built for Elen all be in Wales? Following the construction of these three strongholds Elen decided to have them connected with roads that still exist today. Known as the Sarn Elen (roads of Elen), they run between the three modern cities of Caernarfon, Chester and Carmarthen.

As the emperor could only be absent from Rome for a maximum of seven years, Maximus had to return at the end of this time or risk losing his right to rule. As it was, when Maximus returned to Rome he was forced to lay siege to the city. It went on for a year, until the arrival of Elen's brothers, Cynan and Gadeon. With their help Maximus was able to enter the city and regain the imperial throne. As a way of thanking his brothers-in-law Maximus gave them an army with which they could conquer any lands they saw fit. *The Dream of Macsen Welig* gives no further information on the lands they conquered, but Gadeon decided to return home whilst Cynan (also known as Cynan Meiriadoc) founded a colony in a conquered land he named Llydaw.

CONFUSION 6: BRITTANY/LLYDAW

Geoffrey's *Historia* translated Llydaw into Armorica, the 12th-century name for Brittany in northern France, and ever since Llydaw has been assumed to mean Brittany. This identification has never been confirmed and other references to it in Welsh literature have led historians to suggest that Llydaw was an area in South or Mid-Wales. The Latin *Life of St Cadoc* (c.1070) mentions the emigration of people in the time of Maximus and calls the region Lettau while later Latin texts call it Letavia. The true location lies, quite literally, somewhere between these two arguments.

We found an explanation of why the region was named Llydaw at the end of *The Dream of Macsen Wledig*. Cynan Meiriadoc and his followers killed all the men in the land they had conquered and then, to save their own language from becoming corrupted, cut out the tongues of the native women inhabitants. The land was then called Llydaw – a name that derives from the two Welsh words *lled* (half) and *taw* (silent) – or 'Half Silent', as only the newly arrived Britons were able to speak. This

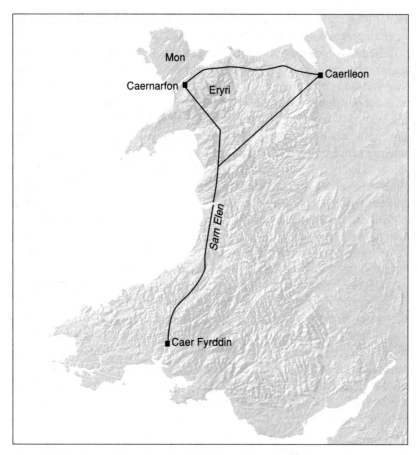

Map 10 The three strongholds of Elen and the Roman roads that link them

drastic measure to preserve the language of the original founders provided a clue to identifying the location of Llydaw. We knew that Cynan came from Caernarfon in North Wales and he would therefore have spoken Welsh, as people still do there today. Was there a region outside Prydein where the inhabitants spoke Welsh? Such a region does exist – today it is known as Cornwall.

The Cornish language has been subject to a revival in recent years and is very similar to Welsh. And not only the Welsh-British language has survived in Cornwall; traditions and folklore are very similar and the church dedications pay witness to a heavy Welsh influence in the area. Historical texts talk of the migration of saints from Wales to Llydaw in the sixth and seventh centuries and it has long been presumed that they went to France. While it is true that the names of some British saints can be found in France, it is not possible to travel more than a few miles in Cornwall before coming across a chapel dedicated to a saint who also has a dedication in Wales – for example, the name of Cynan Meiriadoc, the founder of Llydaw, is preserved in the Cornish village of Camborne, where the parish church is dedicated to St Meriadoc.[3]

If the traditional view, according to which the region called Kernyw is Cornwall, was based on the erroneous translation of Kernyw (the Lleyn Peninsula in North Wales) as Cornubia/Cornwall, had Arthur ever been to Cornwall? Our new identification of the region of Llydaw helped us to understand the origin of the many references to the Arthur's presence in Cornwall. Such references derived not from accounts of Arthur having been in Kernyw, but from Arthur's presence in Llydaw, a region he is said to have visited on at least one occasion in the tale of *Culhwch and Olwen*, the earliest Arthurian source.[4]

THE ARRIVAL OF ARTHUR'S FAMILY IN YNYS PRYDEIN

The events surrounding Maximus's arrival in Prydein and his return to Rome, which we related earlier based on the information contained in the *Brut* and *The Dream of Macsen Welig*, are also described in other Welsh sources. We take up our story again in the important historical text *Historia Brittonum* (attributed to Nennius) where we found the following reference to Maximus: 'The seventh emperor, Maximianus reigned in Britannia. He went forth with all the soldiers of the Britons from Britannia, and slew Gratian, king of the Romans, and held the sovereignty of the whole of Europe. And he was unwilling to send back the soldiers, who had set forth with him, to Britannia, to their wives and to their sons and to their possessions.'[5] The lack of armed men in Britannia left it weak and both Nennius and Gildas state that the Britons sent letters to Rome asking for protection from the Picts and the Scots who were attacking. This period of chaos is also mentioned by Nennius, who tells us that 'after the death of Maximus the tyrant, the rule of the Romans in Britannia being finished, they lived in fear for forty years'.[6]

According to the *Brut*, the remaining nobles of Ynys Prydein decided to bring this 40 years of chaos to an end by sending Cuhelyn, the Archbishop of Llundain (Ludlow) to Llydaw (Cornwall) to look for a ruler of the British royal blood to lead them against the Picts and Scots. Aldwr, the fourth king in descent from Cynan Meiriadoc, was ruler of Llydaw at that time and Cuhelyn informed him of the state of Prydein since Macsen Wledig and Cynan Meiriadoc had taken their armies from the kingdom and left it weakened. Aldwr declined to go to Prydein himself as he had a peaceful kingdom, but gave Cuhelyn 2,000 men with his brother Custennin as prince over them to return to Ynys Prydein.

When Custennin arrived in Prydein with his army the Britons came to meet him where he landed. He also encountered Gwynwas and Melwas, the leaders of the Picts, at an unspecified battlesite where Custennin and the British army slaughtered the Picts. Following his victory, Custennin was made King of Prydein and his coronation took place at Caer Fuddai. The true location of this site is obscure – Geoffrey's *Historia* suggests it was the remains of the Roman town of Silchester in Hampshire – but in our view would it not make more sense for the king to be crowned at a point where all three regions of the kingdom meet? This happened at only one place in the ancient Kingdom of Prydein, the market town of Machynlleth on the banks of the River Dyfi in Mid-Wales, which was also the site chosen by Owain Glyndwr for his own court and parliament in the 15th century.[7]

After taking the throne of Prydein, Custennin was given a wife. Although she is unnamed, we are told she was the daughter of a Roman noble and had been brought up by Cuhelyn the Archbishop. Together Custennin and his wife had three sons: Constans (Constantine), Emrys (Ambrosius) and Uthyr (Uther), of which the latter was later to gain the title Pendragon and become the father of Arthur.

Emrys and Uthyr were given to Archbishop Cuhelin to be fostered – this practice was still carried out in Wales as late as the 18th century – while Constans was brought up in the monastery of St Amphibalus in Caer Wynt.[8] The name Amphibalus is very unusual, as it clearly is not Welsh; *amphibalia* is a rare Latin word used by Gildas to denote a bishop's cloak. However there does exist a Latin text that details the life of St Amphibalus and tells us that he was the confessor of St Alban and that both of them came to North Wales to preach the gospel to the Welsh and the Picts.[9] In his introduction to John Lydgate's 1439 English translation of the Latin and French manuscripts, George Reinecke states that Amphibalus was probably a native of Wales.[10]

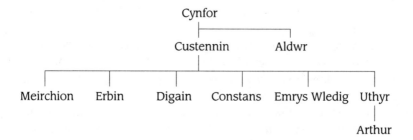

Arthur's family from Llydaw

CONFUSION 7: WINCHESTER/CAER WYNT

The Latin of Geoffrey's *Historia* identifies Caer Wynt – the site of St Amphibalus's monastery – as Winchester, which has led to many Arthurian stories becoming linked to this city and its surroundings, including the site of the stand-off between Arthur and Medrod before the final battle in which both were killed, and the location of the huge Round Table that hangs in the castle there today, with the names of the knights of Round Table painted on it. The Welsh *Brut* mentions Caer Wynt on several occasions, including a reference to St Julian being made bishop of the settlement. St Julian becomes Sulien in Welsh – there is no J in the Welsh alphabet – and St Sulien, along with his brother Mael, is still the patron saint of Corwen in the Dee valley. The *Brut* also mentions Caer Wynt in connection with a battle at a nearby site called Maes Urien (Field of Urien).[11] Maes Urien is named after Urien Rheged – King of Rheged around the time of Arthur and one of the most prominent figures in Welsh history – who is mentioned on several occasions in the folklore of this area, while the name Caer Drewyn (Town of Wyn, or maybe Wynt?), which is attached to the hillfort above the town of Corwen (whose name is suggestive in itself), provides further evidence to suggest that Corwen, which is located near Llangollen in the Dee valley, is the original site of Caer Wynt.

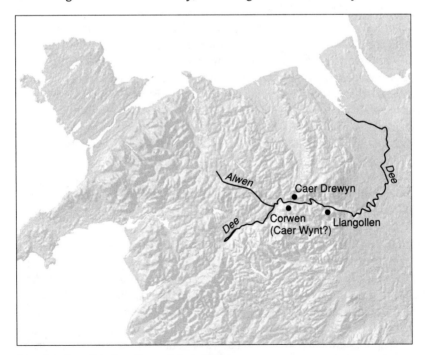

Map 11 Possible location of Caer Wynt

VORTIGERN

The story told in the *Brut* continues by telling us that after Arthur's grandfather Custennin's marriage the remainder of his rule passed quietly for 12 years until he was poisoned by a Pict and died. Following the murder of Custennin we are introduced to one of the most important figures in the history of the British Isles, Vortigern, who was responsible for inviting the Saxons into Britannia. This important event is mentioned in all of the major source texts, including Gildas, Bede, Nennius and the *Anglo-Saxon Chronicle*, but we believe its historical significance has long been misunderstood because it has been located in the wrong place.

Vortigern appears in the *Brut* under his original Welsh name of Gwrtheyrn Gwrtheneu, and in the earlier sources of Nennius and Gildas under the name of Guorthigern. Both of these names have been translated as Vortigern, the name commonly in use today and that we will use from now on. Vortigern is named as the ruler of an area called Erging and Ewias, which correspond to the Archenfield and Ewias areas of modern-day Herefordshire. In Geoffrey's *Historia* these two place names are dropped and Vortigern is called 'ruler of the Gewissi' – Gewissi is the name used by Bede in 731 to refer to the later Saxons who ruled in this area.[12]

The earliest surviving references to both Maximus and Vortigern are recorded on the most important archaeological remain from this period of history in Wales, the ninth-century Pillar of Eliseg. This ancient stone pillar is situated on top of a burial mound next to the ruins of the Cistercian Valle Crucis Abbey, near the town of Llangollen, in the old Welsh Kingdom of Powys, North Wales. The original wording of the inscription on the pillar is now almost impossible to read, and it does not help that a new inscription was carved over it in the 18th century, but fortunately the famous antiquarian Edward Lhuyd made a transcription of it as it was in 1696. The Latin reading of the inscribed stone has been translated and tells us that the pillar was erected by Concenn (c.840), the great-grandson of Eliseg, and commemorates his ancestors, the rulers of Powys. The part of the inscription relating to Vortigern reads: 'Britu, moreover, [was] the son of Guorthigirn [Vortigern], who Germanus blessed and who Severa bore to him, the daughter of Maximus the king of the Romans.'[13] From this we learn that Vortigern was married to Severa, the daughter of Maximus/ Macsen Wledig, the Roman Emperor we have already met. The earliest text to give the story of Vortigern's life is the *Historia Brittonum* of Nennius, and by using this source in conjunction with the Welsh *Brut* we were able to begin to make sense of the life and times of Vortigern.

With Custennin dead an heir had to be found for the throne of Prydein, and the rightful heirs were his three sons: Constans, Emrys and Uthyr.

Constans was a monk and therefore unable to rule, while Emrys and Uthyr were both too young – if either of them were made king, their foster father Archbishop Cuhelin would be required to rule in their place. While the nobles argued over who should succeed, Vortigern saw an opportunity to gain influence over the throne of Ynys Prydein and went to visit Constans in the monastery of Amphibalus in Caer Wynt (Corwen) to tell him of his plan: if Vortigern could persuade the nobles to make Constans the King of Prydein, in return Constans would make Vortigern high steward of the kingdom. Despite protests from the abbot, Constans accepted Vortigern's plan. Vortigern took Constans from the monastery to Llundain (Ludlow) and placed the crown on his head, in spite of the fact that 'not one bishop would perform the ceremony and few approved of the appointment.'[14]

VORTIGERN AND THE PICTS OF POWYS

Vortigern received the title of high steward from Constans as arranged and then, unbeknown to Constans, travelled around the kingdom placing the various tribes under his rule and making strong the castles. Vortigern informed Constans that the Picts were about to stage an uprising and suggested that some of the sons of the leaders of the Picts should be brought to the court at Llundain to act as liaisons with the Pictish race, explaining that if their sons were at the court the Picts of Alban (Powys) would be less likely to pose a threat.

It may seem bizarre to have Picts in Powys, especially in light of the traditional understanding of this period of history, according to which the Picts were in the north of England on the Scottish borders. The origin of the Pictish race is still obscure, but an explanation of how they came to be in Powys is given in an earlier part of the Brut where we are told that the Picts, led by their king Rodric, had come to Alban (Powys) and conquered it in the time of Marius, son of Aviragus (c.AD 70, also known as the British king Gweirydd). Marius eventually defeated the Picts, killing Rodric and most of his army, the remnant of which surrendered. Marius gave this remnant of Rodric's army a part of Alban in which to dwell and after a time they asked the British nobles if they could take their daughters as wives.[15] The nobles considered their request but refused to allow them to marry the women of Prydein. Having had no success with the Britons, the Picts took as wives the women of the Gwyddel (Irish) from Iwerddon (Ireland) instead. This lead to them being referred to as the Gwyddyl Ffichti (Irish Picts) in Welsh texts where they appear on several occasions. We found confirmation of this Pictish settlement in North Wales in a 14th-century manuscript, from Jesus College, Oxford, in which there is a reference to a fifth-century 'king of the Gwyddel Ffichti of Powys'.[16]

Once Vortigern had the Picts at the royal court under his influence he arranged a feast for them, his real motive being to involve them in a plot to kill Constans and gain the throne for himself. When the Picts had become sufficiently drunk, Vortigern told them that he only had the right to rule over the regions of Erging and Ewias and was intending to leave Prydein to seek greater wealth. The Picts were surprised to hear that their friend had such meagre powers and in their drunken state decided that, if they killed Constans, Vortigern would be king and therefore become a useful ally. With that, the Picts entered Constans's chamber, cut off his head and took it to Vortigern, who pretended to be upset at the sight of the dead king. Vortigern's plan had worked: by provoking the Picts in a drunken state to kill the king he had opened up an opportunity to claim the throne for himself.

In a ruse to deflect suspicion for Constans's murder from himself, Vortigern ordered the imprisonment of all the Picts involved, but this was not enough to allay the suspicions of the nobles of Ynys Prydein, nor of Archbishop Cuhelyn. Taking with him his two foster sons – Constans's brothers Emrys and Uthyr – Cuhelyn fled for safety to Llydaw (Cornwall), where Emyr Llydaw, a kinsman of the two brothers, was king. Meanwhile the nobles of Ynys Prydein gathered at Llundain (Ludlow) and condemned the Picts to be hung for their crime. The nobles also decided to entrust the realm to Vortigern, in his role as high steward, until such time as a rightful king could be found to rule over them. (It seems strange that Vortigern was trusted to govern the realm while being suspected of complicity in the murder of Constans, but all the texts agree on this point without further explanation.)

Enraged by the death of their sons, the Pictish nobles decided to make war on Vortigern with the intention of killing him. Meanwhile Vortigern, who was convinced that he would beat the Picts, took the crown and placed it on his own head, thus making himself king. He called upon the nobles of Prydein to help him fight the Picts, but they were angry with him for causing the uprising in the first place and so refused, telling him, quite literally, to fight his own battle. Vortigern 'sought help from foreign nations, but he got almost none'.[17] (By foreign nations we should understand lands outside of Ynys Prydein and therefore east of the River Severn, not lands on mainland Europe.) Having schemed his way to the throne, Vortigern now watched powerless as the northern half of his kingdom degenerated into a state of unrest. Fearing for his safety, he made his way to the southern part of the kingdom, to the chief town of a region called Ceint. It was here that Vortigern met the Saxons.

VORTIGERN AND THE
SAXON INVASION OF BRITAIN

Our research into the texts relating to the Saxon invasion of Britain was to lead us to the conclusion that this is probably one of the most misunderstood episodes in the history of the British Isles. We suggest that the Saxons invaded that part of South Wales mentioned above, the region called Ceint, which was situated in the southeast corner of the Kingdom of Prydein. According to the traditional historical view, however, the Saxon invasion is said to have taken place in Kent, in the southeast corner of England. As we studied the place names contained in the source texts for ourselves we found that the traditional interpretation of events became increasingly untenable. If the conquering Saxons had indeed come from outside the British Isles, we would have expected to find accounts of their invasion in other historical sources, but the absolute lack of any corroborating evidence from Continental chroniclers forced us to think that either the event never happened or that it had taken place somewhere other than Kent. We are not the first to challenge the history books. Several notable scholars have called into question the received understanding of this event and their doubts were summed up over 150 years ago by the English historian J.M. Kemble, who in 1849 said: 'I confess that the more I examine the question, the more completely I am convinced that the received accounts of our migrations, our subsequent fortunes, and ultimate settlement, are devoid of historical truth in every detail.'[18]

The importance of the Saxon invasion of Britain in arriving at a correct understanding of the subsequent history of the British Isles is such that we include here all of the five historical sources on which knowledge of this event is based. The texts speak for themselves, although interpretation of them depends entirely on our understanding of the geographical map to which the place names apply.

Gildas in *De Excidio Britanniae* (c.540):
> They [the Saxons] sailed out, and at the directions of the unlucky tyrant [Vortigern], first fixed their dreadful talons in the eastern part of the realm, as men intending to fight for the country, but more truly to assail it.[19]

Bede in *A History of the English Church and People* (731):
> In his time [Martian, AD 449] the Angles or Saxons came to Britannia at the invitation of King Vortigern in three longships, and were granted lands in the eastern part of the realm on condition that they protected the country: nevertheless their real intention was to subdue it.[20]

Nennius in *Historia Brittonum* (c.800):
> Meanwhile three keels came from Germania, driven in exile in which were Hors and Hengist ... Guorthigirn [Vortigern] received them kindly and handed over to them the realm which in their language is called Tanet, in the British language Ruoihm.[21]

The Anglo-Saxon Chronicle (tenth century):
> 449. Here Martianus and Valentinian succeeded to the kingdom and ruled seven years. In their days Vortigern invited the Angle race here and they came here to Britain in three ships at the place called Ypwines fleot. The king Vortigern gave them land in the south-east of this land on condition that they fought the Picts.[22]

Welsh text of *Brut Y Brenhinedd* [the *Brut*] (not later than 12th century):
> And after they had come to Mynyded Keynt [mountains of Keynt, or Keint] he [Vortigern] saw three ships of marvellous size ... And when the king saw that, he rejoiced and gave the Saxons the land that since then has been called Lyndesei, to dwell in ... the king granted them: land the breadth of an ox-hide for the building. And then they went home and sought out the largest ox-hide they could get, and cut it into one thong as thin as they could, and stretched it as well as they could, and built the city which was called Dinas y Garrei [Town of the Thong], and it is now called Dwong chestyr [Thongchester].[23]

The information on which the present understanding of the Saxon invasion is based is therefore minimal and can be summarized as follows: led by Hengist and Horsa, the Angles/Saxons landed in a region called 'Keynt/ Cent', in the eastern part of the realm of 'Britannia/Britain'. In exchange for their military support, Vortigern gave them the lands of 'Tanet' and 'Lyndesei', where they built the city of 'Dinas y Garrei/Dwong chestyr'. The place names are the key to locating the arrival of the Saxons on the map, but the lack of standardized spelling in the original medieval texts and the subsequent variants this creates, in addition to the further variations of spelling that have occurred in translation, have merely served to add to the confusion. For example, the Welsh consonants *g*, *k* and *c* have the same sound and this is reflected in medieval Welsh texts where these three consonants are interchangeable. The same applies to the consonants *t* and *d*, and the vowels *i* and *y*, which are also interchangeable.

Keynt (variants Keint and Ceint) has long been held to refer to Kent in the southeast of England, but the texts clearly state that this was a region in the southeastern part of Vortigern's realm of Prydein, which as we have seen was Wales and the border counties. This suggested we should look for Keint in the southeast of Wales, in the region known today as Gwent. Gwent was written as Guent in Latin and this suggested to us that the two names Guent and Keint had been confused in the past. Evidence for this was found in one of the *Triads*, regarding a character called Cywryd Ceint (Cywryd of Ceint), who in the various manuscript versions of the *Triad* is called:

Gvryt Gvent
Gwryd gwent
Gweryd Gwent
kywryt geint
gwyrd keint
Gawryd Ceint[24]

Here we had evidence that Gwent and Ceint were interchangeable names for the same place. If this identification were correct, we felt it should be possible to find the other names attached to Ceint in the source material.

The most significant place named in the text is the land called Tanet (variant Danet) given to the Saxons by Vortigern, and a region of Gwent was indeed known as Danet in the past. Under the entry for the year 1171 in the *Brut y Tywysogion* – the *Chronicle of the Princes*, which deals with the period of Welsh history from 688 to 1282 – we found reference to a battle in Llwyn Danet, which is the Welsh name for the Forest of Dean in Gwent.[25] Our new geography seemed to be working. By taking into account the acknowledged variations in medieval spelling, we had found a region called Keynt/Ceint/Gwent in the southeast of Britannia/Prydein, and in this region was a place called Tanet/Danet, exactly as the source texts described.

The next place we needed to locate was Caer Ceint which, according to another Welsh version of the *Brut*, was where Vortigern took up residence when he fled to the region of Ceint for safety. Caer Ceint literally means the 'City (or town) of Ceint', and has been understood to mean the 'city of Kent' and therefore applied to Canterbury in Kent in southeast England. After much searching it occurred to us that the word *Caer*, meaning 'town' or 'city', is the Welsh name for the town of Chester on the Welsh-English border. Similarly, *chester* is an old Saxon word for 'town' – derived from the Roman *castre*, meaning 'settlement' – which still appears as a suffix in the names of English towns such as Colchester and Dorchester. With this in mind we decided to look for a town whose name ended in -chester in the southeast of the ancient realm of Prydein. Within minutes we had found a village named Kenchester (the Town of Ken) on the River Wye to the west of Hereford and north of the Forest of Dean, and the presence of the remains of a Roman settlement on the site suggested that Kenchester had a long history. If the prefix Ken is derived from Keynt, then the name Kenchester is nothing less than an Anglo-Saxonization of the Welsh Caer Keynt or Caer Ceint, both of which can be translated as 'the town of Keynt/Ceint'.

The above account of the Saxon landing from the Welsh Brut, which also appears in translation in Geoffrey's Historia, describes how Vortigern granted the Saxons land on which to build a town called Dinas y Garrei ('City/Town of the Thong'). By the time the Brut was written the name by which the town was known had changed to Dwong chestyr or Thongchester, as had the name Lyndesei, the region in which it was built. In a document known as The Tribal Hidage, written in the tenth century and concerning the Saxon Kingdom of Mercia, we found a reference to an area called Lindes farona. The text also states that within this region was a place called Haethfeld,[26] the site of a battle between King Edwin and Penda in the seventh century. According to Welsh sources, this took place near Welshpool on the River Severn.[27] The region of Lindes approximately corresponded with a part of the modern county of Shropshire, and on the eastern extremity of this county, which was also the eastern extremity of Prydein, are located the small villages of Tong and Tong Sutton. Could these be the site of the 'Thongchester' that was built on the land donated to the Saxons by Vortigern?

The above evidence seemed to confirm our original argument, which was that the simple misunderstanding of the area known in the ancient texts as the 'realm of Britain' meant that one of the most significant historical events in the history of the British Isles has been shoehorned into the county of Kent in the southeast of England. The Saxon invasion of Britain was actually the Saxon invasion of Prydein and took place near the Forest of Dean in Gwent in the southeast of Wales, and the locations mentioned in the source texts can be found in this area in their original form. But the matter was not yet fully resolved. Our reassessment of the Saxon invasion raised a fundamental question: if the Saxons didn't come over from the Continent, where did they originate?

The evidence simply tells us that the Saxons came from somewhere outside Britain/Prydein. However, we found a clue to the true identi-fication of the invading Saxons in a Latin text (c.1019) called The Life of St Goeznovious, which talks of the Saxons persecuting the Britons: 'The Saxons remembering Anglia, an ancient Saxon city, imposed its name on both themselves and the island and called themselves either Angles or Anglici, although to this day they are called Saxons by the Britons.'[28]

Whereas the earliest texts call the invaders 'Saxons', The Life of St Goeznovious informs us that the Saxons and Angles are one and the same people. As we saw in Chapter 2, the Angles inhabited Anglia (the original name for England), a land that bordered the realm of Britannia/Prydein. We suggest therefore that Vortigern's invitation to Hengist and the Saxons to enter his kingdom and his subseqent donations of land to them mark the beginnings of the invasion of the realm of Britain/Prydein – today's Wales and the Marches – and not, as our history books would have us believe, the invasion of Great Britain as we know it today by hoards of Saxons from Germany. The Angles/Saxons may well have originated from Germany, but they were settled in England long before they were invited into Wales by Vortigern around 450.[29]

But to return briefly to our story: with the help of the Saxons Vortigern soon defeated the Picts and in return for their help gave them the land called Lindes in which they built a settlement known as Thongchester. At a feast to celebrate this victory over the Picts, Vortigern got drunk and fell in love with Ronwen, Hengist's daughter, and asked for her hand in marriage. Hengist agreed to this on the understanding that he would receive control over the land of Keint in which the Saxons first landed. Vortigern accepted Hengist's terms and spent the night with Ronwen. But this particular outcome did not please everyone, least of all Gwrangon, who was the ruler of Keint. The three sons of Vortigern by his previous wife were also unhappy at the situation and the nobles of Prydein decided that Vortigern should be replaced by his eldest son Vortimer as their king.

We find an account of the arrangement between Vortigern and Hengist in the *Historia Brittonum*, where Nennius recorded the following advice given to Hengist and the Saxons by their advisor: 'That they should ask for the region which in their language is called Canturguoralen, but in ours Cent [or Chent]. And he gave it to them, Guoyrancgonus [Gwrangon] the while reigning in Cantia [Cent].'[30]

The name of Gwrangon, whose lands were given to Hengist and the Saxons, survived in the place name Caer Wrangon, a town founded by Custennin Fendigaid (Arthur's grandfather) according to *The Tract of the Twenty-Four Mightiest Kings*. We found further evidence that the events surrounding the Saxon invasion took place in Gwent (Keint) in the southeast of the ancient realm of Prydein when we discovered that Caer Wrangon was the original Welsh name for the modern city of Worcester, on the banks of the River Severn.[31] The location of Caer Wrangon in Gwent was also confirmed in a poem from *The Book of Taliesin*: '*Gwenhwys gwallt hiryon am Gaer wyragon*' (Long-haired Gwentians around Caer Wrangon).[32]

The Saxon invasion of Britannia is a pivotal point in the history of Great Britain, but not for the reason commonly assumed. The Saxons were not invaders from Germany, landing in Kent in southeast England, then forcing the Britons back into the hills of Wales and forming the English nation in the lands known today as England. The truth behind this event is far simpler: the Britons never lived in England and 'the Saxons' was simply a British name for the inhabitants of Anglia (England). This distinction between the two races of people living in mainland Britain can be illustrated by the following quote from the 12th-century historian Ordericus Vitalis: 'Anyone who desires to know more fully [about] this and other matters touching what misfortune befell the Britons should read the books of the historian Gildas the Briton and [those] of Bede the Angle.'[33]

The events of the Saxon invasion have been located in the present-day county of Kent because of a failure to understand that the original inhabitants of the land we today call England were Angles/Saxons, not the Britons who lived in the lands we today call Wales. The following table and map (p.61) illustrate how this mistake has affected our understanding of this important event.

THE SAXON INVASION OF BRITAIN

Region/town	Traditional location	Revised location
Keint	Kent	Gwent
Caer Keint	Canterbury	Kenchester
Tanet	Isle of Thanet	Forest of Dean
Lindesei	Lincolnshire	Shropshire
Dinas y Garrei/Thongchester	Caistor	Tong

THE FORGOTTEN WALL OF SEVERUS

Our discovery that the original historical texts described the Saxon invasion of Britain taking place in the southeastern corner of the ancient realm of Prydein, rather than in Kent in southeast England as the history books would have us believe, came as something of a revelation. But our search to uncover the true location and early history of Arthur's realm had further surprises in store for us. Not least of these was the discovery of the forgotten Wall of Severus, a wall whose history and location had been absorbed into the more famous walls of Hadrian and Antoninus in the north of England. How was it possible for a Roman wall over 130 miles in length to disappear from the history books? Once again the answer lies in the fact that the history of the ancient realm of Prydein, the original Kingdom of Britain, has been stretched to fit the map of mainland Britain as we know it today.

Our search to establish the early history of Arthur's kingdom continues with the events following the Saxon invasion. In the *Historia Brittonum*

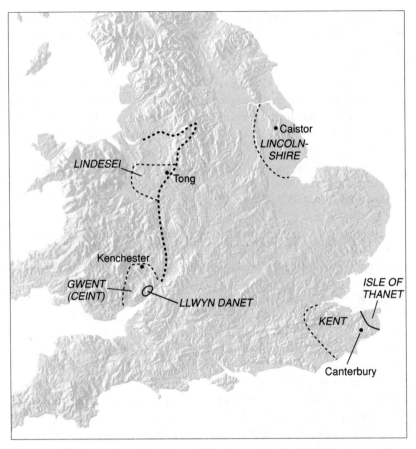

Map 12 The Saxon invasion – traditional and revised locations

Nennius relates how, having obtained the region of Keint (Gwent) for his people, Hengist asked Vortigern if he could bring over his son Octa and his cousin Ossa: 'I will invite my son together with his cousin for they are warlike men, to fight the Scotti [Picts], and give thou to them regions which are in the north, by the wall called Guaul.'[34]

Vortigern agreed to Hengist's request and gave the newcomers land 'in the North', which meant that the Saxons now had land in both the north and south of Vortigern's realm, but where and what was the wall called Guaul? The first reference we could find to this enigmatic structure was in an earlier part of the *Historia Brittonum* where Nennius mentions the construction of the wall called Guaul by the great general and Roman Emperor Septimus Severus. Following his successful campaigns at the eastern end of the empire, Severus came to Britain to conquer the rebellious tribes and died in York in 211. 'In order to safeguard the acquired provinces from barbarian attack, he [Severus] built a wall and rampart from sea to sea through the breadth of Britanniae, that is for 132 miles and it is called in the British language Guaul.'[35]

To understand this reference to the construction of a wall by Severus we turned to a Roman text, the fourth-century *Scriptores Historia Augustae*. It is a little known fact that this one text alone forms the basis of our knowledge of the names of the Romans who built the Hadrian and Antonine Walls, but it also states that another wall was built by Severus.

Hadrian's Wall: He [Hadrian] set out for Britain. There he put right many abuses and was the first to build a wall, eighty miles long, to separate the barbarians and the Romans.[36]

Antonine Wall: Antoninus waged many wars, using his legates. Lollius Urbicus, a legate, conqueured the Britons for him, and when he had driven the barbarians off built another wall, of turf.[37]

Wall of Severus: He [Severus] fortified Britannia, building a wall across the island [realm] from both ends to the Ocean boundary.[38]

The author of the above was evidently aware of three different walls in Britain, of which the first two were built to separate the Romans from the barbarians while the third was built to fortify Britannia, with no mention of barbarians. We found that in all of the early source materials used for the beginnings of British history the only wall ever mentioned is that built by Severus. There is no mention of either Hadrian's or the Antonine Walls in Nennius, Gildas or Bede (who supposedly lived within a few miles of Hadrian's Wall). The consensus view concludes that the third wall was actually a remembrance of Severus refortifying or repairing one of the two northern walls, which would seem to us to be little more than an attempt to reconcile the early source materials with a preconceived idea of what they mean, as it cannot be backed up by any archaeological evidence. Despite the lack of evidence, this theory will be found in every book that touches on the reign of Severus – an example of how, if it is repeated often enough, a theory becomes accepted as fact. The texts clearly state that there was a *third* Roman wall in the British Isles and yet references to 'the wall' in any source have always been ascribed automatically to Hadrian's Wall. As a consequence, the events associated with 'the wall' have been located in the north of mainland Britain. So if the Wall of Severus was neither that of Hadrian or Antoninus, where was it?

We found our first clue in St Jerome's fourth-century Latin translation of the Greek *Chronicle* of Eusebius of Caesarea (c.320). Jerome added material from Roman sources, including the following reference to Severus: '(Anno Abraham 2221) [AD 205] Severus brings war over against the Britanni, where also, in order to safeguard the acquired provinces from barbarian attack, he made a wall from sea to sea for 132 miles.'[39] The same information is contained in other Roman sources: Severus built a wall from sea to sea for 132 miles.[40] Of the two other walls we have mentioned, Hadrian's Wall was built by Hadrian around AD 120 and runs for 73 miles between Carlisle and Newcastle, while the Antonine Wall was built by the Emperor Antonius around AD 140 and is 37 miles long, running between Stirling and Glasgow. The Wall of Severus is not connected with either of these walls in any of the texts or from any archaeological evidence. Non-Roman sources make a similar point. For example, when writing *The History of the English Church and People* in 731, Bede relates the following:

> He [Severus] was compelled to come to Britain by the desertion of nearly all the tribes allied to Rome, and after many critical and hard fought battles he decided to separate that portion of the island under his control from the remaining unconquered peoples. He did this not with a wall, as some imagine, but an earthwork. For a wall is built of stone, but an earthwork such as protects a camp from enemy attack is constructed with sods cut from the earth and raised above the ground level, fronted by the ditch from which the sods were cut and surmounted by a strong palisade of logs. Severus built a rampart and ditch of this type from sea to sea and fortified it by a series of towers.[41]

The Wall of Severus is also mentioned in the Welsh *Brut*, where we are given an indication of its location: 'And he [Severus] caused a deep ditch to be made at public expense from sea to sea between Deifyr and Alban.'[42]

From the above Roman, Saxon and Welsh sources we were able to draw the following conclusions:

- An earthwork/dyke was built by Severus.
- This earthwork stretched from sea to sea.
- It was 132 miles long.
- It separated Deifyr from Alban.

Having established that the Wall of Severus is different from either Hadrian's or the Antonine Wall we needed to find evidence to help us identify a more precise location for it. The *Brut* mentions the Wall of Severus again in relation to a battle between Oswald, King of Northumbria, and Penda, the ruler of Mercia: 'And then they [Oswald and his army] fled to the wall that Severus emperor of Rome had in former times made between Deifyr and Bryneich. And then Cadwallon sent Peanda King of Mercia with a great part of the Army to fight with Oswald. And after he had come there, Peanda surrounded him (lest he should break away from him) in the place that is called in English Hevyn Felt and in the Welsh Maes Nefawl.'[43]

Many scholars have located this battle near Hexham (on Hadrian's Wall) because of the reference to 'the wall', despite the fact that no evidence exists to back up this claim. As we demonstrated earlier when drawing our new map, the Northumbrian kingdoms of Deira and Bernica consisted of the counties of Cheshire and Shropshire to the north of the River Severn and Mercia was the region east of Offa's Dyke and south of the Severn. Add this to the fact that the Welsh texts say that the wall was built between Alban (Powys) and Deifyr (Deira, i.e. Cheshire). We found confirmation that this was indeed the area where the battle was fought in *The Life of St Oswald* (*Vita St Oswaldi*), written in 1162, where we are told that the battle took place at the Welsh-border town of Oswestry in Shropshire: 'This place [the battlesite] is distant from the dyke of King Offa, which divides Anglia and North Wales, scarcely half a mile, from Shrewsbury quite seven miles, and from Wenlock Abbey, towards the south, about sixteen miles.'[44]

As we can see, the above two texts are quite explicit as to where this battle took place. When this information is added to our earlier evidence it would appear that we are looking for an earthwork that runs 132 miles from sea to sea and passes in the vicinity of the market town of Oswestry. Anyone brought up in North Wales is aware of the two famous dykes that exist near the town of Oswestry. The shorter of the two runs for 40 miles from Maesbury, south of Oswestry, to Basingwerk Abbey on the Dee estuary. It is thought to have been built in the eighth century and is known today as Wat's Dyke. The longer one runs for 150 miles from Chepstow on the Severn estuary to Treuddyn in Flintshire and is known today as Offa's Dyke. The length of this dyke is much closer to the 132 miles attributed to the Wall of Severus in the source texts than the 73 miles of Hadrian's Wall. This raises the question: if this dyke is the original Wall of Severus, how did it become known as Offa's Dyke? We came across the earliest reference attributing the Dyke to Offa in the *Life of King Alfred* from 893, which told us that 'there was of late in Mercia a certain strenuous king ... Offa by name, who ordered to be made between Britannia and Mercia, the great dyke from sea to sea'.[45]

It is from this single quote that the name of the Mercian king Offa (ruled 757–96) became attached to the Dyke and the date of its construction estimated at around 780. Historians have long wondered how it was that the Saxons managed to build such a major structure whilst under constant attack from the Welsh and how a people with no history of building huge earthen banks 150 miles long across hilltops had the engineering skill to undertake such a vast project. We were also interested to find that several Roman artefacts had been found within the Dyke in the past, when sections of it had been destroyed to make way for roads or buildings.[46]

With the evidence mounting up we needed to find a link that would connect Severus to Offa's Dyke. We took a closer look at the various texts of Nennius and found something quite startling. In an Irish manuscript compiled in the eleventh century called *Leabhar Breathnach* – a Gaelic version of the *Historia Brittonum* – we read the following: 'Severus was the third king that came to Britannia and it was he that made the *Saxon* ditch against the barbarians i.e. the Cruithnians [Picts], 130 miles long and the name of that ditch among the Britons was Guaul.'[47]

Here was a clear statement that Severus built the Saxon Ditch and, as the Irish manuscript was written after the claim made by Asser in 893 that Offa had built the dyke, the editor of this text used this association to indicate precisely which wall from sea to sea was meant. The only ditch 130 miles long attributed to the Saxons is Offa's Dyke and, as we have already seen, the Picts – or Cruithnians as they are named in the text – are known to have been in this area of North Wales. The presence of Severus in Wales is attested to by a stone inscribed to him that was found in Caernarfon, and it has also been suggested that he rebuilt the walls of Chester during his reign.[48]

From the above evidence we concluded that the wall Severus had built during his time in Britain was in fact the earthwork known today as Offa's Dyke. We also concluded that the original Wall of Severus, which was known to the Britons as Guaul, ran from the Severn estuary in the South to Ruabon (near Wrexham) in the North along the earthwork known today as Offa's Dyke. From Ruabon, where Offa's and Wat's Dykes run very close to each other, it continued northwards along the line of the earthwork known today as Wat's Dyke.

How does all of this relate to Vortigern giving Hengist's family – Hengist's son Octa and his cousin Ossa – land in the north near the wall called Guaul? At the northern end of the wall (Wat's Dyke) there are several place names containing the word Offa.[49] However, we suggest that these refer not to Offa, the King of Mercia, but to Hengist's cousin Ossa, whose name is written in many manuscripts as Offa because of the similar appearance of the letters *s* and *f* in old manuscripts. We believe it was this that led Asser to wrongfully attribute the dyke to Offa in order to claim a Saxon origin for such a marvellous piece of civil engineering, whereas it actually refers to the name of Hengist's cousin Ossa, who was given land in this region by Vortigern.

The implication of our findings for the geography of Dark Age British history is enormous. All of the references in medieval sources to geographical boundaries that incorporate the words 'the wall' have been assumed to refer to Hadrian's Wall – hence, for example, the consensus argument that the Saxon kingdoms of Deira (Deifyr) and Bernica (Bryneich) are in northern England and southern Scotland whereas, according to our new map, Deifyr and Bryneich are areas of Cheshire and Shropshire. When references to 'the wall' are taken to mean Offa's Dyke instead of Hadrian's Wall, a large part of British history for this period begins, for the first time, to make sense.

Present theories on the period of British history known as the Dark Ages are based upon the presumption that the realm of Britannia denotes the whole of mainland Britain, that Keint means Kent and that the Wall of Severus is a reference to Hadrian's Wall. Having dealt with these issues from the source material with the understanding that Britannia and Ynys

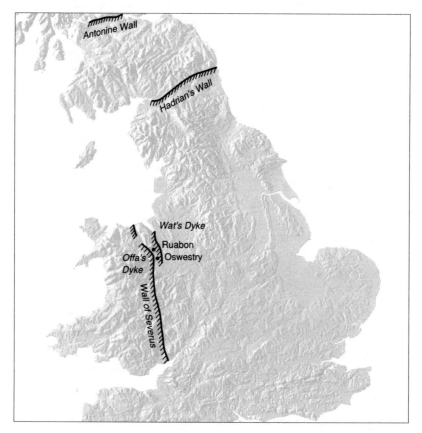

Map 13 The three walls

Prydein refer to the present-day Wales and the border counties of Cheshire, Shropshire and Herefordshire, a new map of this period of British history has emerged. With this revised map it is possible to unlock the truth behind the history of Britain, long hidden in the pages of the *Brut*.

VORTIMER AND THE SAXONS

The next important sequence of events in the early history of Arthur's realm related in the *Brut* concerns Vortimer, who was chosen by the nobles of Prydein to replace his father Vortigern, and the four battles he fought against the Saxons. An additional detail is provided by the *Historia Brittonum* in which Nennius tells us that Vortimer first forced the Saxons into Danet and then fought his four battles. Their names, along with their traditional locations, are as follows:

Saxon sources	Welsh sources	Traditional site in Kent
Creganford	River Derwenydd	Crayford
Aegelesthrep	Rhyd yr Afael	Aylesford
Unknown	In Danet	Unknown
Wippedsfleot	Near the sea in Danet	Unknown

The traditional view of the location of Vortimer's battles is based solely on the assumption that Ceint is Kent, and even these identifications rely on supposition, as pointed out by the great Saxon scholar Sir Frank Stenton in 1943: 'The common identification of Cregan ford with Crayford depends on the bare possibility that all extant manuscripts of the [Anglo-Saxon] Chronicle go back to an original in which the name was misrepresented.'[50]

All four of Vortimer's battles against the Saxons were fought in or near the region called Danet, and it has been suggested that the place name Gwerthefyriwg, which is mentioned in *The Book of Llandaff*, preserves the personal name Gwerthefyr, the Welsh name of Vortimer. This place is situated close to Wonastow, near the Forest of Dean (the ancient region of Danet) in Gwent. In our view all of the sources locate these events in Gwent and nowhere else, which would explain why Vortimer is unknown in southeast England. The potentially confusing reference in the *Historia Brittonum* to this event taking place on the shore of the Gallic Sea is clarified by an entry in the Welsh *Brut* that tells us that Vortigern first saw the three boats of Hengist and Horsa on the Mor Freinc (Sea of the Franks).[51] From this we suggest that around the year 800, the time when Nennius was writing, the Bristol Channel was known to the Welsh as the

Gallic or Frankish Sea; as the Gaulish tribe of the Belgae is known to have lived in the Wiltshire area in Roman times, this identification is not as bizarre as it may at first sound.[52]

With the Saxons back in their own country following his successful campaign against them, Vortimer returned the land to its rightful owners, but shortly afterwards he was poisoned by a retainer in the employ of Ronwen (Vortigern's wife, the daughter of Hengist). Vortimer's dying wish was for a statue of his image to be placed overlooking the harbour from which the Saxons fled. The statue was to contain his ashes and thus scare the Saxons from ever landing in Prydein again. The three chief ports of Ynys Prydein are the subject of a section in *Enwau Ynys Prydein* (The Names of Ynys Prydein, earliest text c.1325.) One of the three ports is Port Ysgewit in Gwent, known today as Portskewett and located near the new bridge over the River Severn. The evidence available suggests that this is the port from which the Saxons fled. Could this also be the port where they first landed and named as Ypwinesfleot in the *Anglo-Saxon Chronicle*? (The traditional identification of this site is Ebbsfleet in Kent.)

The following reference to the burial of Vortimer is made in a *Triad* regarding the three concealments and three disclosures of Ynys Prydein: 'And the third: the bones of Gwerthefyr [Vortimer] the blessed, in the chief ports of this realm. And as long as they remained in that concealment, no Saxon Oppression would ever come to this realm.'[53]

In spite of the protection offered by the relics of the dead British king, the *Brut* tells us that Vortigern 'disclosed the bones of Vortimer' (revealed their whereabouts) for the love of a woman – his wife Ronwen, the daughter of Hengist. This would appear to be a survival of an older tradition, used by both Nennius and the compiler of the *Brut*. According to an additional comment in the *Brut*, however, the Britons ignored Vortimer's request and his remains were buried in Llundain (Ludlow).

THE TREACHERY OF THE LONG KNIVES

Following the death of Vortimer, the nobles of Ynys Prydein reinstated Vortigern as their king and the Saxons sent messengers to ask if they could return to Prydein, to the lands they had previously occupied, if they remained under the rule of the crown of Llundain (Ludlow). Their request was rejected by the nobles of Prydein but the Saxon messengers returned again and asked 'that a set day might be appointed between them, in any place in the realm they might desire, to know how many of them they desired to have in the realm, how many they did not desire.

And if any one of them had done wrong to the Britons they were ready to make it good, in good will, for every wrong it could be proved they had done.'[54]

The meeting was set for May Day at a venue in Maes Mawr yn Cymry (the Great Plain in Wales).[55] (This location is discussed in Chapter 5.) Participants from both sides were to arrive unarmed and discuss a peace agreement, but the Saxons had hidden knives in their shoes and at Hengist's pre-arranged call of 'Draw her Sexes' they proceeded to slaughter all of the nobles of Ynys Prydein. The number killed varies from 300 in the *Historia Brittonum* to 460 in the *Brut*. Vortigern was taken prisoner by the Saxons and only one noble escaped, Eidol the Earl of Caerloyw. Following this treachery, Hengist and his Saxon army captured the cities of Llundain (Ludlow), which was the chief town of Lloegyr, Caer Efrog (Wroxeter), which was the chief town of Alban, Caer Wynt (Corwen) and Caer Lyncoll. In Geoffrey of Monmouth's Latin *Historia* Caer Lyncoll is identified as Lincoln in the east of England, but we will reveal its true location in North Wales in Chapter 6 in connection with Arthur's battle at Caer Llwytcoed. Hengist's massacre of the nobles of Ynys Prydein became known in Welsh as *Brad y Cyllill Hirion* (the Treachery of the Long Knives) and the murder of these British heroes was a turning point in British history. Never again would the Britons trust the Saxons, and from that time forth constant battles were fought between them that continued into the time of Arthur.

SUMMARY

- The region of Llydaw/Armorica referred to in the texts is Cornwall, not Brittany.
- Arthur's grandfather Custennin came from Cornwall, not Brittany.
- The town of Caer Wynt referred to in the texts is Corwen, in the valley of the River Dee in North Wales, not Winchester in Hampshire.
- The Saxon invasion of Britain took place in Gwent (Keynt) in southeast Wales, not Kent in southeast England.
- The Roman Emperor Severus built a wall between the north and south coasts of Ynys Prydein, now erroneously known as Offa's Dyke.
- Vortimer, Vortigern's son, drove the Saxons out of Gwent (Keynt) in southeast Wales, not Kent in southeast England.

The implications of the above are that the origins of an entire nation are in need of an urgent review, starting with the historical geography of the region as found in the early source materials.

CHAPTER FIVE

MERLIN AND UTHYR PENDRAGON

FOLLOWING THE massacre of the nobles of Ynys Prydein at Maes Mawr in Wales – the event known to history as the Treachery of the Long Knives – and his humiliation by Hengist and the Saxons, the *Brut* tells us that Vortigern fled to Cymru (the region of Gwynedd in northwest Wales) where he built a strong fortress.

A more detailed account is given in the *Historia Brittonum*, where we learn that Vortigern was told by his advisors to 'go to the extreme borders of thy kingdom and thou wilt find a fortified citadel to defend thyself, because the nation, which thou hast received in thy kingdom, looks askance at thee and will kill thee by craft and will seize all the regions which thou hast loved together with the whole of thy nation after death'.[1] The actual word used for Vortigern's 'advisors' in Nennius's Latin text is *Magos*, which equates to the better known Magi of the Middle East. This has led to some scholars suggesting that Vortigern's advisors were Druids, for the latter were often compared to the Magi in Classical texts.[2] When Vortigern and his remaining supporters arrived in Gwynedd they found a suitable site to construct a fortress in the mountains of Eryri (Snowdonia),[3] a site known today as Dinas Emrys (Fort of Emrys, a hillfort near Beddgelert). A strange thing happened, however. Every night the materials that had been gathered to build the fortress were taken away by some unknown force. After this had happened for three nights in succession

Vortigern asked his advisors what to do and they told him that: 'Unless thou dost find a child without a father and he be put to death and the citadel be sprinkled with his blood, it will never be built.'[4]

This sequence of events brings us to the point in the *Brut* where we are introduced to one of the most romantic figures in the Arthurian myths, Merlin. More than any other character from the romances he has captured the imaginations of millions as the wise wizard who not only sees into the future but also changes the physical appearance of himself and others. His image, which adorns hundreds of books and posters and has inspired many to write novels and poetry as well as serious studies of his myth, has been adopted by the Western world as the personification of Celtic Wisdom. But what of the real Merlin? Did such a person exist and, if so, where did he come from? The *Brut* and the *Historia Brittonum* tell the story of Merlin in its earliest form, and from the evidence we found there we began to piece together the true history of Merlin and his links with Arthur.

THE YOUNG MERLIN

Acting on his advisors' suggestion, Vortigern sent messengers throughout Britannia to look for a boy 'without a father', and it is at this point Merlin enters our story. After much searching the messengers came across some children playing ball, two of whom were quarrelling. One of the two boys said to the other, 'O fellow without a father, no good will be thine.'[5] The boy's mother, a daughter of the King of Dyfed, was sought out and brought before Vortigern, who asked her who the father of the child was. The woman replied that she did not know for an unseen force had raped her, as she had never been with a man. The *Brut* adds that the boy's mother was a nun at the church of St Peter in Caerfyrddyn, the town where the boy was found.

The story told in the *Historia Brittonum* differs from the *Brut* on this point, saying that the boy was found at a place called Campus Elleti, in a region called Gleguissing[6] – a Latinized form of the Welsh Glywyssing. According to an early Arthurian source, *The Life of St Cadoc* (c.1070), this region of Wales was founded by a certain Glywys. The same source tells us that Glywys abducted the daughter of Brychan, a local ruler. Pursued by Brychan's men, Glywys fled back to his own realm and as he crossed the border he met Arthur, Cai (Kay) and Bedwyr (Bedivere), who helped him fight off the pursuing soldiers. From this we deduced that Glywyssing shared a border with the realm of Brychan, known as Brycheiniog (Brecon), and was therefore located in South Wales.

Caerfyrddyn, the name given in the *Brut* for the town where the boy 'without a father' was found, has long been accepted to be the old Welsh name for Carmarthen in South Wales. As Carmarthen is situated close to the borders of Brycheiniog, it fits the clues given to us in both the *Brut* and the *Historia Brittonum*.

When the boy 'without a father' was taken to Dinas Emrys, the site where Vortigern's castle was being built, he underwent a change of name. As the *Brut* explains: 'And up to that time he was called An ap y lleian and after that he was named Merdyn because he was found in Caer Vyrdyn [Caer Fyrddyn].'[7] According to *The Dream of Macsen Wledig*, Caer Fyrddyn was so named because it had been built by a myriad of men[8] – *myrddyn* is the Welsh word for 'myriad', hence Caer Fyrddyn, or 'City of the Myriad' (*m* and *f* mutate in Welsh). Myrddyn was subsequently rendered into Latin as Merlin.[9] The above extract from the *Brut* also preserves another tradition, not known outside Wales, that of Merlin's original name, An ap y lleian, which translates as either 'the mischance (*anap*) of a nun' or 'An, the son of a nun'.[10] As an early name for Merlin it also appears in the *Stanzas of the Graves*:

> Bedd Ann ap lleian ymnewais fynydd
> lluagor llew Ymrais
> Prif dewin Merddin Embrais.

> (The grave of An ap y lleian on [?] mountain
> Causing gaps in a host, lion of Emrys
> Chief Magician Myrddin Emrys.)[11]

The actual grave of An ap y lleian is mentioned in a manuscript by the bard Grufudd Hiraethog (1545–53), from Denbighshire in North Wales, which tells us where this grave was situated: 'Maen y Bardd [the Bard's Stones] is on the road between Cadair Dinmael and the chapel above the fields within the township of llys An vab y lleian [Court of An ab y lleian]. And within those stones is a little round tomb [where] was found An ab y lleian; and Murddyn y lleian [the nun's ruin] is below that, near a place called Y Llysdir.'[12]

A letter dated 1693 from the Reverend John Lloyd in reply to the parochial queries of a certain Edward Lhwyd gives a similar description of the site where An ab y lleian was buried and includes a drawing of the stones, but the site is not now known despite determined searches, including one of our own, and can be considered lost.[13] The hill named Cadair Dinmael is in the parish of Llanfihangel Glyn Myfyr, to the north of the A5 road between Cerrigydrudion and Corwen (Caer Wynt) in North

Wales, and a tradition of Merlin under his original name of An ap y lleian was evidently well known in the area as other references to him occur in the poetry of the Welsh bards Lewis Glyn Gothi and Lewys Mon.[14]

The bards may have preserved a tradition of Merlin in its oldest form in the hills of North Wales, but it is not the only one. In 1530 a Flintshire man named Elis Gruffydd wrote a chronicle of world history, preserved in the National Library of Wales,[15] within which he recorded traditions he

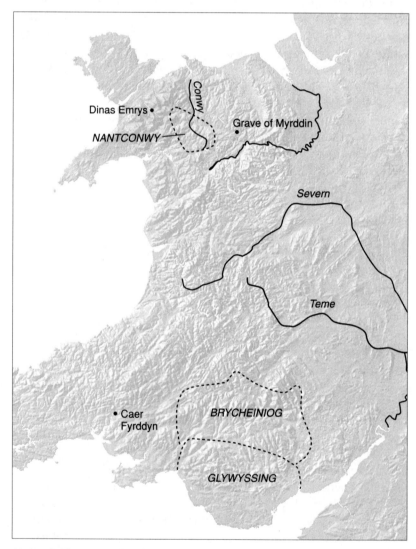

Map 14 Sites associated with Merlin

had found in old books from North Wales. One of these traditions was *The Story of Myrddin Wyllt* (Merlin the Wild).[16] Elis Gruffydd tells us that Merlin (Myrddin) was born in a region called Nantconwy, which is today centred around the upper reaches of the River Conwy, not far from the hill of Cadair Dinmael referred to above. Merlin is described as being 'unstable in mind' and in the summer months would live in the caves and woods on either side of the River Conwy. The tradition goes on to relate that Merlin's sister Gwenddydd came to see him with food and asked him to explain some of the dreams she had been having. This conversation is also paralleled in a very early Welsh poem, and it is quite possible that the tradition copied by Elis Gruffydd is referring to the same event.[17]

In conclusion, we have two different traditions of Merlin's early life: one in Carmarthen in South Wales, and one from the banks of the River Conwy in North Wales, not far from the site of his grave on Cader Dinmael. Both of these are the remnants of an earlier and fuller story of Merlin that is no longer with us, but the one thing that these fragments do show is that Merlin was born and buried in Wales. As we discover more about the true history of Ynys Prydein, we will see that the major events of his life also took place in Wales.

THE RED DRAGON OF WALES

When the young Merlin was taken to the fort at Dinas Emrys in Snowdonia he challenged the wisdom of Vortigern's advisors in having suggested that the blood of a fatherless boy poured over the site would prevent the collapse of the fort. Having persuaded the advisors to admit that they did not know the true reason why the building materials were being spirited away every evening, Merlin told them to dig in the centre of the fort, where they would find an underground lake. The lake was duly found and then Merlin told them that in the lake they would find a tent containing two dragons. When the tent was opened two dragons were found asleep, but when they awoke they started to fight and drove each other from one side of the lake to the other and back again three times. It was then that Merlin delivered his famous prophecy regarding the Red Dragon that symbolized the fortunes of the Britons and the White Dragon that symbolized the Saxons, and the eventual defeat of the White dragon by the Red.[18] It is this event that traditionally led to the Welsh adopting the red dragon on their flag as seen today, and the prophecy was used for political purposes throughout the medieval period. It was also considered to be a danger to the Church, and as such was banned at the Council of Trent in 1543.

THE DEATH OF VORTIGERN

Having delivered his prophecy Merlin ordered Vortigern to leave the site with the following words: 'Nevertheless go thou from this citadel, because thou art not able to build it, and go about many provinces that thou mayest find a secure citadel and I will remain here.'[19] Vortigern proceeded to the 'northern side' of Britannia and arrived at a region called Guunnesi, where he built the fortress known as Caer Gwrtheryn (Town of Vortigern). Guunnesi has been identified as a region of North Wales to the south of Caernarfon on the Lleyn Peninsula.[20] By comparing the Latin and Irish spellings of the name given in different versions of the *Historia Brittonum*, it has been concluded on philological grounds that it would read as Gwynnys or Gwnnys in modern Welsh. As such it is found in the place names Moel Gwynnys, Gwynnys and Cefn Gwynnys, which are all situated in a small area two miles to the south of a short valley next to the sea. Known as Nant Gwrtheyrn (Vortigern's Valley), this valley is hemmed in by cliffs; at one end is a burial mound that is associated with the last days of this British king.

The earliest account of Vortigern's death is found in the *Historia Brittonum*, where we are told that Vortigern fled to Gwrtheyrnion – a region named after himself (near Rhayader in Powys) – to escape from his wives and from St Germanus, who was preaching to him about his unlawful marriage. However, St Germanus pursued Vortigern and stood upon a rock for forty days, praying day and night for Vortigern to convert to the ways of Christ. The rock on which Germanus prayed is to be found at the church of St Harmon (the Welsh name for St Germanus) near Rhayader.

In a further bid to escape from Germanus, Vortigern fled to his fort on the banks of the River Teifi in Dyfed (South Wales). Again Germanus followed him, and on the fourth day caused fire to come down from the heavens and kill Vortigern and his wives. The site of Vortigern's fort is on the summit of an escarpment called Craig Gwrtheyrn (Vortigern's Crag) that towers over the River Teifi near the village of Llanfihangel-ar-Arth in Carmarthenshire. At the bottom of this hill is Ffynnon Armon (the Well of St Garmon).

Meanwhile the *Brut* gives us a different sequence of events, according to which Custennin's sons Emrys and Uthyr returned to Prydein from Llydaw (Cornwall) with an army of 10,000 knights. When they landed in Prydein all of the Britons swore loyalty to them and made Emrys king. Together, Emrys and Uthyr set off to avenge the death of Constans, their elder brother who had been killed by the Picts at Vortigern's instigation. Vortigern fled to Castell Goronw on the banks of the River Wye, where Uthyr and Emrys set his fortress on fire and Vortigern was burnt to death. Castell Goronw can be identified with the earthwork above the village of Ganerew near Monmouth on the summit of the hill Little Doward.

The above are the two accounts of Vortigern's death contained in the two major sources for his life – the *Brut* and the *Historia Brittonum* – but as the compiler of the latter says: '*Alii autem aliter dixerunt*' (others give a different account). These other accounts, we are told, relate how Vortigern died of a broken heart or was swallowed up by the ground when his fortress was burning down.[21] This would seem to indicate that, even in 830 when this text was written, the truth behind the demise of Vortigern was uncertain. Further references to Vortigern's death are to be found within Welsh tradition. For instance, the *Stanzas of the Graves* (first written down in the 12th century) has the following to say:

E bet yn Ystyuacheu
y mae paup yn y amheu
Bet Gurtheyrn Gurtheneu.

(The grave in Ystyfachau
which everyone doubts
is the grave of Gwrtheyrn Gwrthenau.)[22]

Although the location of Ystyfachau is uncertain, it is interesting that the poem says that everyone doubts that the grave in this place is that of Vortigern. Another tradition, recorded in 1773 by Thomas Pennant during his tour around Wales, concerns the burial mound known as Bedd Gwrtheryn (Vortigern's Grave) in the valley of Nant Gwrtheryn on the Lleyn Peninsula (south of Caernarfon in the region of Gwynedd) mentioned previously. When the burial mound was opened it was found to contain the bones of a tall man. Could these have been the remains of the historical Vortigern? The location of Vortigern in this area would seem to be confirmed by the reference to him as [G]wrtheyrn Gwynedd (Vortigern of Gwynedd) in the poem *Armes Prydein*, written c.930.[23]

Having examined these three possible sites for Vortigern's demise, we feel that the Lleyn Peninsula is the location most likely to preserve the true tradition. It is the only location of the three to have an actual grave site named after Vortigern and it is only 15 miles from Dinas Emrys, the site of the fortress he built when he fled to Gwynedd after the Treachery of the Long Knives.

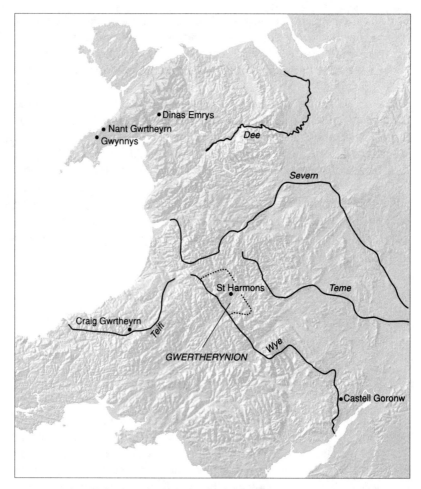

Map 15 Sites linked to the last days of Vortigern

EMRYS AND UTHYR

With Vortigern dead, the *Brut* tells us that Emrys and Uthyr, supported by men from Dyfed, Llydaw and Gwynedd, pursued Hengist and his Saxon army to Maes Beli (the Field/Plain of Beli) where they defeated him in battle. Where was Maes Beli?

The reference to men coming from Dyfed, Llydaw and Gwynedd to support Emrys and Uthyr suggests that Maes Beli was in Alban/Powys, the only region of Ynys Prydein not mentioned. According to Welsh tradition a person named Beli ap Benlli Gawr was killed in battle at a site in Powys, and we learn from the *Historia Brittonum* that his father, Benlli Gawr, was a local chieftain killed by St Germanus (St Garmon) on the summit of Foel Fenlli in the Clwydian hills. The church of St Garmon in the village of Llanarmon yn Ial preserves the name of the victorious saint, and the grave of Beli is mentioned in the *Stanzas of the Graves*:

> *Pieu yr bed yn y Maes Mawr?*
> *Balch y law ar y lafnawr –*
> *Bed Beli ab Benlli Gawr.*

> (Whose is the grave on Maes Mawr?
> Proud with his hand on his sword –
> the grave of Beli ap Benlli Gawr.)[24]

John Jones, a local antiquarian from the turn of the 17th century, copied many older manuscripts and in one written around 1635 he recorded the site of Maes Mawr: 'There is a spot on the mountain between Ial and Ystrad Alun above Rhyd Y Gyfarthfa, called Y Maes Mawr where occurred the battle between Meirion ap Tybion and Beli ap Benlli Gawr; and there Beli ap Benlli was slain. And Meirion erected two standing stones, one at each end of his grave.'[25] The site where these standing stones were placed was called Nant Y Meini (Brook of the Stones) and this name still survives within the large walled enclosure, now covered by a forest plantation, on Nercwys Mountain. This mountain is situated less than three miles from Foel Fenlli (the site of Beli's battle with St Germanus) on the other side of the valley of the River Alun. Local tradition records that Beli's father, Benlli Gawr, was also buried on the same mountain at a place called Bedd Gawr Benlli (Benlli Gawr's Grave). We asked ourselves whether Maes Mawr had originally been known as Maes Beli in memory of Beli's death there in battle, and was therefore the site of Emrys and Uthyr's victory over Hengist and the Saxon army?

Following his defeat at Maes Beli, Hengist fled to a castle at Caer Cynan (the Fort of Cynan). The castle was raided and Eidol, sole survivor of the Treachery of the Long Knives, hunted down Hengist in order to avenge the massacre of his fellow nobles. The two men came face to face and, as they were fighting, Gorlois (first husband to Eigyr, Arthur's mother) stormed the castle with his army. In the confusion Eidol grabbed Hengist by his helmet and dragged him into the British ranks. When the Saxons saw their leader had been captured they fled.

The location of Caer Cynan, where Hengist's last battle took place, is far from certain. In Geoffrey of Monmouth's Latin *Historia* we are told it is 'now called Cunungeburg', which has led to Caer Cynan being identifed as Conisbrough, near Doncaster in South Yorkshire. We have encountered

Cynan earlier; he was brother to Elen (wife of the Roman Emperor Maximus) and son of Eudaf Hen, who had been given the realm of Prydein by Maximus as Elen's 'maiden's fee'. Also known as Cynan Meiriadoc, he had left North Wales to found the British realm of Llydaw (Cornwall). We therefore thought that a more likely location for Caer Cynan than Conisbrough would be the hillfort on Cefn Meiriadog, near St Asaph in North Wales, which is the only place to preserve his name.

Meanwhile Emrys and his army pursued Hengist's son Ossa to Caer Alclud, where Ossa made a stand, but Emrys captured the fort and took Ossa prisoner. Caer Alclud is one of most enigmatic and misunderstood place names of this period of British history, for Caer Alclud (the Fort on the Height of the River Clud) has long been held to refer to the Rock of Dumbarton that overlooks the Clyde estuary near Glasgow on the western coast of Scotland. This has given birth to the idea that a British kingdom existed at Strathclyde in Scotland during the Dark Ages. However, the identification of the River Clud as the River Clyde is not as certain as we are led to believe, for in the 11th-century 'Domesday Book' we find the River Clwyd, which enters the sea on the North Wales coast to the north of St Asaph, spelt Cloit and variously as Cluyt, Cloyth and Cluit.[26] The Welsh *Brut* locates Caer Alclud 'opposite Alban' (Powys in North Wales) and describes its foundation as the work of a pre-Christian king called Efrog (in Latin Ebraucus). It also tells us that a certain Eledenius was made Bishop of Alclud, and the only place linked to him is the village of Llanelidan in the Vale of Clwyd.[27] Our next step was to find a probable site for Caer Alclud near Llanelidan, and the reference to it being built opposite Alban suggested that it was situated on the border of that region. On the border between Powys (Alban) and Gwynedd, which passes through this area, is a hillfort that towers over the River Clwyd near the village of Melin Y Wig, less than three miles from Llanelidan, and this is in all likelihood the original site of Caer Alclud.[28] With this in mind we decided to take a closer look at other references to Caer Alclud in Welsh sources. Though the Gogynfeirdd bards (1100–1282) only make a few references to it, what they do say is of great importance. For example, Gwalchmai (c.1150–70) the chief bard to Owain, Prince of Gwynedd, speaks of his lord thus in a poem:

> *Dychlud clod Brydain bodrydanau*
> *Drygwystlir idaw o Din Alclud gogled*
> *Draig yw yn dyhed drawen yn dehau.*

> (Bears the palm within the four corners of Prydein
> Homage to him from Din Alclud in the North
> And he is a dragon in Dyved in the far away South.)[29]

When used in connection with the realm of Prydein/Britain, Y Gogledd refers specifically to North Wales – as in the above lines by Gwalchmai in praise of Owain Gwynedd – not the north of mainland Britain, a region over which the Prince of Gwynedd had no dominion. Not a single reference in the Welsh texts (which incidentally are the only ones that ever mention Caer Alclud) makes any mention of lands in modern-day Scotland. We therefore believe that the idea of a British kingdom in Scotland has arisen through a simple misunderstanding of the region referred to in the original Welsh texts by the phrase 'Y Gogledd' (the North). (See Appendix 3.)

THE GIANTS' DANCE

After reorganizing his army Emrys returned to Caer Cynan in order to take counsel over what to do with Hengist, who was being held prisoner there by Eidol. It was decided that Hengist should be executed for what he had done to the Britons, so Eidol, the sole survivor of the Treachery of the Long Knives, took him outside of the city and beheaded him, thus avenging himself for his dead comrades. Hengist was then buried under a barrow on a hilltop nearby. Following this Emrys headed for Caer Efrog (Wroxeter) to capture Octa, who surrendered to him. With Octa and Ossa held prisoner and Hengist dead, Emrys travelled to Llundain (Ludlow) and Caer Wynt (Corwen) repairing the churches and returning the land to its rightful owners in the wake of the Saxon destruction of these areas. On completing his duties as leader Emrys left Caer Wynt to go to the site of the Treachery of the Long Knives to pay respect to the dead heroes and build a monument that would last for ever in memory of 'the princes who had been killed, buried in Caer Caradoc beside the monastery of Ambri'.[30]

After seeing the graves Emrys sent messengers across Prydein to look for Merlin/Myrddin, as he wished to ask advice from the prophet concerning the monument he wished to build to commemorate the dead. Some of the messengers knew that Merlin would be at the Spring of Galabes and went straight there. The exact location of this site is uncertain, but according to Layamon's *Brut* – Layamon was the first to translate Geoffrey of Monmouth's *Historia* into English, around 1200 – 'some went straight to [G]Alaban which is a spring in the land of Wales',[31] while the *Historia* states that the spring is in Ewias in the land of the Gewissi. As we have no reason to disbelieve this statement, this important spring may well have been in this southeastern corner of Wales.

Merlin told Emrys to go to Iwerddon[32] (Ireland) and remove a monument called Cor y Cewri (the Circle or Dance of the Giants) from a place called Mynydd Kilara (Kilara Mountain). The stones had supposedly been brought to Ireland by giants from Spain (in other variants Africa) and the *Brut* informs us that they contained magical powers and that when water was run over them and collected it could cure all illnesses. Following this advice Uthyr led 15,000 troops to Ireland and fought on Mynydd Kilara with Gillamuri, the king of that country, and brought the stones back to the monastery of Ambri. Emrys invited all of the nobles of Prydein to a three-day Whitsuntide court at the monastery. On the third and final day the men tried to raise the stones using force alone, but found it impossible. Merlin came forward and raised the stones with ease and 'everybody present recognised that knowledge and skill were stronger than power and strength'.[33]

Geoffrey of Monmouth's Latin *Historia* states that this event took place at Stonehenge, since when the stone circle of the Giants' Dance has been associated with this ancient monument on Salisbury Plain in England, yet we found all the clues necessary to identify the true site within the Welsh *Brut*. The *Brut* also tells us that the Giants' Dance was situated near Caer Caradog, and it was this information that led us to find the true location of the site. There is only one place named Caer Caradog in North Wales and that is a hillfort overlooking the village of Cerrigydrudion in the modern county of Denbighshire. When this place name is translated the identification of this hillfort with the site referred to in the *Brut* becomes certain: Cerrig y drudion – the Stones of the Heroes, a unique place name in Wales. The village of Cerrigydrudion is situated on the A5 road to the west of Cadair Dinmael – the site of the grave of An ap y lleian (Merlin/Myrddin). Leading westward from Cerrigydrudion to the village of Pentrefoelas is a wide open valley that fits the description of the Maes Mawr (Great Plain) given in the *Brut*, and when we made a closer study of the large-scale map for this area we discovered a very interesting place name, Cor Saeson, which can be translated as the Circle of the Saxons.[34]

This seemed to be too good to be true, and a visit to the area the next day provided the greatest shock imaginable. Relying on nothing more than a name on an uninspiring part of the map, we drove to the site. As we came over the brow of the hill we were greeted by mounds of large boulders dotted around the fields. Amazed at this find we promptly followed the nearby footpath and discovered no less than seven of these mounds of enormous boulders and then noticed something interesting: the geology of some of the stones was different from that of the local rock used to build the stone walls in the area. These huge boulders were not indigenous to the site but had been brought here purposefully. We tried to think of other explanations, such as field clearance mounds. This fails on two counts. Firstly, if someone had wanted to clear a field of stones, would they have left them in large piles in the middle of the field? Why bother moving such huge boulders on land that is only good for pasture, for no crops can grow on the side of this bleak hilltop? Secondly, why stack huge boulders one on top of the other, in some cases four boulders high? Why go to such a huge effort if only clearing a field? Were these stones on the hillside on the opposite side of the valley from Caer Caradog and overlooking the village of Cerrigydrudion the original stones of the Giants' Dance?

With all of this evidence we felt sure that we were in the right place. A visit to the local record office told us that the high ground on which Cor Saeson was situated was originally known as Mynydd Main or Mynydd Maen (the Mountain of the Stones) – the word *maen* also has the meaning of 'sacred' and is often used for standing stones.[35]

We also discovered some very interesting traditions associated with the church at Cerrigydrudion, which is dedicated to Mary Magdalene.[36] The church is situated in a very old circular churchyard and a tradition recorded in the parish register states that the church was founded by Ieuan Gwas Padrig (Ieuan the servant of Patrick) in 440, around the same time that the Treachery of the Long Knives took place, according to the *Brut*. It is also recorded that in the church was a *cistfaen* (stone chest) containing the bones of a large person, and a large mound of stones, presumably some sort of cairn, used to exist right next to the church until the middle of the 19th century. On older maps and documents the village is called Llancerrigydrudion – the Sacred Enclosure of the Stones of the Heroes. Could this village be the site of the monastery of Ambri, said in the *Brut* to be situated within the Giants' Dance?

At the other end of the valley near the village of Pentrefoelas – four miles to the west of Cerrigydrudion – is an area called Tre Beddau (the Town of the Graves) and when the main road to Holyhead was built through this area in the 1830s over 40 graves cased in rough stones were uncovered. Could these have been some of the dead from the Treachery of the Long Knives?[37] In the nearby grounds of Foel Las Hall is a large mound, in the side of which a stone was found in 1835. The stone marked the burial place of a certain prince named Levelinus, and part of the inscription on the stone has been translated as 'the Mound of Emrys'.[38] In Latin Emrys is written as Ambrosius and in Geoffrey of Monmouth's Latin *Historia* the monastery of Ambri is written as Ambrius. Could the latter be derived from the name Ambrosius? In other words, could the name Ambri be a Latinization of the Welsh Emrys? If so, the Mound of Emrys is another possible site for the monastery of Ambri.

It is our conclusion that the Treachery of the Long Knives took place in the region of Cerrigydrudion and that the stones of the Giants' Dance

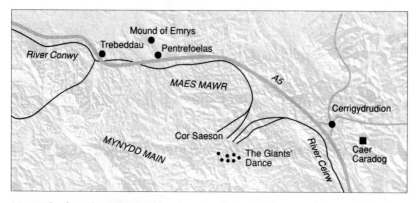

Map 16 The Giants' Dance

survive on a hilltop overlooking the village. Having identified two possible sites for the monastery of Ambri close to our proposed location of the Giants' Dance, we hope that future archaeological research will confirm the validity of our findings.

THE NAMING OF UTHYR PENDRAGON

During this period Pasgen, the son of Vortigern, was in Germania – namely England, the home of the Saxons – forming an army to avenge the death of his father. He landed in Prydein with his army and fought a battle with Emrys, although the *Brut* gives no details as to the location of the site. Emrys was victorious and Pasgen and his army fled to Ireland, where he joined forces with Gillamuri, the Irish king who had been beaten by Uthyr in the battle for the stones of the Giants' Dance. Together they landed at Mynyw (Henfynyw, south of Aberystwyth, not the modern St Davids in Pembrokeshire that is also known as Mynyw in Welsh) and Uthyr became concerned at the size of this army. His brother Emrys was lying ill in Caer Wynt (Corwen) and Uthyr did not have enough men himself to fight off the invaders. While Uthyr was worrying about this a Saxon named Eppa approached Pasgen and offered to kill Emrys in return for land. Using his knowledge of the British language and customs, Eppa disguised himself as a monk and entered Caer Wynt where, under the pretext of being a physician, he prepared a poisoned drink for Emrys and killed him.

Following the murder of Emrys 'there appeared a star of marvellous size with a single tail on it, and on the end of that tail there was a ball of fire in the likeness of a dragon'.[39] At the appearance of this comet Uthyr called his wise men to him and asked of its significance. Merlin began to weep and said:

> O this is the heaviest loss of the race of Britons, one that cannot be made good, for you are bereft of Emrys Wledig. And you are not bereft of the other king, for it is you, excellent Uthyr Pendragon, who are king. And therefore hasten to fight with your enemies and you will conquer them, and you will possess the whole of the realm. And it is you whom the star that you saw signifies and the fiery dragon under it. And the beam which you see extending over Freinc signifies a son of yours, lord, and he shall conquer much of the world. And the other beam signifies a daughter you shall have, and her sons and grandsons shall possess Ynys Prydein, one after the other.[40]

This prophecy not only foretold that Uthyr's son Arthur would conquer foreign lands. As we will see, its last lines have important implications for events later on in the life of Arthur.

Uthyr met Pasgen and Gillamuri in battle and drove them back into their ships, presumably at Henfynyw where they had landed. Following this victory, Uthyr returned to Caer Wynt and had the body of his brother Emrys 'buried beside the monastery of Ambri within the Giants' Circle'.[41] Could this be the reason why the mound at Pentrefoelas is called the Mound of Emrys?

Uthyr called his nobles to unite with him and was crowned as King of Prydein at the monastery of Ambri. Uthyr had two images made of a dragon, to represent the two images described by Merlin in his prophecy to Vortigern at the fort of Dinas Emrys in Snowdonia. One of the images was given to the chief church of Caer Wynt (Corwen) – presumably the monastery of Amphibalus, where Uthyr's brother Constans had been brought up – and the other was borne before him in battle from that time on. This is the story behind the origin of one of the best-known names in the Arthurian myth, Uthyr Pendragon (Head Dragon), which has fascinated readers for centuries.

Following the death of Emrys, Octa and Ossa (Hengist's son and his cousin) linked up with Pasgen and went to Germania (England) to look for more fighting men. They returned to Prydein and conquered lands as far as Caer Efrog (Wroxeter), but as they prepared to attack Caer Efrog itself they encountered the army of Uthyr Pendragon. After a long battle the Saxons fled to a nearby hilltop, 'a strong high place with many stones' called Mount Damen.[42] That night the Saxons barricaded themselves in on the summit of Mount Damen and Uthyr and Gorlois, as they had fewer men than the Saxons, raided the hilltop under the cover of darkness. The attack was successful and Octa and Ossa were captured and the rest of the defeated Saxons scattered. Following this victory Uthyr and his army retired to Caer Alclud and from there he went about his whole realm, and he strengthened the laws until no one dared to do wrong to his fellow.

When he had settled the affairs of his kingdom, Uthyr went to Llundain (Ludlow) and there imprisoned Octa and Ossa. To celebrate his victory over the Saxons, Uthyr held a great Eastertide feast and it is at this feast that he first fell in love with Eigyr (Igraine) and the story of Arthur begins.

SUMMARY

- Merlin (Myrddin), according to all of the known traditions, was born in Wales and the site of his grave is clearly defined in Welsh manuscripts as being situated on a hill named Cader Dinmael in North Wales.
- Caer Alclud, traditionally identified as Dumbarton on the River Clyde in Scotland, is actually on the River Clwyd in North Wales.
- The stone monument known as the Giants' Dance, traditionally identified with Stonehenge, can still in fact be seen near the village of Cerrigydrudion in the county of Denbighshire in North Wales.

CHAPTER SIX

ARTHUR THE BATTLE LEADER

HE ORIGINS of the vast body of legends associated with Arthur can be traced back to the narrative contained in the *Brut* and one mention in the *Historia Brittonum*, commonly ascribed to Nennius. In the following pages we retell the original life of Arthur as related in the Welsh *Brut*, from his miraculous conception, through the sword and the stone incident, and his famous battles to finally his death at the hands of Medrod at Camlan. Some of the other events famously linked to Arthur, such as the adulterous affair between Guinevere and Lancelot and the Lady of the Lake rising from the waters to catch Arthur's sword, are later additions found only in the Continental romances, not in the original story with which we are concerned. Using the new geography of Arthur's Britain established in earlier chapters it is now possible to read the *Brut* and watch the life of Arthur played out on the map in front of us, for without a landscape in which to place his life it will forever remain elusive.

Many of the sites linked to Arthur are still known by their original names and when they are visited the true story comes alive. His final battle at Camlan is no longer simply an entry in a tenth-century set of annals but an actual site where you can stand and picture the battle taking place before you across the exposed moorland.

UTHYR AND EIGYR

We take up our story again at Uthyr's Eastertide feast at Llundain (Ludlow) in celebration of his victory over the Saxons to which he invited all of the nobles of Ynys Prydein. Amongst Uthyr's guests was Gwrlois (Gorlois), the Earl of Kernyw, who had stormed the castle at Caer Cynan and thus helped defeat the Saxon leader Hengist. Gorlois was accompanied to the feast by his beautiful wife Eigyr (Igraine). That evening the only thing on Uthyr's mind was the wife of his ally, and he flirted with her and lavished attention on her the whole evening. Gwrlois was understandably annoyed by this and dragged Eigyr away from the feast and returned to Kernyw (the Lleyn Peninsula) without informing the king. Angered at having the centre of his affections snatched away in such a manner, Uthyr assembled a large army and marched towards Kernyw where he intended to punish Gwrlois for his impudence and win the affections of Eigyr. Aware of the impending battle, Gwrlois fortified two of his castles in Kernyw, putting Eigyr for safekeeping in the castle of Dindagol (known to the romances as Tintagel) and barricading himself in the castle of Dimlot (Latin Dimilioc), known in some Welsh texts as Caer Dunod.[1] When Uthyr arrived in Kernyw he led a ferocious three-day assault against the castles and when this met with no success he decided to surround them and starve the occupants out, waitiing until they fought or died. During this time Uthyr confessed his love for Eigyr to his fellow knight Ulfin of Rhyd y Caradog (the Ford of Caradog), who suggested he should ask Merlin for advice.

What happened next is one of the few occasions in the *Brut* where anything supernatural occurs – Merlin changed the physical appearance of Uthyr to look like Gwrlois and that of Ulfin to look like Gwrlois's man at arms, Jurdan of Dindagol, and himself he made into the likeness of Brithael, the chamberlain of Gwrlois. Under this guise the three men managed to enter the castle of Dindagol undetected. Uthyr went to the chamber of Eigyr, who was delighted to see the man she thought to be her husband safe. Thanks to his disguise, Uthyr finally succeeded in his lust for Eigyr, and it is from this union that Arthur was conceived.

Meanwhile Gwrlois was killed by Uthyr's men whilst trying to fight his way out of the castle of Dunod. When a messenger brought word to Eigyr that her husband had been killed she laughed at the news, for as far as she was concerned the man in her bed was her husband. While still in his disguise, Uthyr told Eigyr that he was going to surrender to Uthyr and put an end to the fighting. When the fighting had ceased, Uthyr was upset that Gwrlois had had to die because of his lust for Eigyr, but nevertheless happy that he had won the woman he desired. Uthyr took Eigyr back to Llundain and six weeks later he held another feast for all of the nobles of Ynys Prydein at which he married Eigyr and made peace with the kinsmen of Gwrlois.[2]

CONFUSION 8: TINTAGEL/DINDAGOL

The castle of Tintagel on the north coast of Cornwall has become synonymous with the location of Arthur's miraculous conception, but as with the other sites described in the *Brut* the true location has been confused by Geoffrey of Monmouth's Latin translation of the original Welsh name. The present castle, which is visited by thousand of tourists every year, was built no earlier than the latter half of the 12th century. The first definite date affixed to the site is in the time of Richard, Earl of Cornwall, who died in 1272.[3] The first documented evidence to link Arthur to the site is unknown and the revival in interest was started by the local priest in 1851![4]

The *Brut* tells us that the castle is called Dindagol and is situated near the sea in the region of Kernyw, which, as we saw in Chapter 3, is the Lleyn Peninsula and the southwest coast of Gwynedd. This narrows down the area in which to look for the original site of Dindagol. No place is now known to have existed anywhere called Dindagol and it is possible that the word may break down into *Din* (fortress) and *Dagol* (a word of uncertain meaning, possibly a personal name), which could refer to any one of the numerous hillforts in the area. However, in other sources we came across another person who was linked to the castle: Mark, King of Cornwall, is mentioned as ruling from Tintagel in two French romances, *Tristan* and *Le Roman de Tristan et Iseut* by Béroul. It was evidence from the latter that enabled us to locate the true site.

The romance tells the tale of a dwarf who discovered a secret about King Mark, but because he was unable to tell anyone his secret the dwarf whispered it to a hawthorn tree: 'I am talking to you, hawthorn bush, not to the barons. Mark has horse's ears!'[5] A Welsh version of this story survives in which King Mark is called March ap Meirchion and said to be the ruler of a part of Gwynedd.[6] This was an important clue as Kernyw is part of Gwynedd and led us to conclude that, in its transmission from Welsh to French to English, March the King of Kernyw had become Mark the King of Cornwall of the later romances. The connection between Mark and horse's ears might be explained when we understand that *march* is also an old Welsh word for horse. We found another clue on the Lleyn Peninsula itself when we discovered the remains of an earthwork, overlooking the sea, called Castellmarch (Castle of March, or Mark). From what little geographical information is given in the texts regarding

Dingagol – namely that it is in Kernyw, overlooks the sea and is associated with March – Castellmarch would therefore appear to be the original site of Arthur's conception.

The castle of Dimilot, the second of Gwrlois's two castles besieged by Uthyr, has been identified with the hillfort of Tregare Rounds in Cornwall, although the true location according to the *Brut* is in northwest Wales. As no place called Dimilot is known in Wales, we had to look at the alternative name given to the site Caer Dunod. The name Dunod occurs twice in connection with Kernyw: first, a cantref – an area of land similar to a hundred in England – of Gwynedd in the region of Kernyw was called Dunoding after its founder Dunod; second, in the *Brut* we are told that a certain Earl of Kernyw named Dunod sent 11,000 virgins to Cynan Meriadoc in his newly founded colony of Llydaw (Cornwall).[7] The only place called Caer Dunod known to exist is near the region of the Giants' Dance, north of the village of Llanfihangel Glyn Myfyr, and is the leading contender for the true location of the castle where Gwrlois was killed. However, there are many unnamed hillforts in the region of the Lleyn Peninsula and closer study of these might uncover further evidence.

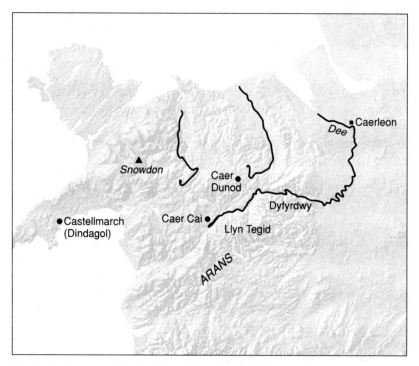

Map 17 Sites associated with Arthur's early life

ARTHUR'S RELATIVES

Gwrlois was the father of Cadwr (Cador), who appears later in the *Brut* as a companion to Arthur. Cadwr was the father of Arthur's successor, Custennin ap Cadwr, who received the crown from the dying king. Gwrlois's wife Eigyr is better known to the romances as Igraine, but the *Brut* identifies her as Eigyr, the daughter of Amlawdd Wledig. This relationship is also implied in *Culhwch and Olwen* where we are told that Culhwch is a cousin to Arthur on his mother's side, and Culhwch's mother is named as Goleuddydd, the daughter of Amlawdd Wledig.[8] The tale also mentions a second brother to Arthur on his mother's side, Gormant ap (son of) Ricca, which implies that Eigyr was once married to Ricca, making three husbands in all.[9] Ricca is a variant name for Rhita Gawr, the chief elder of Kernyw who fought with Arthur for his beard in the Aran Mountains.[10]

In forming a picture of Arthur's early life and the relationship between the immediate members of his family, we used another source in conjunction with the *Brut*. The 14th-century manuscript known as *A Welsh Version of the Birth of Arthur*, which contains similar material to the Merlin part of the Vulgate Cycle, gives details regarding events from the death of Gwrlois to the time of Arthur's coronation. It also gives the following information concerning Gwrlois's family: 'Gwrleis had two daughters by Eigyr, Gwyar and Dioneta. Gwyar was a widow and after the death of her husband Emyr Llydaw (she dwelt) at her father's court with her son, Hywel. Now Uther caused Lleu [Lot], the son of Cynvarch, to marry her, and they had children, two sons, Gwalchmai and Medrawd, and three daughters Gracia, Graeria, and Dioneta. The Duke's [i.e. Gwrlois's] other daughter, Uther caused to be sent to Ynys Afallach and of all in her age she was most skilled in the seven arts.'[11]

The above extract allows to understand the immediate relations of Arthur, introduces the characters who play an important part in the latter part of the legends and makes mention of Ynys Afallach, known to the later romances as the Isle of Avalon. Gwalchmai and Medrawd are better known as Gawain (a knight of the Round Table) and Medrod (Mordred, who mortally wounded Arthur at the Battle of Camlan). To the best of our knowledge the three daughters are unknown outside of this story. Both the *Brut* and the *Welsh Life of Arthur* tell us that Uthyr and Eigyr had another child together, a daughter called Anna. As Anna is named as the mother of Medrod and Gawain in the *Brut*, it would appear that she has been confused with Gwyar, who is named as the mother of these two in other Welsh traditions. This welding together of two characters is not uncommon, especially as in this instance they share a mother.

Arthur's immediate family

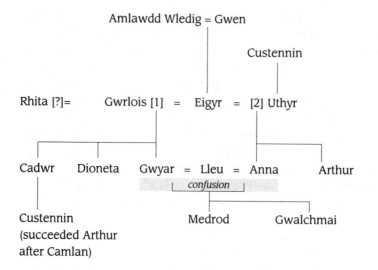

ARTHUR'S EARLY LIFE

Following the wedding feast of Uthyr and Eigyr, Merlin (Myrddin) approached the king and asked for payment in return for having changed his physical appearance so that he could enter the castle of Dindagol to spend the night with Eigyr. Merlin also told Uthyr that his heir would not be recognized in Ynys Prydein because he had been conceived outside of marriage and that it would be better for everyone if this fact was concealed. Merlin asked that the child be given to him at birth so that he could find foster parents to bring the child up as their own. Uthyr told Eigyr of this plan, to which she agreed, and after the child was born a messenger took him to the court of Cynyr Farfog and gave him letters from Uthyr and Merlin explaining the situation. Cynyr took the child, baptized him as Arthur and raised him until he was 14 years old.

Cynyr Farfog, better known to the later romances as Sir Hector, is also referred to in *The Mabinogion* as the father of Cai, known to the romances as Sir Kay.[12] Throughout Welsh literature Cai is portrayed as Arthur's closest companion and as they were foster brothers this is hardly surprising. Cynyr, Cai's father, was Lord of Penllyn, a region that surrounds Llyn Tegid (Lake Bala) near the town of Bala in North Wales. Next to the village of Llanuwchllyn at the southern end of Llyn Tegid and surrounded by forests and the towering peaks of the Aran Mountains are the remains of a Roman fort called Caer Cai (Fort of Cai), which in times gone by was also known as Caer Cynyr (Fort of Cynyr).[13] It was in this beautiful area of North Wales at the headwaters of the River Dee – known to the Welsh as Dyfyrdwy (the Waters of the Goddess) and considered sacred since time immemorial – that Arthur spent the first 14 years of his life. This landscape was briefly described by Edmund Spenser when he wrote about the adoption of Arthur in his most famous work, *The Fairie Queen* (1590), in which he referred to Cynyr as Timon:

Unto old Timon he me brought bylive
    Old Timon, who in youthly years hath been
In warlike feats th' expertest man alive,
    And is the wisest now on earth I ween:
His dwelling is low in a valley green
    Under the foot of Rauran [Aran] mossy hoar
From whence the river Dee, as silver clean,
    His tumbling billows rolls with gentle roar;
There all my days he trained me up in virtous lore.[14]

THE DEATH OF UTHYR PENDRAGON

Soon after his marriage to Eigyr, Uthyr fell ill and the men he had left to guard Octa and Ossa in Llundain (Ludlow) struck a deal with the Saxons; they released them and together they went back to Germania (England). Uthyr was angry at this turn of events, for he believed that the Saxons would return from Germania with an army and try to defeat the Britons once more. He was not wrong.

The Saxons invaded Alban, and Uthyr ordered Lleu ap Cynfarch (Lot), his son-in-law, to meet them with an army. Several battles followed with some won by the Saxons and others by the Britons and this lack of success against his old enemies made Uthyr angry, as he was not used to losing to them. In order to lead by example Uthyr had a litter made for himself and was then carried on it before the army to Dinas Verolam (the Fortress of Verolam) as a sign of defiance to the Saxons. The Saxons had already captured Dinas Verolam and when they heard that Uthyr was half dead and being carried to them on a litter they left the city gates open 'out of disregard and scorn for Uther and his army'.[15]

Carried on his litter, Uthyr entered through the open gates of Dinas Verolam with his army and defeated the Saxons, killing their leaders Octa and Ossa. Following their defeat at Verolam the remaining Saxons regrouped and continued to wage war against Uthyr, but a peace was soon made between them and order was restored to the land. It was during this peace that some of the Saxons dressed themselves as paupers, entered Dinas Verolam and poisoned the fountain from which Uthyr drank. The king was dead within the hour. *The Welsh Life of Arthur* adds the additional information that his death happened in the week of the feast of Martin (Martinmas is on 11 November). The poisoned fountain that had killed Uthyr was covered with stones and a large mound was built over the top of it. The body of the dead king was taken to the Giants' Dance to be buried alongside his brother Emrys, possibly in the Mound of Emrys at Hen Voelas near Pentrefoelas.

CONFUSION 9: ST ALBANS/DINAS VEROLAM

The *Brut* locates Dinas Verolam in Alban, the old Welsh Kingdom of Powys, but the name was translated in Geoffrey of Monmouth's *Historia* as Verolamium and identified as the Roman town that once occupied the present site of St Albans in Hertfordshire. Although there are no traditions to link Uthyr or anybody else from the Arthurian legends to this site, there is a connection between St Alban (after whom the modern town of St Albans is named) and Ynys Prydein. As we saw earlier, St Alban came to North Wales with St Amphibalus (founder of the monastery of Amphibalus at Caer Wynt [Corwen]) to preach the gospel to the Welsh.[16] The actual name Verolam no longer exists, but there is a church dedication from the time of the 'Domesday Book' in Cheshire (part of the old Kingdom of Powys) to St Alban in the village of Tattenhall. Nearby are the fortified hills of Beeston and Peckforton – could one of these sites be the location of the Dinas Verolam named in the Welsh *Brut*?

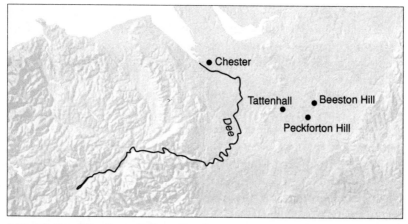

Map 18 *Possible sites of Dinas Verolam*

ARTHUR AND THE SWORD IN THE STONE

After the death of Uthyr the Saxons invaded Ynys Prydein again, this time with the help of the armies of Colcrin (Cholcrin), and according to the *Brut* they conquered land from '[the] Hymyr to Penrhyn Blathaon'.[17] These lands are also mentioned in *The Welsh Birth of Arthur*, where we are told that the Saxons conquered 'from Aber Hwmyr to Mor Katneis' (from the mouth of the Hymyr [Severn] to the Sea of Catneis [the sea off North Wales]).[18] From this we can deduce that Penrhyn Blathaon, a name now lost, was situated somewhere on the shores of the north coast of Wales. This idea was put forward by Dr John Gwenogfryn Evans in 1910, who identified it as the headland of the Wirral peninsula.[19] In the light of our new geography this makes sense and suggests that the Saxons held land from the mouth of the Severn to the tip of the Wirral peninsula, correspond-ing to the lands east of Offa's Dyke (the Wall of Severus) – that is, Mercia.

The *Brut* briefly tells us that Dyfrig (Dubricius), the Archbishop of Caerlleon (Chester), summoned the nobles of Ynys Prydein to meet at Caer Fuddai (Machynlleth) to decide upon a new king, but *The Welsh Birth of Arthur* provides a more detailed description enabling us to build up the following account of the events that transpired at Caer Fuddai.

Dyfrig sought Merlin's advice concerning Uthyr's successor as the latter had advised the nobles on the choice of the two previous kings, and so Merlin came to Caer Fuddai and told the assembled nobles: 'Uther Pendragon died after Martinmas, and it is now near Christmas … gather ye all together and cleanse yourselves by that appointed date and come together to the church, and pray to God in all innocence that he may make clear who is worthy to reign over you.'[20]

Merlin was asked to stay with the nobles at Caer Fuddai over Christmas, but he declined because he had an appointment with his confessor, Bishop Blasius, who was also the scribe of all his prophecies. The nobles arrived at Caer Fuddai on Christmas Eve and amongst them were Cynyr Farfog, Cai and Arthur, who was still unaware that his real father was Uthyr Pendragon. The next morning the nobles entered the church to pray for a leader and when they came out of the church they found 'a four square of Stone, the colour of Marble and a sword embedded in it pointwise'. An inscription on the stone read: 'This sword is a sign to point out a worthy king in the sight of God. None shall pull this sword out except one by the aid of God.'[21] The nobles returned to the church to finish Mass and then began to argue as to who should be the first to try to pull the sword from the stone. Archbishop Dyfrig chose 250 men and ordered them to try to remove the sword, from the oldest down to the youngest. None succeeded in removing the sword and so Dyfrig decided that ten men should guard the stone until another day (the actual day given is missing from the end of the sentence in the manuscript).[22]

When the appointed day came it was made into a great occasion with plays, feasting and jousting. During one of the jousts Cai broke his sword and ordered Arthur to fetch him another. Unable to reach their lodging because of the crowds, Arthur wandered sadly towards the nearby monastery where he came across the sword in the stone. He went to the sword and pulled it out with ease. Hiding the sword under his garments, Arthur took it to Cai, who recognized it and shouted out, 'I am the King! I am the King!'[23] When Cynyr heard this he did not believe Cai and so, together with Arthur, they returned to the location of the stone. When Cynyr asked Cai how he had obtained the sword, Cai admitted that it was Arthur who had retrieved it from the stone. On hearing this, Cynyr told Arthur to return the sword to the stone and withdraw it again, which he did. It is at this point in the story that Arthur learnt of his true identity as the son of Uthyr Pendragon, for when he had withdrawn the sword from the stone Cynyr embraced him and told him the truth about his parents. Cynyr asked that Cai be made seneschal to Arthur, to which Arthur agreed, and then told Arthur that the reason Cai was so ill-bred and bad-mannered was because he had been suckled by another woman while his own mother was nursing Arthur, which explains why Cai is often described as rude and uncouth in Welsh sources.[24]

Cynyr then called the nobles and Archbishop Dyfrig to the stone and asked that Arthur be allowed to try to remove the sword. When Arthur withdrew the sword the nobles became angry, complaining that they would not be ruled over by someone of lowly blood as they were of the blood of Uthyr Pendragon. Swayed by the nobles' anger, Dyfrig ordered Arthur to replace the sword and let them try to remove it. They all failed and Dyfrig decided that they should return at Candlemas (February) to try again. On this occasion the nobles were unable to remove the sword from the stone, whereas Arthur withdrew it once more with ease. Again the nobles asked for another opportunity to try and a date was set for Easter Eve, on which occasion the nobles finally agreed to make Arthur king and Whitsuntide (seven Sundays later) was set as the date for his crowning at Caer Fuddai. Arthur was knighted on Whit Saturday and the following morning was dressed in robes and taken to the sword, which he withdrew from the stone once more before returning to the church where he was crowned by Archbishop Dyfrig. After the ceremony the gathered nobles returned to the site of the stone, but the stone was no longer there and, according to the text, it was never seen again. The Brut provides us with the additional information that Arthur was 15 years old at his crowning and that it occurred 'in the year of the lord 498', but this date does not appear in Geoffrey of Monmouth's Latin translation.[25] Arthur kept the sword, the name of which was Caledfwlch, later translated into the Latin of Geoffrey's *Historia* as Caliburnis, but better known today as Excalibur. This sword became the symbol of Arthur's prowess on the battlefield and in the 12th century the tale of the hand of the Lady in the Lake receiving the sword back into the waters after his death was added to his story.

The significance of the sword in the stone ritual is obscure and appears to have been created in order to confer on Arthur the right to rule – a right which, having been born out of wedlock, he did not possess.[26] From our reading of the texts it is evident that Arthur was not a popular choice as king and it was only after his many victories over the Saxons that he eventually gained the respect of the nobles. This reluctance to accept Arthur as ruler possibly explains why in the earliest historical mention of him he is not referred to as King but as *Dux Bellorum* (Battle Leader).[27]

ARTHUR, *DUX BELLORUM*

Here we take up our story from the Welsh *Brut,* where we are told that following his crowning Arthur gathered an army and set off for Caer Efrog (Wroxeter) to fight the Saxons. Colcrin, the Saxon leader, heard of this and gathered together an army of Scots and Picts and met with Arthur and the Britons on the banks of the River Dulas. In Wales there are several rivers of this name, but the most likely location for this encounter would be one or other of the two rivers named Dulas that join the Dyfi at Machynlleth and that Arthur would have had to cross if he was en route to Caer Efrog. In the ensuing battle many men were killed on both sides, but Arthur gained the victory and Colcrin fled back to Caer Efrog. Arthur surrounded the town and laid siege to it. When Baldulf (Colcrin's brother) heard of this he 'hastened there with six thousand armed men until he was within ten miles of Caer Efrog'.[28] Arthur sent Cadwr (Cador), the son of Gwrleis (Gorlois), to intercept them on the road where he killed large numbers of Baldulf's army.[29] Baldulf escaped, however, and disguising himself as a monk he sneaked into the city of Caer Efrog to see his brother and try to find a way to lift the siege. Meanwhile Cheldric had arrived in Alban with reinforcements from England and was marching towards Caer Efrog. Arthur left for Llundain (Ludlow) to call his nobles about him for advice and it was decided to send for Hywel, the son of Emyr Llydaw, to help them. Hywel (Hoel) arrived from Cornwall with 15,000 men and the combined forces of Arthur and Hywel marched to Caer Llwytcoed where the Saxons were situated.

The *Brut* gives us some extra information at this point regarding the location of Caer Llwytcoed and tells us that 'others call it Lindsey or in another language Caer Lingkoll',[30] which Geoffrey of Monmouth's *Historia* translates as Lincoln, in the east of England. However, it is likely that the region called Lindsey is the same as the region of that name given to Hengist by Vortigern (see page 58) and an area of the old Saxon Kingdom of Mercia on the Welsh borders. The Battle of Llwytcoed is also mentioned in *The Life of Grufudd ap Cynan*, which states that Arthur was defeated, and the implication from the *Brut* would seem to confirm this.[31] The location of Caer Llwytgoed itself is provided by several land grants that mention an area called Llwytgoed in Hopedale on the River Alun to the north of Wrexham.[32] The most obvious fort in this area is Caer Estyn, opposite the remains of Caergwrle Castle.[33]

The British and Saxon armies next met in Coed Celyddon, where the *Brut* relates a strange incident in which the Britons are said to have been wounded by the 'shades of the Oaks' (the meaning of which is uncertain) so Arthur had the oaks cut down.[34] The felled oaks were used to form a barricade within which the Saxons were kept without food or water until they promised to return to Germania (England) and give tribute to Arthur. However, the Saxons soon forgot their promise and returned to Prydein and fought Arthur in a battle at Caer Faddon, better known from the early historical texts as the Battle of Badon.

ARTHUR'S BATTLES

Much of the confusion that has obscured the true identity of the historical Arthur stems from accounts of him having fought against the Saxons and the Picts, which has led to Arthur being identified with sites as far apart as Scotland and southern England. As we have already seen, the Saxons inhabited Anglia (modern-day England), but why was Arthur fighting against the Picts, who supposedly came from Scotland? As we saw in Chapter 4, there is evidence for a Pictish colony in Alban (Powys), which was translated as Albania in the *Historia,* from where it became identifed with Scotland and the confusion began. As we shall show, Arthur did not go to Scotland but to Alban, the old Welsh Kingdom of Powys (which included the English county of Cheshire). Does this mean that the story told in Geoffrey of Monmouth's Latin chronicle is fictional, as many historians would have us believe? On the contrary; as we restored the 'corrected' place names of the *Historia* to their true locations we became convinced that Geoffrey's much maligned chronicle contained more authentic history than previously thought, and as we studied

Arthur's battles in greater detail this conviction was reinforced.

The earliest and possibly most famous of references to the historial Arthur is in the *Historia Brittonum* of Nennius, which contains the following list of his 12 battles:

> Then it was that Arthur was wont to fight against them [the Saxons] in those days along with the kings of Britannia, but he himself was Dux Bellorum [Battle Leader]. The first battle was at the mouth of the river Glein. The second, third, fourth and fifth on another river, which is called Dubglas and is in the region of Linnius. The sixth battle on the river which is called Bassas. The seventh was a battle in the wood of Celidon, that is Cat Coid Celidon. The eighth was the battle at Castellum Guinnion, in which Arthur carried the image of Saint Mary, ever virgin, on his shoulders, and the pagans were put to flight on that day and there was a great slaughter of them through the power of our Lord Jesus Christ and through the power of Saint Mary the Virgin his mother. The ninth battle was fought at the city of the legion. The tenth battle he fought on the shore of the river which is called Tribuit. The eleventh battle occurred on the mountain which is called Agned. The twelfth was the battle on Monte Badonis, in which there fell together in one day nine hundred and sixty men in one onset of Arthur, and no one laid them low save himself alone. And in all the battles he remained victor.[35]

The locations for Arthur's battles can be summarized as follows:
(1)   at the mouth of the River Glein
(2), (3), (4) and (5) on the River Dubglas in the region of Linnuis
(6)   on the River Bassas
(7)   in the wood of Celidon (Coed Celyddon)
(8)   in Castellum Guinnion
(9)   in Urbes Legiones (the City of the Legions)
(10) on the shore of the River Tribruit
(11) on the mountain called Agned (a variant contained within another manuscript gives the site as Mons Breguoin)
(12) on Monte Badonis

Of the above battles those at Dubglas (Dulas), Celidon (Coed Celyddon) and Monte Badonis (Caer Faddon) are mentioned in the *Brut*, but despite many efforts the actual sites of these battles have remained elusive. Writing in 1959, the Reverend A.W. Wade-Evans summed up the situation thus: 'Not one of the sites (so far as I know) has been satisfactorily identified and all attempts to place them would seem to be futile until Arthur's field of activities has been narrowed down within credible and probable limits.'[36]

Now that we have defined the area of Arthur's activities 'within credible limits' it is possible to locate most of the sites by looking in detail at each battle and providing new evidence for those sites that remain obscure.

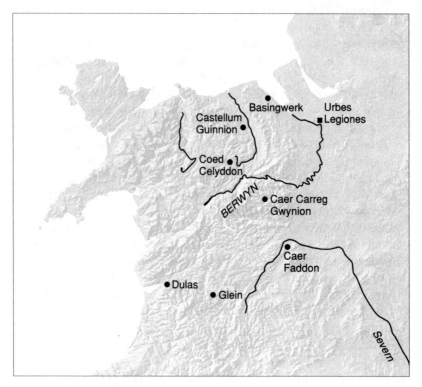

Map 19 Sites of Arthur's battles

(1) MOUTH OF THE RIVER GLEIN

The village of Gleiniant is situated on a river known as Nant Y Gleiniant (Brook of Gleiniant), north of Llanidloes. At the confluence of this river with the River Trannon, near Trefeglwys, are the remains of a Roman road that ran over the hills from Caersws to Pennal, near Machynlleth. This Roman road would have been of strategic importance and in our opinion is a far more likely site for the battle than the River Glen in Lincolnshire, as often cited.[37]

(2), (3), (4) AND (5) RIVER DUBGLAS

Dubglas is a Latinization of the Welsh Dulas, meaning 'Black/Blue Brook' or 'Black Brook', and there are many rivers and streams of this name in Wales. The River Dulas mentioned in connection with Arthur is described in the *Brut* as being between Caer Efrog (Wroxeter) and Caer Fuddai, near

Machynlleth. As discussed earlier, Arthur would have had to cross this river on the way from his crowning in Caer Fuddai to fight the Saxons at Caer Efrog. In our view the obvious choice is therefore the Afon Dulas near Machynlleth.

(6) RIVER BASSAS

We could find no reference to a river of this name anywhere in Britain, but the 'Bas' element of the place name has survived at Bassaleg near Newport in South Wales, Baschurch in Shropshire and Basingwerk Abbey near Holywell. Any of these would make sense, but as the area around Basingwerk has been the site of several battles throughout history it is in our opinion the most likely site for this one.

(7) COED CELYDDON

The site of this battle has never been satisfactorily located, but the general consensus amongst historians is that the word Celyddon derives from Caledonia, and therefore the site has been located in Scotland. Coed Celyddon (the Wood of Celyddon) is also mentioned in connection with Myrddin, who fled there after the Battle of Arderydd. There is a further reference to Coed Celyddon in the Welsh version of the Arthurian romance concerning the elopement of Trystan with Essyllt, the wife of King Mark.[38] As we saw earlier, Mark the King of Cornwall can be identified with March ap Meirchion, who ruled over the part of Gwynedd called Kernyw and who went to see Arthur to ask for help in finding his wife. This suggests that the area covered by the Forest of Celyddon is in North Wales. Around the town of Denbigh several place names exist that suggest that Mark's father, Meirchion, was from the area: Tremeirchion (town of Meirchion), Afon (River) Meirchion and Llys Meirchion (Court of Meirchion). Trystan's name is remembered in the River Tryston that runs into the River Dee near Cynwyd. When the place name and textual evidence are combined, the most likely site for Coed Celyddon is an area of North Wales bounded by Corwen, Cerrigydrudion and Denbigh, and centred on the high ground covered by the Clocaenog Forest plantation.

(8) CASTELLUM GUINNION

This has proven to be the most obscure of the battlesites. The problem has been the meaning of the word Guinnion, but when we understand that Guinnion is simply a Latinized form of the Welsh word Gwynion, identification becomes much easier. An example of the name is to be found in the following entry from the Chester Apprentice Rolls for Ironmongers, 1557–1646: '22 Feb 1613 (1613–14) William son of John Dalbin late of Kayegunnion Co. Denbigh.'[39]

Kayegunnion in Denbighshire is known today as Caeaugwynion Mawr to the south of Denbigh[40] and nearby is a castle mound of unknown origin.[41] Could this be the site of the Castle of Guinnion? Local tradition records people watching a large battle from the hillfort of Penycloddiau overlooking this part of the Vale of Clwyd, which may be a remembrance of this event.[42] There is also a hillfort named Carreg Gwynion situated above the village of Llanarmon Dyfryn Ceiriog in the Berwyn Mountains.[43]

(9) URBES LEGIONES

This site translates as the City of Legions, or in Welsh Caerlleon. There are only two candidates for this site: Caerleon on the Usk in South Wales, and Chester, known in Welsh as Caerlleon. The general consensus is that Chester is the more likely of the two, and in light of our discussion of these two sites in Chapter 3 this would appear almost certain. Chester was one of the most important cities in Ynys Prydein and was the scene of a later battle between the Britons and the Saxons, at the turn of the seventh century.

(10) RIVER TRIBUIT

A poem in *The Black Book of Carmarthen* known as *Who is the Porter?* mentions Arthur and his companions in many fights, one of which is referred to as happening '*Ar traethev Tryvruid*' (on the shores of Tryfrwyd).[44] Tribuit is considered by scholars to be a Latinization of Tryfrwyd. The location of this river is not certain, but apart from Badon and Camlan it is the only battle to be mentioned outside of Nennius's battle list.

(11A) MOUNTAIN OF AGNED

The foundation of this site by the pre-Christian king Efrog is mentioned in the *Brut*: 'And then the king built Caer Efrog, Caer Alclut and Castell Mynydd Agned, which is now called Castell Morynyon [Maidens] on Mynydd Dolurus.'[45]

The mountain of Agned became known as the Castle of the Maidens and in Cheshire not far from Chester is a hillfort called Maidens' Castle, which was known in the 18th century as the Maidens' Tower, and the name Agden is to be found nearby.[46] Could this possibly be a remembrance of the name Agned, which is otherwise unknown?

(11B) MONS BREGUION

This battlesite only appears in the Vatican manuscript of the *Historia Brittonum* in the place of the Mountain of Agned above and it has been suggested that this battle found its way into the list of Arthur's battles by mistake.[47] The name Breguion may be a Latinized form of Brewyn, which was mentioned as a battlesite of Urien Rheged in a poem from *The Book of Taliesin*: *'Kat gellawr brewyn'* (A battle in the huts of Brewyn).[48] The name Brewyn was considered to be a mutated form of Berwyn by T. Gwynn Jones and therefore the Berwyn Mountains might be considered as a possible site,[49] while the Roman settlement of Bravonium at Leintwardine on the Welsh borders has been suggested as another potential candidate.[50]

(12) MONTE BADONIS

The Battle of Badon is mentioned in the earliest source text we possess for this period, the *De Excido* of Gildas, which was copied verbatim by Bede: *'usque ad annum obsessionis Badonici montis'* (up to the year of the siege of the Badonic hill).[51]

For the first time in our study of Arthur we are able to use the evidence from the *Annales Cambriae* (Annals of Wales, written c.955), where under the entry for the year 516 we find:

> *Bellum Badonis in quo Arthur portavit crucem Domini nostri Iesu Christi tribus diebus & tribus noctibus in humeros suos & Brittones victores fuerunt.* (The Battle of Badon, in which Arthur carried the cross of our Lord Jesus Christ for three days and three nights on his shoulders, and the Britons were victorious.)[52]

The *Brut* tells us that the Saxons returned yet again to Ynys Prydein and ravaged the country as far as the River Severn and from there to Caer Faddon. Arthur left Hywel ap Emyr Llydaw, who was ill, in Caer Alclud (Melin Y Wig) and came against the Saxons at Caer Faddon. Dyfrig, the Archbishop of Caerlleon (Chester) went to the top of a high hill and roused the British troops ready for the battle. Arthur put on his armour, a shield named Gwenn that had an image of the Virgin Mary on it, his lance named Ron Gymhynieit (Spear of Command) and Caledfwlch (Excalibur) his sword.[53] The battle lasted two days and during the fighting the Saxons retreated to the top of the mountain. Finally Colcrin and Baldulf were slain, but Celdric fled with what remained of his army.

The two locations usually associated with this battlesite are Bath and the hillfort called Badbury Rings in Dorset, but this identification with sites in the south of England is the result of the Latin translation of the *Historia* being used as the primary source instead of the Welsh *Brut*, which gives the original name Caer Faddon and the site. The geography of the *Brut* places the Saxons on the River Severn and this location can be confirmed by a reference to the Battle of Caer Faddon in the *Dream of Rhonabwy* tale from *The Mabinogion*. According to the text the armies are camped at Rhyd

Y Groes (Ford of the Cross) on the River Severn under a hill called Cefn Digoll.[54] This has been identified as a site near the village of Buttington to the north of Welshpool under Long Mountain that has a hillfort upon it called Caer Digoll.[55] Later in the story we are told that the armies at this ford were due at the Battle of Caer Faddon by midday, implying that the site cannot be far away. The evidence of *The Dream of Rhonabwy* suggests a site either on Long Mountain or the group of isolated steep hills a few miles to the north known as the Breiddin, on the summit of which is a hillfort. As the name Breiddin is similar to Baddon in Welsh pronunciation, could this be a possible site for the battle? The battle is mentioned by some of the bards, but we were unable to glean any additional geographical clues from them other than that it took place in Wales.[56]

SUMMARY

- Arthur was conceived by his parents, Uthyr and Eigyr, at Castellmarch on the Lleyn Peninsula, not Tintagel in Cornwall.
- Arthur was raised by Cynyr Farfog (Sir Hector of the Arthurian romances) in the Aran Mountains near Lake Bala in North Wales.
- Uthyr's victory over the Saxons at Dinas Verolam took place in the old Welsh Kingdom of Powys, not at Verolamium (St Albans) in Hertfordshire.
- The sword in the stone incident and Arthur's crowning both took place at Caer Fuddai (Machynlleth).

With our new understanding of the geography of British history it has been possible to narrow down the sphere of Arthur's activities and suggest new sites for his battles. All of them took place within the northern half of Wales and the Marches, not in Scotland or Lincolnshire, showing that Arthur was protecting a relatively small area from the Saxon and Pictish invasion.

CHAPTER SEVEN

KING ARTHUR AND CAMLAN

AFTER ARTHUR'S victory at Caer Faddon the Britons began to gain the upper hand, halting the Saxon advance and forcing the invaders to retreat. Celdric, the surviving Saxon leader, fled with the remains of his army, but Arthur sent Cadwr (Cador), the Earl of Kernyw, and 10,000 men after him. Cadwr forced the Saxons into Ynys Danet (the Forest of Dean), where they killed Celdric 'and those of the army who escaped being killed were forced to be perpetual captives'.[1] Having conquered the Saxons, Cadwr left Ynys Danet and went to Caer Alclud to help Arthur in his fight against the Scots and the Picts.

Arthur forced the enemy to flee from Caer Alclud to a place named Mwrieff, translated into Latin as Murefensium in Geoffrey of Monmouth's *Historia* and since identified as the Moray Firth near Inverness. A clue to the true location of this region is found in the version of the *Brut* preserved in *The Red Book of Hergest*, which adds the explanation that Mwreiff was also known as Rheged.[2] The location of Rheged has been the cause of much confusion and is discussed in greater detail in Appendix 3. It is sufficient to say that Rheged is a Welsh word for 'march' – as in the Marches (borders) – and the area it covered was an old ecclesiastical region called Marchia, which encompassed the Dee valley between Corwen and Chirk and the town of Oswestry in northern Shropshire.[3]

The Picts and Scots were now in full retreat and, in 'the third flight which Arthur and Hywel made on them',[4] they fled to the lake known as Llyn Llumonwy, a lake that had 60 islands and a river leading from it to the sea called Llevyn. The Picts and Scots remained shut up on the islands in the lake for weeks and were near death from starvation when Gillamuri, King of Ireland, arrived with a great fleet to help them 'for they were descended from the same country and the same language as the Gwyddyl.'[5] (This reference to the Irish, Picts and Scots sharing a common origin not only explains why the Irish came over the sea to help Arthur's beleaguered enemy, but gives us an insight into the other battles fought between the Irish and the Britons.) Leaving the Picts and Scots at Llyn Llumonwy, Arthur set off do battle with Gillamuri and, having defeated him, forced him back to Ireland. (The *Brut* furnishes us with no more details than this.) Arthur then returned to Llyn Llumonwy with the intention of killing the Picts and Scots, but the bishops and nobles of Ynys Prydein persuaded him to have mercy on them and Arthur agreed not to kill them in exchange for their eternal servitude.

From Llyn Llumonwy Arthur went to Caer Efrog where he held a Christmas court at which he set about restoring order to the kingdom following its plunder by the Saxons, Picts and Scots. He rebuilt the churches and returned lands to those who had lost them during the Saxon plunder and compensated them for their loss of livestock. He also distributed lands to his nobles in return for their help in defeating the Saxons.[6]

ARTHUR AND GWENHWYFAR

With his kingdom finally at peace for the first time since his rule had begun, Arthur turned his attention to more personal matters and he married the woman who is described in Welsh poetry as the most beautiful woman of her time – Gwenhwyfar (Guinevere), the daughter of Ogrfan Gawr (Ogrfan the Giant or Chief). The only location we could find asociated with Ogrfan Gawr was in *The Tour of Wales* written by Thomas Pennant in 1773, which mentions that the hillfort at Oswestry (known today as Old Oswestry) was originally called Caer Ogrfan (the Fort of Ogrfan).[7] The *Brut* also tells us that Ogrfan's wife was descended from a Roman of noble lineage and that Gwenhwyfar was brought up by Cadwr (Cador), Earl of Kernyw. The association between Arthur and Gwenhwyfar is found in *Culhwch and Olwen* and the *Triads* as well as many of the other earliest sources where, although often little more than a name, Gwenhwyfar is often cited as the reason for the Battle of Camlan that led to Arthur's downfall.

ARTHUR'S CONTINENTAL CAMPAIGNS

After his reorganization of Prydein and his marriage to Gwenhwyfar, Arthur went to attack his old enemy Gillamuri in Ireland and the *Brut* tells us simply that the campaign was successful and that Arthur defeated Gillamuri for a second time.[8] Following this victory over Gillamuri we come to one of the most complicated and misunderstood parts of Arthur's reign – his Continental campaigns. The *Brut* describes these battles in some detail but they are so different to the rest of the narrative that they have created much confusion and argument. The authenticity of these foreign battles was called into doubt as long ago as the end of the 12th century by William of Newburgh, who accused Geoffrey of Monmouth of having invented the story of Arthur. The issue was again raised by Ranulph Higden in his *Polychronicon* (c.1327–40), where he asked: 'since Geoffrey is the only writer to extol Arthur, many have wondered how it is possible to learn the truth about what is said about him, because if Arthur (as Geoffrey writes) had acquired thirty kingdoms, if he had conquered the kingdom of the Franks, and killed Lucius procurator of the republic of Italy, why do all Roman, French and Saxon historians utterly fail to mention such a man, while recording the minor deeds of lesser men?'[9] It soon became apparent from our own research that when Arthur is said to have crossed into a foreign country he did little more than cross into England. A closer study of the Welsh names for the locations mentioned in the *Brut* might shed further light on this confusion. Our own explanation as to why Arthur is never mentioned by Continental chroniclers is very simple: *he was never there.*

ARTHUR'S CORONATION

On returning to Ynys Prydein from his 'Continental' battles, Arthur held a Whitsuntide court at Caerlleon (Chester) to which he invited the nobles of Ynys Prydein. The splendour of this city is captured in the 15th-century manuscript known as *The Tract of the Twenty-Four Mightiest Kings*, which was evidently influenced by the Continental romances. The *Tract* describes Caerlleon as 'the chief fortress of Ynys Prydein, for the dignity and the state of the realm were there, and the Seven Arts, and the Round Table, and the chief Archbishopric of the three, and the Perilous Chair, and the Thirteen Treasures of Ynys Prydein. At that time it was called a "Second Rome" because it was so beautiful, pleasant, powerful and wealthy.'[10]

The *Brut* describes the feast in some detail, offering us an interesting view on the supposed state of society at that time. Over 30 nobles are named from all over Ynys Prydein and some from beyond the sea, but in the words of the author of the *Brut*, to deal 'with each one separately, would be too tedious'.[11] When the nobles had arrived a special ceremony took place to honour Arthur for his victorious battles against the invaders. The three archbishops of Ynys Prydein enrobed Arthur and placed the crown upon his head, after which Dyfrig (Archbishop of Caerlleon) celebrated Mass. In the procession that followed the end of Mass two archbishops held Arthur's robes while before him walked four sword-bearing nobles, named in the *Brut* as: Arawn ap Kynvarch, King of Alban; Caswallan Llaw Hir, King of Gwynedd; Merrick, King of Dyfed; and Cadwr, the Earl of Kernyw.[12] These four rulers together represent the original four realms of Ynys Prydein – Alban, Cymry (Gwynedd), Lloegyr (Dyfed) and Kernyw – and can all be found independently in Welsh genealogical manuscripts. The fact that the four nobles chosen to bear swords at this ceremony all came from Wales would seem to belie the widely held view that Arthur was the ruler of a realm that stretched from Cornwall in the south to Scotland in the north. Indeed, the presence of the four rulers of Ynys Prydein suggests that Arthur was not himself crowned as ruler of one or other of the four realms, rather that he was crowned for having rid the land of the Saxons, Picts and Scots.

After the crowning ceremony Dyfrig retired from his post as Archbishop of Caerlleon and was replaced by Dewi (better known as St David), an event foretold in Merlin's prophecy that 'Mynyw shall be clothed in the mantle of Caerlleon'.[13] Mynyw is the Welsh name for St Davids in Pembrokeshire, and when St David replaced Dyfrig his bishopric of Mynyw did indeed become clothed in the mantle of Caerlleon. The appointment of other new bishops followed. Morgant was made Bishop of Caer Fuddai (Machynlleth), Julian was made Bishop of Caer Wynt (Corwen), Elidanus became Bishop of Caer Alclud (Melin Y Wig) and, at the entreaty of Hywel ap Emyr Llydaw, Teilio (Bishop of Llandaff) replaced Samson as Archbishop of Caer Efrog (Wroxeter). While the new bishops were being appointed 12 messengers arrived from Rome with a summons for Arthur to appear before the Emperor Lucius the following August.

At this point we leave our story of the historical Arthur while we briefly turn our attention to the mythical Arthur of the romances and the enigma surrounding his most famous court.

THE MYTHICAL COURT OF CAMELOT

In the popular imagination Camelot is intrinsically linked to the Matter of Britain and it has become a byword for all places grand and extravagant.

The true location of this lavish court has never been identified, which has led many people to view Camelot as a fictional creation. In a sense they are right, for Camelot belongs to the world of Arthurian romance and legend.

The Arthurian romance with which most English-speaking people are familiar is the *Morte D'Arthur*, by Thomas Malory, which was first published by William Caxton in 1485. In his introduction to Malory's work Caxton made the following connection between Camelot and Wales: 'And yet of record remayn in wytnesse of hym [Arthur] in Wales, in the toune of Camelot.'[14] However, the earliest Welsh sources made no mention of Camelot and it was not until the latter half of the 12th century that the name first appeared, in the tale of *Lancelot* by Chrétien de Troyes, although of the many different manuscript versions of this tale the name Camelot appears only in some and remains unmentioned in many others. The next appearance of the name came in the anonymous French Grail romance *Perlesvaus*, written at some point between 1200 and 1215. The following passage from this work concerning the location of Camelot differentiates between two places of the same name – there are actually two Camelots! One is the home of the 'widow lady', who appears in many of the Grail romances, and the other is the site of Arthur's court:

> Lords, think not that it is this Camelot whereof these tellers of tales do tell their tales, there, where King Arthur so often held his court. This Camelot that was the Widow lady's stood upon the uttermost headland of the wildest isle of Wales by the sea to the West. Naught was there save the hold and the forest and the waters that were round about it. The other Camelot, of King Arthur's, was situated on the entrance of the kingdom of Logres, and was peopled of folk and was seated at the head of the king's land, for that he had in his governance all lands that on that side marched with his own.[15]

By combining what we can learn from this extract with our new geographical knowledge for this period it is possible to locate the original court of Camelot. The author of *Perlesvaus* tells us that the court is situated at the entrance to the Kingdom of Logres (Lloegyr), a kingdom that the *Brut* describes as being bounded by the River Severn and the coast – basically Wales south of the Severn. The entrance to the Kingdom of Logres and the site of Camelot are therefore somewhere near the River Severn. In his academic edition of *Perlesvaus* published in 1937, Professor Nitze dealt briefly with this matter in his notes and suggested that Camelot should be looked for on the Welsh Marches. He also noted that some of the older names for the River Camlad in this area were Camalet, Camlet,

Kemelet and similar.[16] After drawing attention to this fact he left the argument, unwilling to commit himself to a precise identification. By picking up where Professor Nitze left off we were able to identify the site that gave birth to the 12th-century invention of Arthur's court at Camelot.

Overlooking the River Camlad at its confluence with the River Severn is the town of Montgomery. A closer study of the history of this town proved revealing, for the site of Montgomery has always been a strategic crossing of the River Severn, as evidenced by the nearby hillfort called Ffridd Faldwyn, the Roman fort of Gardden ford, the motte and bailey site known as Hen Domen (the Old Mound), the site of a castle built by Roger de Montgomery in the 11th century and the remains of the 13th-century castle overlooking the town. The important boundary of Offa's Dyke (the Wall of Severus), which passes nearby, makes the town truly fit the description of being 'situated on the entrance of the kingdom of Logres'. When Henry III built Montgomery Castle in 1223, shortly after the tale of *Perlesvaus* was written, a defensive wall was also built encircling the town and we were interested to note that the gate to the north wall was known as Arthur's Gate while the road that runs from the gate into the town centre is still known as Arthur's Street.

We were rapidly becoming certain that Montgomery was the physical location on which the fictional court of Camelot had been modelled, and when we looked to see where the manuscript of *Perlesvaus* came from the jigsaw was complete. The owner of the original manuscript was Earl Thomas of Arundel, one of the Marcher lords, whose major residence on the Welsh border was at Oswestry, to the north of Montgomery. Had the author of *Perlesvaus* written the tale in the Welsh Marches while at the court of Thomas of Arundel? The similarity between *Perlesvaus* and another 13th-century French tale, *Fouke le Fitz Waryn*, which is set along the Welsh border in the vicinity of Oswestry and Llangollen, has been noted by several scholars. Our conclusion is that Camelot was invented at the close of the 12th century based upon a real location – the town of Montgomery – and then appeared in nearly all the subsequent Arthurian romances until it became established as the most famous court of King Arthur.

THE FINAL DAYS OF ARTHUR

We take up our story of the historical Arthur again with the arrival of the imperial summons for him to appear before Emperor Lucius in Rome. Arthur had been condemned by the Roman Senate for his cruelty in conquering neighbouring kingdoms; he was also to be reprimanded for

As this signpost shows, Arthur's lost court of Gelliwig still exists on the map.

A view of Gelliwig. The grove of trees in the middle ground marks the site of Gelliwig. Within the grove sits the ancient manor house of Gelliwig itself.

Nant Gwrtheyrn – Vortigern's Valley. Tradition states that Vortigern sought refuge in this wild and inaccessible valley on the coast of North Wales. The mound rising on the right-hand side against the backdrop of the sea is the location of Castell Gwrtheyrn, Vortigern's castle. In the late 18th century local villagers opened a burial chamber at the site and the bones of a tall male were found within a stone coffin. Was this the grave of Vortigern?

The site of the Giants' Dance on Maes Mawr in Cymry (the Great Plain in Wales). Part of the area is named Cor Saeson (the Circle of the Saxons) and overlooks the village of Cerrigydrudion (the Stones of the Heroes).

The authors resting upon one of the several large mounds of stones that surround Cor Saeson. These stones were located by following the clues given in the Brut in relation to the memorial constructed by Myrddin. The memorial was built to mark the site of the Treachery of the Long Knives, where many nobles of Ynys Prydein were killed.

The high ground on which the stone mounds are situated is known as Mynydd Main (Maen) – the Mountain of Stones. The Welsh word maen *was often used to designate sacred stones.*

The 300-metre-high cliffs of Lliwedd next to the summit of Snowdon, one of the many places where Arthur is supposed to sleep until his country needs him. The mountain pass on the right is called Bwlch y Saetheau (Pass of the Arrows) and is claimed to be the site of Camlan, Arthur's last battle.

The summit of Snowdon, one of the sites where Arthur is said to have fought Rhita Gawr.

Breidden Hill on the Shropshire border with Wales is the probable site of the Battle of Badon.

The parish church of Llangollen
opposite the castle of Dinas Bran
upon the sacred River Dee.

Eliseg's Pillar, dating from the ninth century, traces the lineage of the Princes of Powys back to Vortigern and stands near the site of Valle Crucis Abbey.

The remains of
the Cistercian
monastery of
Valle Crucis.

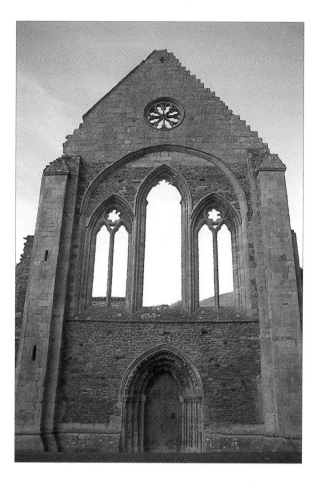

Do the remains of the original Glaestingaburh
lie beneath these ancient walls?

withholding the tribute that Julius Caesar and other emperors had received from Britain. On receiving the notice Arthur asked the assembled nobles for advice and in his address to them he exalted their ancestors who had defied Rome in the past: the brothers Beli and Bran who conquered the Roman armies and brought hostages from Rome, and Elen who, with her Roman husband Macsen and the help of her brothers, had ruled in Rome. He ended his speech by saying that Rome should be paying tribute to them, not the other way round. All of the nobles agreed, a large army was raised from their lands and they marched on Rome.[17]

As Arthur was about to invade Rome a messenger came from Prydein telling him that Medrod had married Gwenhwyfar and taken control of his kingdom. Upon hearing this news Arthur left Hywel (Hoel) in charge of the armies and returned to Prydein to confront Medrod. Meanwhile, Medrod had gathered together a large army of Saxons, Picts and Scots 'and every sort of nation that he knew hated Arthur'.[18] In return for their help in fighting Arthur, Medrod promised them the lands west of the Hwmyr (Severn) and the region of Ceint (Gwent), as Vortigern had done with Hengist and the Saxons 100 years previously. The *Brut* tells us that the total number of Medrod's army was 80,000 men and that this army came to Porth Hamo with the intention of preventing Arthur from landing on the shores of Prydein. A huge battle took place at this site and many of Arthur's men were killed, including Gwalchmai (Gawain) the brother of Medrod, and Arawn (Anguselus), the King of Alban. Medrod and his army fled from the site and Arthur spent the next three days burying his dead comrades near Porth Hamo.

The site of the Battle of Porth Hamo can be identified by locating the grave of Gwalchmai, who was killed in the battle. According to *The Stanzas of the Graves*:

Bet Gwalchmei ym Peryton
ir diliv y dyneton

(The grave of Gwalchmai is in Peryddon
as a reproach to men)[19]

Peryddon is a name used in bardic poetry for the River Dee.[20] Another early reference confirming this region as the location of the grave of Gawain is to be found in the work of William of Malmesbury. Writing about the discovery in 1125 of the gravesite of Walwen (another name for Gawain used in Continental romances) he says: 'At this time was found in the province of Wales called Ros [Rhos] the tomb of Walwen, who was the not degenerate nephew of Arthur by his sister ... The tomb of ... [Walwen] ...

was found in the time of King William upon the sea shore, fourteen feet in length; and here some say he was wounded by his foes and cast out in a shipwreck, but according to others he was killed by his fellow citizens at a public banquet.'[21]

The place name Walwen is found on the banks of the River Dee near the town of Holywell and on the hilltop overlooking this area is a village called Rhosesmor, which literally means 'Rhos by the sea'. This location fits the description given by William of Malmesbury; so, if Walwen is the gravesite of Gwalchmai, where is Porth Hamo? Walwen is itself situated between the remains of two Roman settlements on the shores of the Dee estuary, Prestatyn and Oakenholt, which probably served as harbours. From these three independent pieces of evidence, we conclude that the probable gravesite of Gwalchmai (Gawain) is on the banks of the Dee estuary near the settlement called Walwen and that the harbour referred to as Porth Hamo, where Arthur landed to fight Medrod, is either at Prestatyn or Oakenholt.

Medrod gathered together his scattered army and fled to Caer Wynt (Corwen), which they fortified about them. At this point in the story the *Brut* mentions Gwenhwyfar for the last time, informing us that when she heard of Arthur's return she fled from Caer Efrog (Wroxeter) to Caerlleon ar Wysg (Chester) and became a nun in the church of Julius the martyr to await her death.[22]

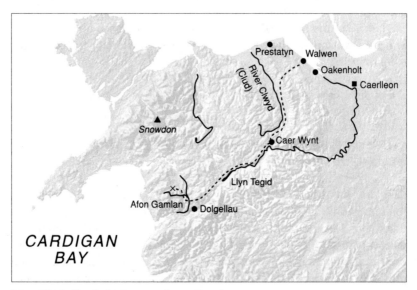

Map 20 Arthur's last campaign – Camlan

When Medrod saw Arthur approaching Caer Wynt, he came out of the city to give battle to Arthur in the open field. (This event was located on Salisbury Plain in Malory's *Morte D'Arthur*, because of the supposed locations of Caer Wynt and Porth Hamo as Winchester and Southampton respectively.) Amidst the slaughter that ensued Medrod retreated with what remained of his army to Kernyw. This time Arthur did not stop to bury his dead and pursued him into that region. He found Medrod waiting for him at the River Gamlan and the final battle of Arthur's reign began.

CAMLAN: ARTHUR'S FINAL BATTLE

The Battle of Camlan is not mentioned outside of Welsh sources and the most likely explanation for this is that it was fought between two Welsh nobles on Welsh soil, so non-Welsh chroniclers would have had little reason to mention it. Nor is it mentioned in the battle list contained in Nennius's *Historia Brittonum*. However Arthur's final battle is found in the *Brut* and bardic poetry as well as in the *Annales Cambriae*, where the entry for the year 539 reads: '*Guieth Camlann in qua Arthur & Medraut corruerunt.*' (The Battle of Camlan in which Arthur and Medrod fell.)[23]

The date of 539 given in the *Annales Cambriae* for the Battle of Camlan differs from that of 542 given in the *Brut* and we can only presume that the event took place at some point between these two dates. (The present state of understanding for the chronology of this period of history is such that it is often impossible to pinpoint the date of events with 100 per cent accuracy.) The battle is also mentioned in *Afallennau*, an early poem concerning Myrddin (Merlin) from *The Black Book of Carmarthen* in which Myrddin prophesies that there would be only seven survivors:

I prophesy that there shall come again
Medrawt [Medrod] and Arthur ruler of hosts
To Camlan ... on a Thursday;
Only seven came from the engagement

...

Then let Gwenhwyfar think upon her crimes.[24]

The attribution of the cause of the battle to Gwenhwyfar is also mentioned in two of the *Triads*, indicating that the idea is of some antiquity.[25] However, *The Dream of Rhonabwy* tells us that the battle was caused by a messenger called Iddog Cordd Prydein (Iddog the embroiler of

Prydein), an envoy between Arthur and Medrod who is said to have delivered the messages between them in such a manner as to provoke the two into battle, although his reason for wanting to do this is not made clear.[26]

The earliest reference to people surviving the battle is given in *Culhwch and Olwen*, which names three men who escaped as Morfran ab Tegid, Sandde Bryd Angel and St Cynwyl.[27] The seven survivors referred to above in Merlin's prophecy are also mentioned in the poetry of two later bards, Dafydd Nanmor and Tudur Aled.[28] A manuscript from 1656 lists the seven survivors as follows: 'Here are the names of the men who escaped the battle of Camlan: Sandde Bryd Angel because of his beauty for he was thought to be an angel; Morfran ap Tegid because of his ugliness for he was thought to be a devil; St Cynfelyn who escaped by the speed of his horse; St Cedwyn by the world's blessing; St Pedrog by the strength of his spear; Derfel Gadarn by his strength; Geneid Hir by his speed. The year of Christ when the battle took place: 542.'[29]

These seven survivors can all be placed in Wales as follows:[30]

Sandde Bryd Angel: confused with Sandde ap Llywarch Hen, who is mentioned along with his brothers protecting the banks of the River Ffraw (Anglesey) in the poetry of Llywarch Hen.

Morfran ap Tegid: son of Tegid Foel, ruler of the region of Penllyn centred upon Llyn Tegid (Lake Bala).

St Cynfelyn: considered to be a later mistake for St Cynwyl below.

St Cynwyl: left Arthur on his horse Hengroen, the name of which survives in the old township of Dinhengroen in Abergele and as the old name for the hillfort of Castell Gawr nearby. He is commemorated at Penrhos on the Lleyn Peninsula, which was originally named Llangynwyl.

St Cedwyn: patron saint of Llangedwen, a chapel under Llanrhaeadr-ym-Mochnant in Powys.

St Pedrog: patron saint of Llanbedrog in Lleyn, where the church is recorded as having contained a relic called Pedrog's spear in 1535, recalling his use of a spear at Camlan. Within the many Welsh manuscripts which preserve genealogies, Pedrog is said to be the son of Clemens, Prince of Kernyw, further reinforcing the identification of Kernyw with the Lleyn Peninsula.[31]

Derfel Gadarn: patron saint of Llandderfel, north of Bala on the River Dee, mentioned in poems by Tudur Aled and Lewis Glyn Gothi as a survivor of Camlan. There survives an interesting account of villagers worshipping a wooden image of this saint that was taken from the church of Llanderfel by the Protestants and burnt at Smithfield in London in 1538.

Geneid Hir: Unknown outside of the above list.

As can be seen, the seven survivors are all from and remembered in Wales and the earliest evidence indicates that the site of the battle is somewhere in Wales, although not everyone agrees on its precise location. For instance, one interesting folk tale locates the battle in the mountains of Snowdonia, supposing Camlan to be a mistake for Cwmllan and siting the battle on a mountain pass between the summits of Snowdon and Lliwedd called Bwlch Y Saethaeu (the Pass of Arrows). Arthur is alleged to have been killed on this pass and today there is a cairn of stones known as Carnedd Arthur (Cairn of Arthur) on the site. The tale tells us that following Arthur's death his knights descended into the cliffs of Lliwedd and went into a cave called Ogof Llanciau Eryri (the Cave of the Youths of Snowdonia) and it is in that cave that they wait for the second coming of Arthur.[32] This is just one of many examples of the 'sleeper in the cave' legend attached to Arthur and found all over Great Britain, for example at Alderley Edge and the Elidon Hills in Scotland.

Despite the Snowdonia legend, the *Brut* tells us that the true location of the Battle of Camlan is named as Afon Gamlan (River Gamlan) in Kernyw. As we have shown, Kernyw consists of the coastal regions of Gwynedd and it was here that we identified the possible site of the battle by simply looking on the map. To the north of Dolgellau in the Rhinog Mountains is situated Afon Gamlan, exactly the same name as that given in the *Brut*. On the upper reaches of this river is a simple bridge known as Pont y Brenhin (Bridge of the King) – could this be a remembrance of the battle? From the evidence furnished by both the texts and the landscape we suggest that the original site of Arthur's last battle was on a tract of high moorland high in the Rhinog Mountains of North Wales.[33] The only reason that the Battle of Camlan has been claimed to have taken place in Cornwall is the translation of Kernyw into Cornubia in Geoffrey of Monmouth's *Historia*.

From various Welsh sources it is possible to build up a picture of what took place on the battlefield at Afon Gamlan: the *Brut* details the people killed and the events of the battle, one of the *Triads* describes the dividing of Arthur's army on three occasions,[34] and references to the battle in the native bardic poetry all suggest that it was a ferocious encounter and a turning point in the history of the Kingdom of Prydein.[35] For an account of what transpired between the end of the battle and Arthur's journey to Avalon we need to turn to the little known manuscript *Vera Historia Morte Arthuri* (The True History of the Death of Arthur), written around 1300.[36] The *Vera Historia* tells us that when the battle was over and Medrod was dead and his army defeated, Arthur looked around the battlefield and saw his dead warriors and gave thanks to Christ and the Virgin Mary for his victory. During the battle Arthur had received a serious wound and he sat down to recover, calling four of his nobles to remove his armour so they could attend to his injuries. Once his armour was removed a tall and handsome youth rode towards them on horseback carrying a shaft of elm. The text explains how the shaft was straight, not knotted or curved, and it had been fired to make it hard and the tip of it was daubed with adders' venom. As the youth rode past Arthur he hurled the elm shaft at the wounded king. The injury inflicted by the spear made Arthur's already serious wounds much worse. In a fit of anger one of Arthur's men threw the spear back at the youth and killed him while Arthur, aware that he was now fatally wounded, asked to be taken to Avalon.[37]

The end of Arthur's life is portrayed as a mix of greed and betrayal – Arthur's greed to conquer foreign lands and his betrayal at the hands of his wife Gwenhwyfar and nephew Medrod culminating in the fateful Battle of Camlan. The evidence from the *Brut* suggests that Medrod and his brother Gwalchmai (Gawain) had a more legitimate right to rule over Ynys Prydein than Arthur, who had been conceived out of wedlock, and it was this that led to the Battle of Camlan. Medrod's and Gwalchmai's right to rule had been upheld by Merlin when he had prophesied that it was these two sons of Anna, Arthur's sister, who were to be future rulers over Ynys Prydein. However, the dying Arthur passed his crown to Custennin, who subsequently killed the two royal sons of Medrod, the rightful heirs to the throne. The issue of Arthur's kingship is confused and it would appear that he was never considered the rightful ruler but was put on the throne during a time of great strife.

It was only after his victories in battle that Arthur gained acceptance from the nobles and the earliest historical reference we have to him says he fought 'alongside' the kings of Ynys Prydein. The true line of descent lay with his sister Anna, and it is through her children that the kingship should have passed. With that in mind we can now view Medrod's battle with Arthur at Camlan as a fight for the true kingship of Ynys Prydein. If Arthur ever did truly gain the crown of Prydein, it was at his special coronation at Caerlleon shortly before his 'foreign campaigns', and the fact that he handed the crown to Custennin provides one final twist. Custennin was the son of Cadwr, who was the child of Gwrlois and Eigyr. This raises the question as to why Uthyr went to such lengths to marry Eigyr. Was it that the right to rule passed down through the female line and Eigyr held the royal bloodline of Ynys Prydein? Was it only by marrying Eigyr that Uthyr could guarantee the crown for his heirs? Once Custennin had killed the two sons of Medrod, was he legitimately the next in line because of his descent from Eigyr? These led to the Battle of Camlan and the death of one of the greatest warriors in history.

SUMMARY

- Arthur's mythical court of Camelot was modelled on the town of Montgomery.
- Arthur's battles with Medrod were a fight for the rightful succession to the crown.
- The site of Arthur's final battle with Medrod at Camlan is in the Rhinog Mountains in North Wales.

The one question that has been the cause of much scratching of heads and stroking of beards is 'Who was Arthur?' He has been identified with anyone bearing a similar name in Welsh genealogical material, a Breton soldier called Riothamus, Owain Ddantgwyn, a son of a Scottish noble and many others too numerous to mention. The simple answer is that Arthur was Arthur. He has a genealogy and a life story, but the only reason these have not been accepted by historians is the absence of any clearly defined locality for Arthur and his activities. Confusion was created when the locations mentioned in the original Arthurian texts were corrupted in their translation from Welsh to Latin.

A close study of the earliest Arthurian texts has narrowed down the sphere of Arthur's activities to North Wales and the Marches. There is no need for Arthur to be anybody else; he is who the texts say he is, a great Dux Bellorum (Battle Leader) who fought the Saxons and gained the crown of Ynys Prydein for his achievements. Conceived out of wedlock, Arthur was raised in secret. When his father Uthyr died, Arthur was the only male blood available, but he was not a popular choice and was considered by the nobles to be an impostor. A better claimant to the crown was Medrod and the Battle of Camlan was a fight for the right to rule Ynys Prydein. Following Arthur's death the kingdom of Ynys Prydein slowly declined and the Saxons overran much of the territory, leaving the Britons cornered in northwest Wales and the mountains of Snowdonia.

With the new understanding of the Arthurian material presented thus far many of the old questions have been answered, but, however, we find ourselves faced with an important question concerning Arthur: where and what is the Isle of Avalon?

PART TWO

PART TWO

CHAPTER EIGHT

THE KEYS TO AVALON

And then there took place the Battle of Camlan between Arthur and Medrawd, and Arthur slew Medrawd, and was himself wounded to death. And from that he died and was buried in a Hall in the Realm of Afallach.[1]

THUS IT WAS that the historical Arthur disappeared into the murky realm of legend. Today his final resting place, named above as the Realm of Afallach (Ynys Afallach in Welsh), is better known to us simply as Avalon, the mere mention of which conjures up a myriad of romantic images that have engrained themselves in our collective psyche – the Misty Isle, the Celtic paradise, the domain of the Old Gods, the mythical realm of Morgan Le Fay, the resting place of kings and the home of the Holy Grail. The historical and mythical references on which this magical realm was founded have been nourished over the years by ecclesiastics, storytellers, politicians, historians, the New Age movement and finally by various tourist boards, all making various claims on Arthur and his associated mythos and all ultimately attempting to make Arthur and Avalon their own. Yet there is still an over-riding feeling that something intrinsic is missing, that the most important questions remain unanswered. What are Avalon's origins? What truth, if any, is there to this obscure tradition that still refuses to be cast aside after centuries of doubt regarding its very existence?

Enough material has been penned regarding Avalon and Arthur to load the shelves of the largest of libraries, and it is enhanced weekly. If the truth be known, apart from the forging of Arthur's sword and his final voyage to be healed, present theories about Avalon give Arthur very little connection with the place, whether mythic or real. When we first approached the subject of Avalon it occurred to us that no one appeared to have addressed a fundamental issue: why has Avalon assumed a position of such importance within the corpus of Arthurian material when it is hardly mentioned in the original texts? It seemed probable to us that the Avalon of Arthurian legend had originally had an identity and mythical lore all of its own, of far greater antiquity than that of Arthur. Furthermore, the naming of Avalon as the setting for the forging of Arthur's magical sword and the healing of his wounds suggested to us that the place itself was of greater importance than the figure of Arthur. Was Avalon purely mythical, or like many mythical realms did it have a physical counterpart?

To our surprise our search for the true Avalon led us not only to its physical location, but also to Avalon's pre-Arthurian identity, its ancient mythic cycle and its connection to the most sacred river in ancient Britain. As we peeled away the subsequent layers of relocation that obscured Avalon's original landscape, it became clear that the true identity of Avalon remained discernible within the modern landscape, complete with the legends that constitute the true Avalonian mythology.

YNYS AFALLACH: THE ISLE OF APPLES?

Our journey in search of Avalon starts with the events surrounding the final moments of Arthur, for it is following the Battle of Camlan that we are first introduced to this enigmatic place that has been obscured by the misinterpretation and corruption of the original Welsh source materials. In Geoffrey of Monmouth's *Historia* we are told that the mortally injured Arthur was taken to Insula Avallonis for his wounds to be healed. However, in the *Brut* and other traditional Welsh sources, the Latin Insula Avallonis reverts to its original Welsh form of Ynys Afallach, which was retained even in the supposed Welsh copies of the *Historia*. As explained earlier, a number of these alleged copies are not in fact copies of the *Historia* at all, for although they contain material that is obviously either taken from or used by Geoffrey they also include elements unrelated to Geoffrey's work. These features, which would appear to come from a much older Welsh tradition, superseded Geoffrey's account in certain Welsh versions of the *Historia Regum Britanniae,* thus ensuring that the name Ynys Afallach was still remembered even after Geoffrey's Latin rendering of Insula Avallonis had made its indelible mark on the world. Despite Geoffrey's famous translation, we will show that the original name for Avalon is the Welsh Ynys Afallach. But what exactly does it mean, and how does it equate to the Latin name?

The root of the problem surrounding the true identity of Avalon has been the misunderstanding of the Welsh word *ynys*. As explained in Chapter 2, *ynys* can mean 'island', but it can also mean 'a kingdom or realm', thereby giving us not the *island* but the *realm* of Afallach. There have however been two schools of thought on the meaning of the word *Afallach*, the first of which holds that it is a common noun meaning 'a place of apples' – from *afall* with perhaps the collective termination -*ach*[2] – and identifies Avalon as the Isle of Apples. (The Welsh language has the forms *afal* (apple) and *afallen* (apple tree), which are attested to in Welsh literature and numerous place names.)[3] In Geoffrey of Monmouth's *Vita Merlin* (Life of Merlin), the Insula Avallonis of the *Historia* becomes Insula Pomorum (Isle of Apples), which suggests that Geoffrey believed the word *Afallach* was derived from the Welsh for 'apple' or 'apple tree' (*afal* or *afall*). He also links the *Historia*'s Insula Avalonis, where Arthur was taken to be healed, to the Insula Pomorum of the *Vita Merlin* by associating Morgan Le Fay and her sisters with the latter in their role as Arthur's healers. So by inference the two are one and the same place. However, in the *Vita Merlin* Geoffrey also transformed the original Avalonis into the Fortunate Island: 'The Island of Apples gets its name "the Fortunate Island"[4] from the fact that it produces all manner of plants spontaneously. There is no cultivation of the land at all beyond that is that which is Nature's work. It produces crops in abundance and grapes without help; and apple trees spring up from the short grass in its woods. All plants, not merely grass alone, grow spontaneously; and men live a hundred years or more.'[5]

This idea of the legendary Fortunate Island was recorded by Pomponius Mela (c. AD 45) in reference to the island of Sena, off the coast of Brittany, which he described as being 'famous for the oracle of a Gaulish God, whose priestesses, living in the holiness of perpetual virginity, are said to be nine in number'.[6] As Geoffrey of Monmouth was a native of the Welsh border lands he would almost certainly have been familiar with the legends attached to the Celtic Otherworld and he amalgamated these with elements from his Classical education, thus merging together two parallel traditions and in doing so creating the existing confusion between the original Welsh Ynys Afallach and the later Latin Insula Avalonis. The misconception that Avalon is the Isle of Apples may have its origins in Geoffrey's writings, but it is the embellishments of subsequent chroniclers that have compounded his mistake and given us the mythical and unlocated Avalon we know today.

THE REALM OF AFALLACH

This brings us to the second school of thought regarding Ynys Afallach and the origin of Avalon. In his *De Antiquitate Glastoniensis Ecclesiae* (Antiquities of the Church of Glastonbury, c.1125?), the medieval historian William of Malmesbury gave two explanations for the the origin of the name Avalon: '[Glastonbury] is also well known by the name of Insula Avaloniae and this is the origin of that name: It was said... that Glasteing found his sow under an apple tree near the ancient church, and because apples were rare in those parts when he first arrived there, he called it Insula Avaloniae in his tongue, that is, Isle of Apples. For avalla in British is translated poma (apples) in Latin. Or it is named after a certain Avalloc who is said to have lived there with his daughters on account of its being a solitary place.'

William's explanation was later reinforced by Giraldus Cambrensis, a monk of Anglo-Welsh parentage: 'Avallonia is so called either from British aval which means apple, because that place abounded with apples, or from a certain [A]vallo, lord of that land.'

In the 12th-century *Prophetiae Merlini* (Prophecies of Merlin), Alanus de Insulis's commentary rendered the site as Ynys Afallach, thereby supporting the case that the name is traditional and not simply a Welsh dress of the Latin Insula Avalonis.[7] In the words of Brynley F. Roberts, writing in 1971: 'since *Afallach* never occurs as a possible common noun except in *Ynys Afallach* (and if it were a common noun here the definite article would be expected: an adjective 'rich in apples', *abhlach*, would give a better meaning), and since the word occurs independently only as a proper name, there seems no reason to reject Avalloc's connection with the island.'[8]

For no apparent reason both William of Malmesbury and Giraldus Cambrensis provided an alternative to the Isle of Apples explanation. Could it be that even as late as the 12th century and despite much propaganda to the contrary Ynys Afallach was still held to be the Realm of Afallach rather than the mythical Isle of Apples? It is already widely recognized that large parts of the Continental Arthurian romances are little more than elaborate rewrites of early Welsh material, yet the subject of Avalon has not been addressed in this Welsh context. Because of this the true origins of Ynys Afallach have been lost in a literary smog, centuries old.

IN SEARCH OF THE LORD OF AVALON

So who was the mysterious Afallach after whom the enigmatic Avalon was named? Where was his realm, mythical or otherwise, and is there any evidence that points to his connection with the mythic Avalonian corpus? At first glance it appeared that very little was known regarding this legendary figure. As we were to discover, however, there was more than enough to establish his connection to the stories that surround the original location of Ynys Afallach. In fact Afallach was obviously a person of some importance, for within the landscape of North Wales we found features attached to both him and members of his immediate family that formed a distinct 'myth in the landscape'.[9] As a consequence, identifying the true location of the Realm of Afallach was relatively straightforward and it quickly became apparent that Afallach was himself directly linked to the historical and mythic material from which had evolved the pagan and Christian mythologies associated with Avalon.

Afallach, or 'Avallo[c]', as he is called in the above extracts from William of Malmesbury and Geraldus Cambrensis, is recorded in early Welsh genealogies, where his name appears in such variants as Aballac, Avallo and Amalech.[10] According to these same genealogies, it is within Afallach's generation that the Christian and pagan traditions first merged for his father is given as Beli Mawr ap Mynogan, a legendary King of Ynys Prydein, while his mother is named as Anna, cousin of the Virgin Mary and daughter of Joseph of Arimathea. Beli Mawr has been equated with (Cuno) Bellinus, a British king who lived in the time of Julius Caesar,[11] and also appears as Beli ab Mynogan in the tale of *Branwen the daughter of Llyr* from *The Mabinogion*.[12] He had four sons, including Afallach, and two daughters, Arianrhod and Penarddun,[13] the first of whom was by the Celtic goddess Don and the second by Anna, the daughter of Joseph of Arimathea. In this context it is of interest to note that in Celtic mythology Don is the Mother of the Gods and her children – Gwydion, Gofannon, Amaethon, Arianrhod and Gilfaethwy[14] – are themselves also considered to be gods.[15] Don's children and a host of other less influential, British god-forms can be found in legends firmly attached to the landscape of North and Mid-Wales.

In the genealogies Afallach is portrayed as a mythical ancestor from whom many of the characters and families encountered within the Arthurian myths descend. He is the father of two daughters, Modron and Gwaltwen, who are referred to as *Fays* (fairies) and said to be lovers of the British kings Urien Rheged and Maelgeyn Gwynedd respectively, both of whom already claimed descent from Afallach. Afallach also had two sons,

Owain and Euddolen, from whom such great British rulers as Cunedda Wledig, Vortigern, Coel Hen, Maelgwn Gwynedd and a host of others descend.[16] Afallach's sister Penarddun (the grand-daughter of Joseph of Arimathea) had children by the Celtic god Llyr, one of whom was Bran, the principal god of the Celtic pantheon. Penarddun's lineage then descended to Eudaf Hen (father of Elen, the wife of Macsen Wledig/Maximus, Emperor of Rome) and on through both the maternal and paternal lines of descent to eventually reconverge in the marriage of Uthyr Pendragon and Eigyr, a union that produced Arthur and his sister Anna.

Having established the status of Afallach within British tradition, our next step was to find geographical references to him and his realm. The following passage within the medieval Welsh text *Y Seint Greal* (The Holy Grail) drew our attention: 'Arthur and Gwalchmei [Gawain] rode until they came to Ynys Avallach, where the Queen had been buried; and they continued for a night along with the hermits, who made them great welcome. Nevertheless it may be known for a truth, that King was not very joyful that night, but his sorrow was renewed, and he said that there was no place in the world, which it was so right for him to honor, as that. The next morning after mass, they departed as straightly as they could towards Caerllion.'[17] Having already identifed the Arthurian Caerlleon as Chester, the statement that they rode 'as straightly as they could towards it' implied that Chester was nearby. So, working on the idea that Ynys Afallach was within striking distance of Chester, the regional town of Gwynedd, we turned to the tenth-century Harleian Genealogies, where we were able to trace the ruling dynasty of Gwynedd back to Aballach (Afallach).[18] From this it seemed reasonable to conclude that Ynys Afallach – the original Realm of Afallach – was within Gwynedd (North Wales).

According to Geoffrey Ashe, author of *King Arthur's Avalon*, 'opinions differ as to whether he [Afallach] had a recognized address on the everyday map.'[19] Yet when we reassessed what we had discovered about Afallach, evidence appeared to be mounting. We had one important factor in our favour in our search for the geographic location of this legendary Lord of Avalon: one of us lives in North Wales within a mile of an impressive hillfort. Sitting astride the highest point of Halkyn Mountain, high above the estuary of the sacred River Dee and opposite the Wirral peninsula, it dominates the western approaches from the Cheshire plain where the Dee divides England from Wales. For some time we had been puzzled by its name, which is given on maps simply as Moel y Gaer (the Hill of the Fort). In common with the many other hills named Moel y Gaer in Wales its original name is also known; it is Caerfallwch (the Fortress of Afallach). As far as we were aware, the name Caerfallwch was the only geographical reference linked to the legendary Afallach.[20] It was also the name of the community nestling in the shadow of this once mighty stronghold and, although this settlement is now more often referred to as Rhosesmor, its original name is applied in various forms to the whole area. The name Caerfallwch can be found on old maps and documents and is used on the village church noticeboard, which still claims to be in the township of Caerfallwch. The land has remembered and the original name has not been forgotten.

YNYS AFALLACH AND THE
THREE PERPETUAL HARMONIES

The next stage of our search to locate the true Avalon was to establish the boundaries of Ynys Afallach. Here we were helped by the Welsh *Triads*, which told us that there were once Three Perpetual Harmonies in Ynys Prydein – that is, three early Celtic monastic sites within which a never-ending song in praise of the Lord was undertaken. The *Triads* inform us that first of these was the monastery of Ynys Afallach, the second at Caer Caradog and the third at Bangor, and that within each of these places 2,400 monks in turns, 100 at a time, spent 24 hours of every day and night ceaselessly in prayer and service to God without rest forever.[21]

The precise location of the Three Perpetual Harmonies has long been debated. However, Ynys Afallach speaks for itself; it is the Welsh rendering of Avalon and there is no reason to believe that the Ynys Afallach mentioned in the *Triads* is not a genuine record of its original location. In an earlier chapter we identifed Caer Caradoc as Cerrigydrudion (the Stones of the Heroes, or Giants' Dance), the site where the nobles of Ynys Prydein had been massacred by the Saxons and a possible location of the monastery of Ambri; the church at Cerrigydrudion was founded around 440, which is in keeping with the period within which the Treachery of the Long Knives took place. Luckily Bangor is not open to misinterpretation and is universally accepted as Bangor-is-y-Coed on the banks of the River Dee in the region of Maelor. One of the most famous early monasteries in the world, Bangor is documented in connection with St Augustine's unsuccessful visit to convert the Celtic Church to Roman custom and with the Battle of Chester, fought between the Britons and the Saxons around 608. Tradition records that the monastery at Bangor was founded by a son of Coel, the first Christian King of Britain. It is worth noting that both St Hilary and, more importantly, St Benedict name Bangor as the 'Mother of all monasteries'.

If we were correct in our belief that Ynys Afallach was the traditional location mentioned in the *Triad*, then somewhere close to Caer Afallach

(Caerfallwch/Rhosesmor) there should be evidence of an early monastic site. This indeed proved to be the case, for in his history of the area Thomas Edwards of Caerfallwch refers to the remains of a chapel of which not a stone remained in his time. Edwards adds that the tradition of the chapel was very imperfect, but that it was said to have been dedicated originally to St Peter and was no doubt supplied from a monastery in the neighbourhood. He also tells us that the last remains of anything of ecclesiastical antiquity were the four fine yew trees on the verge of the ground where the chapel stood; these were cut down in 1799 and converted into household furniture. In the vicinity of the chapel there was a fine spring, called Ffynnon pen y Capel (the Well above the Chapel), a holy well considered to possess miraculous healing qualities and visited by numerous afflicted persons. Within half a mile of Pen y Capel is a farm bearing the name Monachlog, which translates into English as 'monastery', and Edwards tells us that up until some few years previously part of the edifice was discernible. He goes on to record that the walls were over a yard thick and apparently very old and that a descendant of the family which had occupied the place for nearly 200 years asserted that it was formerly surrounded with woods and that the last monk to live there was a very aged man. Edwards also relates that human bones had been found in the field behind a house called Yr Ardd ddu (the Black Garden) – Yr Maes ddu (the Black Field) is a term often applied to old graveyards within Wales. In addition he points to evidence that helps to verify the presence of a monastery, telling us that medicinal herbs in great variety and abundance were to be found near the house and that many coins had been discovered when ploughing the adjacent fields. Coupled with this there is a well kept fish pond on the site that to all intents and purposes is probably monastic in origin. The fact that Monachlog also sits upon Wat's Dyke (the Wall of Severus) should not go unmentioned.

The present farmhouse on the site described by Thomas Edwards still carries the name Monachlog and nestles on the slopes of Caer Afallach in an area known as Cefn Eurgain (Eurgain's Ridge). The Eurgain in question was the daughter of Maelgwn Gwynedd, King of Guenedota (Gwynedd) and the niece of St Asaph. At the foot of Cefn Eurgain is the village of Llaneurgain (the Church of Eurgain) where the parish church is dedicated to her.[22] According to Edwards, it was a fact that ought not to be doubted that it was monks from Monachlog who served the church at Llaneurgain. This would indeed seem likely for he goes on to say that near Monachlog, close to Llwyn Huwcyn (the Halkyn Grove), there was a site now occupied by a farmhouse, called Y Croes (the Cross) as there had been a monastery and a chapel in the locality. It is believed that the cross used to stand on Brynglas (Green Hill). Thomas Edwards certainly did not doubt the antiquity of the place and wonders if the old fabric of Monachlog owed its origin to the favour of St Eurgain. It is widely accepted locally that the site is of considerable historic interest, and its connection with Eurgain suggests that it dates from the Dark Ages.[23] We will return to this area later, again within an Avalonian context, with further evidence concerning its identification. It has to be said, however, that the only way to establish the true origins of Monachlog and the chapel that was once attached to it is by professional archaeological investigation.

Our research into Eurgain and the land known as Ynys Afallach led us to a further, possibly more interesting connection between the two through her father Maelgwn Gwynedd, the king named as Maglocunus by Gildas. Although lawfully married to Sanan (daughter of Cyngen of Powys), Maelgwn had a son called Rhun, whose mother is said to have been Gwallwen, daughter of Afallach, Lord of Avalon. The dates of Maelgwn Gwynedd and his son Rhun make the relationship to the daughter of Afallach untenable, yet the idea of the union of a British king with a daughter of Afallach is not unique. Gwallen's sister Modron is recorded as pairing with Urien Rheged, another British king. As mentioned earlier, the two sisters are described as *Fays*, and Modron is known to be a distinct form of the Celtic Mother Goddess. It is well established that much of the Welsh fairy tradition is derived from the Celtic pagan religion, therefore the chronological impossibility of Gwallwen being Maelgwyn Gwynedd's mistress is not as problematical as it as first seems; in fact it further establishes the importance of Afallach within the Welsh tradition. Two Welsh Dark Age kings considered it important enough to link themselves to Afallach through producing offspring with his fairy/goddess daughters, even though both kings had already descended from him, harking back to the ancient idea of the king having to mate with the

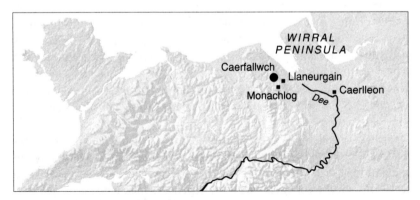

Map 21 *Ynys Afallach and the Three Perpetual Harmonies*

goddess of the land to ensure the fertility of the kingdom; it is interesting that it is represented at such a late date. Both of the sons born of these unions were to become great Welsh heroes who feature within the tales and traditions surrounding Arthur.

We now felt we had identified a geographic location and context in which to place Afallach, and so turned our attention to the other figures associated with Avalon. We discovered that all the main characters of Avalonian mythology, and more importantly the figures upon whom they were based, were to be found within a distinct localized geography.

THE ENIGMA OF MORGAN LE FAY

The death of Arthur has always been shrouded in mystery, but there is perhaps no event more mysterious than the appearance of Morgan Le Fay. Although Geoffrey of Monmouth's account in the *Historia* of events following the Battle of Camlan only makes a brief mention of Avalon and none of Morgan, his *Vita Merlin* (c.1149) goes into more detail. It introduces Morgan for the first time, attaching her to Insula Pomorum (the Isle of Apples) as one of nine sisters who 'exercise a kindly rule over those who come to them from our land. The one who is the first among them has greater skill in healing, as her beauty surpasses that of her sisters. Her name is Morgen, and she has learned the uses of all plants in curing the ills of the body. She knows, too, the art of changing her shape, of flying through the air.'[24]

But from where does the figure of Morgen suddenly appear? At first it would seem that Geoffrey had created a character akin to the nine virgin priestesses on the isle of Senna that we referred to earlier, yet these nine women also appear in very early Welsh poetry: 'the cauldron of the head of Annwn, kindled by the breath of nine virgins.'[25] Annwn is the Welsh name for the Celtic Otherworld, which suggests that Morgen/Morgan Le Fay was based upon the original figure of a Welsh goddess. This came as no surprise for we knew that Geoffrey had used a Welsh text as the basis for his *Historia* and much of his *Vita Merlin*. The latter also tells us that it was Morgan who received Arthur after the Battle of Camlan and, having examined his wound, pronounced that there was hope of recovery but only after a long period of healing.

As we traced the subsequent development of her character it was evident that in many manuscripts Morgen/Morgan was disguised by the mutilation of her name. When she appears within the *Roman de Troie* (c.1160), a French romance, she is portrayed as a fairy who fell in love with the mortal Hector (Cynyr, Arthur's foster father) and developed a great hate for the object of her affections when her love was unreturned. Within Chrétien de Troyes's *Eric et Enide* (c.1168), she is Morgan la Fee, the mistress of Guigomar, Lord of Avalon. She is also believed to be the root of Morgan, named as Arthur's sister within the same work, whereas in Chrétien's *Yvain* she appears as Morgan the Wise. Within Layamon's *Brut* (c.1189–1205), the first English-language rendering of Geoffrey's Latin *Historia*, she appears as Argante in the words spoken by the mortally wounded Arthur to Constantine after the Battle of Camlan: 'And I shall fare to Avalun, to the fairest of all maidens, to Argante the queen, an Elf most fair, and she shall make my wounds all sound; make me all whole with healing draughts.'[26] This obviously corrupt form of her name should read Margante.

Giraldus Cambrensis makes several references to Morganis in an Avalonian context, portraying her as a powerful figure with close links to the twilight world of the gods. With Giraldus, the written word connects Avalonia with Glastonia for the first time. In his *Speculum Ecclesiae* (c.1216), Giraldus relates that 'after the Battle of Camlan the body of Arthur, who had been mortally wounded, was carried off by a certain noble matron, called Morgan, who was his cousin, to the Isle of Avalon, which is now known as Glastonbury'. Giraldus's earlier *De Instructione Principium* (1193–9) explains Morganis's status in Avalon, informing us that she was 'a noble matron who was ruler and patron of those parts and akin to King Arthur by blood', while elsewhere in the same work she is described as 'a certain fairy Goddess ... called Morganis'. At the time Giraldus was writing, the Welsh tradition surrounding Arthur and Ynys Afallach was still remembered by both the Welsh people and the bards. Although Giraldus obviously knew of this original Welsh tradition, he dismissed it as fable to his Norman audience while leaving a record of it within the Welsh account: 'The Bards of Ynys Prydain and its story tellers used to imagine that it was Margan a Goddess of Annwfyn that had hidden him in Ynys Afallach to heal him of his wounds.'[27] As explained above, Annwn (of which Annfwyn is a variant) is the Welsh name for the Celtic Otherworld, and Morgan's links with this mystical realm are confirmed within another manuscript where she is named as 'Morgan, princess of Annwn'.[28]

In contrast to the goddess figure portrayed by Giraldus, the attributes we now associate with Morgan Le Fay have their origin within the Cistercian Vulgate Cycle (c.1220), where Morgan reappears as the youngest daughter of Hoel (Gorlois), Duke of Tintagel (Dindagol), and therefore half-sister of Arthur. It would be unreasonable to expect Cistercian scribes to glorify a figure who was in origin a pagan Celtic goddess, and so she is stripped of her former divinity and transformed into the 'designing and wicked person' familiar to us from modern renderings of the Arthurian legends.[29] As will become clear, despite this assassination of her character 'Margan the Goddess of Annwfyn' has very good reason to be connected with Ynys Afallach.

When discussing the background to Avalonian material in 1926, Professor R.S. Loomis stated: 'Now strangely enough, in the attempts made to explain the name Morgan Le Fay, no one seems to have taken the trouble to find out whether Welsh literature supplied us with a daughter of Afallach.'[30] The point could not have been more succinctly put. As we showed earlier in this chapter, Afallach's daughters are recorded by William of Malmesbury who tells us that Insula Avalonis 'is named after a certain Avalloc [Afallach] who is said to have lived there with his daughters on account of its being a solitary place'.[31] Giraldus Cambrensis reinforced the link between Avalon and Afallach when he stated that Avallonia was named 'from a certain [A]vallo [Afallach], lord of that land'. With the identification of the Welsh Afallach as the Lord of Avalon now apparently indisputable, the search to uncover the identity of his daughters assumed paramount importance.

THE GODDESS OF AVALON

Sitting in the valley at the foot of the mountain named Moel Famau, in the Vale of Clwyd and less than three miles as the crow flies from Caer Afallach, is a ford that crosses the River Alun. Known locally as Rhyd y Gyfarthfa (the Ford of the Barking) this place was of old renowned as a haunt of the Cwn Annwn (Hounds of the Otherworld) and a particular Welsh *Fay*. The local tradition was recorded around 1556 as follows:

> In Denbighshire there is a parish which is called Llanferres, and there is there Rhyd y Gyfarthfa. In the old days the hounds of the countryside used to come together to the side of that ford to bark, and nobody dared go to find out what was there until Urien Rheged came. And when he came to the side of the ford he saw nothing there except a woman washing. And then the hounds ceased barking, and Urien seized the woman and had his will of her; and then she said, "God's blessing on the feet which brought thee here." "Why?" said he. "Because I have been fated to wash here until I should conceive a son by a Christian. And I am daughter to the King of Annfwn, and come thou here at the end of the year and then thou shalt receive the boy." And so he came and he received there a boy and a girl: that is, Owein son of Urien and Morfudd daughter of Urien.'[32]

Who was this 'daughter to the King of Annfwn'? In a *Triad* concerning the womb burdens of Ynys Prydein we are told that the second of the womb burdens of Prydein was Owain and Morfudd, the children of Urien Rheged, and their mother is named as Modron, daughter of Afallach.[33] Immediately the identity of the washer at the ford and daughter of the King of Annwn becomes apparent: she is Modron, and her father the King of Annfwn is none other than Afallach – a clear reference to Afallach's connection with the Celtic Otherworld, which as we saw is itself associated with Avalon (Ynys Afallach). The above account of the episode at the Ford of the Barking, which is the only recorded geographical reference linked to Modron, therefore gives us the mythic father (Afallach) and daughter (Modron) within a defined geographical area. We now had a confirmed location for Afallach, Lord of Avalon and King of the Celtic Otherworld, at Rhyd y Gyfarthfa (the Ford of Barking) which was within a couple of miles of Caer Afallach, the only geographic reference to him.

It is widely accepted that Modron equates to the Celtic Goddess Matrona (the Great Mother), whose name survives in a derived form in that of the Continental River Marne. Matrona's son is named as Maponus, the Continental variant of Mabon, the divine Celtic child. What little is known regarding these two divine figures – the divine mother of the divine son – in their Welsh variants of Modron and Mabon comes to us from the ancient Welsh text of *Culhwch and Olwen*,[34] or more specifically from the section within it known as *The Search for the Mabon*.

The cult of Modron/Matrona has been associated with the cult of the Triple Matron, or the Three Mothers, of which numerous examples are to be found in Romano-Celtic dedications in Britain and Gaul. This connection is also reflected in the landscape of Ynys Afallach, for over-looking the ford where Urien impregnated Modron and rising majestically from the valley floor to dominate the skyline for miles around is the mountain of Moel Famau (the Mountain of the Mothers).[35] Writing of this Moel Famau, Professor John Rhys stated that 'the proper spelling is no doubt Moel Fammau, the Mothers Mountain, the ladies in question being of the class of divine Matres once worshipped by the Celts'.[36] The triple form of the Celtic Goddess often appears as variants of Crone/Mother/Maiden and this relationship is also portrayed within the landscape of the Realm of Afallach over which Moel Fammau reigns. Among the hills surrounding Modron's ford are three mythologically interlinked geographic features: Nant y Wrach[37] (the Valley of the Hag), Bryn Bannon (the Hill of the Maiden Consort) and the Mountain of the Mothers itself, thus giving us Maiden, Mother and Hag, the three faces of the Celtic Goddess.[38] Within Wales many remembrances of the divine Celtic Mothers have come down to us in the form of folk tales and fairy lore. The Tylwyth

Teg (the Fair Tribe, namely the Fairies) are known under various names, among them Bendith y Mamau (the Mothers' Blessing) and just Y Mamau (the Mothers). Professor R.S. Loomis established that legends relating to Modron as the Lady of the Lake and as the divine figure attached to Avalon survived orally in Wales until the end of the 19th century.[39]

We have now seen that Morgan and Modron are intrinsically linked to Avalon, and a closer correlation between these two figures becomes apparent when we consider the variant traditions concerning the mother of Owein and Morfudd. Within Welsh tradition Modron is the mother of these two children by Urien Rheged, yet within the 13th-century *Suite du Merlin* the wife of Urien and mother of Owein is recorded as Morgain la Fee. This relationship is also repeated in Malory's *Morte D'Arthur* and is further enhanced by the reference in the *Historia Meriadoci,* where the wife of Urien is named Oruen. This is an obviously corrupt form of Moruen, but should not be considered unusual as a majority of manuscripts drop the initial of Morgan's name, giving rise to the forms Orain, Ornain, Oruein, Oruain and Orva. In other manuscripts she appears under the variant spellings of Morgain, Morguein, Morgan and Morganz and as such we will meet with her again.[40] Although Welsh tradition clearly stated that Modron was the mother of Owain by Urien, it was now clear that Modron had become the Morgan Le Fay of the romances, which enabled us to understand why the latter is referred to as a fairy goddess and the goddess of Annwn, the Celtic Otherworld.

Our next step was to understand why some texts refer to Morgan as being either akin to Arthur or his sister/half-sister. The Welsh *Brut* names Arthur's sister as Anna, the daughter of Uthyr and Eigyr and mother to Gwalchmai (Gawain) and Medrod. However, in *The Welsh Version of the Birth of Arthur* the mother of Gwalchmai and Medrod is named as Gwyar (the daughter of Eigyr by her first husband Gwrlois), and it would appear that the two characters of Anna and Gwyar became confused as the legends were rewritten and expanded upon. Anna is virtually unknown outside of the *Brut*, but in the *The Welsh Birth of Arthur* we are told that Uthyr sent Gwyar to Ynys Afallach to learn the seven arts and in the poem *Erec et Enide* by Chrétien de Troyes we find reference to Morgan being the lover of Guigomar, the Lord of Avalon.[41] As Gwyar and Morgan Le Fay are both linked to Avalon, we concluded that the later romances that describe Morgan La Fay as the half-sister of Arthur are in all likelihood based upon the figure of Gwyar.

Over the centuries Arthur's sister merged with the ancient figure of Modron the Goddess of Ynys Afallach/Avalon, chief of nine sisters and daughter of Afallach, Lord of Avalon and King of Annwn. Modron was possessed of many supernatural qualities and slowly but surely the attributes of this divine Celtic figure were transferred to the historical figure of Arthur's sister. Eventually this amalgamation gave birth to the schizophrenic figure of Morgan Le Fay, and though her name may be found in various different spellings one is never in doubt when reading of her that we are still in the presence of the Goddess of Avalon. From whichever angle we now looked at the matter, it had become clear that Ynys Afallach was the original name of Avalon and that 'Avalon was the traditional abode of Morgain'.[42]

THE TRUE HISTORY OF THE DEATH OF ARTHUR

Our search for Avalon had brought us to a point where we were certain that the physical location of this mysterious realm was in northeast Wales, when something quite unexpected came to our attention: a Latin text that not only appeared to continue from where Geoffrey of Monmouth had left off, but clearly identified a geographical location for Avalon and in doing so provided the final piece of the jigsaw: 'At length the king, slightly restored by an improvement in his condition, gives orders to be taken to Venodocia [Gwynedd], since he had decided to sojourn in the delightful Isle of Avalon because of the beauty of the place (and for the sake of peace as well as for the easing the pain of his wounds).'[43] We couldn't believe our eyes, for the manuscript clearly stated that Avalon was in Gwynedd, the kingdom that had once stretched across North Wales. Our own research had been confirmed by a little known Latin text, and when we found out where the text came from any doubts we had left simply disappeared.

The manuscript was the *Vera Historia de Morte Arthuri* (The True History of the Death of Arthur), which we referred to briefly in Chapter 7.[44] Dating from around 1300 and known simply as Grays Inn MS. 7, it records events following the Battle of Camlan and the funeral of Arthur. The *Vera Historia* was owned by the Franciscan convent in Chester and a marginal note on the text records that it was given to them by 'frater W. Gyn' (Gwyn), which has led scholars to propose that the text came from the abbey of Aberconwy (Conway) on the North Wales coast.[45] The latter was a Cistercian house, founded in 1198 by Llewelyn the Great of Gwynedd, and the Cistercian monasteries were heavily patronized by the Princes of Wales with whom they often sided in political and religious struggles with English kings. In fact Conway Abbey was the cultural centre of Gwynedd during the rule of the Welsh princes and had property in the city of Chester.

Other, often abbreviated versions of the *Vera Historia* are known to exist in addition to the Grays Inn manuscript, such as that found in the chronicle of the monastery of Hales in Gloucestershire.[46] One such manuscript was incorporated into a first variant copy of Geoffrey of Monmouth's Latin *Historia*, so as to follow on from the Battle of Camlan. In effect the *Vera Historia de Morte Arthuri* would appear to be the missing section from Geoffrey's text, filling in the gap surrounding the death of Arthur and the location of his final destination, Avalon.[47] We could not help but wonder whether what is now known as the *Vera Historia* was in fact traditional material that had once constituted part of that ancient book in the British tongue that Geoffrey used for his source. As of yet no Welsh manuscript of the *Vera Historia* has been found to exist, but as many of the 70-odd Welsh texts that contain the *Brut* have yet to be fully edited it may be that one will come to light in the future.

In light of the fact that the provenance of the *Vera Historia* was traced back to the Welsh Marches, and probably to the courts of the Welsh princes via Conway Abbey or other Welsh Cistercian houses, and that until the dissolution of the monasteries the Cistercians were themselves great patrons of the Welsh bards, it seemed reasonable to conclude that if the original Welsh tradition surrounding the death of Arthur and his interment in Avalon were to have survived anywhere it would almost certainly have been in this environment. This, combined with the fact that events clearly take place within Gwynedd, led us to believe that the *Vera Historia* was a rendering of the original Welsh tradition of the last days of Arthur, for the text gives the fullest detailed account of Arthur's death until the compilation of Vulgate Cycle, which itself evolved from the Cistercian order. In our opinion the *Vera Historia* appears to be a full independent account of Arthur's death and burial, possibly the work of a Welsh cleric well versed in the native tradition. It is not difficult to imagine a Welsh cleric familiar with the courts of the Welsh princes and the stories of the bards, in the twilight days of his people's freedom, hunched over his lectern copying by candlelight the true Welsh tradition of the death of Arthur.

From our point of view the fact that the text confirmed our findings regarding Avalon was enough, but the *Vera Historia de Morte Arthuri* also describes Arthur's death and funeral rites in some detail. On arriving in Avalon Arthur became aware that his wounds were fatal and three bishops came to administer the last rites to him. When Arthur passed away his body was embalmed in balsam and myrrh and prepared for burial. His corpse was then taken to a small chapel dedicated to the Virgin Mary, but because the entrance to the chapel was too small for his body to be taken inside the hermit who resided at the chapel and the bishops who accompanied the body performed the last rites in the chapel while Arthur's body was left outside. During these rites a huge storm rose up and a thick mist descended, making it impossible to see the body of Arthur. After several hours the mist lifted and Arthur's body was gone. The author of the text then says that until his day there existed two different schools of thought concerning the fate of Arthur's body – according to one he was still alive, according to the other he was dead and buried in a tomb near the chapel. This first school of thought could well be related to the idea of Arthur's return, which was used as political propaganda by the English monarchy (see Chapter 10), while the second maintained the Welsh tradition that clearly stated that Arthur was dead (see Appendix 2). The text concludes by telling us that Arthur had ruled over the realm of Britannia for 39 years and that he was succeeded by Cadwr, the son of Constantine (Custennin).

One fascinating aspect of this detailed account of Arthur's final hours is that it leaves the exact whereabouts of his tomb a mystery, a tradition that is also preserved in the *Stanzas of the Graves*, where we are told: '*Anoeth bid bet y Arthur*' (The world's wonder a grave for Arthur).[48] Although the Welsh tradition is unclear about Arthur's final resting place it never suggests that he was alive and about to return.

According to all accounts the destination of Arthur's final journey was Ynys Afallach, the Latin Insula Avallonis or Realm of Avalon, which we had now located in northeast Wales. As most of the events surrounding Arthur's life also had roots in this same area we knew we were establishing a firm foundation from which to continue. It was also common sense; if Arthur was wounded at the Battle of Camlan and taken to Ynys Afallach to have his wounds treated he could not have travelled any great distance. As explained in Chapter 7, the Battle of Camlan took place on Afon Gamlan, north of Dolgellau, and it would seem likely that Arthur had been taken over the hills to Llanuwchllyn and then along the Roman road to Corwen (Caer Wynt), from where he could have been taken either along the Dee valley past Llangollen and down the Dee to its estuary, or over the Clwydian hills towards Caerfallwch. The tradition recorded in the later romances of Arthur's body being carried away on a boat could be a memory of him being ferried down the River Dee. The fact that Derfel, one of the survivors of the Battle of Camlan, is remembered at Llandderfel on the River Dee to the north of Bala suggests that perhaps he accompanied the body to this point and lends some weight to this argument.

We now had a clearer picture of the events surrounding Arthur's final hours, but several other questions concerning Avalon remained unanswered. We had already had glimpses of Ynys Afallach's pre-Arthurian mythology and its identification with Annwn, the Celtic Otherworld, yet we were surprised to find there was much more evidence to support these older Avalonian traditions then either of us would ever have believed. As we will show in the next chapter, there is sufficient evidence to indicate that Ynys Afallach is synonymous with Annwn, the Celtic Otherworld, for historical documents exist to prove that this 'land of the dead' was a physical location in the hills and valleys of North Wales on which the Brythonic Otherworld was centred.

SUMMARY

- The Welsh term Ynys Afallach means 'the Realm of Afallach', a figure who is remembered in the name of the hillfort called Caerfallch near Rhosesmor in northeast Wales.
- Ynys Afallach is named in Welsh tradition as the location of one of the Three Perpetual Harmonies, of which the other two are also in North Wales.
- Afallach is recorded in Welsh genealogies as the legendary ancestor of the kings of Gwynedd. Also named as the King of Annwn, the Celtic Otherworld, he was the father of Modron.
- Modron is the original British form of the Celtic Mother Goddess and is known to the later romances as Morgan Le Fay.
- A medieval text locates Avalon in Gwynedd, the kingdom that once extended across all of North Wales.

CHAPTER NINE

AVALON, ANNWN AND THE CELTIC OTHERWORLD

Denbighshire must once
have been a land rich
in myth and legend.[1]

IN ARTHUR'S TIME and before that, the people of South Wales regarded North Wales as pre-eminently the land of faerie. In the popular imagination, that distant country was the chosen abode of giants, monsters, magicians, and all the creatures of enchantment. Out of it came the fairies, on their visits to the sunny land of the South.[2]

Having established that Avalon was located in Gwynedd our attention was caught by the above superstition, which was maintained until relatively recent times by the people of South Wales for whom North Wales – especially Gwynedd and northern Powys – was considered a strange, supernatural realm of witches, dragons, wizards and fairies. Home to the majority of the legendary tales of *The Mabinogion*, Gwynedd and northern Powys are still exceedingly rich in the legends, folk tales and mythology associated with Annwn, but what exactly is the Celtic Otherworld?

The answer to this question is best addressed in the words of R.S. Loomis. Whilst considering the concept of Annwn among the Welsh as an abode of former divinities, Professor Loomis relates that Annwn was seen as 'a palace which appeared and disappeared in a familiar landscape setting, or as a delightful subterranean region, or as an elysian isle. When Christian clerics identified the king of Annwn with the devil, then of course Annwn had to be hell.'[3] The older form of Annwn was Annwfn, which was originally a Celtic paradise sharing much in common with Avalon. With the spread of Christian influence the home of the old pagan gods, Annwn, became transformed into Hades, the underworld, and equated with Uffren (hell). However in the popular mind Annwn continued to be remembered, eventually metamorphosing into Faerieland and the Land of the Dead.

The realm of Annwn appears in early Welsh tales and poetry, sometimes with an Arthurian connection, as in the poem entitled *The Spoils of Annwn,* where we are told that Arthur entered Annwn to steal a diamond-embellished cauldron. Although the name of the chief to whom the cauldron belongs is not mentioned, certain kings of Annwn can be identified within Welsh sources. For instance, the first branch of *The Mabinogion* relates how Pwyll, Prince of Dyfed (in South Wales), exchanged kingdoms with Arawn, King of Annwn, to help him defeat a rival lord in Annwn named Hafgan. The most famous Lord of Annwn was Gwyn ap Nudd and in *Culhwch and Olwen* we are told that God had set the spirit of the demons of Annwn in Gwyn, lest the world be destroyed. Within Welsh folklore Gwyn ap Nudd is known as King of the Fairies or Plant Annwn (Children of the Otherworld) who are said to fetch the fallen to his realm.[4] He is also portrayed as leading the Cwn Annwn (the Hounds of Annwn), also known as Cwn Bendith y Mamau (the Hounds of the Mothers/Fairies), which were sent from Annwn to hunt out the corpses and souls of the dead. Considered to be omens of death, these spectral hounds came after nightfall foretelling of someone's death, much like the dreaded banshees of Ireland.[5]

Giraldus Cambrensis casts some light on the traditional relationship between Ynys Afallach and Annwn in his Welsh variant *Speculum Ecclesiae.* In our study of Morgan le Fay in Chapter 8 we quoted a short passage from this work in which Giraldus tells us that 'Margan a Goddess of Annwfyn [Annwn]' had hidden Arthur 'in Ynys Afallach to heal him of his wounds', thereby implying that Ynys Afallach and Annwn are one and the same place, or that the one is within the other. We also referred to the correlation between the nine sisters of Morgan who, according to Geoffrey of Monmouth's *Vita Merlin*, were Arthur's healers in the Insula Pomorum (the name given to Ynys Afallach in the *Vita Merlin*) and the nine virgins whose breath kindled the cauldron of the Head of Annwn, recorded within *The Book of Taliesin.*

There are, of course, many correlations between Ynys Afallach/Avalon and Annwn, the Celtic Otherworld as previously established by many eminent scholars such as R.S. Loomis.[6] The related characteristics that firmly associate Avalon as another name for the Otherworld in all probability make Avalon a later name for the same geographic location as Annwn. It has long been assumed that Annwn refers to some non-specific place beyond the realms of the physical world, yet there is plentiful evidence to suggest that our ancestors viewed certain parts of the landscape either as entrances to or areas of Annwn. Annwn only appears in the Welsh sources and there but rarely. Having established the original location of Ynys Afallach and a background to Annwn, we turned to the historical sources to see if we could find any references to enlighten us as to the location of the place that is remembered in folklore and tradition as the realm of the Fairies and the Land of the Dead.

THE WALL AND THE LAND OF THE DEAD

Within his work *The Four Ancient Books of Wales* (1868), William F. Skene refers to a sixth-century text in which Procopius gives an account of his visit to Britannia and relates how in ancient times the Britons had built a long wall that cut off a great portion of the land. The reason the wall was built, explains Procopius, was that the land, the people and all other things were different on either side of it. He goes on to say that the land on the eastern side of the wall was inhabited by people who lived normal lives, and he paints a picture of a very fertile land, with fruit trees and corn fields. He then describes the land on the western side of the wall as being different, adding that it would be impossible for anyone to live there even half an hour because of the innumerable vipers and serpents and all other kinds of wild beasts that infested that place. Procopius continues, telling us that the local inhabitants maintained that anyone who passed over the wall would die immediately, and adds that it was incumbent upon him to record a certain tradition, closely allied to fable, that prevailed in the area. Not wanting to disregard what he has heard in case he should bring upon himself accusations of ignorance when writing about the realm of Britannia, he then records the tradition to which he has been referring: 'They say that the souls of men departed are always conducted to this place.'[7]

Here was a sixth-century chronicle recording an ancient British tradition regarding the location of the Land of the Dead, the Celtic Otherworld. Why this had not been pointed out before returns us to one of the most misunderstood features of the early history of the British Isles, the Wall of Severus. Procopius makes it clear that for the ancient Britons the Land of the Dead was a physical location to the *west* of a wall, and it was to there that the souls of the departed were taken. The text specifically states that the wall has a western and an eastern side, indicating that it runs from north to south, yet for this text to fit the accepted version of early British history the wall referred to by Procopius is generally identified as Hadrian's Wall which, like the Antonine Wall, runs from east to west and therefore has a northern side and a southern side. The misunderstanding surrounding the forgotten Wall of Severus has long led scholars astray, even to the point where the problems it creates have been alleviated simply by changing the original text in translation and inserting 'southern' for eastern and 'northern' for western. In doing so the evidence of a valuable historical source has been dismissed. At the time Procopius was writing there was only one wall running from north to south that divided the realm of Britannia and that was the Wall of Severus, known today as Offa's Dyke (Wat's Dyke).

Having learnt from Procopius that a sixth-century British tradition placed the Land of the Dead to the west of Offa's Dyke, and knowing that this was also the location of the Realm of Afallach (Avalon), we set out to establish whether there was any archaeological evidence for this reference to the Land of the Dead. Once again we were astonished by what we uncovered. The hillfort of Caerfallach, which we referred to in the previous chapter, is located within the modern county of Flintshire, and a short distance away in the county of Denbighshire is Modron's Ford (Rhyd y Gyfarthfa). Until recently these two counties were jointly known as Clwyd, within whose boundaries lay two of the largest concentrations of early burial sites in the United Kingdom. The first runs from Halkyn Mountain along the Flintshire–Delyn plateau and westwards to the North Wales coast, incorporating the land north of the Wheeler valley. The second runs over the moorland of Ruabon Mountain above Llangollen, petering out just south of the River Dee on the northern slopes of the Berwyn Mountains. The name Berwyn is a metathesized form of Bre-wyn (Gwyn's Hill) and this area, which was known locally as Gwyn's Land, also contains Nant Gwyn (Gwyn's Valley) and, just up the Llangollen valley near Corwen (Caer Wynt), is Caer Drewyn (Gwyn's Fort, or Town). The Gwyn after whom these sites are named is none other than Gwyn ap Nudd, Lord of Annwn, and folk tales concerning Gwyn and his subjects abound in this area, as do references to him in the local landscape.[8] What struck us as being of particular significance was that both concentrations of burial sites lie immediately west of Offa's/Wat's Dyke.

In total there are 547 known Bronze Age barrows recorded within the old county of Clwyd as well as burials from earlier and later periods. The most impressive of these early burials is beneath a major landmark known as the Gop cairn, which rises majestically from its central position in the Flintshire plateau concentration high above the River Dee. This giant cairn, 8–14 metres high and 70–100 metres across, is the largest in Wales. (The only cairn larger than this within the United Kingdom is Silbury Hill in Wiltshire, if indeed Silbury Hill is a cairn.) In the past the Gop cairn was thought to date from the Bronze Age, but it equates very well with a Middle to Late Neolithic period. Disturbances at its base have revealed limestone revetment walling and at the turn of the 19th century 14 Neolithic burials were discovered in the caves beneath the cairn. Each individual was buried in a crouching position in a stone chamber against the back wall of the cave, which corresponds very well with other Neolithic cave sites and similar burials within Clwyd. The landscape of the Flintshire plateau was obviously very sacred from the earliest times for the area is home to a multitude of standing stones, holy wells, cave burials and barrows, while local tradition and folklore contain an abundance of Otherworld themes and motifs. The second concentration of burial sites, on Ruabon Mountain above Llangollen, is equally impressive: the high moorland stretches over a vast distance and Ruabon Mountain itself is covered in ancient cairns, barrows and stone circles.

A tradition identifying Ynys Afallach/Avalon as a place for the burial of the dead appears relatively early in Welsh sources in a prophecy attributed to Melkin of Avalon, a Welsh bard said to have flourished during the reign of Maelgwn Gwynedd (c.560). Melkin's prophecy is very unusual and has been described as 'a queer piece of semi-poetical prose, intended to mystify and hardly capable of translation into English'.[9] Nonetheless, the author of those words did translate it, as follows:

Avalon's island, with avidity
Claiming the death of pagans,
More than all in the world beside,
For the entombment of them all,
Honoured by chanting spheres of prophecy:
And for all time to come
Adorned shall it be
By them that praise the Highest.
Abbadare, mighty in Saphat,
Noblest of pagans,
With countless thousands
There had fallen on sleep.

Looking back over the evidence linking Avalon with Annwn we wondered what had marked the boundary to the Land of the Dead before Severus built his wall. The answer to this question was to prove a relatively simple affair. As we explained in Chapter 2, in ancient times the geographical boundaries of kingdoms tended to be established according to naturally occurring features within the landscape, such as drainage basins, impassable mountains, hill tops, etc. One natural feature that was used more often than others to denote a border or border area was a river. From what we had learnt so far there was only one obvious candidate for the river that could have marked the original boundary of Ynys Afallach – that most sacred of rivers, the Dee.

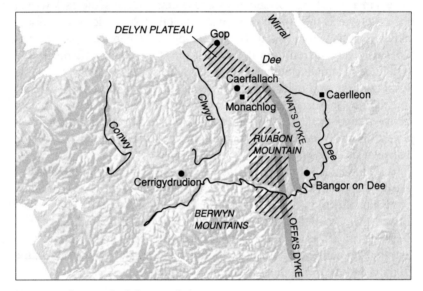

Map 22 The Land of the Dead

THE SACRED RIVER AND THE GODDESS

The River Dee has been regarded as a sacred river since the earliest times, with many myths and legends of the Britons set along her course, but the first recorded mention of the Dee dates from the ancient geographer Ptolemy (c.150) and she has since been recorded in every historical period. In the *Antonine Itinerary* (c.200) she is referred to as the Deva, the feminine of the Celtic word *Devos,* which denotes a goddess, a holy or divine being, or a sacred river.[10] In Roman times the river's name was attached to the city of Chester that stood on her banks, and so within the Roman records Chester became Deva, or the City of the Goddess. It was perhaps for this reason that from a very early period the lands about the River Dee were given the regional name Deifyr (from the Welsh for Deva) or Deira, a province of the Welsh 'Northumbria'. (See Chapter 2.)

As explained earlier, in modern Welsh the sacred River Dee is known as Dyfrdwy (Waters of the Goddess), while an older form of her name is recorded as Aerfen,[11] meaning 'battle goddess' or 'goddess of war', from *aer* (battle) and *fen* or *men* (fate). According to one ancient tradition Aerfen was said to need three human sacrifices each year in order to ensure success in battle, and a tradition relating to the warlike aspect of the goddess of the River Dee was recorded as late as c.1188 by Giraldus Cambrensis in his journey through Wales. Giraldus informs us that 'the local inhabitants maintain that the Dee moves its fords every month and that, as it inclines more towards England or Wales in this change of channel, so they can prognosticate which nation will beat the other or be unsuccessful in war in any particular year.'[12] It is possible that Aerfen may be the original name of the river and that Deva/Dee is a euphemism resulting from the original name of the Goddess being too sacred to be profaned by common use, in much the same way as 'the son of the Mother' could be used in place of the deity's proper name in an everyday, non-sacred context. There is still a remnant of this practice within modern Christianity in that Jesus and Mary are often referred to as 'Our Lord' and 'Our Lady'.

Llyn Aerfen (Aerfen's Lake) is a name applied to Lake Bala, which stands at the headwaters of the Dee. Also known as Llyn Tegid (Tegid's Lake), it is home to another facet of the Goddess of the Dee. Within *Hanes Taliesin* we are told the story of Ceridwen, the wife of Tegid Foel (Tegid the Bald), after whom Tegid's Lake is named. Ceridwen, who dwelt in the midst of Llyn Tegid, was the mother of two children – a son called Morfran,[13] who was a survivor of the Battle of Camlan, and a daughter Creirwy – and her story concerns the birth by magical means of the greatest of Welsh poets Taliesin (Shining or Radiant Brow).[14] In earlier sources Ceridwen is presented as the owner of a cauldron from which came the source of *awen* (poetic inspiration) and there is little doubt that in origin she was a variant of the Goddess of the River Dee. In later times she is referred to as Y Wrach (meaning 'hag' or, as it became in later Welsh, 'witch'), a description that links her with her original form of Aerfen, the goddess of death and battles whose name is still remembered along the banks of the Dee in the village named after her, Aerfen. The Dee's association with war and battle is captured in a late 12th-century Welsh poem in which the poet tells us that, like the mighty cauldrons of Celtic mythology that are said not to cook food for cowards, the waters of the mighty Dee do not agree with those of a faint heart: 'With a coward Dyfrdonwy water [the water of the Dyfrdwy/ Dee] ill agrees.'[15]

It was evident that the warlike aspect of the Celtic Goddess is only one face of her triple personality and so we decided to reappraise the other mythological references attached to this most sacred of rivers. From her source above Lake Bala the River Dee takes in many tributaries in the course of her descent to the sea, among them the River Alun, which runs into the Dee near Pulford. On its descent to the Dee the Alun flows past Moel Famau (the Home of the Celtic Mothers) and continues through Rhyd y Gyfarthfa (the Ford of the Barking), thus linking the geographical location associated with Modron (daughter of Afallach, Lord of the Otherworld) to the Dee, the sacred river of the Goddess. Indeed, the female deity associated with the River Dee from primordial times was in all likelihood Modron, the Brythonic Mother Goddess and mother of Mabon.

Another name used for the Dee in old Welsh sources is Afon Peryddon, which appears in an account of the Battle of Chester as an alternative for Dyfrdwy/Deva. As we saw in Chapter 7, the *Stanzas of the Graves* places the last resting place of Gwalchmai (Gawain) in Peryddon, and the name also occurs within *Armes Prydein* (The Prophecy of Britain), from *The Book of Taliesin*, in which Merlin (Myrddin) 'foretells that they will meet in Aber Peryddon [the estuary of the Dee]'.[16] Aber Peryddon also receives mention in Geoffrey of Monmouth's *Historia*, where we are told that 'the white-haired old man on a white horse will surely divert the river Peryddon, and with a white rod will measure a mill upon it. Cadwaladr shall call upon Cynan, and will bring Alban into the alliance. Then there will be a slaughter of the foreign peoples. Then the rivers will flow with blood.'[17] And in a poem concerning a man of Edeirnion (a region about the River Dee near Corwen), the poet Tudur Aled tells us, 'there is a vision about the Peryddon, that a tall castle/fortress shall be raised there.'[18] Although the ancient name of Peryddon has not been applied to the whole river for many years it has not been completely forgotten by the landscape for there is still a small stream that enters the River Dee near Bodweni known as Nant Beryddon.[19]

From our research it became apparent that the events said to have occurred within the mysterious realm of Afallach/Avalon did indeed take place within the boundary formed by the River Dee. Other events and characters could also be located within this same region, including Ceridwen, the birth of Taliesin, Merlin, Arthur's fostering and Arthur's last voyage, to name but a few. We had also established a historical boundary for the Land of the Dead that matched the boundary of Annwn, the Celtic Otherworld. It has long been claimed that to cross sacred water was to enter the Otherworld, and there is no water in the ancient realm of Prydein more sacred than that of the River Dee.

IN SEARCH OF THE MABON

We had rediscovered the identity of the Goddess to whom the sacred River Dee was dedicated, but what of her son Mabon ap Modron, divine son of the Mother Goddess and grandson of Afallach, Lord of Avalon?

From the surviving evidence Mabon appears to have been a major pre-Christian deity whose legend bears the hallmarks of having at some time been censored or even banned for political or religious purposes. Though fragmentary, there is enough material left to establish his primordial mythology. For instance, Mabon is recorded in such early documents as the Roman *Ravenna Cosmography*, where he is referred to as being the spirit of a particular area of Britannia, the genius loci Maponi. Indeed, the cult of Modron and Mabon is of such great antiquity that it was undoubtedly established long before it was absorbed into the Continental/Classical overlay.

The essence of Mabon's identity is deeply embedded within Celtic culture and his story was obviously well established within the British oral tradition, for he emerges within early Arthurian sources and faint traces of his myth are to be found in the medieval romances and Welsh folklore. There is even evidence of Mabon's story still being extant in medieval times.[20] The most interesting example of this is a reference to a lay entitled *Rey Mabon*, which can be traced back to the Welsh Marches. The manuscript in which the reference to *Rey Mabon* appears belonged to the Benedictine Abbey of St Werburg in Chester in the 14th century and contains a contents list for a large manuscript that is now lost.[21] It is unfortunate that this source contains no further details, but perhaps this is an indication that Mabon's story was so well known that it sufficed just to mention its name without recording or explaining the story.

Until now the myth of the Celtic divine child Mabon has been obscure geographically as well as textually, with archaeological evidence for the Continental variants of Maponus (Mabon) and Matrono (Modron) in Britain appearing only to occur in the area around Hadrian's Wall. As we have shown, however, Modron is clearly associated with an area of northeast Wales, and where we have the Divine Mother should we not also have the Divine Son?

As mentioned earlier, what little is currently known about Mabon comes to us from *The Search for the Mabon*, a section in the ancient Welsh tale of *Culhwch and Olwen*.[22] In his bid to obtain Olwen's hand in marriage, Culhwch enlisted the aid of Arthur, his cousin,[23] in fulfilling the tasks set by Yspadden (Hawthorn), Olwen's father. One was to hunt down a particular boar and secure certain magical treasures from it; to accomplish this they needed to find Mabon ap Modron, the only huntsman in the world who could command the hound Drudwyn, presumably a hound of the Otherworld as it could only be held by the leash of Cwrs Cant Ewin (the Hundred Claws), the collar of Canhastyr Canllaw (the Hundred Hands) and the chain of Kilydd Canhastyr (the Hundred Holds). However, nobody knew where Mabon was, nor whether he was alive or dead, because he had been taken from his mother when only three nights old. As a preliminary to the search for Mabon, Arthur and Culhwch first had to find Mabon's kinsman Eidoel (the only survivor of the Treachery of the Long Knives). Arthur and the warriors of Ynys Prydein set out in search of Eidoel and eventually came to the outer wall of Caer Glini (Glini's Fort), where Eidoel was imprisoned.[24] Having obtained Eidoel's release, Arthur directed him to accompany his men in search of Mabon because he was Mabon's first cousin.

When the companions had taken leave of Arthur they proceeded to Cilgwri, where they asked the Ouzel of Cilgwri about the whereabouts of Mabon. The Ouzel (a variety of blackbird) replied that when he had first come to this place there had been a smith's anvil there. Since then the only work that had been done upon the anvil was carried out every evening with his own beak, yet it had now been worn away so that it was only as big as a nut; and in all that time he had never heard of Mabon ap Modron. Nevertheless the Ouzel told the travellers that there was a creature that God had made before him and that he would guide them to it.

They were taken to the Stag of Rhedynfre, where they again inquired after Mabon. The Stag replied that when he had first come to this place there was one tine on either side of his head and but a single oak sapling. The sapling had grown into an oak with a hundred branches and the tree had eventually fallen, leaving naught but a red stump, and from that day to this he had been there. The Stag related that he had never heard of Mabon, son of Modron, but he knew where there was a creature that God had made before him and would guide them there.

The companions were taken to the Owl of Cwm Cawlwyd, who told them that when he had first come to Cwm Cawlwyd the great valley before them had been a wooded glen, but a race of men had come and laid it waste. Another wood had grown up in its place and the present wood was the third. The Owl was of such a great age that its wings were mere stumps, but he said he could not help as he had not heard of Mabon. However, he would guide them to the creature that was the oldest in the world and which had travelled the furthest.

The Owl guided them to the Eagle of Gwernabwy. When they asked after Mabon the Eagle replied that when he had come to this place long ago there had been a stone from the top of which he was able to peck at the stars every evening. That stone was now less than a handbreadth in height and in all that time he had not heard of Mabon ap Modron. However, the Eagle related that one day whilst out hunting he had flown as far as Llyn Llyw where he had sunk his claws into a magnificent salmon. Unfortunately the salmon was strong and had pulled him down into the depths of the lake. The Eagle had only escaped with great difficulty and so, taking with him the whole of his kindred, he had returned there to destroy the salmon. Seeing this the salmon had sent messengers to make peace with the Eagle, and the salmon had then come to him in person to have 50 tridents removed from his back. The Eagle offered to take the companions to the salmon of Llyn Llyw to ask the whereabouts of Mabon.

The Salmon of Llyn Llyw offered to tell the seekers all he knew and related how he travelled with every tide up the river until he reached the bend by the wall of Caer Loyw, and that there he encountered a distress the like of which he had never encountered in all his life. To convince the companions the Salmon took Cai (Kay) and Gwrhyr (Interpreter of Tongues) upon his shoulders and journeyed to the wall of Caer Loyw, where the two men heard wailing and lamentation coming from the other side. Gwrhyr asked, 'What man laments in this house of stone?' The reply came, 'Mabon son of Modron is imprisoned here,' and Mabon's voice continued, stating that no one had ever been so cruelly imprisoned, not even Lludd Silver-Hand nor Greid son of Eri, and there was no hope of his release, not for gold, silver or worldly wealth. Mabon added that he could only be released by force. The searchers then returned to Arthur and informed him where Mabon son of Modron was imprisoned. Gathering together the warriors of Ynys Prydein, Arthur marched on Caer Loyw while Cai and Bedwyr (Bedivere) returned to Caer Loyw on the shoulders of the salmon. While Arthur's warriors attacked the fortress, Cai broke through the wall and carried Mabon on his back to safety. Having achieved their aim Arthur and his warriors returned home, bringing Mabon, son of Modron with them.

The story was interesting in itself as it is part of the earliest Arthurian tale, but what was more interesting was that it suggested that the whereabouts of Mabon, the Celtic Divine Child, had been lost to human memory. The only way to find the Mabon again was to be guided by a series of ancient animals until those who sought him were finally brought to the Salmon of Llyn Llyw, and for the Celts the salmon symbolized wisdom. In other words the search for the Mabon is essentially a quest for wisdom, a wisdom that would liberate the Divine Child, the son of the Goddess.

THE MYTH IN THE LANDSCAPE

As with many fragments of Celtic mythology the story of Mabon appeared to lack any specific context. However, we felt that the search for Mabon was not as obscure as previously believed. Some suggestions had already been put forward regarding the possible placement of the events described in the tale, yet as we studied the story more closely it became clear that each of the animals visited in the quest for Mabon was instrumental in establishing the original Avalonian mythology. In fact the animals in the tale embody an accepted mythological motif known as the 'Oldest Animals', and the locations associated with them in the search for Mabon constitute a distinct myth in the landscape.[25]

The first of the animals visited in the search for Mabon is the Ouzel of Cilgwri.[26] Cilgwri was an early name for the Wirral peninsula, yet the Cilgwri of *Culhwch and Olwen* is in Tegeingl (Flintshire) and this is the accepted placement for the Blackbird.[27] Independent versions of the Oldest Animals provide further clues to its location. The Welsh for 'blackbird' is *Mwyalchen* and Mwyalchen Gilgwri simply means the Blackbird of Cilgwri, which is the form given within one independent version.[28] The Blackbird is also recorded within the Welsh *Triads* as A Mwyalchen Gelli Gadarn (the Blackbird of the Mighty Grove). Between Caer Afallach and the Dee estuary, and lying on the northern slopes of Halkyn Mountain in Flintshire, is the village of Halkyn, from which the mountain takes its name. In origin it is likely that Halkyn Mountain literally meant the Mountain of the Blackbird, for the earliest form of the name for this area is given in the 'Domesday Book' as Alchene, which would appear to be a corruption of the Welsh Mwyalchen, with the Mighty Grove in question being the old Alchene (or Halkyn) churchyard.[29] This site is in very close proximity to the three sites connected with the monastery of Ynys Afallach: Llwyn Huwcyn (the Halkyn Grove, or Grove of the Blackbird), Y Groes (the Cross) and the site known as Monachlog (the Monastery). Unfortunately, the old church at Halkyn no longer stands. Having been rebuilt in the 1770s on its original site it was demolished in 1877 and a new, grander affair built nearby. The original church, an ancient Celtic chapel dedicated to St Mary, stood on a raised circular site that is still visible and is located within a circle/grove of ancient yews, while on the south side of the site is the ancient holy well known as Ffynnon Fair (the Well of St Mary). This site is inarguably ancient and it has been suggested that it dates from the Bronze Age period, which is of no small importance as it is distinctly within the heartland of Avalon/Ynys Afallach. The identification of this site can be reinforced by some pertinent facts:

- Cilgwri is said to be in Flintshire.
- Halkyn Mountain sits opposite the Wirral peninsula – Cilgwri.
- The search for Mabon led by his kinsman Eidoel appears to start from the mountain whose original form is Mwyalchen (Blackbird) and is home to Mabon's grandfather Afallach, the Lord of Avalon – Caer Afallach.
- Both sites indicate a common origin as to the starting point of the search for the Mabon, the estuary of the sacred River Dee.

The Blackbird guides the party up the river to the Stag of Rhedynfre. Rhedynfre (Fern Hill) appears as the old name for Farndon, Cheshire, which stands alongside the River Dee just over the border from Wales and near a hill by the name of Hart Hill. Farndon was identified as the likely placement for the Rhedynfre of the Mabon Myth by Professor Melville Richards, and this makes total sense in light of its geographical relationship to Cilgwri.[30]

The next stage of the journey in search of Mabon takes us up the River Dee to find the Owl of Cwm Cawlwyd. Welsh tradition mentions a certain person called Caw, and in a manuscript from the Llanstephan Collection in the National Library of Wales Caw is recorded as being the Lord of Cwm Cowlwyd, who resided in the region of Edeirnion in the time of Arthur.[31] Edeirnion covers an area on both sides of the River Dee around the town of Corwen and it is more than likely that the Cwm Cawlwyd named in the search for Mabon was in this region.

The Eagle of Gwernabwy is slightly more obscure. *Gwern* simply means 'alder tree', or on occasion 'swamp', and, unlike the other names associated with the Oldest Animals, Gwe[r]nabwy is only recorded as a personal name. The names Gwenabwy and Gwernabwy are both recorded in early Welsh texts, but only Gwenabwy, the daughter of Caw, is chronologically possible in the context of *Culhwch and Olwen*.[32] It also makes sense in the context of the quest for Mabon in that the companions had already reached the region of Edeirnion and so the seeking out of Gwenabwy, or a lost place named after her, within her father's kingdom would seem to fit in with the unfolding story. (For more on Caw and his family, see Chapter 12.)

Finally we come to the Salmon of Llyn Llyw, or to be more precise Lake Bala, which is fed by several rivers and streams including the following: the Afon Twrch, which on the way to Bala picks up several streams that source from a small lake named Llyn Lliwbran; the Afon Dyfrdwy (Dee) which sources above Bala on Penaran (Height of the Aran); and the Afon Lliw, with Lliw being a variant spelling of Llyw. J.G. Evans identified Llyn Llyw as the old name for Lake Bala, and with the Afon Lliw/Llyw emptying into Bala and Llyn Lliwbran being connected to Bala by the Afon Twrch this seems most likely.[33] This identification is supported by the story itself in that the Salmon of Llyn Llyw is located on the same river as Caer Loyw (Chester), where Mabon was imprisoned. It is significant that the Salmon related how with every tide he went along the river until he came to the bend in the wall at Caer Loyw, because for centuries the River Dee was renowned as one of the best salmon-fishing waters within the United Kingdom, and in the period in which the tale of *Culhwch and Olwen* takes place the tidal bore came up the river past Chester, making its force felt far to the south of the town of Holt.[34]

More evidence supporting the location of the Caer Loyw referred to in the search for Mabon is forthcoming from ancient Welsh genealogies in the person of a certain Tudur Trefor (c.900), who was descended from Cadell Ddyrnllug, Prince of Powys. An imposing figure, Tudur Trefor counted among his titles that of 'Head of the Noble Tribe of the Marches', also known as 'the golden crowned race', and the House of Tudor being counted among his descendants. He is also recorded as Lord of the two Maelors. The realm of Maelor originally ran from Llangollen to Chester and comprised the lands around the middle reaches of the River Dee, an area of some 60 square miles. Maelor was at one time held by the Princes of Powys but it had been conquered and settled by the Saxons during the early Dark Ages. The Princes of Powys recovered this land in later centuries but never completely removed the influence of the early Saxon occupation, hence the realm was known as the two Maelors for it comprised Maelor Saesneg (Saxon Maelor) and Maelor Gymraeg (Welsh Maelor). Within Maelor in the parish of Llangollen is a village named after Tudur Trefor,[35] but what is more interesting is that he is also recorded as King of Caer Loyw (Chester). This has been dismissed as the imagination of genealogists who have wrongly identified Caer Loyw as Gloucester, but as Tudur Trefor's historical kingdom stretched to Chester this ceases to be an imaginary title.[36]

The identification of Caer Loyw as Gloucester resulted in the myth of Mabon becoming detached from the geographical context of the sacred River Dee and references to Modron and Afallach in that area being largely ignored. However, Professor R.S. Loomis noted the reference to Modron at Rhyd y Gyfarthfa (the Ford of the Barking) and also pointed to another reference to Mabon, previously noted by Professor W.J. Gruffydd: 'about 14 miles in a straight line from Moel Famau is the town of Ruabon, originally Rhiw Vabon, the hill of Mabon, Modron's son.'[37] (Ruabon is also approximately the same distance from Caer Afallach, the home of Mabon's grandfather.) In our search for further evidence to establish the myth of Mabon we turned to local ecclesiastical works, amongst which we found a passage that established beyond doubt that the sacred Dee was indeed

Mabon's river for it informed us that 'in AD 1234 the monks of Valle Crucis Abbey did walk over the mountains and paint angels glorious to the venerable Church of Rhiwabon which standeth high above the river of Mabon'.[38] As described in the text, the Church of Ruabon sits high above Modron's river, on the eastern side of Ruabon Mountain, and nearby is an area recorded as Gwald y Madron (Modron's land) – the land of the Celtic Mother Goddess.

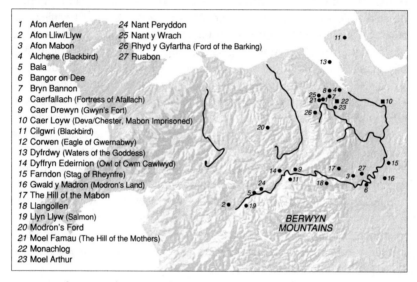

1 Afon Aerfen	24 Nant Peryddon
2 Afon Lliw/Llyw	25 Nant y Wrach
3 Afon Mabon	26 Rhyd y Gyfartha (Ford of the Barking)
4 Alchene (Blackbird)	27 Ruabon
5 Bala	
6 Bangor on Dee	
7 Bryn Bannon	
8 Caerfallach (Fortress of Afallach)	
9 Caer Drewyn (Gwyn's Fort)	
10 Caer Loyw (Deva/Chester, Mabon Imprisoned)	
11 Cilgwri (Blackbird)	
12 Corwen (Eagle of Gwernabwy)	
13 Dyfrdwy (Waters of the Goddess)	
14 Dyffryn Edeirnion (Owl of Cwm Cawlwyd)	
15 Farndon (Stag of Rheynfre)	
16 Gwald y Madron (Modron's Land)	
17 The Hill of the Mabon	
18 Llangollen	
19 Llyn Llyw (Salmon)	
20 Modron's Ford	
21 Moel Famau (The Hill of the Mothers)	
22 Monachlog	
23 Moel Arthur	

Map 23 The sacred river and the myth of the Mabon

When you stand within the ramparts of the once mighty fortress of Afallach above the sacred River Dee, the Waters of the Goddess, the identity of the place ceases to be a purely academic exercise. Before you lies the sacred Vale of Avalon – the Realm of Afallach, or the Celtic Otherworld – and its legendary aura permeates your senses. In whichever direction you turn to take in the beauty of the surrounding landscape, you cannot help but be struck by the myriad ancient mythic and legendary references that greet your eyes. Face east and you overlook the great city of Caerlleon, Arthur's city and the site of one of Arthur's battles. Between that fair city and the Halls of Afallach within which you stand lies the hidden monastery of Ynys Afallach, one of the Three Perpetual Harmonies and the site of the original Avalonian foundation. To the south is the mountain of Mabon, Divine Son of the Divine Mother Goddess, and within the valley beneath it lies the site of Glaestingaburh, the original Glastonbury. In that same direction stands the Castle of the Grail within the land of the Celtic God Bran. Turn to the southwest and you overlook a landscape that remembers the Celtic Goddess in her traditional triplicate form: the Mountain of the Mothers, the Hill of the Maiden Consort and the Valley of the Hag. The hills of Arthur and Benlli nestle in the bosom of the Mothers' Mountain, obscuring from view the Alun valley in which lies the Ford of the Barking, the site where Modron – divine mother of Mabon and daughter of Afallach, King of Annwn – ritually mates with Urien Rheged, thus recreating the marriage of the king to the land. Hiding within the hills of the Vale of Clwyd are Arthur's chapel, Arthur's courts, and numerous other mythical and historical references to the heroes and families that surround the legendary figure of Arthur. In the years since we first realized the importance of Caer Afallach it has become increasingly difficult to read of Arthur, Camlan and the subsequent journey to Avalon without envisaging these events unfolding within the landscape spread before us, events that concluded with Arthur being laid to rest in the Realm of Afallach, otherwise known as the Celtic Otherworld and the Land of the Dead.

So far our search for the original Avalon had led us to reappraise the accepted understanding of Arthur and the history of Dark Age Britain. Our study of ancient Welsh sources had revealed how the original story of Arthur had been expanded, becoming over the centuries more elaborate and more removed from its initial context. In seeking to return Arthur to his true location we had redrawn the map of Arthurian Britain and identified the site of Ynys Afallach, the mythical Avalon. One important question remained, however: how had Avalon become associated with Glastonbury in Somerset?

CHAPTER TEN

THE POLITICS OF ARTHUR AND AVALON

HENRY II, King of England, sat at the head table within the Great Hall, his head resting disinterestedly upon his right fist and a look of boredom etched across his features. God how he hated Wales! The Hall was full of the bustle of the servants dealing with the needs of his entourage and the noise made by his lords, over-indulging and over-boisterous as usual. It had been a relatively dull evening, much the same as any other, the only break to the monotony being the entertainment provided by the two Welsh bards who had recited certain traditions relating to King Arthur. They had appeared from the shadows in the corner of the Great Hall and proceeded to amuse the assembly with arguments over Arthur's final resting place. It had been a strange story, but according to the Welsh tradition Arthur's grave was apparently at Glastonbury. As the bards walked away Henry was sure he noticed a knowing look pass between them, and as they left the Great Hall had the antagonists not turned to each other and smiled? But this did not matter, the seed of an idea had been sown in Henry's mind and the look of boredom on his face evaporated into a smug smile.

On a cold winter morning in 1191 a section of the grounds near to the south door of the newly rebuilt abbey church at Glastonbury in Somerset was roped off and screens erected.[1] The excavation taking place between two tall pillars in the abbey graveyard was apparently a direct result of information given to Henry II by a Welsh bard during his visit to Wales. They were going to dig up King Arthur! Although the exact words spoken by the Welsh bard that evening in the Great Hall will never be known, they had set in motion one of the greatest historical frauds ever perpetrated. In fact the name the bard had given as Arthur's final resting-place was irrelevant, because Henry had understood it as – or perhaps deliberately changed it to – Glastonbury. It is highly unlikely, if not unthinkable, that a Welsh bard would inform an English king of such a secret as the burial place of the legendary Arthur. Perhaps the story had been created retrospectively in support of the exhumation at Glastonbury, which would explain why it did not take place until some years after Henry's death. But what was to be gained from the claim that Arthur was buried at Glastonbury anyway?

Some sources say that Arthur's grave was simply discovered by accident while digging a grave for a monk, whereas Giraldus Cambrensis reports that it was Henry II who had encouraged the monks of Glastonbury to find Arthur's grave.[2] One possible motive for Henry's action is that the finding of Arthur's grave in England would uphold the perverted account of early British history promoted by Geoffrey of Monmouth's *Historia* and the adoption of Arthur as the figurehead for the new political entity of the Angevin realm. Another explanation is that one of the most prevalent legends surrounding Arthur was the idea that he was asleep in a cave and would one day return to save his country in its hour of need,[3] therefore the finding of his grave would not only establish that Arthur was dead but also demolish the legend of his return to save his people and thus eradicate his use as a rallying point by the rebellious Welsh. Here Giraldus's statement that a Welsh bard was the source of Henry's information gives his story a ring of authenticity, for by naming Arthur's burial site the bard acknowledged that Arthur was indeed dead and thus gave voice to a tradition that had always been maintained by the Welsh bards. According to Professor T. Gwynn Jones, the Welsh bards (Gogynfeirdd) never refer to the return of Arthur, nor is there any evidence that they ever believed in Arthur as the once and future king.[4] The once and future kings of the Welsh were Cynan and Cadwaladr, not Arthur, and although no mention is made in early Welsh material of Arthur returning in his country's hour of need, in 1187 Henry II christened his grandson Arthur in an attempt to identify him with the legendary British king returning to unite his people.[5] In fact the vast majority of the reports regarding Arthur's supposed return flowed from the pens of chroniclers in the employ of the Anglo-Norman monarchy. To all intents and purposes they were simply creating a self-fulfilling prophecy because the Welsh took up the idea and, adapting it to their own advantage, turned it against its creators. They did this so effectively that the English conviction that the Welsh were sufficiently gullible to believe in Arthur's return was recorded as late as 1530.[6]

But to return to Arthur's supposed exhumation, the precise date of which is open to debate. Some sources give the year as 1191 and others 1190, whereas Giraldus states that the exhumation occurred within King Henry's lifetime, but as Henry II died in July 1189 this confuses the issue further still.[7] Present scholarship favours 1191, and this would appear to be the most likely date.[8] Giraldus reports the finding of a lead cross which was attached to a stone slab with its inscribed face turned inwards. The inscription read:

> Hic iacet sepultus inclytus rex Arthurus cum Wenneveria uxore sua secunda in insula Avallonia.

> (Here lies buried the famous King Arthurus with Wenneveria his second wife in the isle of Avalonia.)[9]

The wording on the cross was reinterpreted by later chroniclers such as Ralph of Coggeshall who, 30 years after the event, gave the inscription as 'Here lies the famous King Arthurus, buried in the isle of Avalon.'[10] Ralph of Coggeshall's rendering of the inscription agrees closely with those of the later reports by Leland and Camden,[11] but traditions relating to the inscription are confused. Although Leland and Camden probably made an accurate record of the inscription on the cross that was in existence at their time, it was certainly not the one talked of by Giraldus for the original version recorded by him was quite exceptional in that it described Guinevere as Arthur's second wife, a statement dropped by the later chroniclers.[12] Unfortunately neither the cross nor the bones that were dug up at Glastonbury Abbey are in existence today, which is not really surprising as it is now widely accepted that the finding of Arthur's alleged grave was a medieval fraud. As the arguments have been addressed at length by many scholars we need not tally over long in dealing with them here.[13] Giraldus Cambrensis (1145–1223) provides the nearest we have to an eyewitness account, telling us that in his lifetime, when Henry II was reigning in England, strenuous efforts were made to locate the grave of the renowned King Arthur at Glastonbury. Eventually some remains were found, deep within the earth, sixteen feet deep to be precise, in a hollowed-out oak bole. The remains were taken into the abbey church and there placed in a marble tomb. And so it was that the mighty Arthur came to be the property of the now famous Somerset monastery.

Another possible motive for the miraculous discovery of Arthur's remains revolves around the greatest crisis to face Glastonbury Abbey since its founding by King Ine of Wessex (688–726).[14] On the feast of

St Urban, 25 May 1184, a fire swept through the abbey virtually destroying the entire foundation. At that time the abbey belonged to the Crown and therefore Henry II installed his own steward Ralph Fitz-Stephen to set about the job of rebuilding. In their zeal to finance the reconstruction of their abbey the monks appear to have adopted a practice common among religious establishments in need of funds – namely, the exploitation of that most marketable of medieval religious commodities, holy relics. For following the fire the relics of numerous saints miraculously appeared out of the Glastonbury closet, especially Celtic saints such as St Patrick, St Indract, St Bridgit and St Gildas, who it was claimed had all been interred at Glastonbury despite the fact that many were known to be buried elsewhere. No doubt the propaganda surrounding the discovery of King Arthur's grave did much to further increase Glastonbury's prestige, bolster its coffers and increase its market share of the pilgrim trade, but it was not the primary motive behind the events taking place in Somerset in 1190–91.

THE POLITICAL BACKGROUND

When William, Duke of Normandy, invaded England in 1066 he brought with him a large contingent of Bretons, descendants of Welsh migrants and no friends of the Saxons, who were given Saxon lands as reward for their services. As William I of England he went to great lengths to establish that it was he who was the legitimate heir to Edward the Confessor rather than the defeated Harold. To consolidate his recent conquest he adopted an astute policy of adaptation and amalgamation that was continued by William's son Henry I – who married a grand-daughter of Edward the Confessor to further the link between the new dynasty and their Saxon predecessors – and later by Henry's grandson, Henry of Anjou, who as Henry II founded the Anglo-Angevin dynasty known to history as the Plantagenets.[15] The Anglo-Norman kings needed to establish their divine right to rule, thus legalizing their claim to the English throne. As they had acquired the kingdom by conquest it required some rewriting of history to justify their claims, so the new monarchy and its allies encouraged their scribes to validate the line of Anglo-Norman descent from legendary predecessors such as Arthur.

The rewriting of history by the victor is nothing new, but Henry I seems to have excelled in this, for William of Malmesbury recorded that 'they would write nothing but what would please him and do nothing but what he commanded'.[16] It was out of this background that Geoffrey of Monmouth's *Historia Regum Britanniae* emerged. Contrary to the view held by some Arthurian scholars, Geoffrey did not invent anything but simply did as he was asked and translated into Latin an ancient Welsh manuscript. It is likely that Robert of Gloucester, to whom the majority of the copies of the *Historia* are dedicated, was well aware of the existence of Geoffrey's source. Illegitimate son of Henry I and virtual kingmaker of Henry II, Robert held sway over the Welsh Marches and western counties of England. King of the West in all but title, he was virtually a law unto himself. Furthermore, as both Robert's mother and wife were Welsh, it is quite possible that the ancient book Walter of Oxford gave Geoffrey to translate had originally come from Wales via Robert's family connections.

The Anglo-Norman monarchy was in a greatly inferior position to its Continental rivals, the Kings of France, not only because the latter were their feudal overlords, but because the newly founded English dynasty lacked a noble and heroic figure such as Charlemagne and the divine rights of sacred kingship afforded by Clovis. To overcome this they needed a mythos of their own and so, at what appears to have been the instigation of Robert of Gloucester, Geoffrey's *Historia* was adopted as the new Anglo-Norman political mythology. In a brilliant propaganda coup they made the history of the British kings their own. With the true British monarchy penned up in Wales, Geoffrey's chronicle legitimized the claims of the Norman conquerors by tracing their descent from Trojan stock, which was something the original kings of the Britons had always claimed to be. By spreading the geography of ancient Britain beyond the confines of its homeland, the *Historia* incorporated the domains of the new monarchy into the history of the British kings. It also took Arthur away from his Welsh roots and turned him into a figurehead in an attempt to unite Briton, Saxon and Norman into one nation. So effective was the reworking of history in Geoffrey's Latin *Historia* that it 'became the foundation of a great historical myth which supported racial and dynastic aspirations for over five hundred years'.[17]

Some scholars maintain that the Arthurian romances proliferated mainly because of the activities of three men, all patronized by Robert of Gloucester – Walter of Oxford, Geoffrey of Monmouth and Caradoc of Llancavarn (who took up the story of Britain from where Geoffrey left off). It has even been suggested that 12th-century writers invented the Arthurian legend in order to flatter the Anglo-Norman monarchy. However, while there is no doubt that it was the influence of Geoffrey's *Historia* that put Arthur firmly into the literary domain, there is equally no doubt that the royal household of Henry II adopted the Arthurian romances for purely political purposes,[18] exploiting them for their own greater glory as they attempted to recreate themselves as the successors to the kings of the Britons and give their fledgling dynasty a history to rival that of the Continental Capetians.[19] Much was made of the historical account provided by the *Historia*, especially the links between Britain and Brittany – according to Geoffrey's chronicle both had been ruled by Arthur – for the Plantagenet kings were exploiting their own links with Brittany in an attempt to unite their lands on the Continent with those of the British Isles into one coherent dynastic whole. To this end Henry II had himself elected High King of Ireland and had his son Geoffrey marry the daughter of the Duke of Brittany, thereby reinforcing the Breton–British link. The political motivations of Henry II were to establish a firm basis for the new Angevin dynasty, which was under threat from the Capetian monarchy in France, who regarded themselves as continuing the succession of the Merovingian and Carlovingian lines and repeatedly laid claim to the English throne. Yet it was Edward I who more than any of his predecessors adopted the Arthurian legends, turning them to his own advantage and using Geoffrey of Monmouth's *Historia* as a weapon with which to beat his political foes. Surrounding himself with the Arthurian mythos, he took up Arthur's mantle to the point where he even styled himself Arthurus Redivivus (Arthur Returned).[20]

The story of Arthur's burial at Glastonbury did not end with the propaganda coup of the first exhumation; 90 years on it was politically necessary for Arthur to be brought out of the Glastonbury closet and dusted down. In 1277 Edward successfully led a campaign against North Wales and in November of that year Llewelyn, Prince of Wales, was forced to pay him homage, and the aftermath of the campaign necessitated it being re-established that Arthur was interred at Glastonbury. So on 19 April 1278 Edward I, accompanied by Queen Eleanor, went to the abbey and ordered Arthur's tomb to be opened in order to reiterate his royal household's connection with the most renowned of British kings.[21] The event is recorded in the *Annals of Waverly*:

The Lord Edward ... the Lady Eleanor, came to Glastonbury ... to celebrate Easter ... The following Tuesday ... at dusk, the Lord King had the tomb of the famous King Arthur opened. Wherein, in two caskets painted with their pictures and arms, were found separately, the bones of the said King, which were of great size, and those of Queen Guinevere, which were of marvelous beauty ... On the following day ... The Lord King replaced the bones of the King, and the Queen those of the Queen, each in their own casket, having wrapped them in costly silk. When they had been sealed they ordered the tomb to be placed forthwith in front of the high altar, after the removal of the skulls for the veneration of the people.

It has long been held that this event was simply to remind the Welsh that Arthur was dead, not that they needed reminding as they had never believed anything else. The real significance of this second exhumation was that it took place at Easter, coinciding with the Feast of the Resurrection. As has been impressively suggested, did Edward mean to imply he was the second Arthur?[22]

As part of his coronation oath, Edward I had sworn to preserve the rights of the Crown, which included the English monarchy's authority over the imperium. This was part of the justification for Edward's annexation of Wales and was also behind the Crown's assertion of its right to rule Scotland.[23] In the case of Scotland, the Scots had approached the Court of Rome protesting at the injuries perpetrated against them by the English. In response the Pope had written to Edward in 1299, setting out his reasons for supporting Scottish independence. Edward had commanded his scribes to collect historic materials to prove his right to rule over Scotland, which culminated in 1301 in a letter addressed to Pope Boniface VIII to which over 100 English barons affixed their seals. The claims made within Edward I's reply were drawn from the pages of Geoffrey's *Historia*, judiciously edited to suit Edward's purpose. Great play was made of the fact that within the *Historia* Arthur handed over the kingdom of the Scots to Anguselus; it neglected to mention the fact that he was handing it back to its rightful ruler.

EDWARD I, THE TRUE CROSS
AND THE CROWN OF ARTHUR

> Through our great power we commit wrongs and violence against these people [the Welsh]; yet everybody knows that they have a hereditary right to their lands.
>
> *Henry I* [24]

Probably the most important event with an Arthurian connection in the reign of Edward I took place in June 1283 in Aber Conway, Gwynedd. Edward I sat smugly overlooking the throng before him in the hall, the look of victory stamped on his features. At last he had achieved the impossible. He had broken Gwynedd, the last bastion of the British, and was about to fulfil in part the pledge made by Henry I in 1114 'to exterminate all the Britons completely so that the Brittannic name should never more be remembered'.[25] More than that, as his reward he was about to have laid before him the most sacred objects that the Welsh possessed.

Suddenly the humdrum noise of the assembled dignitaries abated and a near silence descended, apart from the occasional shuffling of feet and a few whispered conversations. The steward of the hall banged his staff three times and the great doors swung open, allowing entry to the small party on the opposite side. As this group entered the room Edward I rose to his feet without a word and stood glaring triumphantly over the seven approaching figures. A figure broke away from the party and advanced towards the king head bowed, not in homage, as the assembled English believed, but in shame. The figure introduced himself to King Edward as Einion ap Ynor and related that, as promised, he brought with him the safeguard of his nation, the relics on which Wales had long depended for succour in its hour of need, artefacts that had been carried before her princes, exalted by her bards and regarded with the utmost devotion of the people. The regalia of the House of Gwynedd that Einion had brought with him had been sold not for 30 pieces of silver but for 'privileges' granted to them and their heirs.[26] 'And thus, says the chronicler, the glory of the Welsh, although against their will, was transferred to the English.'[27]

It was of no small consequence that, following his conquest of Gwynedd, Edward had demanded the royal regalia of the House of Gwynedd, which consisted of Llewelyn's personal seal, the seal of his wife Eleanor de Montfort, and the two most precious relics of Wales – the Croes Naidd and, most importantly of all, the Crown of Arthur. The Croes Naidd was said to be a piece of the True Cross upon which Jesus had been crucified, which was kept within a reliquary in the shape of a Celtic cross known as the Cross of Refuge.[28] Apparently Llewelyn, the last true Prince of Wales, was carrying the Croes Naidd when he was taken by deceit and murdered in cold blood near Builth. His head had been severed from his body and taken to Aber Conway, where it was presented to Edward I before being removed to London and taken in procession through the streets to the Tower, where it was impaled upon a spike in plain view. This grisly trophy soon had company: the severed head of Dafydd, Llewelyn's brother, was also brought to the Tower to join his brother for a final time, their lifeless eyes looking out over the capital of a foreign land. But of even greater importance to Edward I and the English monarchy was the final piece of the jigsaw they had been assembling for generations. Finally they had in their possession the relic belonging to the figure that they themselves had created as the symbol of British kingship: the Crown of Arthur.[29]

Edward I, or 'Longshanks' as he was known, was a shrewd propagandist and aware that it would take more than the eradication of Llewelyn and his successors to bring North Wales under his control. He took care to keep Llewelyn's heirs out of the way by imprisoning his sons and consigning his daughter to Sempringham nunnery, where she eventually died. More importantly he won a massive psychological victory by obtaining possession of the sacred relics and made great political capital from it. To celebrate his conquest of Wales, Edward held a Round Table at Nevyn in Carnarvonshire, from 27–29 July 1284.

On the Friday following Easter of 1285 a strange event took place in London. Flanked by 14 bishops, John Pecham, the Archbishop of Canterbury, stood in ecclesiastical splendour before the Tower of London. In his hands was one of the most sacred relics of the Welsh, the Croes Naidd, the True Cross. As the procession made its way towards Westminster Abbey its form became clear. Following the Archbishop's party were Edward I and his queen, Eleanor of Castile; slightly in front of them was Alfonso, Edward's 12-year-old son, who was not destined to see another year. Laid on a gold-embroidered cushion held firmly in Alfonso's hands was that most awe inspiring relic, the Crown of Arthur, especially regilded for the occasion. Behind the royal party and the immediate retainers came all the magnates and dignitaries of the Plantagenet court and as they walked through the streets in pilgrimage the crowd that had gathered to witness the spectacle fell silent. When the procession arrived at the great abbey the Crown of Arthur was offered at the shrine of Edward the Confessor. Edward I was undoubtedly aware of the symbolic victory he had achieved, because invested in the crown that he had in his possession was the sovereignty of Wales and the national identity of the last remnant of the Britons, Arthur's people. Following its presentation at the shrine nothing more is heard of this important Welsh relic and the fate of the Crown of Arthur remains a mystery.

From that time on Edward kept the Croes Naidd as his private property, carrying it with him constantly, including during his Scottish campaigns. During his son Edward II's reign the Croes Naidd resided within the King's Chapel in the Tower of London, where it became a focus of pilgrimage. Then during the reign of Edward III, after an unsuccessful attempt to establish a Round Table, the King founded the Order of the Garter in 1348 and the Croes Naidd was presented as a gift to the chapel of the Order, St George's Chapel in Windsor Castle. The Order regarded the Croes Naidd as its chief treasure and again the cross became the centre of pilgrimage. Sadly, during the Reformation the Croes Naidd disappeared from the records and is believed to have been broken up for its precious metal and jewels. Today all that remains of the Croes Naidd, once the glory of Wales and the chief relic of the Order of the Garter, is the image of it retained in the ceiling bosses of St George's Chapel.[30]

Edward I plundered Wales of more than its most important physical relics. According to bardic tradition he also instituted the massacre and persecution of the bards, those repositories of the history, genealogy and oral tradition of Wales. By the time of Llewellyn, the last Prince of Wales, the bards had committed much of their lore to written form. The poetry of later bards such as Guto'r Glyn records that following the conquest of Wales Edward I had all the great books of Welsh history taken to the Tower of London and burnt.[31] The burning of the books in the Tower is also mentioned by William Salesbury, who adds that the books that remained were likewise destroyed during the rebellion of Owen Glyndwr and that none escaped that was not irrevocably maimed, torn or mangled. This wholesale destruction of Welsh history could account for the loss of the original book that Geoffrey of Monmouth translated as the *Historia Regum Britanniae*. Why would an English king bother himself with the eradication of the bardic tradition? Obviously a profession that literally sang the praises of the true British kings posed a threat to Edward and his political ambitions. More than that, the bardic tradition preserved a purer form of the historical tradition that had been adopted by the Plantagenets in an attempt to make it their own. In spite of Edward's conquest of Wales, the centuries that followed saw the Welsh bardic tradition continue its association with the Cistercian houses of North Wales, such as Valle Crucis Abbey and Aber Conway Abbey, and much of the material that survived the ravages of English occupation was saved by their patronage.

Was it more than coincidence that the national relics of Wales were relinquished at Aber Conway, which Edward I had used as a base during his final conquest of Gwynedd? Founded in 1198 by Llewelyn the Great of Gwynedd, Aber Conway Abbey was one of the most important abbeys in North Wales and a great patron of the Welsh bards. After the suppression of Gwynedd it was relocated from its original site around 1284 to make way for the imposing fortress built by Edward as a permanent symbol of English domination. It was from this background that the text known as the *Vera Historia de Morte Arthuri* emerged. As already explained, the *Vera Historia* relates the events surrounding Arthur's death and his final journey to Avalon, which it places in Gwynedd. Although it dates from the late 13th century, the evidence points to the earliest manuscripts being copies of an earlier text recording the genuine Welsh tradition regarding the death and burial of Arthur. With his enthusiasm for things Arthurian, Edward I would almost certainly have been made aware of the existence of such a tradition during his early Welsh campaign and it is our belief that the tradition recorded in what is now known as the *Vera Historia* was probably a major contributory factor to the events surrounding the spectacle of Arthur's second exhumation at Glastonbury. Not only did it prove that Arthur could not return to save his people, but it removed him definitively from his Welsh homeland and reinforced Glastonbury's claim to be his final resting place, the mystical Avalon.

ARTHUR AND GLASTONBURY

The validity of Arthur's association with Glastonbury has long been debated but scholars generally agree that there is no tangible evidence to connect either Arthur or Avalon with this Somerset town. In short, Glastonbury's claim to be the Avalon of Arthurian legend relies upon two things: the identification in early sources of Avalon as the burial place of Arthur, and the exhumation of Arthur's alleged remains in the abbey grounds in the late 12th century. But these early sources clearly do not say that Arthur was buried in Glastonbury; he was buried in Avalon. However, because of the effectiveness of the Anglo-Norman propaganda, Glastonbury remains firmly identified with both Arthur and Avalon. Meanwhile scholarly debate has revolved around Glastonbury because there has never been a serious alternative.

The background to Arthur's emergence as a political pawn within the Glastonbury context is complicated and fragmentary, yet enough can be gleaned from textual sources to establish certain facts. When Geoffrey wrote his *Historia* around 1135, not only did he fail to associate Glastonbury with Avalon/Ynys Afallach, but he made no mention of Glastonbury whatsoever. William of Malmesbury, who examined the Glastonbury records in the 1120s, makes no link between Avalon and Glastonbury, not because Arthur was unknown to him or the other Anglo-Norman writers, but because Arthur had yet to be fully adopted by them. Nor did William have any knowledge of Glastonbury as being Arthur's burial place, for he states that 'the tomb of Arthur is nowhere beheld'. Even Saxon chronicles make hardly any reference to Glastonbury, nor do the Welsh bards. How was it then that this monastic establishment assumed such great significance within the Arthurian mythos when it is barely mentioned in early historical records?

The earliest text to supposedly connect Arthur with Glastonbury is the *Life of St Gildas* (1150) by Caradoc of Llancarfan, the text of which is pre-served in a Durham manuscript of a later date. In this work Caradoc refers to a certain Glastonia, which has been taken to mean Glastonbury in Somerset, yet this interpretation is supposition more than anything else. It should also be borne in mind that Caradoc's patron was Robert of Gloucester, whose political motives we have already explained. Nonetheless, Caradoc's *Life of St Gildas* has been used to connect Arthur, Guinevere, St Gildas and Melwas with Somerset. Because of this Melwas is assumed to be a mythical character and the story of his kidnapping of Guinevere is believed to have no historical basis, yet – as we shall show in Chapter 12 – when returned to his correct location Melwas takes on the substance of a verifiable historical figure whose realm is outlined by the Welsh bards.

Other stories allegedly linking Arthur with Glastonbury are to be found in William of Malmesbury's *De Antiquitate Glastoniensis Ecclesiae* (Antiquities of the Church of Glastonbury), but these are additions inserted piecemeal in the hundred or so years following William's death. As E.K. Chambers noted, 'the process of interpolating the *De Antiquitate* was a gradual one, and extended well into the thirteenth century'.[32] From this it would appear that the Glastonbury propagandists used William's *De Antiquitate* as a basis from which to create an antiquity for their own foundation. Not satisfied with simply laying claim to Arthur, however, they also professed to be the home of Avalon, St Joseph of Arimathea and the origins of Christianity in Britain. In the process the genuine Avalon had become definitively separated both from its original geographical location in North Wales and from its true identity as the realm of Afallach, otherwise known as Annwn, the Celtic Otherworld. The revelation contained in the 13th-century *Vera Historia* that identifies Arthur's burial in Avalon within the ancient region of Gwynedd has been described as a counterblast to Glastonbury's claims, and indeed it is.[33]

Having established the location of the original Avalon it became obvious that Glastonbury did not in fact create the mythical stories that we now associate with it but absorbed an already existing tradition that had simply been added to the melting pot of Glastonbury lore. Even the supposed foundation legend from which Glastonbury claims to take its name appears to be suspect. According to R.F. Treharne, author of *The Glastonbury Legends*: 'Grievous though the loss be, we must therefore dismiss Arthur, whether as hero or as king, from any proven historical connection with Glastonbury.'[34]

CHAPTER ELEVEN

IN SEARCH
OF
GLAESTINGABURH

W E HAD reached a point in our search for Avalon where we had established that this mythical realm was located in the ancient region of Gwynedd in North Wales, in an area referred to as the Realm of Afallach that was also the geographical location associated with Annwn, the Celtic Otherworld and the Land of the Dead. It was to here that the mortally wounded Arthur had been taken after his final battle at Camlan. However, for political motives it was deemed expedient in the 12th century to relocate Arthur's final resting place to a site in England, so the discovery of Arthur's alleged remains had been staged at Glastonbury in Somerset. As a result of this medieval fraud Glastonbury has become synonymous with Avalon and in absorbing the traditions associated with this ancient realm had assumed a position of unwarranted significance in the story of Arthur. Our research revealed to us that the merging of Glastonbury with Avalon had further confused things by amalgamating two separate traditions – one associated with the *realm* of Avalon and another associated with a *town* located within that realm. Unfortunately the pre-eminence assumed by Glastonbury in both Arthurian and Avalonian tradition has obscured the true identity of the town which is referred to in some sources by the Saxon name of Glaestingaburh, and the similarity between the two names has simply compounded the confusion. With this in mind we set out in search of the town whose mantle had been worn by Glastonbury for the last 800 years.

The oldest name associated with Avalon is Ynys Wydrin, which has mistakenly been taken to mean the Isle of Glass. In the opinion of P.C. Bartrum 'this unsatisfactory explanation of "glassy" shows the falsity of the supposed etymology of the names Glastonbury and Ynys Wydrin.'[1] The rendering of *Wydir* (*Witrin* or *Vitrin*) as 'glass' is a result of the confusion caused by Caradoc of Llancarfan when writing his biography of Gildas. In giving his explanation of the name Glastonia he said, 'Glastonia, that is, Urbs Vitrea [the Glass City], which took its name from glass, is a city with a name originally in the British speech' and 'Glastonia was of old called *Ynisgutrin* and is still called so by the British inhabitants. *Ynis* in British speech is *insula* in Latin; *gutrin* is *vitrea* [glassy]. But after the coming of the English ... It was renamed *Glastigberi* ... that is *glas* [glass] in the English, *vitrum* in Latin, and *beria*, a city, whence *Glastiberia*, that is, *Vitrea Civitas* [the Glassy City].' Within the original British (Welsh) language *glas* can be interpreted as 'green/blue', as 'glass' or as the personal name Glas or Glast.

William of Malmesbury helped to dispel some of the confusion sown by Caradoc for he twice mentions a charter recording that a certain king gave five hides of land at Ineswitrin to Abbott Worgret.[2] There are academic reasons for regarding this charter as genuine and therefore it was of interest that when William referred to this same charter in his *De Antiquitate* he gave a variant of Ineswitrin, recording the name as Yneswitherim. In later Welsh this would be Ynys Wytherin, which in all probability derives from the Welsh personal name Gwytherin (Latin Victorinus), thus giving the meaning as 'the Island/Realm of Gwytherin'.[3] Wydrin was therefore simply a corrupt form of Ynys Wytherin, the original name of the town before it received the Saxon name Glaestingaburh (the Town of the Glaestings). Giraldus Cambrensis reiterated this information, but with one important difference: he placed Ynys Wydrin within an Avalonian context.[4] This struck us as particularly interesting in view of an interpolation in William of Malmesbury's *De Antiquitate* according to which Ynswitrin was given to Joseph of Arimathea by the pagan King Arviragus. If Ynys Witrin was situated in Avalon, then it was evident that the story of St Joseph of Arimathea belonged there too, and not in Glastonbury, Somerset. How did Ynys Witrin get the name Glaestingaburh/Glastonia? In finding the answer to that question we discovered that the original Glaestingaburh was indeed in the Realm of Afallach.

THE FOUNDING OF GLAESTINGABURH

[Glasteing] following his pigs as far as Wellis and from there through the pathless and watery way, called Sugewege, that is 'Sow's Way', he found his sow near the church of which we are speaking, suckling under an apple tree, whence it has reached us that the apples of that apple tree are called Ealdcyrcenas epple, that is 'Old Church Apples'. For that reason, also, the sow was called Ealdecyrce Suge [Old Church Sow], which, wonderful to relate, had eight feet, whereas other sows have four. Here, therefore, Glasteing, after entering that island [or realm] saw it abounding in many ways with good things, came to live in it with all his family, and spent the course of his life there. And from his progeny and family which succeeded him, that place is said to have been populated.[5]

The above account of the founding of the town of Glaestingaburh by a certain individual named Glast (or Glasteing) is contained in William of Malmesbury's history of Glastonbury, *De Antiquitate Glastoniensis Ecclesiae*, and therefore has long been claimed to be the foundation legend of the Somerset town of that name. At first glance that seems a reasonable enough claim – after all, William's book recounts the history of Glastonbury – yet when we studied the evidence more closely we found that apart from the 'Glast' element in their names the only link between Glastonbury and the Glaestingaburh founded by Glast was the inclusion of this passage in *De Antiquitate*, which William himself admits was drawn from many sources. The name Glaestingaburh simply means 'the town of the descendants of Glast', and the Anglo-Saxon form of the name is recorded in several variants, including Glastingaburi, Glastingei, Glestingaburuh and Glaestingbiri, to which can be added the forms Glastenic, Glassymbyri, Glastonia and other similar renderings from various early sources.[6] The question remained: who was this person Glast who had had a town named after him, and where did he come from?

One of the later interpolations in *De Antiquitate* informs us that Glast was a great-grandson of Cunedda Wledig (c.370), although, as we were to find out, the interpolator was dealing with unfamiliar material for he incorrectly named Glast's lineal descendants as Glast's brothers. Glast is referred to in the tenth-century Welsh pedigree in the Harleian manuscripts,[7] while his great-grandfather Cunedda is mentioned in the *Historia Brittonum*[8] in connection with one of his descendants, Maelgwn Gwynedd (d. 547), who as we saw in a previous chapter was reputed to be the lover of one of the daughters of Afallach: 'Maelgwn, the great King, was reigning among the Britons in the region of Gwynedd, for his ancestor, Cunedag [Cunedda], with his sons, whose number was eight, had come previously from the northern part, that is from the region which is called Manaw Gododdin, one hundred and forty-six years before Maelgwn reigned. And with great slaughter they drove out from those regions the Scotti who never returned again to inhabit them.'[9]

The descendants of Cunedda

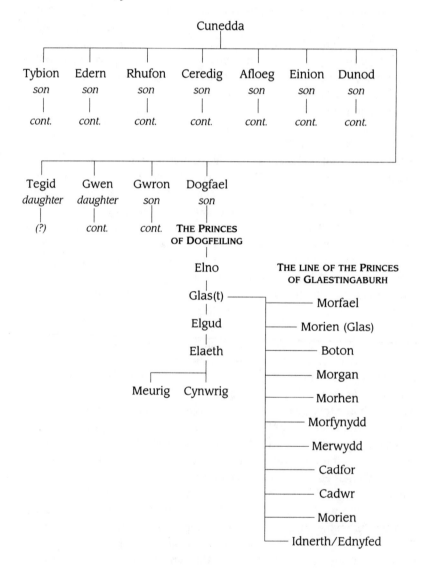

The Harleian genealogies told us more about Cunedda's sons and how they divided up between them the land they had conquered: 'These are the names of the sons of Cunedda, whose number was nine: (1) Tybion, the first-born, who died in the region called Manaw Gododdin and did not come hither with his father and his aforesaid brothers. Meirion, his son, divided the possessions among his brothers. (2) Ysfael, (3) Rhufon, (4) Dunod, (5) Ceredig, (6) Afloeg, (7) Einion Yrth, (8) Dogfael, (9) Edern. This is their boundary: From the river which is called Dyfrdwy [Dee], to another river, the Teifi; and they held very many districts in the western part of Britain.'[10] All the sons named in the Harleian genealogies, except Tybion and Einion Yrth, gave their names to the regions allotted to them in North and West Wales. The areas covered by these kingdoms were as follows.

In Cardigan Bay, West Wales:
• *Meirionydd*: from Mawddach to the River Dovey, given to Meirion (son of Tybion).
• *Ceredigion*: an area between the River Dovey and the River Teifi, given to Ceredig.
• *Afloegion*: a coastal region from Abersoch to Abererch, given to Afloeg.
• *Dunoding*: an area from Erch to Mawddach, given to Dunod.

East of the Conway:
• *Rhufoniog*: the area between the rivers Elwy, Clwyd and Clywedog, given to Rhufon.
• *Dogfeiling*: an area lying to the east of Rhufoniog that embraced the southern section of the Vale of Clwyd, between Bodfari and Derwen, given to Dogfael.[11]
• *Edeirnion*: an area to the south of Dogfeiling, lying on both sides of the River Dee in the area around Corwen and extending to the Berwyn Mountains, given to Edern.[12]
• *Rhos*: an area extending from the River Conway in the south to the River Clwyd in the north, and from the River Elwy in the east to the sea in the west, given to and ruled over by Einion Yrth.[13]

And finally:
• *Ysfeilion*: the eastern horn of Anglesey, given to Ysfael.[14]

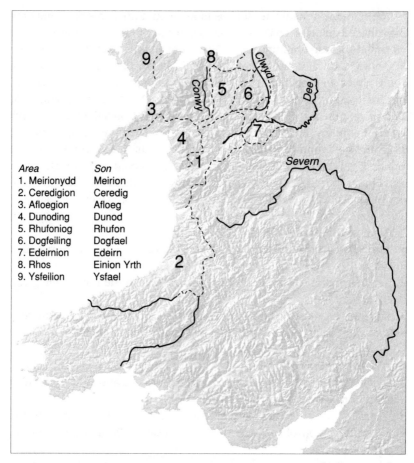

Area	Son
1. Meirionydd	Meirion
2. Ceredigion	Ceredig
3. Afloegion	Afloeg
4. Dunoding	Dunod
5. Rhufoniog	Rhufon
6. Dogfeiling	Dogfael
7. Edeirnion	Edeirn
8. Rhos	Einion Yrth
9. Ysfeilion	Ysfael

Map 24 The sons of Cunedda in Wales

As shown on the map, the area occupied by Cunedda's descendants extended from the mouth of the River Clwyd to the mouth of the River Teifi in the west, and from the Dee in the north to the Teifi in the south, the only exceptions being the areas of Arfon, Arllechwedd, Llyn and an enclave in the Isle of Mon (Anglesey).

Later sources inform us that Cunedda fathered more children, including two daughters named Gwen and Tegeingl (or Tegid). Gwen became the wife of Amlawdd Wledig and mother to Eigyr (wife of Uthyr Pendragon and mother of the famous Arthur).[15] Little is known of Tegeingl other than that a cantref, then in Gwynedd, bears the same name.[16] Cunedda is accredited with four more sons – Gwron, Coel, Arwystl and Mael – but the general opinion is that, except for Gwron, these sons are entirely fictitious.[17] Cunedda is also named as the founder of one of the Three Saintly Lineages of Ynys Prydain because of his descendants producing a large number of saints in subsequent generations.[18]

A partial list of the names of Cunedda's great-grandsons reads like a veritable Who's Who of early British history, for it includes Glast, Arthur, Cynlas Goch,[19] Maelgwn Gwynedd[20] and Caradog Freichfras.[21] (See genealogical chart page 228.) Like their forebears, these figures can all be located in the region conquered by Cunedda.

Glast (or Glas) was a descendant of Cunedda's son Dogfael. Dogfeiling, the area of land given to Dogfael by Cunedda, embraced the southern part of what is now called Dyffryn Clwyd (the Vale of Clwyd), and from the Harleian manuscripts we learnt that this region had been ruled over by the descendants of Glast, through his son Elgud. More importantly, we discovered that a second line had ruled over Glaestingaburh through another of Glast's sons, named Morfael. The earliest documentary record of Glast we could find was contained in a genealogy within the priceless Harleian MS. 3859. Predating the work of William of Malmesbury, the genealogy was written in 958 and survives in a manuscript dated around 1100, where Glast's descendants are called Glaestings and their city or town is named as Glaestingaburh.[22] Within the genealogy, Glas(t) is said to be the father of Morfael and this descent continues through 11 generations to Idnerth (or Ednyfed), who would appear to be the last of the line of the Princes of Glaestingaburh. At the end of this genealogy appears the following: 'Whence are the Glastings(?) Who came [through the town] which is called Loytcoyt.'[23] William of Malmesbury's De Antiquitate contains a similar reference: 'This is that Glasteing, who [came] through the midland Angles, otherwise the town which is called Escebtiorne.' And the same pedigree is also found in the Hanesyn Hen tract,[24] written by Grufudd Hiraethog: 'Whence the Glastonians who came from Caer Lwyd Coed[25] to the city called Aldud today.'[26] The similarity of these three quotes indicates a common origin, and a suggested composite reading is: 'Whence are the Glastings who came from Caer Loytcoyt through the midland Angles to the town called Aldud today.'

The town referred to by the name Loytcoyt (modern Welsh Lwydcoed) has long been identified with the city of Lichfield (modern Welsh Maes y Cyrph). The fact that Lichfield was a bishopric could explain why the name Loytcoyt was changed to Escebtiorne in the De Antiquate (Esceb in modern Welsh is esgob, meaning 'bishop', hence 'Bishop's Town'). The reference to the 'midland Angles' has also been used to further the argument in favour of Lichfield as Glast is supposed to have passed through this region on his way to Glastonbury, yet there is scant evidence to suggest that what is known today as the Midlands maintained any such identification during the Dark Ages. At the time the texts referred to above were written the name Y Berfeddwlad (the Middle Country, Midlands, or the Lands Between) designated an area of Ynys Prydein situated between the Dee and the Conway comprising the cantrefs of Rhos, Rhufoniog, Tegeingl and Dogfeiling. A reference to this area is contained in a Welsh text dated around 1160 – 'through the middle country till he came to Chester'[27] – and we concluded that this was indeed the *'mediterraneos'* or 'Midlands' alluded to in the interpolated *De Antiquitate*. Our conclusion was confirmed when we discovered a reference to the placename Loydcoyd (Loytcoyt) in *The Survey of Denbigh* of 1334. This seemed a viable alternative to the traditional argument that Loytcoyt was Lichfield, especially as Loydcoyd was in the cantref of Rhos, one of the four cantrefs that constituted the Middle Lands (Y Berfeddwlad), and was ruled over by the descendants of Cunedda.[28]

Having identified the figure of Glast as well as several locations in North Wales associated with him we felt we now had an explanation for the reference to Wellis in the confusing story of Glast and the Sow's Way that William of Malmesbury had cited as the foundation legend for Glaestingaburh. It was not the cathedral city of Wells in Somerset, as Glastonbury tradition maintained, but simply a Latin rendering of Wales – namely Wellis or Wallis. A village by the name of Mochdre shed a little more light on the story of the Sow's Way, for *moch* is Welsh for pigs, hogs or swine, and thus in translation Mochdre means 'Town of Pigs'. Situated a few miles from Loydcoyd, Mochdre is noted for its mention in *The Mabinogion* where it lies on the route taken by Gwydion (son of the Celtic goddess Arianrhod) who, having obtained the sacred swine from Pryderi (the hero of *The Mabinogi*), drives them north. Each location referred to in the text is a remembrance of the route his journey took. In brief the story is recorded as follows:

> And that night they journeyed as far as the uplands of Ceredigiawn, the place which for that reason is still called Mochdref. And on the morrow they pushed ahead; over Elenid they came. And that night they were between Ceri and Arwystli, in the township which is likewise for that reason called Mochdref. And thence they journeyed on, and that night they went as far as a commot [an area of land] in Powys which is likewise for that reason called Mochnant, and they were there that night. And thence they journeyed as far as the cantref of Rhos, and they were there that night in the township which is still called Mochdref.[29]

The journey described here gives us a clearly defined route running through the heart of the region of Wales we have shown to be the home of the descendants of Cunedda. The hills and valleys of this region are crisscrossed with numerous ancient trackways and drovers' roads, some of prehistoric origin, along which are to be found many place names associated with the sow or pig, and we believe that the route described above can be identified as the Sow's Way referred to in the *De Antiquitate*. In fact, the tradition recorded in the Harleian manuscript and the interpolated *De Antiquitate* appeared to provide an accurate record of Glast's journey, which we were now able to trace on the map. We suggest that the route taken by Glast went from Loydcoyd, near Mochdre in the cantref of Rhos, through Y Berfeddwlad (the Middle Country, or Midlands) into the Dee valley and eventually led to the Vale of Llangollen. He may have travelled part of the way along the ancient trackway known as Stryt y Hwch (Street of the Sow, or Sow's Way) that runs from Marchwiel parish in a westerly direction towards the Middle Country and the Vale of Llangollen and ends up on Bryn Afallen (Hill of Apples, or Apple Hill) in the parish of Ruabon.[30] Another of the old trackways from the Middle Country

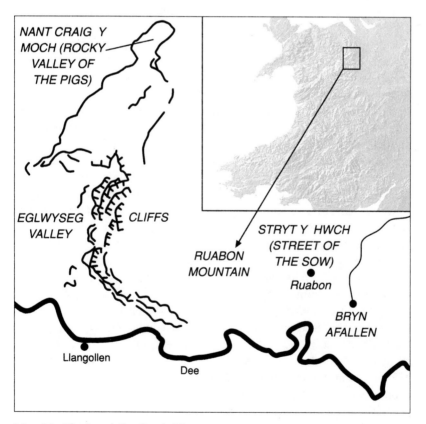

Map 25 Glast and the Sow's Way

leads across Ruabon Mountain above Llangollen, passing through Nant Craig y Moch (Rocky Valley of the Pigs, or Pigs' Hollow) before continuing down the Eglwyseg valley past Valle Crucis Abbey and Castell Dinas Bran on its way to Llangollen. The fact that the area around the Vale of Llangollen and Eglwyseg valley bordered Dogfeiling, the domain of Glast's ancestors, convinced us that this was where we needed to look for the original location of Glaestingaburh. Even so, we were unprepared for how obvious the site of the true Glaestingaburh was to prove to be and how much of its early semi-legendary material had remained independently attached to its place of origin.

ST COLLEN AND GLAESTINGABURH

The route taken centuries ago by Glast follows the course of the sacred River Dee and brings us into the Vale of Llangollen, one of the most picturesque spots on earth, beloved by the Welsh bards and English poets alike. This has been hallowed ground since pre-Christian times and is still held to be so by those who have an intimate knowledge of the area. In and around the parish of Llangollen are some of the places we had come across earlier in our quest for Avalon, such as the Wall of Severus and the Ruabon Mountain prehistoric burial concentrations. The area teems with stories of Arthur and his knights, and the references to giants, fairies, demons and devils that abound in the surrounding landscape enhance the mystical nature of the panorama. The name Llangollen means the 'church' or 'enclosure' (Llan) of Collen (Gollen) and the church of St Collen sits in the centre of this famous parish, home of the international Eisteddfodd – essentially a congress of Welsh bards, with competitions in music, literature, art and folk-dancing as a celebration of Welsh culture. Langollen is visited by thousands of tourists every year who come to appreciate the beauty of the landscape and the Welsh cultural tradition. But the thing that interested us most about it now was the apparent connection between its patron saint and Glaestingaburh.

What little is known regarding St Collen's links with Glaestingaburh comes from two versions of *Buchedd Collen* (The Life of Collen) in which we are told that St Collen was Abbot of Glaestingaburh (or Glassymbyri, the variant used in *Buchedd Collen*). The text tells us that Collen was chosen as abbot three months after arriving at the abbey and taking the religious habit. Shortly afterwards he adopted the life of a hermit, taking upon himself 'a life that was heavier and harder than being abbot', which he pursued for three years before returning to the abbey where he remained for a further five, at which point we are told he became angry with the men of the land and cursed them for wrongdoing.[31] The story then tells us that St Collen retired to the mountain above Glaestingaburh and was there confronted by Gwyn ap Nudd, King of the Fairies and Lord of Annwn (the Celtic Otherworld), who appears as a mythical being in several early Welsh sources alongside Arthur.[32] As previously related, the mountain range to the south of the valley of Valle Crucis and Llangollen is known as the Berwyn Mountains (*Berwyn* means 'the Hill of Gwyn'), and of old this area was known as Gwyn's Land.[33] The story of the meeting between St Collen and Gwyn ap Nudd is recorded as follows:

Collen was passing a period of mortification as a hermit, in a cell under a rock on a mountain. There he one day overheard two men talking about Gwyn ap Nudd, and giving him this twofold kingly character. Collen cried out to the men to go away and hold their tongues, instead of talking about Devils. For this Collen was rebuked, as the king of fairyland had an objection to such language. The Saint was summoned to meet the king on the hill top at noon, and after repeated refusals, he finally went there; but he carried a flask of holy water with him. And when he came there he saw the fairest Castle he had ever beheld, and around it the best appointed troops, and numbers of minstrels and every kind of music of voice and string, and steeds with youths upon them, the comeliest in the world, and maidens of elegant aspect, sprightly, light of foot, of graceful apparel, and in the bloom of youth; and every magnificence becoming the court of a puissant sovereign. And he beheld a courteous man on the top of the Castle who bade him enter, saying that the king was waiting for him to come to meet. And Collen went into the Castle, and when he came there the king was sitting in a golden chair. And he welcomed Collen honourably, and desired him to eat, assuring him that besides what he saw, he should have the most luxurious of every dainty and delicacy that the mind could desire, and should be supplied with every drink and liquor that the heart could wish; and that there should be in readiness for him every luxury of courtesy and service, of banquet and of honourable entertainment, of rank and of presents, and every aspect and welcome due to a man of his wisdom. 'I will not eat the leaves of the trees,' said Collen. 'Didst thou ever see men of better equipment than these of red and blue?' asked the king. 'Their equipment is good enough,' said Collen, 'for such equipment as it is.' 'What kind of equipment is that?' said the king. Then said Collen, 'The red on the one part signifies burning, and the blue on the other signifies coldness.' And with that Collen drew out his flask and threw the holy water on their heads, whereupon they vanished from his sight, so that there was neither

Castle nor troops, nor men, nor maidens, nor music, nor song nor steeds, nor youths, nor banquet, nor the appearance of anything whatever but the green hillocks.[34]

The story continues that having vanquished Gwyn ap Nudd, St Collen prayed to God for somewhere that he might live peacefully. He was told to go out that morning and travel until he came across a horse, which he was to then mount and ride over as large an area as he could encompass in a day and that this would then be 'his sanctuary until Doomsday'. So on the morning after his confrontation with Gwyn ap Nudd St Collen left his cell on the mountain above Glaestingaburh and the *Buchedd Collen* relates that he met the miraculous horse at a place named Rhysfa Maes Cadfarch (the Course of the Charger's Field).[35] The legend continues by telling us that Collen then rode the horse for the remainder of the day, thus defining the area that was to be his sanctuary (parish). At its centre he made the cell in which he spent the rest of his days, and it was there that he was laid to rest.

In the parish church of Llangollen, which is dedicated to St Collen, can be found an inscription recording his line of descent, revealing that, like Glast, he was a descendant of Cunedda: 'St Collen son of Gwennog, son of Coleddog, son of Cawdraf, son of Caradog Freichfras, son of Llyr Marini, son of Einion Yrth, son of Cunedda Wledig, by Ethni Wyddeles daughter of Lord of Cwl, in the kingdom of Ireland. Which Saint was buried here.'[36] The tomb of St Collen at Llangollen is mentioned in the Rural Dean's report of 1749: 'There is a building adjoining the tower, westward, called the Old Church, in which the tutelar saint Collen lies.' In 1771 Thomas Pennant described the tombstone, or what were said to be its much worn remains, as lying in the belfry of Llangollen Church, where it had been thrown at some point between 1749 and 1771; it was a recumbent figure of an ecclesiastic, said to represent St Collen. In fact it is believed that the alabaster figure known as St Collen was originally in the possession of Valle Crucis Abbey, from where it was removed to the parish church at Llangollen, which was owned by the abbey. The magnificent carvings that decorate Llangollen Church were also rescued from the Abbey of Valle Crucis following the Reformation, including the beautiful oak carvings that enrich the church ceiling. Indeed, many churches in the surrounding area retain pieces of this once great abbey.

Further references to St Collen are plentiful in and around the Vale of Llangollen. The parish church at Ruabon, which lies four miles downstream from Llangollen, is now dedicated to St Mary but its original dedication was to St Collen,[37] as evidenced in the land grants of Valle Crucis Abbey to which the church was granted in 1274. In 1699 the antiquarian Edward Lhwyd recorded another site associated with St Collen in the township of Dinhinlle Isaf, which is in the south of the parish of Ruabon. 'Capel Collen is the name of a field, wherein is a cross, they celebrate the wake of the saint in the Parish of Ruabon'. This chapel is also mentioned in the Norwich Taxatio of 1254 – 'Capel Collen (in Maelor)' – although it is not clear whether the notice of the Norwich Taxatio is referring to the site of the extinct chapel that lies less than a mile to the southeast in Dinhinlle Isaf or to the present church in Ruabon. It has been suggested that the latter was built on the site of an earlier church and dedicated to St Mary (*Assumptu Baetae Mariae*) by the monks of Valle Crucis – mentioned in the previous chapter, the church at Ruabon sits 'high above the river of Mabon'. The reference to the cross and to St Collen's wakes being held there point to the very early Capel Collen in Dinhinlle Isaf as being the most likely location for St Collen's cell, although Ruabon Church itself also fits the evidence.

Edward Lhuyd records a further site associated with St Collen as 'Clawdd Collen on Cefn Ucha, in the township of Pengwern: a short dyke, similar to Offa's Dyke.'[38] There is also a legend connecting the saint to the Eglwyseg valley, in which Valle Crucis Abbey stands. The legend relates how, long ago, there was a giantess popularly known as Cawres y Bwlch (the Giantess of the Pass) who dwelt at Bwlch Rhiwfelen (Rhiwfelen Pass), an elevation commanding an extensive view of the surrounding countryside. The giantess had a penchant for devouring every human being who attempted to travel through the pass. St Collen lived nearby and, determined to rid the district of this pest, proceeded towards the pass. When the giantess showed herself St Collen challenged her and they immediately began to fight, the saint chopping off her right arm with his sword. She retrieved her dismembered limb and attacked St Collen with it, so the saint cut off her other arm. The giantess then cried aloud to Arthur to come to her aid out of his stronghold in the Eglwyseg rocks, but the saint slew her. Having achieved his victory, St Collen washed the blood stains from himself in a nearby well on the mountain, which is known to this day as Ffynnon Gollen (Collen's Well).[39] Ffynnon Collen is situated just below the pass of Bwlch Rhiwfelen, known today as Horseshoe Pass, on the Valle Crucis side of a hill called Cyrn-y-Brain. What particularly interested us about this story was the reference to Arthur's stronghold in the Eglwyseg rocks, thus linking him to the area around Glaestingaburh. Crowning the Eglwyseg valley is a 200-foot cliff now named Craig Arthur but of old called Cadair Arthur (Arthur's Throne, or Chair). In the vicinity to the south of Llangollen there is also Ffynnon Arthur (Arthur's Well) and numerous other geographical references to this ancient hero, his knights and adventures.

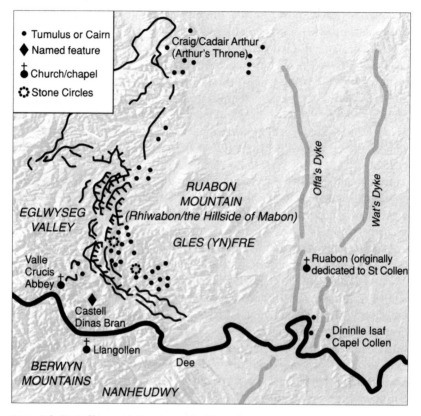

Map 26 St Collen and Gwyn ap Nudd

St Collen is said to have had his hermit's cell on the high ground above Valle Crucis Abbey and the town of Llangollen. We have come across this high ground in earlier chapters in our search for Avalon; it is called Ruabon Mountain, or the Mountain of Mabon. Up until the 17th century it was also known as Glasfre, derived from *Glas* (the personal name) and *fre* (a mutated form of *tre*, meaning 'town') to give us the 'Town of Glas'. It has also been suggested that Glasfre is an abbreviated form of Glesynfre, again meaning 'Town of Glas', but which in early Welsh dictionaries is also given as an alternative name for Ynys Afallach. As we had discovered earlier, the name Ynys Afallach – the Realm of Afallach, or Avalon – designated the geographical location of the Celtic Otherworld. This gave new meaning to the story of St Collen's encounter on Ruabon Mountain with Gwyn ap Nudd, Lord of Annwn, for it now seemed to portray a symbolic confrontation between the Christian faith and the old Celtic religion, or even the Christianization of an important pagan site.

St Collen's burial place has always traditionally been at Llangollen, in the cantref of Nanheudwy in Powys Fadog, now Denbighshire, yet it is also claimed that he was buried in Glastonbury, Somerset. Similarly, the location of St Collen's confrontation with Gwyn ap Nudd is claimed to be the hill known as Glastonbury Tor, while St Collen's half-day ride around the boundary of his parish, which clearly ends at Llangollen, is also claimed to have begun at Glastonbury, some 200 miles away as the crow flies. (Of the latter claim, a footnote in *Lives of the British Saints* reads, 'there must be some mistake here, as the "sanctuary" meant is surely Llangollen.') We believe that these and similar claims concern the body of tradition that has been attributed to Glastonbury and yet rightfully belongs to Glaestingaburh.

But what of Glaestingaburh itself? As we established, the original site of Glaestingaburh had to be in or near the boundaries of the Kingdom of Dogfeiling, as this was the area that had been ruled over by Glast and his descendants following the founding of Glaestingaburh, the 'town of the Glaestings'. The abbot of Glaestingaburh Abbey had at one time been St Collen who had spent most of his life in the vicinity of Llangollen, the town which bears his name. Not only was the parish of Llangollen the site of the saint's sanctuary, it was the location of his hermit's cell and his last resting place. A number of legends also linked St Collen to the area. The evidence we had examined thus far therefore pointed to Glaestingaburh as being located in the Vale of Llangollen, somewhere in the area around Valle Crucis Abbey and the town of Llangollen itself, and the most likely site appeared to be the Eglwyseg valley, which bordered Dogfeiling and Llangollen. Furthermore, we were convinced that Glaestingaburh Abbey was an original Celtic/Saxon foundation over which the later Valle Crucis Abbey had been built around the year 1200.

CHAPTER TWELVE

AVALON: THE WORLD'S END

THE EARLY stages of our search for Arthur and Avalon had focused on disentangling the confusing geography of Britain promoted by Geoffrey of Monmouth's *Historia*. We had now reached a point in our research into the ancient site of Glaestingaburth where we had something equally confusing to contend with: certain traditions belonging to the area of North Wales in which Glaestingaburh was situated had been translocated to Somerset, where they had been absorbed into the Glastonbury corpus. As we had already established that Arthur's primary sphere of activity was North Wales and the Marches and that the discovery of his alleged remains at Glastonbury was nothing more than a carefully stage-managed political fraud, we decided to re-examine some of the traditional stories claiming to link Arthur with Glastonbury to see whether they could shed any further light on the history of Glaestingaburh and the surrounding area.

ARTHUR AND GLAESTINGABURH ABBEY

The first such tradition to attract our attention was an interpolation within William of Malmesbury's history of Glastonbury, *De Antiquitate Glastoniensis Ecclesiae*, concerning certain grants of land made by Arthur to the abbey of

Glastonia. Although the interpolation is widely held to relate Glastonbury Abbey's acquisition of the lands of Brent and Polden, we felt certain that it originally related to the abbey of Glaestingaburh in the Vale of Llangollen. The story recounts that while Arthur was at Caerlleon he decorated with honours a powerful youth named Ider, the son of a certain King Nuth (Nudd). Ider was then sent to test his prowess against three giants living on Mount Ranae who were renowned for their ill deeds. The youth set off for the mountain ahead of Arthur and his comrades, attacked the giants, and having slain all three in a fearsome combat collapsed with exhaustion. When Arthur arrived at the scene of the fight he saw Ider's body lying on the ground and, thinking him dead, began to mourn for him. Holding himself responsible for Ider's death because he had not come to his aid in time, Arthur turned for home in anguish, leaving Ider's body where it lay until arrangements could be made to collect it. On his way back to Caerleon Arthur passed through Glastonia and there arranged for 24 monks to pray for the soul of his lost friend. He also bestowed upon the monks many possessions and lands for their sustenance.[1] An addition in the margin of the text adds: 'Thus Brent was given, and Poldone with the adjacent territory.'

A similar story is recorded within the mid-14th century Latin history of Glastonbury Abbey, written by a certain John of Glastonbury about whom little if anything is known. Again, the story supposedly explains how the lands of Brent Knoll and Polden were granted to the abbey, yet the version contained in John of Glastonbury's *Chronica* differed in some details from the interpolation in the *De Antiquitate*. Not least of these was the statement that the mountains of Areynes to which Ider ap Nudd was sent were in North Wales – '*Nortwalliam in monte de Areynes*'. The *Chronica* also stated that Arthur's gifts of land to the monks included the territories of Brentmareis and Pouldon, which were later stolen by the pagan Saxons who, once converted to the Christian faith, restored them to the abbey.

In spite of the fact that both stories purported to relate to Glastonbury Abbey, they clearly seemed to be set in North Wales for in both versions Ider's investiture is given as taking place at Caerlleon (Chester). Furthermore, from his family name it appeared that Ider ap Nudd was the brother of Gwyn ap Nudd, the Lord of Annwn who St Collen had encountered on Ruabon Mountain above Glaestingaburh.[2] Traditionally the fight between Ider and the giants is located on Brent Knoll, a hill in Somerset, following the margin note in the *De Antiquitate* that says that the Mount named Ranae was now called Brentecnol, yet the *Chronica* explicitly states that the Monte de Areynes was in North Wales. It has been suggested that Mount Ranae means 'Mount of Frogs', which was rendered as Areynes (Mount of Spiders) because of a misreading of 'Mons

Aranearum' for 'Mons [A]Renarum', though neither of these forms appears.

There are many folk tales and legends attached to specific locations in the hills and mountains of old Gwynedd and Powys relating to Arthur's battles with various giants and hags. One in particular seemed to shed some light on the location of Ider's fight with the three giants, and that was Arthur's famous encounter with the giant Rhita Gawr, described as 'king of Gwynedd in the time of Arthur'.[3] Referred to briefly in Chapter 3, the battle between Arthur and Rhita took place on Aran Benllyn, or the 'Height of the Head of the Lake', the lake in question being Bala, also known as Penllyn. Arthur won the fight and, according to Geoffrey of Monmouth's *Historia*, he slew Rhita Gawr upon Aravius Mons.[4] In variants of the tale the fight is said to have taken place on Bwlch y Groes (the Pass of the Cross) between Mawddwy and Penllyn in Meirionedd. There the defeated Rhita was buried and even today local inhabitants point to Mynydd Aran Mawr (Great Aran Mountain) in Penllyn under Bwlch y Groes as the location of Bedd Rhita Gawr (the grave of Rhita Gawr). Like the Monte de Areynes referred to in the *Chronica* and the Ranae referred to in the *De Antiquitate*, Geoffrey of Monmouth's Aravius Mons would appear to be a Latinization of the original Welsh Mynydd Aran, the Aran Mountains in North Wales.

We now began to see the story in a new light. In Arthur's time access between Caerlleon (Chester) and North Wales was most likely to have been

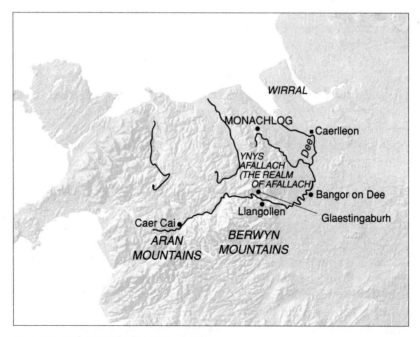

Map 27 Arthur and Glaestingaburh

along one of the old Roman roads. One such road from Chester went via Holt, through the Vale of Llangollen, continuing past Lake Bala and Caer Cai (where Arthur was fostered as a child) and eventually ran through a valley between Penaran and Aran Penllyn – namely, the Aran Mountains. Returning along this route Arthur would have passed through Glaestingaburh where he may well have given the abbey lands at Pouldon, for a Poulton does in fact exist within easy distance of Llangollen along the River Dee and was recorded within the 'Domesday Book' as part of the hundred of Broxton.

THE ABDUCTION OF GWENHWYFAR

We next turned our attention to the story of the abduction of Arthur's wife Gwenhwyfar by a certain Melwas. It is supposedly the earliest tradition to link Arthur with Glastonbury. The earliest complete version of this story is recorded by Caradoc of Llancarfan within his *Vita Gildae* (Life of Gildas) around 1135 and is also mentioned in later works and appears on an archivolt of Modena Cathedral in Italy, which predates Caradoc's account.

In his *Life of Gildas*, Caradoc tells us that Gildas arrived at 'Glastonia, at the time when King Melvas was reigning in the summer country'. Gildas was greatly welcomed by the Abbot of Glastonia and proceeded to teach the brethren and people the heavenly doctrine. We are also told that it was while he was in Glastonia Gildas wrote his history of the Kings of Britain. Caradoc then identifies Glastonia as Urbs Vitrea (the Glassy City), thereby establishing the erroneous tradition that Glastonia took its name from glass, and continues by telling the reader that Glastonia was of old called Ynisgutrin (Ynys Wydrin).[5] He resumes his account of the abduction of Gwenhwyfar by telling us that, while Gildas was resident at the abbey, Glastonia was besieged by the 'tyrant Arthur' and a large army because his wife Gwenhwyfar had been taken there when she had been carried off by the wicked King Melwas. Caradoc details the protection afforded by the invulnerable position, complete with fortifications of thickets, reed, river and marsh. Caradoc also calls Arthur 'the rebellious king' and explains how he had searched for Gwenhwyfar for a whole year until he learnt that she was at Glastonia. He had then roused the armies of the whole of Cornubia (Kernyw) and Dibneria (Dyfnaint) and prepared for war. The Abbot of Glastonia, 'attended by the clergy and Gildas the Wise, stepped in between the contending armies, and in a peaceable manner advised his king, Melvas, to restore the ravished lady'. Gwenhwyfar was restored to Arthur in peace and goodwill, and afterwards both Melwas and Arthur gave the Abbot of Glastonia many domains and subsequently both kings came to visit the 'temple of St Mary' to pray. The kings returned reconciled to one another and promised 'reverently to obey the most venerable abbot of Glastonia, and never to violate the most sacred place nor even the districts adjoining the chief's seat'.[6]

In order to have a fuller understanding of the story we sought out further variants of the tale, turning first to Chrétien de Troyes's Arthurian romance *Lancelot* in which Melwas is called Meleagant. The story is further romanticized and Chrétien offers some interesting information about the place to which Gwynhwyfar was taken: 'I assure you, my lords, that Meleagant, a tall, strapping knight who is the king of Gorres' son, has seized her [Gwynhwyfar] and taken her into the kingdrom from which no stranger returns, but is forced to stay in the land in servitude and exile.'[7] Chrétien further informs us that Meleagant defeated Cai in a wood and carried Gwenhwyfar off to his land called Goirre and that Lancelot went in search of her, eventually securing her freedom. In the earlier romance *Erec et Enide*, Chrétien referred to the same character but under a different name: 'With those I have mentioned came Maheloas, a great baron, lord of the Isle of glass.'[8]

We found that the tale of the abduction of Gwenhwyfar was also well known to the Welsh bards, those inheritors of the early British oral tradition, and their accounts of this event not only established the location of Glaestingaburh, but also provided further evidence regarding the three ancient realms of Ynys Prydein – Cymru, Alban and Lloegyr.

The bard who made the most frequent reference to Melwas was the Welsh poet Tudur Aled, a Franciscan monk who flourished around 1480 to 1520, and whose poems exalting Valle Crucis Abbey made the place much celebrated in his day.[9] Tudur spent much of his youth in the locality of Valle Crucis and wrote many poems concerning important people and places in and around the Vale of Llangollen, including Nanheudwy, the cantref in which Llangollen stands. Here he learnt of the traditions and stories associated with Melwas, and it is obvious from Tudur Aled's poetry that Melwas was a very important figure within local tradition, for he compares his presence to that of the stars. Within Tudur's poem entitled *Edeirnion* we found what we felt to be the most important reference to Melwas from any source, because it clearly defined the boundaries to the kingdom over which Melwas ruled.[10] Edeirnion, which takes its name from one of the sons of Cunedda, is an area neighbouring Llangollen along the River Dee and in his poem Tudur relates that Melwas was the ruler of two Maelors, and from south of Maelor to Tren and from Tren as far as the Hafren.

As explained earlier, the two Maelors comprised Maelor Saesneg (Saxon Maelor) and Maelor Gymraeg (Welsh Maelor) and originally ran from Llangollen to Chester, being made up of the lands around the middle reaches of the River Dee. Tren was a town on the River Roden, a tributary of the Hafren (Severn),[11] which it joins near Viroconium (Wroxeter/Caer Efrog). The 15th-century poet Guto'r Glyn, the bard of Valle Crucis Abbey, also referred to Melwas within the context of Maelor.[12] Our research into the name Maelor underlined Melwas's connection with this area for we learnt that it means 'the territory belonging to Mael',[13] and Melwas's name originally took the form Maelguas and/or Mailguas, from *Mael, a guass*,[14] which suggested that the Maelor over which he ruled was actually named after Melwas.

We discovered further material referring to Melwas and the abduction of Gwenhwyfar in a bardic poem contained in *The Myvyrian Archaiology* (1870), whose editors gave the poem the title *A Conversation Between Arthur and His Second Wife Gwenhwyfar*. This text survives in two manuscripts – one from Wynnstay Hall on the eastern side of Ruabon

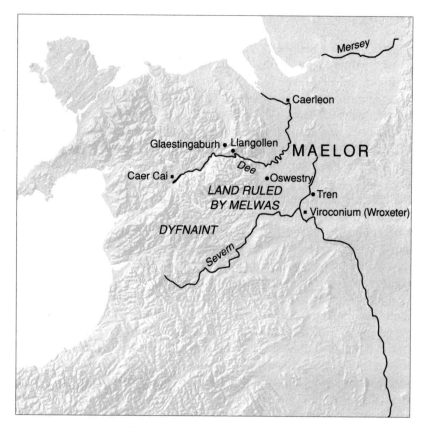

Map 28 The realm of Melwas

Mountain, the other from the Llanstephan manuscripts[15] – and comparisons between the two have established that both are copies of a much older original from around 1150 or earlier.[16] In a reference to Gwenhwyfar as 'the girl carried off by Melwas, a prince from Alban', we again found confirmation of the area ruled by Melwas, for, as previously explained, Alban was the Welsh name given to the region of Ynys Prydein corresponding to the modern counties of Cheshire and northern Powys. Although fragmentary, the text tells us that during a feast an altercation took place between Cai and Melwas 'of Ynys Wydrin', followed by a conversation that appears to be between Melwas, Cai and Gwenhwyfar in which boasts were made and refuted. During these exchanges Melwas was asked where he had seen Gwenhwyfar before, to which he replied that he had seen her in a court in the land of Dyfneint – the implication being that Melwas had had a previous liaison with Gwenhwyfar and this was his reason for adbucting her. Long confused with Devon, the Dyfnaint connected to the Arthurian tradition is an area around Lake Vyrnwy, bordering the original realm of Kernyw, and according to one of the manuscripts the feast described in the poem takes place at the court of Geraint, son of Erbin and Prince of Dyfnaint, who was Arthur's first cousin.[17] The inclusion of Arthur's foster brother Cai in the poem interested us too because he is associated with Caer Cai, also known as Caer Cynyr (Cynyr being Cai's father), which is located near Lake Bala , and it is from Bala that the River Dee flows down through the Edeirnion valley, passing Corwen and Llangollen on its way to Chester and the sea.

A reference found in two poems attributed to the bard Dafydd ap Gwilym (14th century) sheds more light on the location of Gwenhwyfar's abduction: 'A window like this ... through which Melwas came at Caerlleon, from great love, without fear... near the house of the giant Ogrfan's daughter [Gwenhwyfar].'[18] The Caerlleon referred to is Chester, 20 miles down the River Dee from Llangollen, site of Arthur's coronation and one of the most important cities in Dark Age Britain. The house of the giant Ogrfan, Gwenhwyfar's father, can be identified with two possible locations. Caer Ogrfan (the Fortress/Stronghold of Ogrfan) was the name of an impressive hillfort known today as Old Oswestry, situated about a mile north of Oswestry on the Shropshire–Wales border. Thomas Pennant recorded it as Caer Ogyrfan in 1773 and several other references regarding the site exist.[19] Another Caer Ogrfan is also recorded on the border between Wales and Shropshire, this being Knucklas Castle near Knighton. A local tradition holds that it was here that Arthur married Gwenhwyfar, and in some texts Knucklas Castle is also called Castell Pendragon. Both place names locate the otherwise legendary figure of Ogrfan within ten miles of Glaestingaburh and within easy reach of

Chester. The name of his daughter is remembered in the locality too, for in a field on the banks of the River Dee near Llangollen is the base of an old stone cross. Named Croes Gwenhwyfar (Guinevere's Cross),[20] the cross is the only known site to bear her name, although it is recorded that Gwenhwyfar was buried at Glastonia, the nearby abbey of Glaestingaburh.

It was the work of a bard with connections to Valle Crucis Abbey, Dafydd ap Edmund,[21] that next caught our attention, for it added a new dimension to the story of Gwenhwyfar's abduction: 'Melwas, the thief that by magic and enchantment took a girl to the end of the world: to the green wood that deceiver went.' At first glance this seemed to be a semi-legendary account of the event, with the reference to the 'end of the world' simply added as a flourish to the story. A closer examination of the original Welsh text convinced us otherwise. It stated: *'Aeth a bun i eitha' byd: I'r coed ir ai'r hocedydd.'*[22]

Eitha' byd translates literally as 'the extremity of the world' and in the vicinity of Glaestingaburh is an area known as World's End. It is situated at the head of the Eglwyseg valley in which sits Valle Crucis Abbey, and the river that flows off the eastern side of this tract of high ground is called Afon Eitha (the River at the Extremity of the World), which reinforces the link between the poem and this particular part of the landscape. Welsh poets frequently use puns or word-plays within their work, often in reference to place names. The 'green wood' of Dafydd ap Edmund's poem is *coed ir* in the original Welsh – *ir* is an Old Welsh word for 'green', but it can also mean 'fresh'. A modern Welsh rendering of 'green' or 'fresh' wood is Coed Glas and a site so named exists opposite World's End. In the same area is a cliff known by the name Craig y Forwyn (the Rock/Cliff of the Maidens). These places are all within the heartland of Maelor, part of the kingdom ascribed to Melwas, and appear to be linked through a play on words with the events related in the abduction of Gwenhwyfar in a manuscript by David Johns dated 1587. Referring to 'the sleep of Melwas in the green cloak', Johns describes Melwas as being 'in a cloak of the same colour as the leaves, waiting for Gwenhwyfar and her hand maidens on may day. They had come to seek birch to welcome the summer. This story says that he went away from her for a time. He was a man of Scotland, one of the Britons and a Prince... there.'[23] Or are the place names themselves remembrances of the event?

A composite version of the story of Gwenhwyfar's abduction was given by Lewis Morris in 1875: ' Arthur left her at home, and she having a former intimacy with Melwas, a Prince of North Britain, they continued it so that she with her maids of honour went to the wood a-Maying, where Melwas was to lie in wait for her among the bushes with a suit of clothes on him made of green leaves of trees. When the queen and her maids came to the place appointed, Melwas started up and carried the queen away in his arms to his companions; and all the maids of honour ran away in fright, taking him to be a satyr, or wild man of the wood.'[24]

The above are virtually all we are left with from Welsh, Latin and French sources regarding the story of the abduction of Gwenhwyfar by Melwas. The latter is a potentially confusing figure, however. Although we had established that the kingdom of Melwas was clearly located in North Wales, he has assumed a number of other identities. For example, in the work of Geoffrey of Monmouth he appears under a number of variant names, including Melga, who is said to be king of the Picts, and Guanius, said to be king of the Huns. These two figures first occur in Geoffrey's *Historia* in the story of St Ursula, in which they abuduct her and her companions in what could be a possible parallel to the Gwenhwyfar abduction. The two kings are also said to lead expeditions of Picts and Scots from Ireland. In the Welsh versions of the *Historia* they are called Gwynwas and Melwas, and they are also recorded in the list of princes attending Arthur's special coronation, on which occasion they are named Malvasius and Gunvasius and titled respectively King of Iceland and King of Orc (said to be the Orkneys). In fact, when we take everything into account we find that Melwas is variously identified as king of the Picts, king of the Huns, King of Iceland, King of the Orkneys, a prince of North Britain, a prince in Alban and a man of Scotland, who is claimed to rule over Glastonbury in Somerset where he takes the abudcted Gwenhwyfar. Melwas is also attributed with leading raiding parties of Picts and Scots from Ireland and yet attends the coronation of Arthur, whose lands he raids and whose life he either abducts by force or runs away with. How did the figure we had identified as Melwas or Maelor correlate with his chameleonlike character?

It was here that our new map of Arthurian Britain came to our aid for we knew that following the appearance of Geoffrey of Monmouth's *Historia* the region of northeast Wales known as Alban had been mistakenly identified as Scotland. Therefore the naming of Melwas as King of Alban simply meant that he ruled over that area of Ynys Prydein, which corresponds to the modern counties of northern Powys and Cheshire. His naming as 'a man of Scotland' was also straightforward for Cunedda had captured this northern region of Ynys Prydein from the Scotti. Similarly, many Welsh references to Ysgotland refer to those areas of Wales that had for some time been, and in some cases still were, the land of the Scotti. Likewise, there were enclaves of Picts and Saxons in this region of North Wales, which could account for the variants of Melwas being named as king of the Picts. Finally, the naming of Melwas as a prince in North Britain also places him in North Wales, for as we explained earlier the term Y Gogledd of the texts referred to the north of Ynys Prydein – Gogledd Cymri is still used to describe North Wales.

The confusion surrounding the figure of Melwas had been heightened by Caradoc's reference to him as having reigned in 'the summer country' (Latin *aestiva regio*), which has been interpreted to mean Somerset (Gwald yr Haf in Welsh). In fact the summer country (Welsh *hafod*) played an important part in the way of life of the early Welsh for it was the common practice of the princes and nobles to have both a winter and a summer residence. The winter residence or *maerdref* was a permanent settlement where the court was situated and the main agricultural activity took place. The summer residence or *hafod* was located in the highest areas of the district, and the land of the summer pasture. The annual migration of the court, retainers, livestock and possessions from the lowland regions to the upland areas was part of the traditional way of life, and also explains in

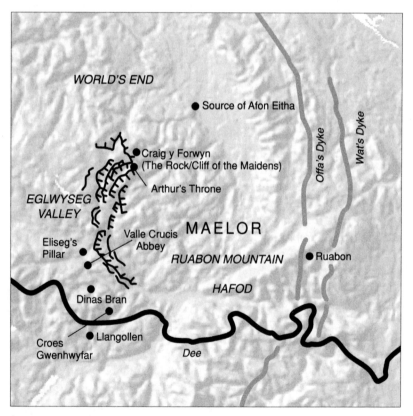

Map 29 *The abduction of Gwenhwyfar*

part how the Welsh princes remained independent for so long.[25] In fact the high ground around World's End and the western side of Ruabon Mountain – the area also known as Glas[yn]fre or Ynys Afallach – was also known as Hafod (the Summer Lands) and the township of Hafod exists to this day upon Ruabon Mountain. Could *hafod* have been the original Welsh word that Caradoc of Llancarfan rendered as *aestiva regio*?

The semi-legendary story of Gwenhwyfar's abduction now began to take on a more historical quality. We felt we could even trace it on the map. The majority of the manuscripts relating to the original tale were either connected to the Abbey of Valle Crucis or written by Welsh bards associated with it and, as we had earlier established that Glaestingaburh was located in the vicinity of Llangollen and Valle Crucis, a coherent story began to emerge as follows. Gwenhwyfar was abducted by Melwas, Lord of Alban, who took her to the *hafod* on Eitha' byd, the natural fortress at the 'extremity of the world' at the head of the Eglwyseg valley above Glaestingaburh. Melwas kept Gwenhwyfar there for a year, at which time Arthur eventually received word of her whereabouts. Arthur raised an army in Kernyw and, en route to Maelor, the kingdom of Melwas, he was joined by the men of Dyfnaint, who were probably led by his cousin Geraint, son of Erbin. They proceeded past Lake Bala, in all likelihood picking up reinforcements from Arthur's foster brother Cai, and continued along the Dee, passing through the Edeirnion before arriving in the Eglwyseg valley. Once there the Abbot of Glaestingaburh and Gildas the Wise attempted to prevent bloodshed by mediating between the two warlords. As Arthur had already had problems with war bands of Scotti from this area led by Gildas's brothers, he agreed to a truce. Gwenhwyfar was returned to her husband and both Melwas and Arthur rewarded the Abbot of Glastonia with grants of land and privileges.

ST GILDAS

Caradoc of Llancarfan's *Life of St Gildas* (c.1140) tells us that St Gildas was the historian of the Britons and spent many years in Glastonia before passing out of this life in the year 512. Our research into Caradoc's account of the abduction of Gwenhwyfar had convinced us that St Gildas was connected with Glaestingaburh and the Eglwyseg valley, yet the confusion surrounding the true identity of Glastonia had led to the saint long being linked with Glastonbury, a link reinforced by an interpolation within William of Malmesbury's *De Antiquitate* to the effect that Gildas was buried in front of the altar in the Old Church.[26] Caradoc's *Life of St Gildas* was also the main source for the more detailed account of the saint's life that appears within John of Glastonbury's *Chronica*, a history of Glastonbury containing new material that reinforced Gildas's association with this Somerset town.[27] The *Chronica* tells us that Gildas was the son of a King of Scocie named Kau. One of the 23 brothers who were warlike soldiers, he was the most outstanding preacher in the whole Kingdom of Britannia. John of Glastonbury also relates how Gildas's elder brother Hueil plagued Arthur from Scocia, burning villages and carrying off many spoils, until Arthur pursued him and caused his death. When news of his brother's death reached Gildas he wept with grief and immediately returned to Britannia. Arthur then came to Gildas with a great host and Gildas granted him pardon – although, as explained in Chapter 2, Gildas is said to have thrown his histories regarding Arthur into the sea in a pique of anger over his brother's death. The *Chronica* relates Gildas's further adventures and his arrival in Glastonia where he was received with the appropriate honours. While there he wrote his *Historias de Regibus Britanniae* (History of the Kings of Britain).[28] He then decided to lead a hermit's life and so built a church dedicated to the Holy Trinity, which the *Chronica* informs us is now called the Chapel Adventurous. Eventually Gildas became ill and knowing that his death was near he called for the Abbot of Glastonia and asked that after his death his body should be taken to the monastery and there be buried, a request that was satisfied.

As we had already established that the abduction of Gwenhwyfar recorded by Caradoc of Llancarfan took place in the Vale of Llangollen and surrounding area, we decided to look for more substantial evidence of Gildas's presence in this region. Putting to one side the account of Gildas's life contained within John of Glastonbury's *Chronica* we turned our attention to two other texts recounting the life of the saint: a life of Gildas written by a monk in Brittany,[29] and the *Life of St Gildas* attributed to Caradoc of Llancarfan.[30] We were immediately struck by the apparent confusion surrounding the origins of Gildas. In the 'life' from Brittany Gildas is said to have been born in the district of Arecluta and to be the son of Caunus (Caw). Gildas is given four brothers including Cuillus (Huail), an active warrior who succeeds to the kingdom upon his father's death, and Mailocus (Maelog/Meilig), who was consecrated to sacred literature and retired to Llowes in Elfael (an area of southern Powys in Radnorshire), where he built a monastery and eventually died.[31] His remaining brothers – Egreas (Eugrad) and Alleccus – and his sister Peteova (Peithien) retired to a remote place where they built oratories near to each other. The particular foundations attributed to these children of Caw are known to be the parishes of Llaneugrad and Llanallgo in Twrcelyn, an area of land in northeast Anglesey in the neighbourhood of Llancadog (the Monastery of

Cadog).[32] According to Caradoc's *Life of Gildas*, the saint was one of the 24 sons of Nau, King of Scotia, who directed Gildas into the study of literature. It also told us that Gildas's brothers were constantly rising up against Arthur, refusing to accept him as their overlord, and the brother named Hueil subsequently died at Arthur's hand in Ruthin. Caradoc then related Gildas's arrival in Glastonia, the abduction of Gwenhwyfar by Melwas and the other details that John of Glastonbury had inserted into his own chronicle. (The remaining details from the 'lives of Gildas' have been the subject of much debate, in particular concerning the works ascribed to Gildas and the apparent merging of two texts of differing dates.)

We then looked into the names of these people and places, consulting a number of texts to see what they could tell us about the family of Gildas and the locations associated with them. The only specific geographic references we could find to Caw, the father of Gildas, came from two sources. First, the Llanstephan manuscripts, which talk of the children of Caw o Dwrcelyn, Lord of Cwm Cowlwyd, who in the time of Arthur resided in the region known as the Edeirnion.[33] Second, the chronicle of Elis Gruffydd (c.1530), which states that 'Caw of Prydain was a chieftain who ruled over the Edeirnion'. The Edeirnion lay to the south of the Kingdom of Dogfeiling, on both sides of the River Dee in the area around Corwen, and extended as far as the Berwyn Mountains, while Dwrcelyn (variant Twrcelyn) is an area of Anglesey.[34] We also noted that Giraldus Cambrensis referred to Gildas's brother Hueil as *'princeps Albaniae'* (a prince of Alban), and as the texts informed us that Hueil inherited his father's Kingdom of Edeirnion this gave us further proof that the name Alban had once applied to northern Powys.

From the *Life of St Cadog* we learnt that when Cadog was returning from a pilgrimage to Albania, commonly called Scocia, he had halted this side of Mons Bannauc (Mynydd Bannog) and resided there seven years to convert the population. While he was building his monastery Cadog unearthed an enormous collarbone and an angel told Cadog that it was the collarbone of Cawr (a giant), who would be raised from the dead to do the digging for him for as long as he lived. These events apparently came to pass and the giant begged Cadog to save him from returning to hell. Cawr then told Cadog that his name was Cau Pritdin (Caw of Prydein) and recited how he had plundered the nearby coasts with his robbers and how eventually the local king pursued him, destroying both him and his army.

If we were to translate these events from St Cadog's life onto a modern map the goal of his pilgrimage would be located in northern Powys, anciently known as Albania or Scocia. As for the mountain referred to as Mynydd Bannog, this was a major landmark in Y Berfeddwlad (the Middle

Country or Midlands) and a natural point of reference. It is a geographical feature mentioned in several texts,[35] often linked with a magical pair of oxen, the Ychain Bannog.[36] An early geographical reference to Mynydd Bannog is found in *Canu Llywarch*. Llywarch Hen was a bard, first cousin of Urien Rheged and the subject of a lost saga of Powys. There is a body of poetry remaining that is attributed to him. The information regarding Mynnydd Bannog gleaned from this poetry is important as almost all references place him and his family in the area of Penllyn, Llangollen and northern Powys, so Bannog was a location familiar to him. He talks of Llanfawr (Lanfor) beyond Bannawg, where the River Clwyd meets the River Clywedog, before going on in the next stanza to talk of the River Dee.[37] The rivers Clwyd and Clywedog are still known by these names and both have their source on the high ground known by the name of Craig Bron Bannog that dominates the skyline to the north of the Edeirnion valley, known to be the kingdom of Caw, Gildas's father. *Bannog* means 'horned' and the Clwyd has its source between the double-peaked summit that gives Craig Bron Bannog its name.[38] The Lanfor mentioned in the text is on the River Dee near Lake Bala. Although the reference to Bannog Mountain places the above events from the life of St Cadog in an identifiable location in North Wales, the confusion surrounding the name Alban has for decades led scholars to try to place this mountain in Scotland. Similarly, the River Clwyd has often been confused with the River Clyde in Scotland because of the resemblance between the names of Clwyd and Clyde.[39] As a result Gildas's birthplace of Arecluta has been identified as Alclud on Clydeside, whereas Arecluta means 'Clywdside' and is a reference to the Vale of Clwyd.

So it was that, whilst returning from a pilgrimage to Alban, Cadog arrived in the Edeirnion, the land of Caw, halting this side (south) of Mons Bannauc (Mynydd Bannog). When Caw told Cadog how he had plundered the nearby coasts with his robbers and how eventually the local king had pursued him, destroying him and his army, he was relating his raids along the North Wales coast, in all probability launched from his other stronghold of Dwrcelyn in Anglesey. Furthermore, when Hueil the Prince of Alban inherited his father's kingdom he inherited the region of Edeirnion, from where he was recorded as 'often swooping from Scotia', harassing Arthur until the latter eventually killed him.

Professor Lloyd quite rightly points out that both the severity of Gildas's tyrade against the rulers of Britannia (Wales) and the fact that he actually addressed the five kings concerned by name suggests that he could not have been dwelling in the same land and must have written it at a safe distance, probably beyond Chester. Knowing that the sons of Caw refused to accept Arthur as their overlord, and having established that the

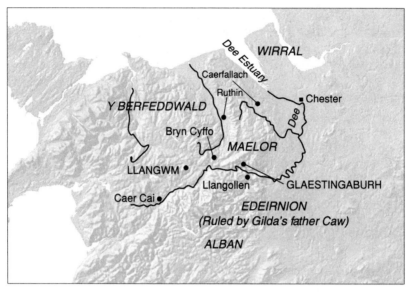

Map 30 The family of St Gildas

geographic distribution of Gildas's family was within Powys (Alban) and other regions of northeast Wales, it is likely that Gildas was writing from within his family's stronghold in northern Powys and the Edernion. Evidence to support this comes from the sites connected with Gildas's two sons, Gwynnog and Noethon. Gwynnog is commemorated at Llanwnnog, a parish in Montgomeryshire that adjoins Penstrowed, whose patron is Gwrhei, the brother of Gildas,[40] while both Gwynnog and Noethon are recorded as local saints at Llangwn Dinmael in Denbighshire, near the Edernion. Furthermore, the neighbouring area of Maelor along the River Dee was under the control of another Prince of Alban, Melwas, who had also had a confrontation with Arthur. From this we concluded that when Gildas came to Glastonia (Glaestingaburh) he was in fact coming home, back to the land of his birth to pass his final days within the bosom and protection of his own family before being laid to rest in the hallowed ground of Glaestingaburh Abbey. But one question remained: why did Gildas intervene between Melwas and Arthur? He was certainly no friend of Arthur and in fact had every reason to wish him ill. Could the answer lie in the fact that Gildas had a brother named Mailocus/Maelog, otherwise known as Melwas?

As we continued our research into the legendary lore of Arthur and Avalon we chanced upon an ancient text that was to send us off in an entirely new direction. We were aware that Glastonbury had long claimed to be associated with St Joseph of Arimathea and the Holy Grail, but we had never considered this to be anything more than legend because of medieval Glastonbury's reputation for chicanery, in particular the spurious exhumation of Arthur. But one sentence that we came across in an obscure Welsh variant of the story of the Holy Grail caused us to radically reassess this view: 'St Joseph of Arimathea was buried in the monastery of Glas in Alban.'

CHAPTER THIRTEEN

THE GRAIL LAND

THE STORY of the Holy Grail and how it came to be in the possession of Joseph of Arimathea was first related in Robert de Boron's French romance *Joseph d'Arimathie*, compiled some time between 1180 and 1199, in which the Grail is described as the cup used by Jesus at the Last Supper. It is believed that Robert made use of material from the Apocryphal Gospels to bring the narrative to a point where St Joseph and his followers set out to dwell in far-off lands. (The Apocryphal Gospels were Gospels which, for various reasons, were omitted from the final canon of the Bible when it was established in the fourth century.) According to the story, Joseph died in the land where he had been born,[1] but before dying he gave guardianship of the Grail to Hebron (Bron), husband of his sister Enygeus (Eurgain), who then proceeded westward with the Grail and finally settled in a place whose identity is obscure. Hebron's son Alain continued westward, although all we are told is that he would have an heir who would be the guardian of the sacred vessel. Apparently Robert de Boron planned a cycle of three romances, the second of which was Merlin and the third of which told how the Grail came to Britain, but unfortunately the cycle was never completed.

A few years later the story of Joseph and the Holy Grail was further elaborated in *L'Estoire del Saint Graal*, the first volume of the Vulgate Cycle of Arthurian romances. Written between 1205 and 1216 by monks of the

Cistercian Order, *L'Estoire del Saint Graal* presented Lancelot as the protagonist and his son Galahad, the Grail Knight. It also clarified Robert de Boron's oblique references to far-off lands by informing us that St Joseph and his followers landed in Norgales (North Wales), bringing with them the Holy Grail, and that on his arrival St Joseph was imprisoned by Crudel, a tyrannical king of North Wales. This last detail was to be recorded in nearly every version of the story from the Vulgate Cycle onwards, as evidenced in Richard Pynson's verse *Lyfe of Joseph of Armathia*, published in 1520:

> They fortuned to a countre of a tyraunt kene,
>   Called wales, there was a kyng that tyme;
> They landed all, as the boke telleth, on an ester euyn,
> xxxi yere after the passyon, about the houre of nyne.[2]

L'Estoire del Saint Graal also relates that following his release from imprisonment by a certain Evalach (Afallach), St Joseph and his party spent 15 years wandering through various parts of Britain before eventually returning to Castle Galafort where both Joseph and his son Josephes died. The guardianship of the Grail was handed by Josephes to Alain, son of Bron (Hebron), who continued to Terre Foraine where he built the Castle of Corbenic to house the Grail. We are told that both the Castle of Corbenic and the Grail remained in the possession of his lineage until the time of Arthur.

From the evidence provided by texts such as *L'Estoire del Saint Graal* it was clear that at the beginning of the 13th century there existed a coherent story regarding the arrival in Britain of Joseph of Arimathea and the Holy Grail, the principal elements of which are in the main reiterated in all the source texts. It was also clear that the story was set in North Wales. Yet the frequently voiced presumption that the legend of St Joseph of Arimathea had simply been invented as a piece of Glastonbury propaganda led Professor R.S. Loomis to comment in 1963 that the 'array of evidence which has impressed not only credulous enthusiasts but also a few highly respected scholars ... [has] ... led them to believe that the early history of the Grail originated as a piece of Glastonbury propaganda, deliberately fabricated to enhance the prestige and increase the revenues of the holy house of Avalon, in much the same way as the exhumation of the skeletons of Arthur and Guinevere was planned and carried out for similar ends'.[3] Professor Loomis adds that the underpinning of this theory collapses when tested, for despite the legend being attached to Glastonbury the abbey's list of relics contained no supposed dish or chalice in any way associated with the Last Supper or the Passion of Christ.

In view of Glastonbury's reputation for forgery, the mere fact that the abbey never purported to own such a relic alone speaks volumes. Professor Loomis also points out that the author of the Grail romance *Perlesvaus* professed to have used as his source a book from 'the holy house of Avalon': 'The Latin from whence this history was drawn into romance was taken in the Isle [Realm] of Avalon, in the holy house of religion that standeth at the head of the Moors Adventurous.'[4] If this is the case, how did the story of Joseph of Arimathea become so inextricably associated with Glastonbury in Somerset?

ST JOSEPH OF ARIMATHEA
AND THE GLASTONBURY LEGEND

The legend of St Joseph of Arimathea was first linked to Glastonbury in the 13th century when an anonymous monk at Glastonbury Abbey added a marginal note regarding Joseph's arrival in Britain to William of Malmesbury's *De Antiquitate*. The exact date of this interpolation is obscure, although dates around the mid-13th century have been suggested,[5] thereby placing it some decades after the story of Joseph and the Grail related in *L'Estoire del Saint Graal*. In fact the legend of Joseph of Arimathea as it is popularly known today corresponds closely in many respects to this interpolated story. According to the latter, Joseph arrived in Britain with 11 followers 63 years after the incarnation of the Lord, 15 since the Assumption of the Blessed Virgin Mary. The local king, a pagan, gave them a certain island called Ynys Witrin that lay on the edges of his kingdom and was surrounded by forest and marsh. Subsequently two other pagan kings granted them 12 portions of land. The 12 saints were then visited in a vision by the angel Gabriel who instructed them to build a church in honour of the Virgin Mary, which they duly built according to the angel's directions, completing it in the 31st year after the Passion of our Lord. As the church was the first one in the kingdom, Christ distinguished it by dedicating it himself in his mother's name. The saints continued to dwell in the chapel for many years, eventually ending their days in that blessed spot, after which Ynys Witrin reverted to its previously wild state. A note to the margin of the surviving *De Antiquitate* records that Joseph of Arimathea was accompanied by his son Josephes on this journey and further that St Joseph died in Britain, citing the Grail legend as its source.

It is widely acknowledged that only the core of the *De Antiquitate* is the original work of William of Malmesbury and that the interpolations, including the above story of Joseph of Arimathea, were added in the 100 or so years after it was written. Close study of the text has, however, led scholars to regard the reference to 12 disciples of Saints Philip and James arriving in Britain in the 63rd year of Our Lord's Incarnation and their being given 12 portions of land by three pagan kings to be William of Malmesbury's own work, although William added the comment that the story was a matter of opinion.

The Glastonbury legend of Joseph of Arimathea was next taken up by John of Tinmouth, who, within his 14th-century *Life of St Patrick,* gave an identity to the previously anonymous pagan king who had granted Ynys Witrin to Joseph and his followers by naming him as Arviragus. The story was subsequently reiterated by a monk of Malmesbury who added to it that Joseph of Arimathea had been laid to rest in Glastonbury, with two phials full of the blood and sweat of Christ. Yet another interpolation within *De Antiquitate* identified the remaining two unnamed pagan kings as Marius and Coillus, adding that Coillus had a son named Lucius, the first Christian king of Britain. However, when we examined what the sources had to say about these kings it was clear that they had no connection with Glastonbury. Arviragus, Marius, Coillus and Lucius appear in Geoffrey of Monmouth's *Historia* and the Welsh tradition recorded in the *Brut* gives their names as Gweirydd, Meurig, Coel and Lles. The latter tradition has been dismissed on the grounds that the names were taken from the *Historia*, yet as we have already shown Geoffrey was translating a Welsh text. Arviragus is recorded as a British chief who revolted against Rome in the reign of the Emperor Domitian (AD 81–96) and Juvenal further makes its clear that he was a thorn in the side of the Roman forces.[6] According to the Welsh *Brut* Caer Loyw (Chester) was founded in honour of British King Gweirydd (Arviragus)[7] by Emperor Claudius and Geoffrey of Monmouth (or Geoffrey's original source) relates that Caer Loyw is where Arviragus was buried, while tradition states that it was Arviragus's successor, his son Marius, who built the walls of Chester.[8] Robert Chester records Arviragus as the King of Venedotia (Gwynedd) and thereby relates the only tradition to place Arviragus in an exact geographical setting.[9] The lands granted to St Joseph of Arimathea by Arviragus and Marius would therefore have been in this region and not in Somerset, thus supporting the evidence of the *Vera Historia.*

It was also in the 14th century that John of Glastonbury gave the first full account of the Glastonbury legend within the pages of his *Chronica*,[10] based upon the fragmentary material of William of Malmesbury's *De Antiquitate* and numerous other sources to which he seems to have applied a fertile imagination. When John wrote his account he not only had available to him the Glastonbury records but also what he described in his own words as 'the book which is called The Holy Grail'. In the main, the story of Joseph of Arimathea presented within John's chronicle agrees with other known texts, including *L'Estoire del Saint Graal*, from which he had taken extracts while omitting certain points. He also made a number of additions, including the assertion that St Joseph was *paranymphos* (guardian) to the Virgin Mary.[11] John also professed to quote from a work entitled *De Sancto Joseph ab Arimathea* by Emperor Theodosius (379–395).[12]

The story of Joseph of Arimathea that appeared in John of Glastonbury's *Chronica* tells us that St Philip sent to Britain 12 of his disciples, over whom he had set St Joseph and his son Josephes. More than 600 followers accompanied them, all men and women who had taken a vow to abstain from their spouses until they reached the land appointed to them. Only 150 kept their oath and these, at the Lord's command, crossed the sea with St Joseph and Josephes, making landfall in Britain on the morning of Easter Eve. When the remainder of his followers repented the Lord sent them a ship constructed by King Solomon and, accompanied by Nasciens, a duke from Medorum who had been baptized by Joseph in the city of Saraz, they thus rejoined their companions. Mordrain, the King of Saraz who had been baptized by St Joseph along with Nasciens, later received a vision of the Lord within which he was shown the wounds of the Crucifixion. Feeling great sympathy for the figure before him, Mordrain asked who had committed such a thing and the Lord replied: 'The faithless King of Nortwallie [North Wales] has done these things to me.' Adding that this king had also imprisoned Joseph and his companions, the Lord directed Mordrain to hasten to North Wales to avenge his servants and free them from their chains. Mordrain raised an army and, guided by God, journeyed to North Wales, where, upon his arrival, he commanded the Welsh king to release God's servants. The king refused, ordering Mordrain to leave his land without delay, at which Mordrain and Nasciens waged war against the Welsh, eventually securing the release of Joseph and his companions.

St Joseph, Josephes and ten companions subsequently travelled through Britannia preaching the faith of Christ.[13] They eventually came to King Arviragus who, although refusing to relinquish his ancestral traditions, granted the 12 an island on the edge of his kingdom, surrounded by forests, thickets and swamps, which the inhabitants called Ynswytryn. John of Glastonbury informs us that the twelvefold band of men entered Avallonia (Avalon) with Joseph of Arimathea as their chief, accompanied by his son Josephes. He then identifies Glastonbury with Avalon by adding that the right to Glastonia is held by these original 12.

John continues with an account of the vision in which the Archangel Gabriel directed the 12 to build a church in honour of the Holy Mother of God, the ever virgin Mary. He then tells us that they constructed a chapel of wattles, the first church in the land, in the 31st year after the Lord's

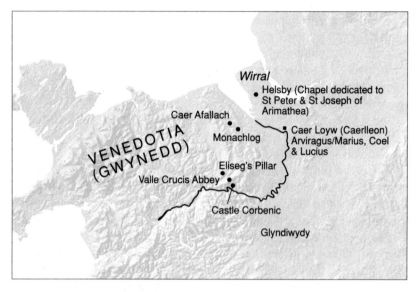

Map 31 St Joseph's arrival in Britain

Passion and 15 years after the Assumption of the glorious Virgin, the year of their arrival. The chapel was adorned with the manifold power of God, and the Son of God distinguished it by dedicating it in his own presence in honour of his mother. The twelve saints were subsequently granted a hide of land each by Marius, son of Arviragus, and Coillus, son of Marius, and the 12 hides took their name from these grants. After several years the saints passed away and St Joseph was buried next to the oratory, to which John adds the enigmatic detail that Joseph was buried 'on a two-forked line'. The sacred site then reverted to being a den of wild beasts, until it would please the Virgin to restore it to the memory of the faithful.

The *Chronica* also includes a genealogy of Arthur that uses the same sequence as the pedigree of Galahad found in *L'Estoire del Saint Graal*. The genealogy begins with Helaius nepos Joseph[14] and continues from father to son through Josue, Aminadab and Castellors to Manael who fathered Lambord and Urlard. Lambord had a son who fathered Ygernam (Eigyr), with whom Uthyr Pendragon fathered the noble and famous King Arthur. John continues with another genealogy showing a line of descent from Petrus (Peter), cousin of Joseph of Arimathea, through to Loth, who takes as his wife Arthur's sister with whom he fathered Walwanum (Gawain) and three other sons.[15] Later John again returns to the story of St Joseph of Arimathea by introducing the strange prophecy of Melchinus (Melkin), the use of which was to provide the means for establishing the ecclesiastical precedence of the British Church.

MELKIN, THE BARD OF AVALON

The strange prophecy of Melkin concerning the burial place of St Joseph of Arimathea in the Island/Realm of Avalon first comes to light in John of Glastonbury's *Chronica*. The prophecy transforms the Grail into a dignified and honourable relic, describing it as two cruets that contained the blood and sweat of Jesus, thus appearing to be the root of the tradition of the two cruets. The Latin of the original also has certain archaic oddities within it, leading one commentator to describe it as 'a queer piece of semi-poetical prose, intended to mystify and hardly capable of translation into English'.[16] This – along with the fact that it states that Joseph was buried in a pagan cemetery and other contradictory elements – prompted the Glastonbury scholar Geoffrey Ashe to comment: 'The prophecy looks as if it might well embody something handed down from Celtic era by way of Wales.'[17] Indeed there is in existence a note putting forward a very strong case for the authenticity of Melkin's prophecy and among the reasons given is that it was from a partially interpolated and misunderstood Welsh model.[18]

Avalon's island [realm], with avidity
Claiming the death of pagans,
More than all in the world beside,
For the entombment of them all,
Honoured by chanting spheres of prophecy:
And for all time to come
Adorned shall it be
By them that praise the Highest.
Abbadare, mighty in Saphat,
Noblest of pagans,
With countless thousands
There had fallen on sleep.
Amid these Joseph in marble,
Of Arimathea by name,
Hath found perpetual sleep:
And he lies on a two-forked line
Next the south quarter of an oratory
Fashioned of wattles
For the adoring of a mighty Virgin
By the aforesaid sphere-betokened
Dwellers in that place, thirteen in all.
For Joseph hath with him
In his sarcophagus

Two cruets, white and silver,
Filled with blood and sweat
Of the Prophet Jesus.
When his sarcophagus
Shall be found entire, intact,
In time to come, it shall be seen
And shall be open unto all the world:
Thenceforth nor water nor the dew of heaven
Shall fail the dwellers in that ancient isle [realm].
For a long while before
The day of judgement in Josaphat
Open shall these things be
And declared to living men.[19]

Melkin is often described as an enigmatic figure yet his works appear to have been held in very high regard by scholars of the past, for John Bale wrote of him: 'Melkin of Avalon, a British prophet. Some call him Mevin ... Capgrave, Hardyng and Leland count him among the stars of British antiquity.'[20]

The first surviving mention of Melkin outside the Glastonbury corpus is to be found in John Hardyng's *Chronicle of English History*,[21] in which Melkin is referred to as 'Mewynus, The Cronycler in Britayne tonge full fyne'.[22] Written in the mid-15th century, Hardyng's English verse *Chronicle* covers the history of Britain from Albion through to the time of composition and was used as a source by both Malory and Spenser. Hardyng was an exception to those medieval chroniclers who, when writing of the time of Arthur, simply followed the path laid down by Geoffrey of Monmouth and relied very little upon the material of the romances. He writes of Joseph of Arimathea bringing Christianity to Britain and, citing Melkin as his source, relates that Joseph of Arimathea baptized the pagan king Arviragus and gave him St George's arms to bear as his own. This particular development concerning the conversion of Arviragus by St Joseph struck us as odd because it has no precedent – before Hardyng, Arviragus always maintained his pagan status. According to Hardyng, Joseph arrived in Britain in AD 63, bringing with him the two phials containing the blood and sweat of Christ. King Arviragus granted Joseph 12 hides of land at Mewetryne, now called Glastonbury(!), and this was where Joseph was buried. Hardyng goes on to relate a story about a crucifix, made by Joseph, and a pagan king of North Wales called Agrestes, who appears to be a mixture of Crudel, King of North Wales of the earlier legend, and Agrestes, King of Kamaalot. The pagan king apparently threw this lifelike crucifix into the sea off Caerlleon (Chester), for which he was burnt to death.[23] It is

Dinas Bran, the original Castle of the Grail, sits high above the Abbey of Valle Crucis, dominating the skyline from the valley below.

Another view of Valle Crucis.

An early Christian/ Celtic Wheel Cross from the Valle Crucis Abbey.

The natural fortress at World's End where Melwas abducted Gwenhwyfar. The rocks in view are Craig y Forwyn (the Cliff of the Maiden).

Caer Drewyn, the fortress of Gwyn ap Nudd overlooking the River Dee near Corwen.

Moel Arthur and Moel Famau viewed from Caer Afallach (the Fortress of Afallach).

Caer Afallach. The Halls of Afallach whence, according to Welsh tradition, Arthur was taken following the Battle of Camlan.

The Wirral peninsula viewed from Caer Afallach: this is the original Wirral referred to as the landing place of St Joseph of Arimathea in the Glastonbury texts. These traditions were corrupted and relocated in Somerset, resulting in the name Wearyall Hill.

Castell Dinas Bran – the Castle Corbenic of the Grail Romances and home to the Holy Grail.

Another view of Dinas Bran.

Wat's Dyke, the wall spoken of by Procopius, which marks the boundary of the Land of the Dead where it passes over the slopes of Caer Afallach.

not known whether Hardyng had seen John of Glastonbury's Melkin passage, but the additional material Hardyng credits to Melkin suggests that there was a work ascribed to the latter in circulation.[24]

Melkin next appears in Capgrave's *Nova Legenda Angliae*, in which there is a life of Joseph of Arimathea taken verbatim from John's *Chronica*,[25] but the most important pre-Dissolution witness to the tradition of Melkin is John Leland, who reported that he had found in Glastonbury's library an ancient fragment of Melkin's *Historia* from which he had taken notes. It would therefore appear that prior to the Dissolution of the Monasteries in the 16th century the library had housed documents, other than John of Glastonbury's *Chronica*, that contained a record of Melkin and his writing. Moreover, these fragments from Melkin appear to contain a number of details that do not appear within the prophecy itself. Leland states that Melkin was anciently known as one of the most famous and erudite of British writers and that his later obscurity was a result of the Saxon invasions. Leyland also notes that Melkin was born in Wales, trained as a bard and wrote a work entitled *Historiola de Rebus Britannicis* in the typical form of his country, a comment that possibly refers to prophecy. He also tells us that Melkin believed Joseph of Arimathea was laid to rest at Glastonbury and oddly that Melkin had flourished before Merlin.

The historian John Bale also talks of Melkin, citing Capgrave, Hardyng and Leyland as his main sources, yet he includes additional details about Melkin not found within the works of these three. For instance, he credits Melkin with skills as an astrologer and geometer, which would seem to indicate that Bale actually saw material credited to Melkin that is now lost. This latter possibility is reinforced by Bale's assertion that Melkin wrote a work entitled *De Arthurii Mensa Rotunda*. The fact that this text is not mentioned by Leland when he uses Melkin as his authority for information regarding Arthur and his court in *Assertio Arturii* would seem to suggest yet another book attributed to Melkin existed and was known to Bale and had been seen by Leyland before he compiled this work. Bale also states that Melkin wrote a third book entitled *De Rebus Brytannicis*. In a work published in 1619[26] the historian John Pits also credits Melkin with three works, although he gives different titles from those named by Bale: *Antiquitatibus Britannicis*, *De Gestis Britannorum* and *De Regis Arthurii Mensa Rotunda*.

The above had shed a little more light on the enigmatic figure of Melkin of Avalon: he was a Welshman, a trained bard and prophet, and the author of at least three historical works. Moreover, our belief that the obscure nature of his prophecy and its archaic form pointed to a genuinely ancient Welsh traditional source had been borne out by the comments of

Capgrave, Hardyng, John of Glastonbury, Pits and Leland. Nor should Melkin's prophecy be dismissed out of hand because its author's full works are now lost to us, for Bale and Pits inform us that Melkin lived in the middle of the sixth century, in the reign of Maelgwn Gwynedd, near to the close of the Arthurian Age, and the evidence gleaned from past historians and chroniclers suggests that the legend of St Joseph of Arimathea was already in existence at that time. In fact Professor J.P. Carley suggests that Melkin of Avalon derives from Maelgwn Gwynedd, for both were renowned as bards and prophets.[27] Furthermore, Professor Carley points out the obvious route whereby a corrupted form of Maelgwn's Latin name – Mailcunus – could easily have evolved into Melkinus.[28]

Maelgwn Gwynedd, whom we encountered in an earlier chaper, descended from Cunedda Wledig and died in 547. He ruled over much of North Wales and was recorded as being superior to almost all the kings of Britannia. Although berated for his evil deeds by Gildas within his *Epistola*, at some point Maelgwyn vowed to publish to the world and to become a monk for ever. Professor J. Rhys and A. W. Wade-Evans believe it was St Cadog who persuaded him to become a monk, for recorded in the *Life of St Cadog* is the statement that Maelgwn had chosen Cadog as his confessor.[29] Having established earlier that Maelgwn ruled in Gwynedd (Venodocium), and that according to the *Vera Historia* Avalon was indeed within this domain, it seemed to us that Melkinus Avalonius (Melkin of Avalon) and Mailcunus Guenedota (Maelgwn Gwynedd) did indeed equate to one and the same person. The variant spellings of the name Melkin include Mevinus, Melkinus Avalonius, Mewynus, Mewyn, Melchin and Melchinus, and in the course of our research into the bard of Avalon we came across a place recorded in the 'Domesday Book' under the name of Melchanstone, which can be translated as the town or settlement of Melchan/Melkin, namely Melchan's Tone (Town). Although the exact location of Melchanstone is no longer known, it is mentioned within the 'Doomsday Book' in connection with an identifiable place called Picton[30] that lies only a few miles from Caerfallwch, at the heart of Ynys Afallach, the original Realm of Avalon.

The fact that the tradition regarding Melkin of Avalon was a late addition to the Glastonbury corpus – it was not associated with the Somerset town until it appeared in John of Glastonbury's 14th-century *Chronica* – struck us as further evidence of the piecemeal arrival of genuine Avalonian material from its original location in northeast Wales. This translocation of material also explained the reference to St Joseph being laid to rest within a large pagan cemetery, for the cemetery referred to was in all likelihood the Land of the Dead that lay to the west of the Wall on the high ground above Glaestingaburh.

ARTHUR, WIRRAL AND AVALON

A further victim of the removal of Avalonian material from Wales to Somerset was the Wirral peninsula, which forms one side of the Dee estuary north of Chester and has become the 'Wearyall Hill' of the Glastonbury version of the legend of Joseph of Arimathea. As R.F. Treharne relates in *The Glastonbury Legends*, following their arrival in Britain Joseph and his companions approached Glastonbury Tor 'across the marsh, all weary with their long journeying, they rested on the rise about a mile to the south-west of Glastonbury, and ever since their halting-place has been called "Wearyall Hill". At the foot of the Tor, St Joseph stopped to pray: before he knelt, he thrust his staff into the ground and lo!, a miracle! The staff immediately took root and budded; it was a sign from heaven that he reached Journey's End.'[31] As Treharne points out, however, this detail was not added to the Glastonbury legend until well after the 16th century.[32] Why 'Wearyall Hill' should have been added at such a late date became clear when we studied the following rendition by John of Glastonbury of a story from within the 13th-century *Perlesvaus*.

The story opens with John of Glastonbury informing us that 'there was at that time in Wirral (Wirale), within the island [realm] of Avalonia (insulam Auallonie) a monastery of holy virgins, dedicated in the name of the Apostle Peter, wherein Arthur oftentimes rested and abode, attracted by the amenity of the place'.[33] The story continues that one night when the king was in residence an angel appeared to him, calling his name and telling him to arise at dawn and to go to the hermitage of St Mary Magdalene of Bekery on the island to learn what was occurring at that place. The king arose and informed his knight Gawain (Gwalchmai) of the visitation, but Gawain suggested that the king's vision was naught but a trifle. The vision was repeated the following night. Again Arthur ignored the angel's voice, but assented that if the angel came a third time he would do as directed. In preparation Arthur instructed his squire to be ready to leave early the following morning. That night the squire had a dream that he had come to the hermitage and upon entering the chapel he saw a body upon a bier surrounded by many candles. Among them upon the altar were two golden candlesticks and, unable to resist the temptation, the squire stole one of them. As he attempted to leave the chapel the squire was wounded grievously in the groin and yelled out in pain, awaking Arthur, who immediately went to his bedside. The squire recounted his dream to Arthur and then, pulling his cloak from around him, he showed Arthur both the candlestick and the steel in his groin. Thereupon the squire took his last breath and expired, and was buried among the nuns at Wirale. As testimony to the veracity of this incident,

John declares that the candlestick and knife remain 'to this day' in the Treasury of the King of England at Westminster.

The *Perlesvaus* (c.1220) names the place of Arthur's retreat as Cardueil, which is believed by some to be Carlisle, though on the basis of very questionable evidence. However, in *Yvain* (Owein ap Rheged), Chrétien de Troyes talks of *'Carduel en Gales'* (Carduel in Wales); further comparisons between Continental and Welsh sources indicate that Cardueil is a Continental rendering of the Welsh Caerlleon (Chester).[34] Chester sits at the southern end of the Wirral peninsula and the above argument regarding the identification of Cardueil, Caerliwelydd or Caerliel can be applied to further references to this town, including that in Marie de France's *Lanval*, where Cardueil is placed within close proximity of Avalon. In fact there is no difficulty in Chester being known as Caer Loyw, Caerlleon, Caerliel and Cardueil, for the latter two are simply renderings of the Welsh Caerlleon.[35]

Here was a tale universally accepted as being derived from the earlier Grail romance *Perlesvaus*, or a source common to both, that had been incorporated within the Glastonbury material at a later date. Some minor topographical details had been changed – such as the insertion of Bekery into John of Glastonbury's account – to make it fit into its new Glastonbury context. The story narrated within John's *Chronica* contains further distinct differences, for within *Perlesvaus* Arthur is said to be at the Great Hall at Cardueil, the candlestick is said to have been given to St Paul's in London and the chapel is named as St Augustine's in the White Forest,[36] not the hermitage of St Mary Magdalene.[37] It seemed that we had two variants of the same tale, each with supposedly conflicting evidence that could be explained away as Glastonbury propaganda, but in this instance that is not necessarily so. The chapel of St Augustine in the White Forest was also mentioned in *Perlesvaus* as being 'where dwells the holyiest hermit in Wales'. In the version contained within *The High History of the Holy Grail* it is said that 'the most worshipful hermit that is in the kingdom of Wales, hath his dwelling beside the chapel'.

The story is related within a third text, namely *Fouke le Fitz Waryn*, a prose redaction of a lost original verse set in the Welsh Marches that is believed to derive from the same source as *Perlesvaus*. The name Blanche launde or Blanche ville (White Town) identifies the location as the village of Whittington and its surrounding area in the Marches of North Wales:

For in this country [Blaunche launde] was the chapel
Of Saint Austen, which was beautiful,

Where Kahuz the son of Yweyn dreamed
That he stole a candlestick.

We reviewed the evidence point by point. The opening sentence of John of Glastonbury's version of the story located Wirral within Avalon. We had already identified Avalon as an area of northeastern Wales bordering the River Dee, which indeed incorporated 'Wirral' – the Wirral peninsula – and there was at one time an ancient chapel dedicated to St Peter, near Helsby on the Wirral. Could this have been the 'monastery of holy virgins, dedicated in the name of the Apostle Peter' referred to by John of Glastonbury? Nor was this the only mention of Wirral in Arthurian material, for in certain romances Arthur's nephew Gawain is attached to the Wirral, notably during his quest for the Green Chapel in *Sir Gawain and the Green Knight*. In this story he is recorded as leaving Camelot and travelling through the Kingdom of Logres to North Wales where he crosses over 'the fords by the foreland over at Holyhead, till he came to the wilderness of Wirral, where but few dwell who love God and man of true heart'. The ford at Holyhead evidently refers to the old ford over the River Dee between Maes Glas (Greenfield) near Holywell and the Wirral peninsula.[38]

So what gave John of Glastonbury the idea to rework this story from the Grail romances and relocate it in a Somerset context? We believe that the answer is explained in his opening reference to Wirral being in Avalon, for if Glastonbury was supposed to be Avalon then Wirral needed to be incorporated into the Glastonbury corpus too. Except for the Glastonbury rendering of the story, however, all variants place these events in that part of North Wales in which the Wirral peninsula is situated and that we had identified as the original Avalon. The Wirral tradition therefore appeared to have a sound basis, especially as it was also attached to the arrival of St Joseph in Britain, and once we realized that the present-day version of the tradition relating to the Holy Thorn on Wearyall Hill, so beloved by tourists, was a piece of early 18th-century commercialism devised by a local Glastonbury innkeeper we were in no doubt: Wirral had always belonged to Avalon. The additional fact that the Glastonbury Thorn and Wearyall Hill did not appear within the Glastonbury legend until after the 16th century led us to conclude that the Wirral belonged to the original Avalonian tradition and must have been linked to St Joseph and Arthur in a now lost source.

KING LUCIUS AND THE PAPAL
MISSIONARIES PHAGAN AND DERUVIAN

King Lucius, grandson of Arviragus, the pagan king who granted Ynys Witrin to Joseph of Arimathea, first appears in an extract from the *Liber Pontificalis*, recorded between AD 483 and 492;[39] reference is made to a letter from 'Lucio of Britannio' to Pope Eleutherius.[40] Lucius's letter to the Pope is also referred to by Bede in his Chronicle of 725, in which he records 'Lucius, King of Britannia sent a letter to Eleutherius Bishop of Rome asking that he might be made a Christian'. In his *Ecclesiastical History* of 731 Bede further wrote: 'In their time whilst Eleutherius, a holy man, presided over the Roman church, Lucius, king of the Britons, sent a letter entreating that by his command he might be made a Christian. He soon obtained his pious request, and the Britons preserved the faith which they had received.' A date of between 169 and 180 has been ascribed to Lucius's letter, but as Eleutherius was Pope from 174/5–192 a date of between 175 and 180 would seem to be more precise.[41]

Lucius's open attitude to Christianity and the background to his letter to the Pope are recorded elsewhere. For instance, the annals for AD 183, which were written from ancient records, tell us 'the British king Lucius never showed himself adverse to Christianity, or an [open] enemy: But [rather] admiring the miracles of the Christians and likewise their integrity of life, he seemed somewhat favourable to them.'[42] Further on the annals tell us that Lucius 'would have embraced Christianity already before this had he not been bound fast by the superstition of his ancestors as in a serpent's coils'.[43] Other records tell us:

he [Lucius] learnt from Imperial Legates that several senators had become Christians, among others a man called Pertinax and [one called] Trebellius; and that the Emperor himself, Marcus Aurelius, having obtained a victory through their prayers, had [begun to] look kindly on the Christians. Learning these [facts] and others, Lucius sent an embassy to Eleutherius the Pope, through Elvanus and Medwin, Britons; asking [Eleutherius] to open through them and their priests an approach [request] to [the king's] conversion to Christianity. This [request] he obtained. For the same Pope sent Fugatius and Donatianus[44] to Britain to initiate the king and others into the sacred mysteries, they being already slightly acquainted with Christianity. This command they fulfilled energetically.[45]

The Pope's response to King Lucius's letter is recorded within William of Malmesbury's *De Antiquitate*, in a chapter entitled 'How Saints Phagan and

Deruvian converted the Britons to the Faith, and arrived in the Island [Realm] of Avalon'. In brief the text tells how 'annals worthy of credence' relate that Lucius, king of the Britons, sent to Pope Eleutherius asking him to send missionaries to instruct the Britons in the Christian faith. In response the Pope sent two most saintly men – Phagan and Deruvian – who baptized Lucius and his people in AD 166 and then made their way through Britain preaching and baptizing. Eventually the two holy men penetrated the deserted interior and arrived in the Isle (Realm) of Avalonia, where they discovered an old church that had been built, so they were told, by the hands of Christ's disciples. Joyous at finding the remains of a house of prayer, Phagan and Deruvian gave thanks to God and remained in Insula Avalonia for nine years. Upon examining their new abode they discovered evidence that Christians had inhabited the place in former times. Within 'ancient writings' they found the story of how St Phillip had sent 12 disciples to Britain and how, once there, the 12 had been instructed by revelation to build a chapel, which was dedicated by the Son of God in honour of His mother. Within these ancient writings they also found an account of the deeds performed by the original 12 and how three pagan kings had granted them 12 portions of land for their sustenance. Because the disciples of St Phillip had loved this place above all others, Phagan and Deruvian chose 12 of their own, who, with the permission of King Lucius, inhabited the aforesaid island/realm. The 12 appointed by Phagan and Deruvian took to a life as anchorites in the same locations inhabited by the original 12, regularly meeting in the old church in order to worship. And so these 12 companions and their successors inhabited the island/realm of Avalon until the coming of St Patrick, building an oratory of stone that they dedicated to the apostles St Peter and St Paul.

A similar story is repeated by John of Glastonbury, with the additional information that Phagan and Deruvian also built an oratory in honour of St Michael the Archangel on 'Montis qui eminet' (supposedly Glastonbury Tor), and that the saints then returned to Rome to ask the Pope to confirm their actions. Having been granted 30 years' indulgence for pilgrims that would visit the old church and St Michael's on the Tor, they returned to Britain with many others and strengthened the British in the faith of Christ. In light of our research, the reference to the oratory dedicated to St Michael the Archangel appears to be little more than a fictitious addition to promote the Norman chapel of St Michael's on the Tor at Glastonbury as a pilgrim destination.

The early introduction of Christianity to Britain is reiterated in a letter written between 1125 and 1130 by the Chapter of St Andrew's and St David's to Pope Honorius II.[46] In this letter, which is referred to within Giraldus Cambrensis's De Invectionibus (c.1203), the Chapter insists that their church had been an archbishopric since the days of Pope Eleutherius, who had sent Fagan and Duvian to King Lucius, and that these saints had founded three archbishoprics and 27 bishoprics in their kingdom.[47] Phagan and Deruvian are also recorded within Geoffrey of Monmouth's *Historia* under the Latinized names Faganus and Duvianus and within the Welsh *Brut* as Ffagan and Dwywan. Drawing on information from his 'book in the British tongue', Geoffrey adds that Lles (Lucius), the son of Coel (Coillus), succeeded to the crown upon the death of his father and sent letters to Pope Eleutherius requesting instruction in the Christian religion. In reply the Pope sent two religious doctors, Ffagan (Phagan) and Dwywan (Deruvian), who baptized the king. The people were then baptized following the king's example and the two religious doctors almost eradicated paganism within the realm. They also rededicated the pagan temples to God and his saints, and in doing so replaced the three pagan archflamens of Lundain, Caer Efrog and Caerlleon with three archbishoprics and the 28 pagan flamens with 28 bishoprics. Lucius also accorded the Christian churches – the rededicated pagan temples – a variety of rights and privileges.[48] Under the Welsh form of his name, Ffagan is remembered at St Fagan's near Cardiff. According to the *Brut*, when King Lucius died he was buried in the cathedral church in Caer Gloyw (Chester) in AD 156.

As we reviewed the evidence we had assembled relating to the arrival in Britain of Joseph of Arimathea the following composite picture began to emerge. Accompanied by his followers, St Joseph of Arimathea arrived in Britain with the Holy Grail on Easter Eve, 31 years after the passion of Christ. They made landfall on the Wirral peninsula in North Wales. The highest point on the Wirral, which may at one time have been known as Wirral Hill, is now called Heswall Hill, and evidence for Joseph's association with this area came in the form of a reference to a now extinct chapel at Heswall that had originally been dedicated to St Peter the Apostle and St Joseph of Arimathea.[49] Shortly after his arrival St Joseph was captured and imprisoned by Crudel, a king of North Wales. After his release, St Joseph and his followers were granted an area of land known as Ynys Witrin (Ynys Wytherin) on the edge of the Kingdom of Arviragus, the King of Gwynedd, who ruled from Chester (Caer Loyw), which was built for him by the Emperor Claudius. Arviragus's sons Marius (who built the walls of Chester) and Coillus made further grants of land to the followers of Joseph. As we had established earlier, an area of Venedotia (Gwynedd) was known Ynys Afallach (Avalon) and had also been known as Ynys Wytherin (Gwytherin) in early sources. Then there were the references to the sixth-century figure of Melkin of Avalon, who appears to have been the same person as Maelgwn Gwynedd, as well as the enigmatic but seemingly genuine prophecy that contains the earliest recorded reference to St Joseph, the two true cruets containing the blood and sweat of Christ, and St Joseph's burial in the pagan cemetery known as the Land of the Dead, otherwise known as Annwn, the Celtic Otherworld.

THE VALE OF THE CROSS
AND THE GRAIL CASTLE

Never – not even at Glastonbury – have I felt the spirit of what Spengler would call the springtime of our Faustian culture as powerfully as in this holy ground.

J. Cowper Powys

These words could not more adequately render the atmosphere of sanctity that surrounds the area known as 'Glyndyvrdwy' (Glen of the Sacred Waters), where the River Dee runs through the deep heavily wooded ravine between Edeirnion to the great plain of Maelor and where still stands the Abbey of Valle Crucis. Nor did the poet J. Cowper Powys realize that when he wrote the above words he unconsciously touched a gossamer thread that leads back through the centuries to the origins of this place. Indeed, unknown to him he was actually standing on the land that constituted the original Glaestingaburh. It is almost ironic that this place has drawn poets to comment time and again on the sanctity of this blessed spot and, despite the fact that they were unaware of its true history, they never failed to recognize this most holy of sites.

The name Valle Crucis is Latin in origin and, like its Welsh equivalent Pantygroes, means 'Vale of the Cross'. The sacred Vale of the Cross is itself said to take its name from the ninth-century Eliseg's Pillar, which was formerly capped with a Celtic cross. As explained earlier, the pillar was erected in honour of his ancestors by Cyngen, last of the old line of the Kings of Powys, and the genealogy inscribed upon it traced the lineage of these kings back to Vortigern, otherwise known by the Welsh name of Gwytherin. In fact it occurred to us that Ynys Wytherin (the realm of Vortigern/Gwytherin later glossed Ynys Witrin) is an area of land on the edge of the Kingdom of Arviragus given to him by St Joseph of Arimathea. The testimony of Eliseg's Pillar suggested that this pillar – the only reference to him cast in stone – most likely stood within Ynys Gwytherin. This became even more plausible when we came across a reference from the early Welsh poem *Armes Prydein* that referred to Vortigern as Gwytheyrn Gwynedd (Vortigern of Gwynedd). Indeed, there is a local tradition concerning a Dark Age settlement in the vicinity. Having narrowed our search for the location of the original monastery of Glaestingaburh to the Eglywseg valley near Llangollen, we now needed to find archaeological evidence of an early monastic establishment in the area and the obvious place to start was the records of the Cistercian Valle Crucis Abbey. It was amidst the reports of a series of digs undertaken on the site between 1888 and 1900 that we found the evidence we were looking for.

In 1865 the Reverend H.T. Owen, vicar of the private chapel at nearby Trevor Hall, became custodian of the ruins of Valle Crucis Abbey and the fact that the site is in such good condition today is primarily the result of his efforts in clearing away debris and preserving what remained of the ruins. During this work the Reverend Owen made several very interesting finds, including elaborately engraved tombstones and an Arabic copy of the Koran, but what interested us most was the excavation of the abbey cloister, which he had begun in an attempt to find the well used by the monks. Having uncovered the well he continued digging and found evidence of a Saxon building that clearly predated the foundation date of about 1200 generally attributed to the abbey – a date that has always been treated with caution because of the proximity of the ninth-century Eliseg's Pillar, which itself suggests that the area was in use long before 1200. Using a water pump to drain their excavations, Owen and his team dug deeper still, uncovering vestiges of Roman occupation including masonry, hypocausts, tiles and coins. The discovery that the site had been in continuous use from Roman times to the 13th century was exciting enough, but then Owen uncovered something that had quite phenomenal implications. Underneath the layer left by the Roman occupation of the site he found the burnt remains of an oak foundation.

In light of our previous research there seemed to be only one possible explanation for the existence of a pre-Roman wooden building on this ancient religious site on the floor of the Eglywseg valley, below Castell Dinas Bran, the Grail Castle of the Arthurian romances. Could these ancient wooden foundations be the remains of the chapel built by Joseph of Arimathea, guardian of the Holy Grail? If this were indeed the case then the wooden foundations uncovered by the Reverend Owen beneath the cloister of Valle Crucis Abbey are the remains of one of the world's very first Christian churches. In this context it is perhaps no coincidence that the hill above Valle Crucis Abbey has long been known as Rhuabon, the Hill of Mabon, for in certain early Welsh texts Mabon is the Welsh name for Christ. Perhaps it is no coincidence either that the river that runs off the mountain is to this day known as Afon Christionydd, the River of Christianity.

We watched the sun as it rose slowly over Mabon's Hill and the land of Modron and its first rays illuminated the Vale of Llangollen. In the dawn light the mist rose wraithlike from the valley floor, obscuring the ruins of Valle Crucis Abbey and the waters of the sacred River Dee, the primordial Waters of the Goddess. Above the sea of mist stood an island crowned by the dark silhouette of the timeworn walls of Castell Dinas Bran. For a while we contemplated the view in silence, for when seen like this in the early morning light the ancient stronghold of Dinas Bran evokes the archetypal image of the magical Grail Castle, the Castle of Wonders spoken of in the Arthurian romances, more eloquently than any words. When we finally broke the silence it was to reminisce about our quest for the historical Arthur and to talk of the ancient sites to which it had taken us: to the site of the Monastery of Ambri and the great stones of the Giants' Dance; to Arthur's realm of Kernyw on the western coast of Wales; to Caer Cai, where Arthur spent his youth; and to the ancient town of Montgomery, which had been the model for the mythical Camelot. Our thoughts then turned to our search for the mystical realm of Avalon in which we now stood, and to Annwn, the Celtic Otherworld, whose myths were written on the landscape around us. Our thoughts turned also to Glaestingaburh, the Town of the Glaestings, and the thriving Dark Age settlement that had once graced the valley below us. There too, hidden from view on the mist-shrouded valley floor, were the ruins of Valle Crucis Abbey, beneath which lay the remains of what is possibly Joseph of Arimathea's wooden church. But therein lies another story, a story that would lead us to discover something tucked away in the hills and valleys of North Wales that would call into question the origins of Christianity itself.

APPENDIX ONE:
THE GEOGRAPHY OF ARTHUR'S RELATIVES

Using Welsh source material, we have compiled an extended genealogy to show the names of Arthur's relatives and associates from Eudaf Hen in the fourth century down to the saints of the seventh. The names of all of Arthur's uncles, aunts, grandparents, cousins and nephews have been included and are listed below. We have kept the accompanying notes as brief as possible; for more information about these people we recommend Peter Bartrum's *A Welsh Classical Dictionary* and Rachel Bromwich's *Trioedd Ynys Prydein*. The bracketed numbers at the end of some of the entries correspond to numbered points on the map, showing the locations linked to these characters in the Welsh sources.

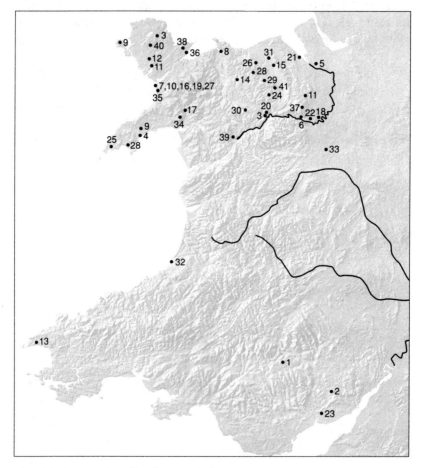

Map 32 Geography of Arthur's relatives

Having established that Arthur was Welsh and primarily linked to North Wales, we intend this appendix to serve by way of a final piece of evidence. For, if Arthur was from Cornwall, Scotland or Somerset, would his family have been located in Wales for generations before and after him? The myth is recorded in the landscape and the landscape doesn't forget. We feel the map speaks for itself.

Ap   Son of
Ferch Daughter of

Aldwr ap Cynfor Brother to Custennin Fendigaid and the fourth King of Llydaw after Cynan Meiriadoc.
Amlawdd Wledig Husband to Gwen ferch Cunedda and father of Arthur's mother Eigyr.
Anarawn ap Cynfarch Brother to Urien and a Bishop of Llydaw.
Anna ferch Uthyr Sister to Arthur, wife to Llew and mother of Medrod. Sometimes identified as Gwyar, the exact relationship between Anna and Arthur is uncertain.
Arawn ap Cynfarch Brother of Urien, the *Brut* tells us he was the King of Ysgotland and that he was killed at Porth Hamo. Also mentioned in the *Triads* as one of the three womb burdens of Ynys Prydein.
Arthur Sites dedicated to him all over Wales!
Bicanus Father of St Illtud and husband to Rhienwylydd.
Brychan Father of many saints. Gives his name to the Kingdom of Brycheiniog (Brecon in South Wales) (1).
Bugi ap Gwynllyw Husband to Perferren.
Cadog, St The *Life of Saint Cadog* contains one of the earliest references to Arthur and locates him in the region of Brycheiniog in South Wales. He is also comemmorated in several church dedications in South Wales (2).
Cadwy ap Geraint Named as one of the 42 counsellors of Arthur in *Culhwch and Olwen* and father of Peredur.
Caradog Freichfras ap Tywanedd Chief elder in Kernyw and named as one of the three favourites of Arthur in the *Triads*.
Caw Father of many children including two sons, Gildas and Huail, and a daughter called Cywyllog. A ruler in both the Edeirnion valley and the cantref of Twrcelyn in Anglesey (3).
Cawrdaf ap Caradog Freichfras One of the 42 counsellors of Arthur in *The Dream of Rhonabwy* and commerated in Abererch on the Lleyn Peninsula and Llangoed in Anglesey (4).
Ceneu ap Coel Included in the pedigrees of the Men of the North.
Cilydd ap Cyleddon Wledig Husband to Goleuddydd and father of Culhwch, the main character in *Culhwch and Olwen*.

Coel Hen *or* **Coel Godebog** One of the Men of the North. Husband of Ystradwel and prominent in the *Brut*. Coel Godebog was the Earl of Caer Loyw (5).

Coleddog ap Cawrdaf Grandson of Caradog Freichfras and grandfather of St Collen.

Collen, St, ap Pedrwn Patron saint of Llangollen and Abbot of 'Glasymbyri' (6).

Constans ap Custennin Fendigaid Uncle of Arthur and brother to Uthyr.

Culhwch ap Cilydd First cousin to Arthur and hero of the tale of *Culhwch and Olwen*.

Cunneda Wledig Husband to Gwawl and father to many sons who gave their names to many regions in North Wales.

Custennin ap Macsen Wledig Son of Elen. Linked to Caernarfon where he is said to be buried (7).

Custennin Fendigaid (Gorneu) ap Cynfor Father to Meirchion, Erbin, St Digain, Constans, Emrys and Uthyr Pendragon, and therefore grandfather to Arthur. Possibly to be identified with St Custennin, the patron saint of Llangystennin, near Llandudno (8).

Cybi, St, ap Selyf Patron of Caergybi (Holyhead) and Llangybi near Pwllheli (9).

Cynan Meiriadoc ap Eudaf Hen Mentioned in *The Dream of Macsen Wledig* at Caernarfon when Macsen Wledig arrived. Founded the colony of Llydaw (10).

Cynfarch Oer ap Meirchion Gul Father of Urien Rheged and husband to Nyfain.

Cynfor ap Tudwal Father of Custennin Fendigaid.

Cyngar ap Geraint Patron saint of Hope and Llangefni (11).

Cynwal ap Ffrwdwr Father of Amlawdd Wledig.

Cynyr of Caer Gawch Father of Gwen and Non and therefore grandfather of St David.

Cywyllog *or* **Cwyllog ferch Caw** Wife of Medrod and patron of Llangwyllog in Anglesey (12).

Denw ferch Lleuddun Lwyddog Wife of Owain and mother of Kentigern.

Dewi, St Son of Non and the patron saint of Wales. Commemorated at many sites in South Wales, including St Davids and Henfynyw (13).

Digain, St, ap Custennin Uncle to Arthur and patron saint of Llangernyw in Denbighshire (14).

Diheufyr ap Hawystyl Gloff Patron saint of Bodfari in the Vale of Clwyd (15).

Dyfwn ferch Glywys Sister to Gwynllyw and aunt to St Cadog.

Eigyr ferch Amlawdd Wledig Wife of Uthyr Pendragon and mother to Arthur.

Elen ferch Eudaf Wife of Macsen Wledig. Associated with Caernarfon and other sites in the region, she gave her name to the ancient road Sarn Elen (16).

Eliffer Gosgorddfawr Father of Gwrgi and Peredur. Mentioned in the *Triads*.

Emrys Wledig ap Custennin *aka* **Ambrosius Aurelianus** Brother to Uthyr and therefore uncle of Arthur. Named by Gildas and Bede. Linked to Dinas Emrys and buried in the Giants' Dance (17).

Erbin ap Custennin Mentioned in *The Mabinogion* as the uncle of Arthur and was originally the patron saint of Erbistock on the River Dee (18).

Essyllt Wife of March who ran off with Trystan. She is mentioned as one of the ladies present at Arthur's court in *Culhwch and Olwen*.

Eudaf Hen Placed at Caernarfon in *The Dream of Macsen Wledig*. He is the father of Cynan, Gadeon and Elen Luyddog (19).

Ffrwdwr ap Morfawr Father of Cynwal.

Gadeon ap Eudaf Hen Mentioned in *The Dream of Macsen Wledig* in relation to Caernarfon. He was the father of Ystradwel who married Coel Hen.

Geraint ap Erbin Appears in early poetry and mentioned in *Geraint Son of Erbin* as a cousin to Arthur and a warrior in his court. Was the father of several saints.

Gildas ap Caw Writer of *De Excido Britannia* and linked to the Edeirnion valley (20).

Glywys ap Solor Mentioned with Arthur in the *Life of St Cadoc*. Father of Gwynllyw.

Goleuddydd ferch Amlawdd Wledig Wife to Cilydd and mother of Culhwch.

Gwalchmai ap Gwyar Gawain of the romances, nephew to Arthur. Buried at Walwen on the banks of the River Dee (21).

Gwawl ferch Coel Hen Wife to Cunedda Wledig and mother to his many sons.

Gwen ferch Cunedda Wife of Amlawdd Wledig.

Gwen ferch Cynyr Wife of Selyf and mother of St Cybi. Sister to Non the mother of St David. Also known as Tonwen.

Gwenhwyfar ferch Ogrfan Gawr Wife to Arthur and remembered at Croes Gwenhwyfar near Llangollen (22).

Gwennog Father of St Collen.

Gwrgi ap Eliffer Gosgorddfawr Brother to Peredur with whom he fought at the Battle of Arderydd.

Gwrwst Ledlwm ap Ceneu Released from prison by Arthur in *Culhwch and Olwen*. Father of Meirchion Gul and Eliffer Gosgorddfawr.

Gwynllyw ap Glywys Father of St Cadoc. Commemorated at Newport (23).

Hawystyl Gloff ap Owain Ddantgwyn Husband to Tywanedd and father of several saints.

Huail ap Caw Killed by Arthur and remembered at Maen Huail in Ruthin (24).

Iestyn ap Geraint Founder of Llaniestyn in Anglesey and Llaniestyn in Lleyn (25).

Illtud, St Numerous sites dedicated to him in the southern half of Wales.

Kentigern, St Known in Welsh as Cyndeyrn Garthwys, Chief Bishop of Penrhyn Rhianedd. Linked to the foundation of Llanelwy (St Asaph) and other churches in the area (26).

Llew ap Cynfarch Brother of Urien and husband to Anna, Arthur's sister.

Macsen Wledig Roman Emperor (Latin name, Maximus) who appears in *The Dream of Macsen Wledig* and is named as husband of Elen. Linked to Caernarfon, Caer Fyrddin and Caerlleon. Mentioned in Gildas, Nennius and Bede (27).

March ap Meirchion Cousin of Arthur. Linked to Henllan, and Castellmarch (28).

Marchell ferch Hawystyl Gloff The patron saint of Llanfarchell, now called Whitchurch near Denbigh in the Vale of Clwyd. Also located at Capel Marchell near Llanrwst (29).

Medrod ap Llew Nephew to Arthur and his adversary at the Battle of Camlan. His wife was Cywyllog. Remembered in the River Medrad near Llangwm (30).

Meirchion ap Custennin Uncle to Arthur. His name is remembered in Tremeirchion, Afon Meirchion and Llys Meirchion, all near Denbigh. Father of March (31).

Meirchion Gul ap Gwrwst Ledlwm Father of Cynfarch Oer. Named in the Men of the North genealogy.

Morfawr ap Gadeon Also known as Gwrfawr, father of Tudwal.

Non ferch Cynyr Sister to Gwen and the mother of St Dewi (David). Commemorated in several church dedications in the southern half of Wales (32).

Nor ab Owain Finddu Father of Solor.

Nyfain ferch Brychan Wife to Cynfarch Oer and the mother of Urien Rheged. Mentioned in the *Triads*.

Ogryfan Gawr Father of Gwenhwyfar, linked to Caer Ogryfan at Oswestry (33).

Olwen ferch Ysbadden Pencawr Became the wife of Culhwch after many adventures detailed in *Culhwch and Olwen*.

Owain ab Urien Prominent in Arthurian myths. Father of Cyndeyrn
  Garthwys (St Kentigern).
Owain Finddu ap Macsen Wledig Son of Elen. Mentioned in the *Triads,
  Life of St Cadoc*. Legend of his death near Beddgelert (34).
Peblig ap Macsen Wledig Son of Elen. Saint of Llanbeblig near
  Caernarfon (35).
Peredur ab Cadwy One of the 42 counsellors of Arthur named in
  The Dream of Rhonabwy. Also mentioned in the *Triads*.
Peredur ap Eliffer Brother to Gwrgi, fought at Battle of Arderydd and is
  named as Dux Venedotia (Duke of Gwynedd) in the *Annales Cambriae*.
Rhieinwylydd ferch Amlawdd Wledig Wife to Bicanus and mother of
  St Illtud.
Selfan ap Geraint Saint located near Penmon on Anglesey (36).
Selyf ap Erbin Father of St Cybi by Gwen.
Severa Named on Eliseg's Pillar as Vortigern's wife and daughter to
  Maximus, the Latin name of Macsen Wledig (37).
Solor ap Nor Father of Glywys.
Sylwein Daughter of Geraint and patron saint of Llanfihangel Dinsylwy
  near Penmon in Anglesey (38).
Tudur Patron saint of Darowen in Cyfeiliog and Eglwys Dudur in
  Llanuwchllyn and remembered at a well called Ffynon Dudur near
  Llanelidan in the Vale of Clwyd (39).
Tudwal Son of Morfawr/Gwrfawr and father of Cynfor.
Tyfrydog Patron saint of Llandyfrydog in Anglesey (40).
Tyrnog Patron saint of Llandyrnog in the Vale of Clwyd (41).
Tywanedd ferch Amlawdd Wledig Wife to Hawystyl Gloff and mother
  of Caradog Freichfras. Mentioned in the Men of the North material.
Urien Rheged Mentioned in the *Triads*, early poetry and many Arthurian
  sources, along with his son Owain.
Uthyr Pendragon Father of Arthur.
Ystradwel ferch Gadeon Wife of Coel Hen. Linked to the inheritance
  of Gwynedd.

Arthur's extended family tree

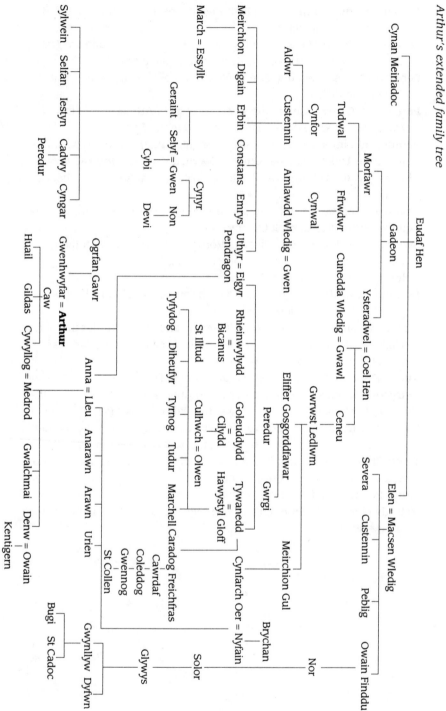

APPENDIX TWO:
THE UNKNOWN ARTHUR

In Part One of this book we followed the story of Arthur as told in early Welsh sources and in the original Welsh *Brut*, which Geoffrey of Monmouth translated into Latin as *Historia Regum Britanniae*. In this appendix we shall be looking at some of the lesser known events of Arthur's life not to be found in the *Brut* but preserved in various sources including the poetry and folklore of Wales. In the *Brut* we find several occasions where years pass by between events without commentary. Is it possible that some of these lesser known aspects of Arthur's life took place in these years, between his battles with the Saxons? What follows is a small selection of these missing pieces of Arthur's life as well as the location of his various courts and the legend of Arthur sleeping in a cave ready to return as the 'once and future king'.

THE DEATH OF HUAIL

Published for the first time below is an English translation from the *Chronicle* of Elis Gruffydd (written around 1530) concerning the death of Huail, the brother of the historian Gildas, at the hands of Arthur. This story is little known outside of Wales and by translating the exact text of the manuscript we find details and place names that will help to throw further light on this tradition. The translation has been made as literal as possible and therefore reads awkwardly in places; some punctuation has been added in order to help it read more easily.

> Because some of the authors have shown the origin of a Saxon, he who is called Cerdic, who reigned as king of the West Saxons, in the year of Christ 522. This which is thought to be [and the story professes] that was around the fifth year of the reign of Arthur, he, as the *Polychronicon* shows, sustained a great war against Arthur. And in the end there was agreement and union between them in the time he made homage and an oath to be a loyal supporter to King Arthur, who gave Cerdic two lands, those which are today called Hampshire and Somerset.
>
> And from this time on there was a covenant and peace between Arthur and Cerdic. And because it was him that finished putting everything in order he remained in the lands that are today called North Wales. In this place and time there were many marvels in this part of the realm, especially in the island the French book calls Surloes, that which the story professes is called today Ynys Mon [Anglesey]. In the time, as

the story shows, there was a bridge [or causeway] over the Menai around about the place that is called today Bon y Don [Bridge of Don], at that place there were certain of men in armour guarding it all the time. And the king of this island made many cruel battles against Arthur, those which would be too long to relate at this time. Those who lamented of reading this story worked to read the book of the conquest, the Sangreal.

Also some of the books show that there was a lord living in the country called Edeirnion or in that area called Caw, he who some of the books call Caw of Prydein, to whom there were two sons of many. The one who was called Gildas ap Caw, he was a respectable scholar who preached and made many books against the wickedness of the Britons, books which are accepted and praised amongst the scholars since then to today.

And the second son was called Huail ap Caw, he was a cheeky and wanton man, who according to the story happened to give his affection and love to one of the mistresses of Arthur, who took jealousy between Huail and his mistress. Because of this Arthur took a long sword and went secretly to near the house of the mistress to watch Huail, who came to the place with Arthur there. In this place after a long conversation they struck with their two swords and they fought like two lions. In this place after long fighting it happened that Huail landed a blow to Arthur on one of his knees and wounded him badly. Nevertheless, the story shows the reconciliation of Arthur and Huail before going from this place under the condition that Huail did not taunt this blow to Arthur, under pain of his head. And so they left; and so Arthur went home to his court, that was in a town which the story of the Sangreal calls Caerhass, that which the story professes is today called Caerwys. In this place he was nursed back to health from his wound, but from this, so the story goes, he had a slight lameness whilst he lived.

And in a short time after he became healthy from his wound there fell a love between himself and a girl from the town that was called Rhuthun [Ruthin]. To this place he went dressed in the clothes of a girl, in these clothes it happened that Huail discovered him playing dance amongst the girls and recognized him because of his lameness. In the time he said like this: 'The dancing were very good were it not for the knee.' This Arthur heard and he knew that it was about him these words were said. Because of this Arthur left the company and secretly went to his court.

He caused Huail to be fetched to his side at this place, and he questioned him cruelly for breaking his oath; and in a short time after a number of words to him he commanded to take him and go with him to the market of the town and caused his head to be cut off on the stone that was lying on the ground of the road. This was fulfilled accordingly. And because of this, to remember this deed the stone was called from then to today, Maen Huail [the Stone of Huail].

And in this time according to some of the stories Arthur made a court in the place which is today called Nannerch. And again the place is called the Court of Arthur. And to him it is said that the church was his chapel, the one that has been called for a long time Capel Gwial [the Chapel of Sticks].

And in that quarter of the kingdom Arthur and his soldiers made a lot of warfare especially from the place that the stories of the Sangreal call Sdrettmares, the place it is thought and the story professes we today call Ystrad March, while in Surloes, or Ynys Mon ...[1]

The opening part of the story tells us that Arthur fought against Cerdic, king of the West Saxons in the fifth year of Arthur's reign in 522, and uses as its source the *Polychronicon*, a large Latin chronicle written by Ranulph Higden, a monk from the abbey at Chester, and finished in 1327. In Book V we find the original reference to Cerdic receiving Somerset and Hampshire, but the *Polychronicon* adds 'which he [Arthur] after called West Saxon', implying that the identification of Hampshire and Somerset with this area is a later addition. Another point of interest in the *Polychronicon* is the battle list from Nennius's *Historia Brittonum*, in which Higden elaborates on the battlesite on the River Dulas, identifying it with a river running through the town of Wigan in Lancashire – an early example of Arthurian guesswork or the record of an old tradition?[2]

The next section contains material that is very obscure but also very important. Because of the peace made with the Saxons, Arthur is said to have remained in North Wales – here we have a 16th-century text preserving a local tradition unknown elsewhere. One of the most interesting parts of the extract are the several references to the *Sangreal*, which could mean any of the many French Grail romances written by this time. The story of the knights guarding the ford can be found in Malory's *Morte D'Arthur*.[3] The reference to Arthur fighting battles with the King of Anglesey at Bon Y Don is again unheard of elsewhere, but as we know that Arthur was primarily linked to North Wales they take on a new importance. One of the earliest Welsh Arthurian poems tells of Cai fighting Palug's Cat – a monster cat – on Anglesey, so do we have in this chronicle a record of a historical event regarding Arthur on the island? How we wish that Elis Gruffydd had expanded upon the battles 'which would be too long to relate at this time'.

The full story of Huail and Arthur is detailed and easy to follow, but the oldest reference we have to animosity between Arthur and Huail can be found in *Culhwch and Olwen*, where Huail is mentioned on two occasions: 'Huail ap Caw (he never submitted to a lords hand.)' and 'Huail his uncle stabbed him and therefore there was hatred between Arthur and Huail because of the wound'.[4] The poor relationship between Arthur and Huail appears again in the *Vita Gildae* (Life of Gildas) written by Caradoc of Llancarfan (c.1150), which says of Huail that he is 'destined and hoped for to become king by the locals'.[5] This is just one example of many Welsh traditions where Arthur is not portrayed as the great king of the romances but a tyrannical ruler not liked by the local populace. The actual stone called Maen Huail in the chronicle is still situated on the town square in Ruthin, outside a bank. The plaque above it reads:

MAEN HUAIL
On which tradition states King Arthur
Beheaded Huail, brother of Gildas the
Historian.

The last lines of the passage tell us that Arthur fought many of his battles from an area called Ystrad March. This was the Welsh name given to the Cistercian Abbey of Strata Marcella, situated to the north of Welshpool near the River Severn. This is exactly the same area in which the Battle of Badon took place according to the description in *The Dream of Rhonabwy*. In recording the local traditions of North Wales from both oral and written sources in his *Chronicle*, Elis Gruffydd may just have left us one of the most detailed and important pieces of evidence regarding the historical Arthur.

THE COURTS OF ARTHUR

In light of the previous evidence the two courts of Arthur in North Wales named by Elis Gruffydd must be looked at more closely. The first at Caerwys is said to be confirmed by the mention of Caerhaas in the French book *Sangreal* and we do indeed find another reference to the site in the tale of *Erec and Enide* by Chrétien de Troyes, where mention is made of the courts of Quarrois and Quaraduel. The second of these courts is also spelt 'Rotelan' and 'Rodelen' and many scholars have identified it with Rhuddlan in North Wales, which suggests that the other court is also in the area.[6] The oldest name for Caerwys is recorded in the 'Domesday Book' as Cairos and the similarity with Quarrois is obvious. The entry in Elis Gruffydd's *Chronicle* is therefore confirmed by a 12th-century tale of

Chrétien de Troyes and the 'Domesday Book', written in 1086.

The other court of Arthur is placed at Nannerch, three miles distant from Caerwys in the valley of the River Wheeler. The name of Arthur's chapel, Capel y Gwial in Nannerch, is also mentioned in the *Parochialia* of Edward Lhwyd written in 1697 and in a manuscript of Angharad Llwyd, a local scholar from the first half of the 19th century. The exact location of this site is currently unknown.

One of the *Triads* also mentions courts of Arthur as yet unidentified:

Three Tribal thrones of Ynys Prydein:
- Arthur as Chief Prince in Caerlleon ar Wysg, and Dewi as Chief Bishop and Maelgwyn Gwynedd as Chief Elder;
- Arthur as Chief Prince in Kelliwig in Kernyw, and Bishop Bytwini as Chief Bishop, and Caradog Freichfras as Chief Elder;
- Arthur as Chief Prince in Penrhyn Rhianydd in the North, and Gerthmwl Wledig as Chief Elder and Cynderyn Garthwys as Chief Bishop.[7]

As we saw in Chapter 3, the court of Caerlleon ar Wysg was located at Chester on the banks of the River Dee. The locations of Arthur's other courts at Kelliwig (Gelliwig) and Penrhyn Rhianydd are identified below.

GELLIWIG

The earliest tale of Arthur, *Culhwch and Olwen,* mentions Gelliwig on several occasions and so this is therefore his earliest recorded court and one of the earliest place names linked to Arthur. Because Kernyw, the realm most closely associated with Arthur, is generally identified as Cornwall the current leading contender for the site of Arthur's court at Gelliwig is the hillfort of Kelly Rounds on the northern coast of Cornwall, based purely on the slight similarity of the name. However, we found Gelliwig mentioned in the poetry of the Gogynfeirdd bards:

I Arthur loyw deml wrth aur wledig
A'I lwysgall awen lys Gelliwig.

(Like unto soverign Arthur, whose temple shone with gold,
He at Gelliwig, whose court was the noble cell of the muse.)[8]

We also found a mention of Gelliwig in a poem by the Welsh bard Gutun Owain: '*Lle Kawn Gelliwic Kwynedd*' (We find Gelliwig in Gwynedd).[9]

We were encouraged by this as Kernyw comprised the coastal region of Gwynedd and the Lleyn Peninsula, so we decided to look for the original site of this court in this area. After a long study of the maps of the Lleyn

Peninsula we found the place name Gelliwig in relation to two properties south of the village of Botwnnog near the end of the Lleyn Peninsula. Set in a fertile plain near the coast at Porth Neigwl (Hell's Mouth) are the remains of a small deciduous wood – Gelliwig means 'woodland' or 'forest' – and a large house called Plas Gelliwig (the Hall of Gelliwig) and Gelliwig Farm. Any trace of the original settlement of Arthur has long since disappeared, but the fact that the place name exists in its original form in the old Welsh kingdom of Kernyw suggests that the landscape does not forget places of importance from our past.

PENRHYN RHIANEDD

Arthur's court at Penrhyn Rhianedd is very obscure and unknown outside of Welsh tradition. Its location in Y Gogledd has led many to look for it in Scotland, but as we have seen, Y Gogledd simply means 'the North' and is referring to North Wales, not Scotland. By using the evidence contained within the above *Triad* we soon found ourselves again pointing to a site on the modern map.

The first element of the place name – Penrhyn – is a common Welsh geographical term for a headland. The second element – Rhianedd – is found elsewhere in Welsh tradition and provides the key to the location of Arthur's Court. The traditions associated with Maelgwn Gwynedd (one of the chief elders of the *Triad*) tell of a yellow plague that will rise out of a place called Morfa Rhianedd and cause his death. In another tale we are told of a race over Morfa Rhianedd in which the winner finds a pot of gold, and finally we are told that it is the 'burial place of Maidens', hence its name Rhianedd, a Welsh word for 'maidens'.

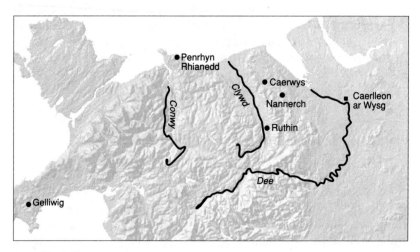

Map 33 Arthur's courts

Morfa Rhianedd translates as the 'Seastrand of the Maidens' and is located on the North Wales coast between Llandudno and Colwyn Bay; on this stretch of coast is the town of Penrhyn Bay – could this be the original 'Penrhyn on the Rhianedd'? Half a mile inland from Penrhyn Bay is the hillfort named Dinarth (the Fortress of the Bear, or possibly Arthur) – could this be the original site of Arthur's court?[10] This identification was confirmed when we looked at the history of the Chief Bishop of the court, Cynderyn Garthwys (better known to history as St Kentigern), who was also attached to Maelgwyn Gwynedd at Deganwy and the foundation of the nearby monastic establishment of Llanelwy (St Asaph).[11]

ARTHUR'S MISTRESSES

The mistresses of Arthur are not mentioned outside of Welsh material and only the briefest allusions exist to them in the Welsh. They are named in one of the *Triads* as follows:

Indec verch Arvy Hir
A Garven verch Henin Hen
A Gvyl verch Endavt

(Indeg daughter of Garwy Hir [tall]
and Garwen [fairleg] daughter of Henin the old
and Gwyl [modest] daughter of Gendrawd [big chin])

Of the women named above the easiest to identify and locate is Garwen. Her burial site is mentioned in the *Stanzas of the Graves* along with that of Rhun and Lledin as being in the Morfa. Rhun was the son of Maelgwyn Gwynedd, who held court at Degannwy, and Lledin is remembered in the place name Rhiw Lledin, near Llandudno. The Morfa talked of is therefore Morfa Rhianedd (the Seastrand of Maidens), which as we saw earlier stretched across the coast near Llandudno. Indeg is mentioned as one of the women of Arthur's court in *Culhwch and Olwen*, which shows an early date for the origin of this tradition. Her father was Garwy Hir, who was known in Welsh tradition as a great lover, and in a poem by the Gogynfeirdd bard Hywel ab Einion Llygliw, we are told that the centre of his affections was Myfanwy Fychan, who lived in the castle of Dinas Bran that overlooks the town of Llangollen. The final mistress Gwyl is not known outside of this *Triad*. There is no mention of mistresses in the *Brut* and this *Triad* has preserved a very early knowledge of Arthur's personal life not recorded elsewhere.

ARTHUR'S CHILDREN

As well as its famous list of Arthur's twelve battles the *Historia Brittonum* of Nennius contains other references to Arthur. One of these concerns a stone mound (in the region of Builth in Mid-Wales) containing a stone that is superimposed with the footprint of Arthur's dog Cafall or Caball that was involved in the hunt for the boar named Trwyth and is mentioned in *Culhwch and Olwen*. Another reference is to a marvel in the region of Erging (modern Herefordshire) concerning the grave of Llygad Amr, who was killed by his father Arthur, for every time the grave is measured it is a different size. Amr is one of several sons of Arthur to be mentioned in Welsh tradition:

Amhar/Amr Killed by his father and buried in Llygad Amr in Herefordshire. Also mentioned in *Culhwch and Olwen*.

Gwydre Killed by the boar Twrch Trwyth in the Preseleu mountains in West Wales, according to *Culhwch and Olwen*.

Llacheu His death at Llongborth is mentioned in an early poem from *The Black Book of Carmarthen*. He is the only son of Arthur to have made it into the later Arthurian romances, where he was called Loholt, the son of Arthur in *Erec et Enide* by Chrétien de Troyes. He is also mentioned in *Perlesvaus*.

Cydfan He is mentioned in a Welsh manuscript regarding the Children of Iaen, who is also mentioned in *Culhwch and Olwen* and unknown outside of North Wales. Iaen had a daughter called Elerich, mother of Cydfan ab Arthur. The implication here is that Arthur had a son called Cydfan by Elerich, who is otherwise unknown.

Arthur is also said to have had a daughter called Archfedd who is only mentioned in one source, a collection of genealogies called *Bonedd Y Saint* (Lineage of the Saints): 'Efadier and Gwrial, the children of Llawfrodedd Farchog and Archfedd the daughter of Arthur, their mother.'[12] Nothing else is known about the two children referred to here, but Llawfrodedd is named as a member of Arthur's court in *Culhwch and Olwen* and as one of Arthur's 42 counsellors in *The Dream of Rhonabwy*. These two tales from *The Mabinogion* preserve some of the earliest and most authentic traditions regarding the historical Arthur.

ARTHUR AND THE HEAD OF BRAN

The tradition concerning Arthur and the head of Bran is to be found in the *Triad* entitled *The Three Unfortunate Concealments and Disclosures of Ynys Prydein*:

> The head of Bran Fendigaid, son of Llyr, which was concealed in Gwynfryn in Llundain, with its face towards Frainc. And as long as it was in the position in which it was put there, no Saxon oppresion would ever come to this kingdom.
>
> And Arthur disclosed the head of Bran Fendigaid from Gwynfryn, because it did not seem right to him that this kingdom should be defended by the strength of anyone but by his own.

The story of how and where the head of Bran Fendigaid was buried is told in the Second Branch of *The Mabinogion*, in a tale called *Branwen the Daughter of Llyr*. According to the tale Bran went to Ireland to rescue his sister Branwen and whilst in battle with her captives was injured in his foot by a poisoned arrow. He told his companions to cut off his head and take it back to Ynys Prydein, and so they returned to Prydein and spent seven years feasting with Bran's head at Harlech, for his head still spoke. From Harlech they carried Bran's head to a palace on the island of Gwales in Penfro (the island of Grassholm off the coast of Pembrokeshire). For 80 years the magical powers of Bran's head provided food and drink for the entourage and time passed by very quickly. From the island the head was taken to Gwynfryn (White Hill) in Llundain (Ludlow), as directed by Bran himself. The story ends by saying that no oppression could come from across the sea to Ynys Prydein as long as the head remained concealed, which suggests that the *Triad* and the tale of *Branwen* share a common tradition.

Arthur's removal of the head is only found in this *Triad* and the implication is that his action was instrumental in his downfall. The site of Gwynfryn has long been identified as the Tower of London because of the confusion between Llundain and London and this raises an interesting question concerning the ravens at the Tower, for tradition states that if the ravens ever leave the Tower England will be invaded and conquered. This tradition parallels the story of Bran's head very closely, but as *bran* is the Welsh word for 'raven', could this be a garbled remembrance of the Bran story?

The early date of the Welsh tradition concerning Bran's head is attested to by the inclusion of the two other concealments and disclosures from the *Triad* – the dragons of Dinas Emrys and the resting place of the bones of Vortimer, both mentioned earlier in this book – in the *Historia Brittonum* attributed to Nennius (c.800). The tradition can therefore be traced back at least to the eighth century and probably has its origins much further back in time.

THE MYTH OF THE ONCE AND FUTURE KING

One of the most intriguing myths associated with Arthur is the idea that he is asleep in a cave and will one day return to save the country in its hour of need. The motif of a hero sleeping in a cave is found in mythical traditions across the world, but why and when did it become associated with Arthur?

The poetry of the Gogynfeirdd bards has provided many valuable clues in identifying people and events from the Arthurian legends and it is within their poetry that we find the Welsh point of view concerning Arthur's supposed immortality. In fact, the Gogynfeirdd never refer to the return of Arthur and are often quite explicit as to his mortal end:

Maredut marw yw heuyd
Mal modur Arthur arthreyd

(Maredudd also is dead,
as is sovereign Arthur.)[13]

It was poetry such as this that led Professor T. Gwynn Jones to conclude in 1927: 'There is no evidence whatever in these poems that the bards believed the tradition that Arthur was not dead, and that he would one day return to free his people from bondage.'[14]

If there was no bardic tradition for Arthur's return, where did the idea come from? Elis Gruffydd gives us a clue in his *Chronicle* of 1530: 'And yet they [the English] talk more about him than we [the Welsh] do; for they say and firmly believe that he will rise again to be king.'[15] In fact the concept of Arthur waiting in some kind of otherworld to return and rescue the nation in its hour of need originated in the 12th century with the Normans, who were also responsible for turning Arthur into the chivalrous king we know today. The original 'once and future king' of the Welsh was Cadwaladr, the last king of the Britons, of whom Welsh poetry tells us that he would return to rescue Prydein from its enemies.[16] Not wanting to encourage the idea of a native Welsh king returning to drive them out of Wales, the Normans simply replaced Cadwaladr with Arthur (whom they had already made one of their own) and used the concept to further their own cause.

In the 15th century the Welsh were to turn the Norman invention of Arthur's return against its creators, using it for their own propaganda during the rise to power of Henry VII in 1485. For the first time since Cadwaladr, a descendant of the original British royal bloodline was on the throne, not only of Wales but of England as well. Henry VII named his eldest son Arthur and the country awaited the return of Arthur to the throne of Britain, but his premature death in 1502 meant that this expected return never happened. The Norman propaganda of Arthur's return was used by the Welsh Tudors to gain acceptance in England, while in Wales poetry comparing Henry with Cadwaladr was used to appeal to the Welsh. As a consequence, the idea of Arthur's return was not entertained widely in Wales until the late fifteenth century, and even then it only took root slowly. The English, however, had been fed the myth from two different dynasties – the Normans and the Tudors – and therefore the legend of the 'once and future king' was much stronger than in Wales.

APPENDIX THREE:
THE 'LOST' KINGDOMS OF NORTHERN BRITAIN

In the course of the our research for this book we came across many references to the 'North British Kingdoms' and the 'Men of the North'. Recent history books appeared to offer little consensus and much conjecture about the significance of these terms. It soon became clear that if we were to make any sense of them, the entire concept of the 'North British Kingdoms' would need fresh scrutiny. And so, aided by our new geographical understanding of this period, that is exactly what we did. This section summarizes some of the most important points arising from our research. (We intend to publish a more detailed account of our findings in the not too distant future.)

Within the early Welsh texts there are many references to places in and people from Y Gogledd (the North); they also mention a genealogical tract entitled *Bonedd Gwyr y Gogledd* (The Lineage of the Men of the North). Standard history books about the Dark Ages tell us that all these references relate to southern Scotland, where there once existed a British-Welsh-speaking kingdom. Sometimes referred to as the 'Old North', this kingdom was presumed to have been located in the area of the Rock of Dumbarton on the River Clyde near Glasgow.

The fact that our history books refer to the location of this kingdom with such certainty is surprising, for one very simple reason – not one of the people or place names linked to Y Gogledd can be positively identified with a site in Scotland. Another reason for finding fault with the traditional argument is that nowhere within Scottish folklore is there a remembrance of the kingdom or its people. The only places where references to any of the people or locations connected to Y Gogledd can be found are in North Wales.

So how has this theoretical anomaly been explained away? Despite the lack of textual evidence, historians have conjectured that the references to many of the people and place names linked to Y Gogledd can be found within North Wales because of a Dark Age exodus that relocated them there. The theory goes that at some point in the eighth century the 'North Britons' of Y Gogledd were forced south to join their fellow Welsh-speakers in Wales. The refugees brought all of their stories and histories with them, writing new poems and stories to relocate their heroes within the landscape of North Wales. Yet, in spite of this and other tortuous arguments that try to make the evidence to fit the theory, the fact remains that not one of the primary locations named as being in Y Gogledd can be positively identified with a single site in Scotland.

We tried to find out what had gone wrong and discovered that the crux of the problem could be traced back to the simple misunderstanding of one word, *ynys*. As we have seen, *ynys* can mean 'island', but another meaning for it is 'realm'. All references in the source materials to Y Gogledd (the North) of Ynys Prydein have been taken to refer to the north of the island of Britain as we understand it today, hence the bizarre theory that a Welsh-speaking kingdom existed in Scotland. Having already established that the term Ynys Prydein only ever referred to Wales and the Marches, we reread the texts in the belief that Y Gogledd might mean North Wales. (The modern Welsh name for North Wales is Gogledd Cymru, which has led to people in South Wales giving those from the North the nickname Gogs!) We quickly came to the conclusion that the supposed secondary localizations of characters in North Wales were not secondary at all, but the original locations. The discovery of the original locations of these 'North British Kingdoms' has proved invaluable for our understanding of Dark Age history and the time of Arthur.

RHEGED

The exact location of Rheged has long proved elusive, a fact that prompted the scholar J. Gwenogfryn Evans to call the kingdom, 'a sort of Wandering Jew among Welsh Archaeologists'.[1] Where once the boundaries of the kingdom were thought to have stretched from the Mersey to Inverness, the currently accepted theory is that Rheged encompassed Carlisle and the Dumfries and Galloway region of southern Scotland.

Given that Rheged was ruled over by the great king Urien Rheged, if the current theory is correct we might expect to find place names and folklore associated with him in Scotland, but not one tradition or place name relates to him outside Wales, where Urien is mentioned on several occasions in the poetry of Llywarch Hen (c.700), which is set in Powys. As we saw in Chapter 8, he also appears in the folklore of North Wales where tales describe him having raped Modron, the daugher of Afallach, at a ford near the village of Llanferres in Denbighshire. However, this type of evidence has again been explained away as secondary localization and the futile hunt for place names and other references in Scotland has continued, despite the fact that J. Gwenogfryn Evans provided ample evidence for the location of Rheged in North Wales as far back as 1910.

J. Gwenogfryn Evans argued that the name Rheged was a mutated form of Rhedeg, which in modern Welsh means 'run' or 'march' and is therefore related to the area of the Welsh borders still known today as the 'Marches'. Evidence to support this identification – as with so many of the findings of this book – can be found in the poetry of the Gogynfeirdd. A poem by

Hywel ab Owain Gwynedd (1140–72) suggests the true location of Rheged:

Esgynneis ar velyn o vaelyenyt
Hyd ynhir Reged rwg nos ymy a dyt

(I mounted a bay from Maelienydd
At last came to Rheged, rode day and night)[2]

According to these verses, Rheged lay a good day's ride from Maelienydd, the region of Mid-Wales that surrounds the village of Llanbister near Llandrindod Wells. As Rheged is said to be in the North we can presume that the narrator of the poem rode in that direction. It was in this northern area that J. Gwenogfryn Evans located Rheged, suggesting that the perimeters of the kingdom were roughly the same as those of the Domesday hundred of Mersete on the Welsh borders, an area that in turn corresponded with the medieval deaneries of Marchia and Edeirnion, part of the diocese of St Asaph. The name Marchia is derived from the same root as marches and is therefore merely an Anglicized version of Rheged. We know that the Edeirnion covered the region around the Dee valley and the northern half of the Berwyn Mountains.[3] Moreover, folklore often connects Urien Rheged to this area, which is about 50 miles – or a day's ride north – from Maelienydd. A further reference to Rheged in a poem by

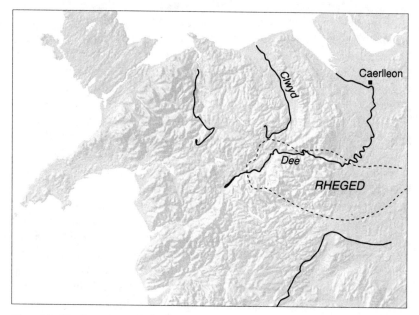

Map 34 The location of Rheged in North Wales

the 13th-century bard Llygad Gwr places it in or near the region of Maelor on the Welsh border.[4]

Which, we wonder, makes the most sense? A supposed kingdom in Scotland for which there is no definitive evidence and that lies in a region possessing no associations whatsoever with that kingdom's ruler? Or an area in North Wales rich with folklore and place names related to the ruler and confirmed by geographical references from 12th-century Welsh bards? We must conclude that, as Rheged is unknown outside Welsh material, it is only Geoffrey's Latin mistranslation of Rheged into Mureifensium (Morayshire) and the misguided ideas concerning the location of Y Gogledd that have led to it being identified with a part of Scotland.

THE GODODDIN

The Gododdin is one of the earliest Welsh poems, composed in the sixth century and preserved in the 14th-century Book of Aneirin. It describes a battle between the men of Deira and Bernica and the men of Gwynedd at a site called Catraeth. Traditional commentary on this poem would have us believe that the men of Deira and Bernica were from the northeast of England and southern Scotland, and that the men of Gwynedd (North Wales) met them in battle at Catterick in Yorkshire.

As we discovered in Chapter 3, if the descriptions offered by the bards are taken into account, the true locations of the ancient Kingdoms of Deira and Bernica correspond with areas that lie within the modern counties of Shropshire and Cheshire. As Gwynedd is the old name for North Wales, a battle between these neighbouring regions would make much sense. However, that still leaves Catraeth.

The name 'Catraeth' breaks down into two elements: cat and traeth. Sir John Rhys points out that cat is cognate with cad, which means 'battle', and traeth is still in modern usage, meaning 'shore' or 'beach'.[5] Therefore 'Catraeth' simply means the Battle Shore. However, Catterick in Yorkshire is 50 miles inland!

J. Gwenogfryn Evans draws our attention to 'the lands of Catraeth' in North Wales within a 12th-century poem by Elidir Sais: 'Gallas dreis ar direw catraeth' (able to take by force the lands of Catraeth).[6] These lands were captured by Rodri ap Owain Gwynedd (d.1195), who never left Wales yet waged many battles against his half-brother Dafydd on both the Menai Straits near Anglesey and the River Conwy. All of the available evidence suggests that the lands of Catraeth lie somewhere along the North Wales coast, possibly on an estuary. This is further confirmed by reference in The

Gododdin to the battle taking place at Mordei, which means that it took place near the sea (*mor* is Welsh for 'sea').[7]

We are not the first to quetion the accepted ideas regarding this battlesite or to suggest a location on the North Wales coast: our old friend J. Gwenogfryn Evans also studied *The Book of Aneirin* and came to a similar conclusion. Unfortunately he peppered his deductions with bizarre ideas on chronology in order to try to prove his point, which led to everybody dismissing the rest of his argument, despite the fact that the evidence he used from the bardic poetry is as valid today as it was 90 years ago. He suggested that Catraeth was on the shores of the Menai Straits at Castle Aber Lleiniog, on the island of Anglesey.

It is worth noting that the handful of place names preserved within *The Book of Aneirin* the few that can be located include Rhufoniog (a region to the west of Denbigh), the River Aled near Denbigh, the town of Caerwys and Rhyd Ben Clwyd (the ford at the head of the River Clwyd), all of which are in North Wales.

MANAW GODODDIN

The location of the other lost Kingdom of the North, Manaw Gododdin, is even more obscure than Rheged. Current theories place it in the vicinity of the Firth of Forth in Scotland. We dealt in Chapter 11 with the traditions concerning the migration of Cunedda Wledig and his sons from this region to the western parts of Wales.

The word *Gododdin* has long been thought to be a Welsh rendering of Otadini, the name given to a Scottish tribe by Ptolemy (c.140),[8] yet despite the weakness of this argument it has been adhered to tightly, for without it there is no evidence to place Gododdin or Manaw in Scotland and the whole idea of the 'Northern British Kingdoms' collapses. It should also be noted that the phrase *Manaw Gododdin* only appears in a single instance in one manuscript, all other references being to either *Manaw* or *Gododdin* but never the two together.

By revisiting Welsh bardic poetry, we can find some clues as to the original location of Manaw. In a poem from *The Red Book of Hergest* entitled *Cyfoesi Myrddin a Gwenddydd I Chwaer* (A Conversation between Merlin and his sister Gwenddydd), we find the following line: '*Mervin vrych o dir Manaw*' (Mervyn Frych from the land of Manaw).[9] Merfyn Frych was Prince of Gwynedd (d.844), which suggests that Manaw was a region of that kingdom. Other references to Manaw in Welsh bardic poetry always mention it in the context of North Wales,[10] and there is one reference from outside the works of the bards which also reinforces this suggestion. In the

12th-century *Life of St Gildas* by Caradoc of Llancarfan we are told that Gildas's elder brother Huail was killed by Arthur in Manaw,[11] but – as we saw in Appendix Two – local tradition states that he was killed in Ruthin. Does this mean that Ruthin in North Wales once lay within the province of Manaw? It is difficult to establish the precise boundaries of Manaw, but we can be certain that it was never located in Scotland as that identification contradicts all of the evidence available from the source materials.

Scotland has a history all of its own and the grafting of all this Dark Age material onto its landscape has done nothing but cause confusion. In view of this, we may well ask how such misidentifications have become so established as to appear in every history book published within the last hundred years. Sadly, it has long been an accepted practice to place an event within a conjectured time and place in order to create a seemingly coherent depictation of events, which often involves the manipulation of pieces of evidence, ultimately contradicting the overall picture. It is surprising and not a little unsettling to discover that the general understanding of an important part of history has been based on little more than supposition.

The present clouded understanding of the Dark Ages can only be cleared up by reassessing the geography of the events. Then and only then can we begin to understand the history of our ancestors. The whole concept of a Northern British Kingdom was based on nothing more than the misunderstanding of the geography. As this book has shown, many of the references to 'The Wall' relate to the Wall of Severus (Offa's Dyke in Wales), not Hadrian's Wall on the English–Scottish border. When this fact is combined with the original location of the Kingdoms of Deira and Bernica in Cheshire and northern Shropshire, a whole corpus of evidence begins to make sense in its original North Wales context.

APPENDIX FOUR:
SOURCE MATERIALS

We firmly believe that people should be encouraged to examine the Arthurian source materials for themselves. To that end, this appendix aims to give a brief overview of the sources and to guide the reader to the publications in which the original texts and translations appear.

When considering source material, it is important to distinguish between the date of authorship and the date of the oldest manuscript in which the text has survived. Nennius, for example, wrote the *Historia Brittonum* around 800, but the earliest manuscript to preserve his text dates from about 1100. Sadly none of the surviving manuscripts of the earliest source texts (including Roman and other Classical sources) were transcribed in the hands of their authors.

References to author and year (e.g. Wade-Evans, 1938) can be found in more detail in the Bibliography. Abbreviations used below are:

MS.   manuscript,

MSS.   manuscripts (plural),

UWP   University of Wales Press.

GILDAS (C.AD 540)

A Welsh monk who lived in the sixth century, Gildas is the author of the earliest British document to have survived. His work can be divided into two parts, *De Excidio et Conquesta Britanniae* and the *Epistola*. The *Epistola* was written around 540 and mentions several Welsh kings known from other sources. The authorship and date of *De Excidio* has been a subject of some controversy, with one faction of scholars believing it to date from as late as about 708. (For a discussion of the theory behind this date see A.W. Wade-Evans's *The Emergence of England and Wales*, 1959.) Whichever date is correct, the work still predates Bede and was consulted by him in his *History of the English Church* (see below).

The standard edition for the work of both Gildas and Nennius (see below) is *Monumenta Germaniae Historica*, *Chronica Minora*, Vol. III, edited by Theodore Mommsen, Berlin, 1894. This edition is written entirely in Latin, notes and all, and is not widely available. It is still, however, considered to be the best version of the text that we have (although it does seem a shame that we still have to rely on an edition over 100 years old in order to access one of the most important works from the Dark Age of British history).

A later edition of the Latin text of Gildas's work, including a facing translation and copious notes, was edited by Hugh Williams in two volumes – *Gildas Part I* and *Part II* – for the Cymmrodorion Record Series, 1899–1901. This edition also included the two versions of the life of Gildas, one from Brittany and the other by Caradoc of Llancarfan. It also includes facing translations and a summary of references to Gildas from early manuscripts. The latest edition to include an English translation and notes is *Gildas*, edited by M. Winterbottom, *Arthurian Sources*, Vol. 7, Philimore, 1978.

BEDE (AD 731)

Bede was an English monk whose writings have survived in very early MSS. He wrote many works, including a chronicle, biographies of saints and commentaries on the Gospels, but the work that is of most interest is his history of the English Church. Written from an anti-British point of view, it is a major source for the period. A detailed academic edition was edited by C. Plummer in 1898 as *Baedae Opera Historica*, Oxford University Press. This in turn was translated by Leo Sherley-Price in *A History of the English Church and People*, Penguin, 1968.

NENNIUS (C.AD 820)

There are over 35 different manuscripts of a work called *Historia Brittonum* in Latin and five versions in Irish. The text consists of a series of extracts starting with the Trojan origin of the Britons through to the Saxon kings of the eighth century. It is the source for the famous list of the 12 battles of Arthur against the Saxons and his first verifiable historical mention.

The work is commonly ascribed to Nennius as the earliest date of compilation is derived from the mention of his name in the introduction to the Harleian MS. 3859: 'I Nennius, disciple of Elvodugus, have undertaken to write some extracts – up to the fourth year of king Merfyn ruler of Gwynedd' (c.830). The aforementioned Elvodugus is referred to in the *Annales Cambriae* as the Bishop of Gwynedd in North Wales; this, combined with brief references to Nennius in other sources, has led to the suggestion that Nennius was a monk from Bangor in North Wales. Other manuscripts of the *Historia Brittonum* offer different introductions: 'Samuel child of my master, Beulan in the thirtieth year of Anarawad, king of Mon, who now rules the realm of Gwynedd.' (AD 907–8, Cambridge Corpus Christi MS.139), and: 'Here begins the History of the Britons, edited by Mark the Anchorite, of the same race, a holy Bishop in the fifth year of King Edmund.' (AD 943–4, Vatican text.)

The earliest surviving manuscript of the *Historia Brittonum* (c.900) was housed in the Chartres city library in France. In the introduction we are told: 'Here begin excerpts of the son of Urien found in the book of Saint Germanus, and concerning the origin and genealogy of the Britons, and concerning the Ages of the World.' If the 'son of Urien' is the same person as Rhun ap Urien mentioned in some later versions, the manuscript may possibly date from the first half of the seventh century.

The Latin text was published in the journal *Révue Celtique*, Vol. XV, 1894 by Duchesne. An English translation with notes was published by A.W. Wade-Evans in the journal *Archaeologica Cambrensis*, 1937, pp.64–85, but it is the 1938 translation by Wade-Evans that has been used throughout this book.

All five Irish texts were edited together by A.G. Van Hamel in *Lebor Bretnach*, The Stationery Office, Dublin, 1932, an edition that also included the Latin text from the Harleian MS. John Morris edited and translated a version in *Nennius, Arthurian Sources,* Vol. 8, Philimore, 1980. The most recent Latin edition is the Vatican manuscript edited by David Dumville, *The Historia Brittonum* 3: *The Vatican Recension*, Boydell and Brewer, 1985.

THE *ANNALES CAMBRIAE* (TENTH CENTURY)

This important chronicle can be found in four manuscripts. Three of these (A, B and C) were edited together in the Rolls edition of John ab Ithel in 1860. A fourth text (D) was edited by Thomas Jones in *Cronica Wallia* and other documents from Exeter Cathedral Library MS. 3514, 1946. An English translation can be found in Wade-Evans 1938 and in John Morris's edition of Nennius (see above).

THE *ANGLO-SAXON CHRONICLE* (TENTH CENTURY)

The edition of six of the remaining seven MSS. published in the two-volume Rolls Series edition of 1861 will soon be superseded by the collaborative edition edited by Boydell and Brewer. This involves each manuscript being edited individually. At the time of going to press four of the seven have been completed (MSS. A, B, D and F in a facsimile copy). The most recent English translation of *The Anglo-Saxon Chronicle*, edited by Michael Swanton, includes variants from different manuscripts, contains a very full and up-to-date bibliography and was published by Dent in 1996.

Another important source from this era is *The Life of King Alfred* by Asser (c.890). The Latin text can be found in Asser's *Life of King Alfred*, second edition, edited by D. Whitelock, Oxford, 1959. An English translation by Keynes and Lapidge is in *Alfred the Great: Asser's Life of King Alfred and other Contemporary Sources*, Penguin, 1983.

LIVES OF THE SAINTS

Accounts of the lives of a majority of the Welsh saints are edited and translated in *Vitae Sanctorum Britanniae et Genealogiae* by A.W. Wade-Evans, UWP, 1944. *The Lives of the British Saints,* edited by Sabine Baring-Gould and John Fisher in four volumes (published by the Society of the Cymmrodorion, 1908–13), gives information about all of the saints connected to Wales, whether famous or obscure. Although a little dated in places it is still the standard starting point as it collects together many lives and other important documents in their original form and/or in translation. Other works that are very useful include: *The Saints of Gwynedd* by Molly Miller, Boydell, 1979, which provides a detailed study of this area of North Wales; *Welsh Christian Origins* by A.W. Wade-Evans, Alden, 1934; and E.G. Bowen's *The Settlements of the Celtic Saints in Wales*, UWP, 1954 and *Saints, Seaways and Settlements,* UWP, 1969. Attention should also be drawn to the Bollandists, a group within the Jesuit movement who have been publishing the lives of saints from all over the world since the 17th century. Their 61-volume library of saints' lives is known as *Acta Sanctorum* and is almost exclusively written in Latin. They also publish a journal called *Analecta Bollandina*, which occasionally deals with material relevant to Britain.

THE *HISTORIA* AND *BRUT Y BRENHINEDD*

The first critical edition of Geoffrey of Monmouth's Latin *Historia* was *The Historia Regum Britanniae* of *Geoffrey of Monmouth* edited by Acton Griscom in 1929: this edition was based upon Cambridge MS. 1709 and listed variants from two other manuscripts. The most recent text to be printed is taken from Bern MS. 568 and edited by Neil Wright in *Historia Regum Brittaniae* I, Bern, Burgerbibliothek, MS. 568, Boydell and Brewer, 1984. Some of the surviving Latin texts which differ from the standard version of the text have been grouped together by scholars and become collectively known as the variant edition. These can be found in Jacob Hammer's *Geoffrey of Monmouth's Historia Regum Brittaniae, A variant edition edited from the MSS*, The Medieval Academy of America, 1951. Another edition containing these variants is *Historia Regum Britanniae II, The First Variant Version: A Critical Edition*, edited by Neil Wright, Boydell and Brewer, 1986. A catalogue of the surviving Latin manuscripts has been compiled by Julia Crick in *Historia Regum Britanniae III, A Summary Catalogue of the Manuscripts*, Boydell and Brewer, 1989.

The text of the *Brut* referred to as *Brut Tysilio* in *The Myvyrian Archaiology* (3 vols. 1801–06, reprinted as one volume in 1870) is from Jesus College, Oxford MS. 28 which in itself is a copy of Jesus College, Oxford MS. 61. This was translated in 1811 by Peter Roberts in *The History of The Kings of Britain*, which was superseded by the translation in Griscom, 1929. The version in *The Red Book of Hergest* was edited by John Rhys and John Gwenogfryn Evans in *The Text of the Bruts from the Red Book of Hergest*, Oxford, 1890. Included in Griscom's 1929 edition was an English translation by the Reverend R.E. Jones of the Welsh text of Jesus College MS. 61, which fortunately left the proper names in their original form. The text of Cotton Cleopatra, B.V., was published with variants from *The Black Book of Basingwerk* along with an accompanying translation in 1937, but unfortunately the translation used the commonly accepted names instead of the originals and as it was these that were used in the index it can be quite frustrating to consult. This edition had a very small print run of only 400. The version taken from the earliest surviving Welsh MS. (c.1200) was edited by Henry Lewis in *Brut Dingestow*, UWP, 1942, with detailed notes (in Welsh). Extracts from Llanstephan MS. 1 with notes in English were edited by Brynley F. Roberts in *Brut Y Brenhinedd*, Dublin Institute of Advanced Celtic Studies, 1971, which also includes a very useful essay entitled 'The *Historia Regum Britanniae* in Wales'.

The only English version currently available is *The History of the Kings of Britain*, translated by Lewis Thorpe, Penguin, 1966, which translates the Latin text published by Griscom in 1929. The index to this translation also lists the Welsh equivalents for place names used in the Jesus College MS. as reproduced in Griscom, 1929 and is very useful. The standard discussion of this work is *The Legendary History of Britain* by J.P.S. Tatlock, University of California Press, 1950.

Two articles from academic journals that we consider essential reading are: 'The Book of Basingwerk and MS. Cotton Cleopatra, B.V.' by the Reverend Acton Griscom in *Y Cymmrodor*, Vol. XXXV, pp.49–116 and continued in Vol. XXXVI, pp.1–33; and 'The Welsh Versions of Geoffrey of Monmouth' by Edmund Reiss in *The Welsh Historical Review*, Vol. IV, 1968, pp.97–128.

THE MABINOGION

The tales collectively known as *The Mabinogion* survive primarily in two Welsh manuscripts known as *The White Book of Rhydderch* and *The Red Book of Hergest*. These have been published in diplomatic editions (in which the text is reproduced in type exactly as it is on the manuscript), including: *Llyfr Gwyn Rhydderch,* edited by J.G. Evans, 1907, reprinted with a new introduction (in Welsh) by R.M. Jones, UWP, 1973; and *The Text of The Mabinogion and Other Welsh Tales from the Red Book of Hergest,* edited by John Rhys and John Gwenogfryn Evans, Oxford, 1887.

The best English translation of *The Mabinogion* is the 1948 Everyman edition by Gwyn Jones and Thomas Jones. In 1993 a revised edition included an index of proper names, which is very useful. It contains an excellent introduction to the tales and an appendix of variant readings from the different manuscripts makes it suitable for those who which to study the texts in more detail.

Most of the individual tales have been edited separately and published with detailed notes. *Culhwch and Olwen, The Oldest Arthurian Tale*, edited by R. Bromwich and S. Evans, UWP, 1992, is an edition of the Welsh text with variant readings and includes an introduction and detailed notes in English. *The Dream of Rhonabwy* was edited by Melville Richards and published in 1948 by UWP under the title *Breudwyt Ronabwy* with detailed notes (in Welsh). Of the three romances *Owain* and *Geraint* have been edited and published with English notes by the Dublin Institute of Advanced Celtic Studies. *The Dream of Macsen Wledig* was edited by Ifor Williams with notes (in Welsh) in *Breuddwyd Maxen*, third edition, Bangor, 1928.

THE *TRIADS*

These have been edited with a translation, commentary and notes by Rachel Bromwich in *Trioedd Ynys Prydein*, second edition, UWP, 1978 (at the time of going to print a third edition was imminent and eagerly awaited). Also included in this work are invaluable and extensive notes on the characters and places mentioned in the *Triads*. A collection of *Triads* called the Third Series, only known to exist in later manuscripts, has been edited and translated by Rachel Bromwich in 'Trioedd Ynys Prydain: The Myvyrian "Third Series"', *The Transactions of the Honourable Society of Cymmrodorion*, 1968, Part II, pp.299–338 and 1969, Part I, pp.127–56.

WELSH BARDIC POETRY

The earliest Welsh poetry is found primarily in four major MSS.

A facsimile edition of *The Book of Taliesin* was published by J. Gwenogfryn Evans in 1910; this edition also included a text transcript. Individual poems from *The Book of Taliesin* have also been edited, the most important of which is the prophecy *Armes Prydein*, published with an English translation and notes by Rachel Bromwich, Dublin Institute of Advanced Studies, 1972. Some of the poems were also translated by John Matthews in *Taliesin: Shamanism and the Bardic Mysteries in Britain and Ireland*, Aquarian Press, 1991.

A facsimile edition of *The Book of Aneirin*, edited by Daniel Huws, was published by National Library of Wales, as *Llyfr Aneirin*, in 1989. An edition of the poem including notes (in Welsh) was published in 1938 under the title *Canu Aneirin*, by Ifor Williams; it was later translated by Kenneth Jackson in *The Oldest Scottish Poem, The Gododdin*, Edinburgh, 1969 and again by A.O.H. Jarman in *Y Gododdin*, Gomer Press, 1988.

In 1923 J. Gwenogfryn Evans published an emended text with a translation that is primarily of curiosity value only, although it was in the introduction to this work that he first put forward the idea that the Battle of Catraeth took place on Anglesey, using evidence from the poetry of the Gogynfeirdd to prove his point.

A diplomatic edition of *The Black Book of Carmarthen* was edited by J. Gwenogfryn Evans in 1906. The most recent edition is *Llyfyr Du Caerfyrddin*, edited with notes (in Welsh) by A.O.H. Jarman, UWP, 1982.

The Red Book of Hergest was edited by J. G. Evans, 1911. See below.

The poetry of Llywarch Hen has now been edited and translated with detailed notes by Jenny Rowlands in *Early Welsh Saga Poetry*, Boydell and Brewer, 1990.

EARLY ARTHURIAN POETRY

Arthur is mentioned on several occasions in the earliest Welsh poetry in circumstances that differ to those described in the *Brut*. Most of these pre-Norman and often obscure poetic references are little more than a line long.

The Book of Taliesin (1910 edition) mentions Arthur in four different poems: *Marwnad Uthyr Ben* (Death of the Wonderful Head/Uthyr Pendragon?) p.71; *Kanu Y Meirch* (Song of the Horses) p.48; *Cad Goddeu* (The Battle of the Trees) p.23; this is translated in *The Mabinogi and Other Medieval Welsh Tales*, University of California Press, 1977, pp.184–7; and

Preiddau Annwn (The Spoils of Annwn) edited and translated in 'Preiddau Annwn and the Figure of Taliesin' by Marged Haycock, *Studia Celtica*, Vol. XVIII/XIX, 1983–4, p.54.

The Black Book of Carmarthen mentions Arthur on several occasions. The following references are to the original Welsh text in the 1982 edition of *Llyfr Du Caerfyrddin,* edited by A.O.H. Jarman:

• Dialogue between Arthur and the Porter, pp.66–7
• Geraint ab Erbin poem regarding the battle at Llongborth, p.48
• Also mentioned in passing on pp.71 and 77.
• *Stanzas of the Graves*, p.41. (For a detailed consideration of these stanzas see Thomas Jones, *Stanzas of the Graves*, The Sir John Rhys Memorial Lecture, 1967, *Proceedings of the British Academy*, Vol. LIII, pp.97–137.)

The Book of Anerein is generally regarded to contain the earliest ever reference to Arthur in literature, when a warrior is praised for his courage: '*Ceni bei ef Arthur*' (though he was no Arthur). See the edition edited by Sir Ifor Williams, *Canu Aneirin*, UWP,1938, p.49, line 1,242.

Two other early poems include references to Arthur in addition to those manuscripts mentioned above. The first deals with the abduction of Gwenhwyfar by Melwas and appeared under the title *A Conversation Between Arthur and His Second Wife Gwenhwyfar* when it was printed in *The Myvyrian Archaiology* in 1870, although this title is not given in the original manuscripts. These manuscripts (Llanstephan MS. 122 and Wynnstay MS. 1) were edited by Evan D. Jones in *The Bulletin of the Board of Celtic Studies*, Vol.VIII, 1936–7, pp.203–8 and translated by Mary Williams in *Speculum*, Vol.13, 1938, pp.38–51.

The second poem is called *The Prophecy of the Eagle*. It concerns Arthur's conversation with an eagle who turns out to be Eliwlat ap Madoc ap Uthyr and therefore Arthur's own nephew. The conversation turns to matters of good and evil and the eagle tells Arthur that his sins can be absolved by praying to Christ. See *Ymddiddan Arthur a'r Eryr*, edited by Ifor Williams, *The Bulletin of the Board of Celtic Studies*, Vol.II, pp.269–86. Also of note is a translation by Patrick Sims-Williams in *The Early Welsh Arthurian Poems*, *Arthur of the Welsh*, edited by Bromwich, Jarman and Roberts, UWP, 1991.

Many of the other characters associated with Arthur can also be found in references in the early Welsh poetry. Gwenhwyfar, Cai, Trystan, March, Urien, Owain and many others appear in contexts not found in the *Brut* or any of the later romances. These early Welsh poems preserve some of the earliest and most authentic traditions concerning Arthur and early British history.

THE POETRY OF THE GOGYNFEIRDD (1100–1282)

The oldest manuscript of Gogynfeirdd poetry was found in 1910 at the bottom of a wardrobe in Porthmadog, North Wales! It was edited by John Morris-Jones and T.H. Parry in *Llawysgrif Hendregadredd*, UWP, 1933. As this edition is easily available it has been used (wherever possible) for the references in this book.

The collected poetry of the Gogynfeirdd, based on other manuscripts, appears in *The Myvyrian Archaiology*, second edition, Gee and Son, 1870, pp.140–356. This section was printed separately by Edward Anwyl in *The Poetry of the Gogynfeirdd*, Gee and Son, 1909. *The Poetry of the Red Book of Hergest*, edited by J. Gwenogfryn Evans, contains many of the Gogynfeirdd poems, with the rest appearing in a companion volume *Poetry By Medieval Welsh Bards*, 1926, which contains an index to the proper names found in both volumes.

It is only since 1991 that all of the Gogynfeirdd poetry has finally been published in an academic form, with very detailed notes, in the seven-volume series *Cyfres Beirdd Y Tywysgion* (Series of the Poets of the Princes) under the editorship of R.G. Gruffydd (all notes in Welsh).

The few available translations of the poetry of the Gogynfeirdd can be found in: *Early Welsh Poetry,* edited by Joseph Clancy, London,1970; *Welsh Verse*, edited by Tony Conran, Seren, third edition, 1992 (originally published as *The Penguin Book of Welsh Verse*, 1967); and *The Oxford Book of Welsh Verse in English*, edited by Gwyn Jones, Oxford University Press, 1977. A detailed bibliography of English translations by Patrick Sims-Williams can be found in the journal *Ysgrifiau Beirniadol*, Vol. XIII, 1985, pp.39–47.

Now that the whole corpus of poetry has been edited to an academic level it is hoped that popular translations will be published, thus bringing the important information contained within these poems to a wider audience.

The poems of the later bards have been collected together on an individual basis. The three volumes used most frequently in this book are:

- *Guto'r Glyn – Gwaith Guto Glyn*, edited by Ifor Williams and J. Lloyd Williams, UWP, 1937.
- *Gutun Owain – L'Œuvre Poetique de Gutun Owain*, edited by E. Bachellery, 2 vols, Paris, 1950–51 (notes and translations in French).
- *Tudur Aled – Gwaith Tudur Aled*, edited by T. Gwynn Jones, UWP, 2 vols, 1926.

GENEALOGICAL MATERIAL

Peter Bartrum's *Early Welsh Genealogical Tracts*, UWP, 1966, brings together edited versions of all of the surviving early texts and is regarded as the standard work on its subject. Peter Bartrum is also responsible for the 18-volume *Welsh Genealogies AD 300–1400* and the 12-volume *Welsh Genealogies AD 1400–1500*. His latest work, *A Welsh Classical Dictionary, People in History and Myth up to about AD 1000,* is the product of a lifetime's research and the starting point for any serious study into early Welsh material and the origins of Arthur.

PLACE-NAME STUDIES

These are not as far advanced in Wales as they are in England, which has excellent studies for each county published by the English Place-Name Society; seven volumes cover Cheshire alone, and two volumes cover Shropshire. Place-name studies of many areas of Wales have yet to be published, but some of those that have been consulted in this book are listed below:

- B.G. Charles, *The Place-Names of Pembrokeshire*, National Library of Wales, 2 vols, 1992.
- Hywel Wyn Owen, *The Place-Names of East Flintshire*, UWP, 1994.
- Ellis Davies, *Flintshire Place-Names*, UWP, 1955.
- John Lloyd-Jones, *Enwau Lleoedd Sir Garnarfon*, Cardiff, 1928.
- Gwynedd O. Pierce, *The Place-Names of Dinas Powys Hundred*, UWP, 1968.
- Elwyn Davies, *A Gazetteer of Welsh Place-Names*, UWP, 1968.

General books about Welsh place-names, including translations, can be found in most bookshops in Wales.

FOLKLORE

The folklore of Wales has been well documented. Some of the major works are:

- Gwynn Jones, *Welsh Folklore and Folk Custom*, Methuen, 1930.
- Rev Elias Owen, *Welsh Folklore*, Woodall, Minshall and Co., 1896.
- John Rhys, *Celtic Folklore, Welsh & Manx*, 2 vols, Clarendon Press, 1901.
- Wirt Sykes, *British Goblins*, Sampson Low, 1880 (reprinted by EP Publishing, 1973).

ARTHURIAN STUDIES

Many Arthurian titles can be found on the shelves. Below is a selection of what we consider to be the most useful studies.

Arthur of Britain by E.K. Chambers, Sidgwick and Jackson, 1927 (reprint 1966), was the first serious study and in our opinion it is still the best. It includes an appendix of the most important manuscripts concerning Arthur printed in Latin and French.

Many of these works have been translated and published in the very useful *King Arthur in Legend and History*, edited by Richard White, Dent, 1997. This work also includes extracts from some of the lesser known Arthurian romances not found in *Arthur of Britain*.

The Figure of Arthur by Richard Barber, Boydell, 1972, is a very good discussion of the available evidence and devotes a large part to early Welsh sources. Similarly *Arthur of the Welsh*, edited by Rachel Bromwich, A.O.H. Jarman and Brynley F. Roberts, UWP, 1991, deals with the Welsh material in detail. All of the works by Roger Sherman Loomis are a valuable aid to study, especially his *Wales and the Arthurian Legend*, UWP, 1956 and *Arthurian Literature in the Middle Ages*, Clarendon Press, 1959.

Articles published in academic journals that are very useful include the following:

- Thomas Jones, 'The Early Evolution of The Legend of Arthur', *Nottingham Mediaeval Studies*, Vol.VIII, 1964, pp.3–21.
- Rachel Bromwich, 'Concepts of Arthur', *Studia Celtica*, Vol.X–XI, 1975–6, pp.163–81.
- Brynley F. Roberts, 'Geoffrey of Monmouth and the Welsh Historical Tradition', *Nottingham Medieval Studies*, Vol.XX, 1976, pp.29–40.
- T. Gwynn Jones, 'Some Arthurian Matter in Keltic', *Aberystwyth Studies*, Vol.VIII, 1927, pp.37–93, which, although a little dated, is still a very good overall discussion on early Welsh and Irish texts regarding Arthur.

Another valuable source of information is the annual *Arthurian Literature* published by Boydell and Brewer, currently at Volume XVII. Volume I, 1982, contains the Latin text with a facing English translation of the very important text *Vera Historia de Morte Arthur* (The True History of the Death of Arthur).

Studies of the Arthurian myth that have caused discussion in the last decade include *King Arthur – The True Story* by Graham Philips and Martin Keatman, Century, 1992. This work was a step in the right direction but its inaccurate details and complete lack of footnotes means that its use for further study is strictly limited. The authors identified Arthur with Owain Ddantgwyn, a prince over the district of Rhos in North Wales.

The theories of Alan Wilson and Baram Blackett concerning two possible Arthurs, both from South Wales, are detailed (with the help of Adrian Gilbert) in *The Holy Kingdom*, Bantam, 1998. Wilson and Blackett question the current understanding of geography from this period, but they try to identify Arthur with similar sounding names in Welsh genealogies and in doing so create more problems than they claim to solve. *The Journey to Avalon* by Chris Barber and David Pykitt, Blorenge, 1993, offers another theory that uses some of Wilson and Blackett's research and also makes good use of the various traditions regarding the early saints in order to locate Arthur in Wales. Both of the above works build theories around interpreting one name in a genealogy as Arthur and turning all the other names around this into accepted forms such as Uthyr, which as we have shown is unnecessary.

The most recent book to appear claiming to have solved the enigma of Arthur is Alistair Moffat's *Arthur and the Lost Kingdoms*, Weidenfeld & Nicholson, 1999. This deals with Arthur in one chapter and relies solely on the idea of a North British Kingdom existing on the Scottish borders, which as we have shown in Appendix 3 never existed.

THE ULTIMATE RESOURCE!

We hope that readers will be encouraged to consult the literary sources listed above and embark on their own quests for Arthur. To that end, a Welsh dictionary and a Latin dictionary will ease the way in the study. Out on the field, some good Ordnance Survey maps, a pair of stout walking boots, an enquiring mind and a little bit of inspiration will provide everything else. Good luck!

SELECT BIBLIOGRAPHY

Anwyl, E., *The Poetry of the Gogynfeirdd From the Myvyrian Archaiology of Wales*, Gee & Son, 1909.

Asher, Geoffrey, *From Caesar to Arthur*, Collins, 1960.

Bachellery, E., *L'Œuvre Poetique de Gutun Owain*, Librairie Ancienne Honoré Champion, 2 vols, 1950 and 1951.

Baring-Gould, Sabine, and Fisher, John, *The Lives of the British Saints*, The Honourable Society of the Cymmrodorion, 4 vols, 1907–13.

Bartrum, Peter C., *Early Welsh Genealogical Tracts*, University of Wales Press, 1966.

——, 'Y Pedwar Ar Hugain A Farnwyd Yn Gadarnaf (The Twenty-Four Kings Judged to be the Mightiest)', *Études Celtiques*, Vol.12, 1968–71, pp.157–94.

——, *A Welsh Classical Dictionary, People in History and Legend up to about AD 1000*, The National Library of Wales, 1993.

Bell, Alexander (ed.), *L'Estoire des Engleis by Geffrei Gaimar*, Anglo-Norman Texts XIV–XVI, Oxford, 1968.

Blake, Steve, with additions by Scott Lloyd, *The Myth in the Landscape/The Search for the Mabon*, unpublished, 1990.

Bromwich, Rachel, *Armes Prydein*, Dublin Institute of Advanced Studies, 1972.

——, *Trioedd Ynys Prydein*, University of Wales Press, second edition, 1978.

Budden, C.W., *Rambles Round the Old Churches of Wirral*, 1922.

Carley, J.P. and Townsend, D., *The Chronicle of Glastonbury Abbey*, Boydell and Brewer, 1985.

Chambers, E.K., *Arthur of Britain*, Sidgwick and Jackson, 1927.

Clarke, Basil, *Life of Merlin*, University of Wales Press, 1973.

Conran, Tony, *Welsh Verse*, Seren, 3rd edition, 1992.

Davies, Ellis, *Flintshire Placenames*, University of Wales Press, 1959.

Davies, R.R., *Domination and Conquest*, Cambridge University Press, 1990.

Evans, D.S., *A Mediaeval Prince of Wales: The Life of Gruffud ap Cynan*, Llanerch, 1990.

Evans, John Gwenogfryn, *The Book of Taliesin Facsimile and Text*, Llanbedrog, 1910.

——, *The Book of Aneirin, Vol.II*, Llanbedrog, 1922.

——, *Poetry by Medieval Welsh Bards*, Llanbedrog, 1926.

Evans, Sebastian, *The High History of the Holy Grail*, James Clarke & Co., 1910.

Ford, Patrick K., *The Mabinogi and Other Medieval Welsh Tales*, University of California Press, 1977.

Gerould, G. Hall, 'King Arthur and Politics', *Speculum*, Vol. 2, January 1927, pp.33–51.

Griscom, Acton, *The Historia Regum Britanniae of Geoffrey of Monmouth*, Longmans, Green and Co., 1929.

Jarman, A.O.H., *Llyfr Du Caerfyrddin*, University of Wales Press, 1982.

Jones, Gwyn and Jones, Thomas, *The Mabinogion*, Everyman, 1993.

Jones, T. Gwyn, *Gwaith Tudur Aled*, University of Wales Press, 2 vols, 1926.

——, *Welsh Folklore and Folk Custom*, Methuen, 1930.

Jones, Thomas, *Brut y Tywysogyon, Red Book of Hergest Version*, University of Wales Press, 1955.

——, ' A Sixteenth-Century Version of the Arthurian Cave Legend', *Studies in Language and Literature in Honour of Margaret Schlauch*, Warsaw, 1966, pp.175–85.

——, *Stanzas of the Graves*, The John Rhys Memorial Lecture, *Proceedings of the British Academy*, Vol.LIII, pp.97–137, 1967.

Kennedy, E.D., 'Johyn Hardyng and the Holy Grail', *Arthurian Literature* VIII, Boydell and Brewer, 1989, pp.185–206.

Lagorio, V.M., 'The Evolving Legend of St Joseph of Glastonbury', *Speculum*, Vol.46, 1971, pp.209–31.

Lapidge, Michael, 'An Edition of the *Vera Historia de Morte Arthuri*', *Arthurian Literature* I, pp.79–93, 1981.

Lomax, Frank, *The Antiquities of Glastonbury by William of Malmesbury*, facsimile reprint, Llanerch, 1992.

Loomis, R.S., *Celtic Myth and Arthurian Romance*, Colombia University Press, 1926.

——, 'Edward I, Arthurian Enthusiast', *Speculum*, Vol.28, 1953, pp.114–27.

——, *Wales and the Arthurian Legend*, University of Wales Press, 1956.

——, *The Grail from Celtic Myth to Christian Symbol*, Columbia University Press, 1963.

MacDougall, H., *Racial Myth in English History*, University Press of New England, London, 1982.

Mann, J., and Penman, R.G., *Literary Sources for Roman Britain*, Lactor 11, 1978.

Morris-Jones, John and Parry-Williams, T.H., *Llawysgrif Hendregadredd*, University of Wales Press, 1971.

The Myvyrian Archaiology, second edition, Gee & Son, 1870.

Nitze, W.A., and Jenkins, T.A., *Perlesvaus*, Chicago, 2 vols, 1937.

Parry, John Jay, *Brut y Brenhinedd, Cotton Cleopatra Version*, The Medieval Academy of America, 1937.

Parsons, J.C., 'The Second Exhumation of King Arthur's Remains at Glastonbury, 19 April 1278', *Arthurian Literature* XII, Boydell and Brewer, 1987, pp.173–177.

Price, G. Vernon, *Valle Crucis Abbey*, Brython Press, 1952.

Rees, William, *An Historical Atlas of Wales*, Faber and Faber, 1959.

Rhys, John, *The Hibbert Lectures, Lectures on the Origin and Growth of Religon as Illustrated by Celtic Heathendom*, Williams and Norgate, 1886.

——, *Celtic Folklore*, Clarendon Press, 2 vols, 1901.

Rhys, John and Evans, John Gwenogfryn, *The Text of the Book of Llan Dav Reproduced from the Gwysaney Manuscript*, original 1893, National Library of Wales Press facsimile copy, 1979.

Richards, Melville, *Breudwyt Ronabwy*, University of Wales Press, 1948.

——, 'Arthurian Onosmatics', *The Transactions of the Honourable Society of the Cymmrodorion*, 1969, pp.250–64.

Riddy, Felicity, 'Glastonbury, Joseph of Arimathea and the Grail in John Hardyng's Chronicle', *The Archaeology and History of Glastonbury Abbey*, eds. Lesley Adams and James P. Carley, Boydell and Brewer, 1991.

Roberts, Brynley F., *Brut Y Brenhinedd, Llanstephan MS. 1 Version*, Dublin Institute for Advanced Studies, 1971.

Robinson, J.A., *Two Glastonbury Legends*, Cambridge University Press, 1926.

Salway, Peter, *Roman Britain*, Clarendon Press, 1991.

Sherley-Price, Leo, *Bede, A History of the English Church and People*, Penguin, 1968.

Skeat, Reverend W.W., *Joseph of Arimathie*, Early English Text Society, 1871.

Sommer, H.O., *The Vulgate Version of the Arthurian Romances*, Washington, 7 vols, 1908–16.

Stenton, Frank M., *Anglo-Saxon England*, Clarendon Press, 1971.

Swanton, Michael, *The Anglo-Saxon Chronicle*, J.M. Dent, 1996.

Thorpe, L., *The History of the Kings of Britain*, Penguin, 1966.

——, *Gerald of Wales, The Journey Through Wales/The Description of Wales*, Penguin, 1978.

Treharne, R.F., *The Glastonbury Legends*, Cresset, 1967.

Van Hamel, A.G., *Lebor Bretnach, The Irish Version of the Historia Brittonum Ascribed to Nennius*, The Stationery Office, Dublin, 1932.

Vinaver, Eugene, *The Works of Sir Thomas Malory*, Clarendon Press, 3 vols, 1947.

Wade-Evans, A.W., *Welsh Christian Origins*, Alden, 1934.

——, *Nennius's History of the Britons*, SPCK, 1938.

——, *Vitae Sanctorum Brittaniae et Genealogiae*, University of Wales Press, 1944.

——, *The Emergence of England and Wales*, Heffer, 2nd edition, 1959.

White, Richard, *King Arthur in Legend and History*, J.M. Dent, 1997.

Williams, Hugh, *Gildas*, Cymmrodorion Record Series no. 3, Vol.I, 1899, Vol.II, 1901.

Williams, Ifor and Williams, John Llewelyn, *Gwaith Guto'r Glyn*, University of Wales Press, 1937.

Williams, Robert, *Y Seint Greal*, Jones (Wales) Publishers, original 1876, 1987 facsimile reprint.

NOTES

1 THE ARTHURIAN ENIGMA

1 Wade-Evans, 1959, p.v.
2 Dendrochronology; the science of dating events and environmental variations by means of the comparative study of the growth rings in (ancient) timber.
3 Vinaver, 1947, Vol.I, p.cxiii.
4 Treharne, 1967, p.121.
5 Loomis, 1963, p.266.
6 Wade-Evans, 1959, p.v.

2 THE MYTH OF ARTHUR

1 Thorpe, 1966, pp.51–2.
2 This cycle comprises the works known as *Estoire Del Sainte Graal, The Prose Lancelot, The Queste for the Sainte Graal, Mort Artu, The Vulgate Merlin* and *The Vulgate Merlin Continuation.* The whole series of texts was edited in seven volumes by H.O. Sommer in *The Vulgate Version of the Arthurian Romances,* Carnegie Institute, Washington, 1908–16.
3 Clarke, 1973, p.32; for a more detailed examination of Geoffrey of Monmouth's life see pp.26–35.
4 Gildas was also attributed authorship for some versions of the *Historia Brittonum,* usually attributed to Nennius.
5 Griscom, 1929, p.219. Translation from Thorpe, 1966, p.51.
6 Walter the Archdeacon of Oxford has often been confused with Walter Map, who was deacon to Henry II 50 years later and is mentioned in some of the Grail romances. They are not the same person.
7 Griscom, 1929, p.536, Thorpe, 1966, p.284.
8 Thorpe, 1966, p.51.
9 Chambers, 1927, p.262. [s.a. 1152], *Gaufridus Arthur, qui transtulerat historiam de regibus Britonum de Britannico in Latinum, fit episcopus Sancti asaph in Norgualis.*
10 French text from Bell, p.204, lines 6448–53. Translation from *Lestoire Des Engles,* Vol.II, edited by Sir T.D. Hardy & C.T. Martin, Rolls edition, 1889, p.203.
11 Chambers, 1927, p.55.
12 Reiss, Edmund, 'The Welsh Versions of Geoffrey of Monmouth's *Historia', Welsh History Review,* Vol.4, 1968, pp.97–128.
13 For a detailed look at attitudes towards the *Brut* in Wales throughout history, see the Appendix to Roberts, 1971.
14 '"The "Book of Basingwerk" and MS. Cotton Cleopatra', B.V. in *Y Cymmrodor,* Vol. XXXV, 1925, pp.49–109 and continued in Vol.XXXVI, 1926, pp.1–33.
15 See Appendix 4 for a more detailed examination of the texts mentioned here.
16 Griscom, 1929, p.260. Thorpe, 1966, pp.80 and 122.
17 Rhys and Evans, 1893, p.118, lines 13–14.
18 Ibid., p.120, lines 5–6.
19 Ibid., p.192, lines 4–7.
20 Palmer, A.N., 'Offa's and Wat's Dykes', *Archaeologia Cambrensis,* 1909, p.158.
21 Williams, 1901, p.397, n.3.
22 *The Bulletin of the Board of Celtic Studies,* Vol.XVII, pp.268–9 and references therein (article in Welsh).
23 According to Williams, 1901, p.412, *insula* also had a derived meaning: 'a piece of

dedicated land especially in the case of monasteries, was in Britain termed *insula*, or in the British tongue *inis'* (modern Welsh *ynys*).

24 Evans, J.G., 1926, p.421.
25 Originally published in Welsh in *The Bulletin of the Board of Celtic Studies*, Vol.XVII, 1958, pp.237-52 under the title 'Datblygiadau Cynnar Chwedl Arthur'; see note below for translation.
26 'The Early Evolution of the Legend of Arthur', translated by Gerald Morgan in *Nottingham Medieval Studies*, Vol.VIII, p.3.
27 *Peredur, Geraint ab Erbin* and *Owain* from *The Mabinogion* contain similar material to *Perceval, Erec et Enid* and *Yvain* written in the latter half of the 12th century by Chrétien de Troyes. Arguments still rage as to which came first, the Welsh or the French – or did they both come from a common source now lost? For an English translation of Chrétien's work see *Arthurian Romances*, Chrétien de Troyes, translated by Owen, D.D.R., Everyman, revised edition, 1993.
28 Jones and Jones, 1993, p.ix.
29 Bromwich, 1978, pp.lxx–lxxxviii.
30 Ibid., p.274.
31 See Appendix 4 for more information on these works.
32 Jones, T. Gwyn 'Some Arthurian Material in Keltic', *Aberystwyth Studies*, Vol.VIII, p.43. Jones notes a reference to Arthur at Caer Fenlli in a 13th-century poem by Bleddyn Fardd and the fact that the local tradition remembered this association, attached to the hillfort on the summit of Foel Fenlli, a hill in the Clwydian range in North Wales.
33 Thorpe, 1978, p.251.
34 Bartrum, 1993. See also Appendix Four.
35 For the texts and translations, see Wade-Evans, 1944. For English translations of the Arthurian sections, see White, 1997, pp.13–18.
36 Although often ascribed to Nennius, he was by no means the only author. This is dealt with in more detail in Appendix Four.
37 Thorpe, 1978, p.259. For more on this murder see Appendix Two.

3 THE KEYS TO ARTHUR'S KINGDOM

1 Rees, 1959, plate 52.
2 Lloyd, John E., *Owen Glendower*, Clarendon Press, 1931, p.93 and references therein.
3 Davies, R.R., *The Revolt of Owain Glyn Dwr*, Oxford University Press, 1995, p.167.
4 Lloyd, 1931, p.95 n.1 and references therein.
5 Williams, H., 1901, p.399.
6 Ibid., p.398n. The fact that Rhodri's sons were considered kings by the Welsh explains why the Latin texts refer to the three divisions as *Tria Regne* (Three Kingdoms).
7 Loomis, 1953, passim.
8 Wade-Evans, 1959.
9 For example, his English translation of the Chartres Text of *Historia Brittonum* in *Archaeologia Cambrensis*, 1937, pp.64–85 and the lives of the Welsh Saints in Wade-Evans, 1944.
10 Evans, J.G., 'Taliesin: Or the Critic Criticised', *Y Cymmrodor*, Vol.XXXIV, 1924.
11 Evans, J.G., 1926, p.viii.
12 Bromwich, 1978, pp.228–9.
13 These two bishops are discussed in more detail in Chapter 14.
14 Parry, 1937, p.88.
15 Thorpe, 1966, p.77.
16 Juvenal, *The Sixteen Satires*, translated by Peter Green, Penguin, revised 1974, p.109.

17 Stokes, Francis Griffin, *Who's Who in Shakespeare*, George G. Harrap, 1924 (1989 Bracken reprint), p.24.

18 Bartrum, 1993, p.456 and references therein regarding the 14th-century *Eulogium Historiarum*.

19 Wade-Evans, 1938, pp.72–3.

20 Parry, p.201.

21 Thorpe, 1966, p.226.

22 Bartrum, 1968, pp.178–9.

23 Jones, T., 1955, pp.14–15.

24 Swanton, 1996, p.119.

25 Evans, David, ed., *Drych Y Prif Oesoedd*, Gan Theophilus Evans, Y Rhan Gyntaf, University of Wales Press, 1960, p.8 for original Welsh text.

26 Williams and Williams, 1937, p.114, line 71.

27 Anwyl, 1909, p.194.

28 Ibid., p.195.

29 Both translations by Jones, T. Gwynn in *The Cheshire Sheaf*, 20 May 1925, p.38.

30 Evans, J.G., 1922, p.xix.

31 Evans, J.G., 1926, p.399.

32 Evans, J.G., 1922, p.xix.

33 Morris-Jones and Parry-Williams, 1971, p.90.

34 Dumville, D.N., ed., *Historia Brittonum 3: The Vatican Recension*, Boydell and Brewer, 1985, p.105, §27.

35 Owen, Hugh, 'Peniarth MS.118 fos 829–837', *Y Cymmrodor*, Vol.XXVII, 1917, p.129.

36 Parry, 1937, p.48.

37 Further evidence for this identification may come from Ptolemy's reference to the Dee estuary being named Seteia. Claudius Ptolemy, *The Geography*, translated and edited by Edward Luther Stevenson, 1932 (1991, Dover reprint), p.49. Is Caitness a British variant of this otherwise unknown name?

4 BRITAIN BEFORE ARTHUR

1 Bromwich, 1978, p.452 and references therein.

2 Jones and Jones, 1993, p.72. The three adjacent islands are also mentioned in *Enwau Ynys Prydein* and are named as Mon, Manaw and Weir, which correspond to Anglesey, Man and Lundy. Some variants replace Mon with Orc, which suggests that Orc refers to Anglesey, not the Orkneys as is commonly stated for the want of a better suggestion. Bromwich, 1978, pp.228–32.

3 Bartrum, 1993, pp.474–5.

4 Jones and Jones, 1993, p.107. Arthur and two companions go to Llydaw to seek the two dogs of Glythfyr Ledewig.

5 Wade-Evans, 1938, p.49, §27.

6 Ibid., 1938, p.53, §31.

7 Near to Machynlleth at Pennal is another important site of Roman origin that might be the original site of Caer Fuddai, which later moved across the river to Machynlleth.

8 Thomas Pennant (1726–98), the famous Welsh antiquarian who 'according to an old custom prevalent at the time, was put out to be nursed at a farm house called Pentre'. Davies, Ellis, 'Thomas Pennant', *Journal of the Historical Society of the Church in Wales*, Vol.II, p.87.

9 Reinecke, George, ed., *Saint Albon and Saint Amphibalus by John Lydgate*, Garland, 1985, p.156, line 599.

10 Ibid., p.xxvii.

11 Parry, 1937, p.96.

12 Sherley-Price, 1968, p.151.

13 Bartrum, 1966, pp.2–3.

14 Parry, 1937, p.107.

15 Ibid., pp.85–6.

16 Bartrum, 1966, p.47.

17 Parry, 1937, p.110.

18 Kemble, J.M., *The Saxons in England*, 1849, pp.22–3. Quoted from Wade-Evans, 1959, p.1.

19 Williams, 1899, p.55.

20 Sherley-Price, 1968, pp. 55–6.

21 Wade-Evans, 1938, pp.53–4, §31.

22 Swanton, 1996, p.13.

23 Parry, 1937, pp.110–12.

24 Bromwich, 1978, p.154. For details of the individual manuscripts see pp. xi–lxii.

25 Jones, T., 1955, p.153.

26 Morris, John, *Arthurian Period Sources, Vol.5, Genealogies and Texts*, Phillimore, 1995, p.144.

27 Bromwich, 1978, pp.151–2.

28 White, 1997, p.13. For the Latin text see Chambers, 1927, pp.242–3.

29 Myers, J.N.L., *The English Settlements*, Oxford, 1986, pp.84–7.

30 Wade-Evans, 1938, p.60, §38.

31 Bartrum, 1968, p.181.

32 Evans, J.G., 1910, p.41, line 25.

33 *Historia Ecclesiastica*, xii, 47. Original Latin extract in Chambers, 1927, pp.258–9.

34 Wade-Evans, 1938, p.60, §38.

35 Ibid., p.48, §23.

36 Mann and Penman, 1978, p.33.

37 Ibid.

38 *Scriptores Historia Augustae*, XVIII, 2.

39 Wade-Evans, 1938, p.48 n.2.

40 These other Roman sources can be found listed in Mann and Penman, 1978, p.58.

41 Sherley-Price, 1968, p.43.

42 Parry, 1937, p.88. *A pheri a oruc gwneithur clawd dwfyn y rwg deiuyr ar alban o gyffredyn dreul or mor pwy gilyd.*

43 Parry, p.210–11. Basingwerk text p.195. *Ac yna y ffoassant hyt y Mur awnathoed seuerus amherrawdyr ruvein gynt rwng deivyr a bryneich. Ac yna yd anvones catwallawn peanda brenhin Mers a llu gantho; y ymlad ac oswallt. A gwedy ev dyvot hyt yno; y ogilchynv a oruc peanda ydaw rac y didor yganthaw. Yny lle a elwyr yn saesnec hevyn felt; ac yn gkymraec maes nefawl.*

44 The original Latin text is: *Distatque locus iste a fossa regis Offae, quae Angliam et Waliam borealem dividit, miliario non ferme dimidio, et Scropesbyri miliario integre septimo, ab abbatia vero Waneloc versus plagam meridianam miliario circiter sextodecimo.* Arnold,Thomas, ed., *The Works of Simeon of Durham, Historia Regum*, Rolls edition, cap. xiv, i. p.353. Translation in Palmer, A.N., 'Offa's and Wat's Dykes', *Archaeologia Cambrensis*, 1909, p.159. Note that the dyke separates *North* Wales from *Anglia*.

45 Ibid., p.158.

46 Ibid., p.162, n.2.

47 Van Hamel, pp.31–2.

48 Collingwood, R.G., and Myers, J.N.L., *Roman Britain and the English Settlements*, Clarendon Press, 1937, second edition, p.156.

49 A.N. Palmer, op. cit., pp.167–8.

50 Stenton, 1971, p.17.

51 Wade-Evans, 1938, p.67, §44. Parry, 1937, p.110.

52 Salway, 1991, Map V.

53 Bromwich, 1978, p.89.

54 Parry, 1937, p.118.

55 Ibid.

5 MERLIN AND UTHYR PENDRAGON

1 Wade-Evans, 1938, p.62, §40.

2 For example see Kendrick, T.D., *The Druids*, Methuen, 1927, p.93 for an extract from the *Orations* (XLIX) of Dion Chrysostom. 'The Persians, I think, have men called Magi … the Egyptians, their priests … and the Indians their Brahmins. On the other hand, the Kelts have men called Druids, who concern themselves with divination and all branches of Wisdom.'

3 Wade-Evans, 1938, p.62, §40.

4 Ibid.

5 Ibid., p.63, §41.

6 Ibid.

7 Parry, 1937, p.124. *Ac an ab y lleian y gelwit ymab kyn no hynny. Ac o hynny allan y dodet arnaw Merdyn. O achos y gaffael yngkaer vyrdyn.* The Basingwerk text gives *An ap y lleian.*

8 Jones and Jones, 1993, p.72.

9 Later on in the *Historia Brittonum* the child says that his name is Emrys, the son of a Roman noble. This has caused a large amount of confusion as it contradicts what is said previously about Emrys. This confusion is over 1,200 years old, causing scholars throughout the ages to invent other Merlins to get around the problem, which has led to us having at least four different Merlins! We know that the *Historia Brittonum* was a compilation of early sources and it might be easier to accept this confusion as a scribal mistake instead of coming up with more ingenious methods of trying to accommodate it and in turn creating more confusion.

10 Sims-Williams, Patrick, *The Bulletin of the Board of Celtic Studies*, Vol.XXVIII, 1978, pp.90–3.

11 Jones, Thomas, 1967, pp.136–7, #17.

12 Bartrum, 1993, p.495.

13 Davies, Canon Ellis, *Prehistoric and Roman Remains of Denbighshire*, Cardiff, 1929, p.282.

14 Sims-Williams, 1978.

15 The manuscript consists of 2,500 folio pages and is catalogued as NLW 5276D.

16 Jones, Thomas, 'The Story of Myrddin and the Five Dreams of Gwendydd', *Études Celtiques*, Vol.VIII, 1958, pp.328–45. The English translation can also be found in Stewart, R.J., and Matthews, John, eds., *Merlin Through the Ages*, Blandford, 1995, pp.38–43.

17 Evans, 1911, pp.1–4. Stewart and Matthews, op. cit. pp.32–8.

18 The story of how the dragons came to be under Dinas Emrys in the first place is told in *The Tale of Lludd and Llefelys* from *The Mabinogion*, Jones and Jones, 1993, pp.75–9.

19 Wade-Evans, 1938, p.65.

20 Richards, Melville, 'Nennius's *Regio Guunnesi*', *The Transactions of the Caernarvonshire Historical Society*, 1963, pp.20–27.

21 Wade-Evans, 1938, p.70, §48.

22 Jones, Thomas, 1967, p.125, #40.

23 Bromwich, 1972, p.1, line 27.

24 Jones, Thomas, 1967, p.133, #73.

25 Bartrum, 1993, p.37.

26 Davies, 1959, p.36.

27 It is worth noting that near the village is a place called Plas-yr-Esgob (Palace of the Bishop), Grid Ref. SJ 109 501.

28 During our research we also considered Rhuddlan, at the mouth of the River Clwyd, and the town of Ruthin as possible sites, but the references to the border with Alban and the proximity of the Elidan place name finally swayed us to Melin Y Wig.

29 Morris-Jones and Parry-Williams, 1971, p.21. Translation from Evans, 1910, p.xvii.

30 Parry, 1937, p.119.

31 Barron, W.R.J., and Weinberg, S.C., *Layamon's Brut*, Longman, 1995, p.439.

32 The name Iwerddon is also preserved on a hill south of Betws y Coed nearby, Grid Ref. 788 524. The inhabitants of Iwerddon are called Gwyddel and the village under this hill is named Dolwyddelan – the Meadow of the Gwyddel. Another mountain ridge north of Blaenau Ffestiniog preserves the name Iwerddon as does the lake on it, Grid Ref. 685 478.

33 Parry, 1937, pp.146–7.

34 It is also worth noting that the Maes Mawr estate is less than five miles away, near the village of Maerdy.

35 Denbighshire Record Office, Ref. QSD/DE/26A.

36 Only three other Magdelene dedications are known in North Wales – at Harlech, Gwaunysgor and Penley.

37 *Archaeologia Cambrensis*, 1847, p.31. Amongst the graves was a stone inscribed to Brochmael, which Sir John Rhys thought could corrspond with either of the Brochmaels mentioned in the *Annales Cambriae* at 616 and 662. *Y Cymmrodor*, Vol.XVIII, 1905, pp.15–17.

38 RCAM Denbighshire, p.74. Also referred to in the handwritten parish history of Cerrigydrudion and Pentrefoelas. *Historical Notes Regarding Cerrigydrudion* in the Denbighshire County Record Office, Ref. PD/85/1/13 fos.16–18.

39 Parry, 1937, p.148.

40 Ibid., pp.148–9.

41 Ibid., p.149.

42 Ibid., p.150.

43 Ibid.

6 ARTHUR THE BATTLE LEADER

1 Parry, 1937, p.151, n.6.

2 In the Welsh Grail romance, this wedding is said to have taken place six weeks after the death of Gwrlois. *Y Seint Greal*, edited and translated by Williams, Robert, 1876 (facsimile reprint, Jones [Wales] Publishers, 1987), p.663.

3 Van der Geest, Aad, 'Tintagel', *The Journal of the Pendragon Society*, Vol.XXVI, Summer 1997, p.6.

4 Fairburn, Neil, *A Traveller's Guide to the Kingdoms of Arthur*, Evans Brothers, 1983, p.144.

5 Béroul, *The Romance of Tristan*, translated by Alan S. Fedrick, Penguin, 1970, p.77.

6 Edited in Bartrum, Peter C., 'Pedwar Iarddur', *The National Library of Wales Journal*, Vol.XX, pp.373–6 from a manuscript by Gruffudd Hiraethog (Peniarth MS. 134, pp.131–2), translation in Bartrum, 1993, p.451.

7   See Chapter 4.

8   Jones and Jones, 1993, p. 80.

9   Ibid., p.86.

10   Bartrum, 1993, p.293.

11   Davies, J.H., 'A Welsh Version of the Birth of Arthur', *Y Cymmrodor*, Vol.XXIV, p.258.

12   Jones and Jones, 1993, p.87.

13   Caer Gynar is found as an alternative to Caer Cai in the poetry of William Llyn and Ieuan Brydydd Hir. See Bromwich, 1978, p.307 and references therein.

14   Morris, R., ed., *The Works of Edmund Spenser*, Macmillan, 1912, Book I, Canto ix, p.4.

15   Parry, 1937, pp.154–5.

16   St Alban is also mentioned in some of the earliest manuscripts dealing with the foundation of Freemasonry and is often said to be the founder of the craft in England. See Mackey, Albert, *The History of Freemasonry*, Gramercy reprint, 1996, pp.90–94.

17   Parry, 1937, p.156.

18   Davies, op. cit. p.259.

19   Evans, J.G., 1910, p.120.

20   Davies, op cit. p.260.

21   Ibid., p.261.

22   Ibid., p.262.

23   Ibid.

24   See Bartrum, 1993, pp.91–4 and references therein for examples.

25   Parry, 1937, p.157.

26   The veneration of a sword stuck in the ground is practised by some Kurdish tribes and it has been suggested that the two traditions may be linked. See Izady, Mehrdad R., *The Kurds: A Concise Handbook*, Taylor & Francis, 1992, p.151.

27   Wade-Evans, 1938, p.75, n.56.

28   Parry, 1937, p.157.

29   This battle could have taken place on any of the four Roman roads that radiate out from Wroxeter.

30   Parry, 1937, p.158.

31   Evans, D. Simon, ed. *Historia Grufudd ap Kynan*, University of Wales Press, 1977, pp.11–12. Translation in D. Simon Evans, *A Mediaeval Welsh Prince of Wales – The Life of Grufydd ap Cynan*, Llanerch, 1996, p.64.

32   Davies, 1959, pp.98–9.

33   Another possibility is the hillfort near Llay.

34   Parry, 1937, p.158.

35   Wade-Evans, 1938, p.75, n.56.

36   Wade-Evans, 1959, p.73.

37   The location of the River Gleni as mentioned in Bede (II.14) as the site of the baptism of Edwin might yield to further research. The idea that it is situated at Glendale in Northumberland is founded on very doubtful grounds.

38   The Welsh text was edited by Ifor Williams in *The Bulletin of the Board of Celtic Studies*, Vol.V, 1930, pp.115–29 and translated by Tom Peete Cross in *Studies in Philology*, Vol.17, 1920, pp.93–110.

39   *The Cheshire Sheaf*, March 1910, p.22.

40   Grid Ref. SJ 051 642.

41   RCAM Vol.IV, Denbighshire, 1914, pp.135–6.

42   Lewis, J.B., 'An Account of the Penbedw Papers in the Flintshire Record Office', *Flintshire Historical Society Publications*, Vol.25, 1971–2, p.125.

43 Grid Ref. SJ 151 341.

44 Jarman, 1982, p.67, line 48.

45 Parry, 1937, p.28.

46 On the B5395 to the north of Whitchurch, SJ 511 439.

47 Suggested by Kenneth Jackson in Loomis, Roger, ed., *Arthurian Literature in the Middle Ages*, Clarendon Press, 1959, pp.4 and 7.

48 Bartrum, 1993, p.56.

49 Jones, T. Gwynn, 1930, p.52.

50 Originally by Alfred Anscombe in 1905 in *Zeitschrift für Celtische Philologie*, Vol.V (1905), pp.103–23.

51 Williams, 1899, pp.60–1.

52 Bartrum, 1993, p.87.

53 There has been much discussion about the shield of Arthur and its confusion with another relic linked to him, his mantle (*llen*). This is referred to in *Culhwch and Olwen* and is also one of the 13 treasures of Ynys Prydein. See Bromwich, 1978, pp.240–49 for further discussion.

54 Jones and Jones, 1993, p.117.

55 Richards, 1948, pp.37–8 and references therein.

56 For example, *In Praise of Owain Gwynedd* by Cynddelw Brydydd Mawr (1155–1200) *Fal gwaith Fadon fawr wriawr oriain* (As at Badon fawr, valiant war-cry). Welsh text in Morris-Jones and Parry-Williams, 1971, p.84, line 10. Translation from Jones T. Gwyn, ed., *The Oxford Book of Welsh Verse in English*, Oxford University Press, 1983, p.26.

7 KING ARTHUR AND CAMLAN

1   Parry, 1937, p.160.

2   Rhys, John and Evans, J.G., eds., *The Text of the Bruts from the Red Book of Hergest*, Oxford, 1890, p.191, line 30.

3   Evans, J.G., 1910, pp.xiii–xiv.

4   Parry, 1937, p.161.

5   Ibid., n.8.

6   According to Parry, 1937, p.163, the lands were distributed to Urien, Arawn and Lleu, who are all mentioned elsewhere in Welsh tradition. Urien is very prominent and is found in more early material than Arthur. For early poetry concerning Urien, see Caerwyn Williams, J.E., *The Poems of Taliesin*, Dublin Institute for Advanced Studies, 1968.

7   Pennant, Thomas, *A Tour in Wales*, London, 1784 (1991, Bridge Books, facsimile reprint), Vol.I, p.271.

8   Parry, 1937, p.163.

9   *Polychronicon*, Rolls edition, 1875, Vol.V, p.332.

10 Bartrum, 1968, p.179. The seven arts in Classical times were defined as geometry, astronomy, logic, rhetoric, music, architecture and grammar. The Thirteen Treasures of Ynys Prydein are named in several manuscripts, although their purpose is uncertain. See Bromwich, 1978, Appendix III, pp.240–49.

11 Parry, 1937, p.169. See also Chapter IX.12 in Thorpe, 1966, pp.226–8.

12 Ibid., p.170.

13 Ibid., p.125.

14 Vinaver, 1947, p.cxiii.

15 Evans, S., 1910, pp.269–70.

16 Nitze and Jenkins, 1937, Vol.II, p.197.

17 As we indicated earlier in this chapter, the precise nature of Arthur's supposed 'foreign' campaigns is at present uncertain. Further study of the place names employed in the original Welsh sources should help to clarify this matter. It is also interesting to note that most of the lands supposedly conquered by Arthur in these 'foreign campaigns' belong to the Angevin empire of Henry I: coincidence?
18 Parry, 1937, p.191.
19 Jones, T., 1967, p.118–9.
20 Bromwich, 1972, pp.xxxiv–xl.
21 Bartrum, 1993, p.303.
22 Parry, 1937, p.191.
23 Bartrum, 1993, p.97.
24 Ibid., p.98 and references quoted therein.
25 Bromwich, 1978, pp.144 and 206.
26 Jones and Jones, 1993, p.116.
27 Ibid., p.86.
28 Bromwich, 1978, p.161.
29 Bartrum, 1993, p.98.
30 For further information and references to the seven survivors see their respective entries in Bartrum, 1993.
31 Bartrum, 1966, p.60, Bonedd Y Saint §39. For other 'Cornish' saints linked to Gwynedd, see Miller, Molly, *The Saints of Gwynedd*, Boydell and Brewer, 1979, pp.68–9.
32 Rhys, J., 1891, pp.473–4.
33 Grid Ref. SH 677 248.
34 Bromwich, 1978, p.159.
35 Evans, 1926, p.393 and references therein.
36 Lapidge, 1981.
37 Ibid., pp.84–7 for the Latin text with a facing translation.

8 THE KEYS TO AVALON

1 Bromwich, 1978, p.133.
2 Ibid., p.267.
3 The Welsh word for orchard is *perllan* and appears as such from the 16th century, in glossaries.
4 Clarke, 1973, pp.17 and 182, line 908, *Insula pomorum que Fortunata vocatur.*
5 Ibid., p.101.
6 Rhys, 1886, pp.195–6, Rhys, 1891, p.331, note1 and Loomis, 1956, p.155.
7 Translation of Alanus de Insulis's *Prophetiae Merlini* in *The Bulletin of the Board of Celtic Studies*, Vol.XXII (XVIIc).
8 Roberts, 1971, pp.49–50.
9 Blake, Steve, *Myth in Landscape – In Search of the Mabon*, 1990, unpublished.
10 Bartrum, 1993, p.5.
11 Wade-Evans, 1938, p.46, §19.
12 Jones and Jones, 1993, p.21.
13 Bartrum, 1993, pp.38–9.
14 Through Gilfaethwy, Don later appears in Arthurian romance as Do, Doon, Dos de Carduel, Du, Deu and God. Loomis, 1926, p.359.
15 Sir John Rhys equated her with the Irish Danu or Donu. He also suggested that Beli was the consort of the goddess Don and the possible father to her other children (Rhys, 1886, pp.89–92). P.C. Bartrum states: 'However we cannot deduce that Don was the

mother of all Beli's sons or that Beli was the father of all Don's children' (Bartrum, 1993, p.204).

16 Bartrum, 1966, pp.9–11, §1, §10.

17 Williams, R., 1876, p.684.

18 Bartrum, 1966, pp.9–11, and §1.

19 Ashe, Geoffrey, *King Arthur's Avalon*, Collins, 1957.

20 Davies, 1959, p.28. See also Evans-Gunther, Charles, 'Arthur, The Clwyd Connection', *Journal of the Pendragon Society*, Vol.XXIV/I, February 1994, pp.4–7.

21 Bromwich, 1978, p.217–19. Ynys Afallach, Caer Caradog and Bangor-is-y-Coed are all early Welsh foundations in close proximity to one another in North Wales. In light of the evidence put forward regarding Ynys Afallach in this and the following chapters, we believe that this *Triad* records the traditional sites and can now be viewed in its correct context.

22 Baring-Gould and Fisher, 1907–13, Vol.II, p.474.

23 The Royal Commission report on ancient monuments in Flintshire (1910) suggested that the site was probably a medieval monastic grange from the evidence of the place name and the fact that bodies had been unearthed nearby. We believe that in the light of the new evidence the site is much older.

24 Clarke, 1973, p.101.

25 Bartrum, 1993, p.548.

26 *Layamon's Brut*, edited and translated by Barron, W.R.J. and Weinberg, S.C., Longman, 1995, p.733.

27 From Llanstephan MS. 4, edited and translated by Lewis, Timothy and Bruce, J. Douglas in *Révue Celtique*, Vol.33, 1912, p.443.

28 Bartrum, 1993, p.488.

29 Rhys, 1901, p.374.

30 Loomis, 1926, p.192.

31 Within his *Vita Merlin*, Geoffrey of Monmouth names Morgan's sisters to whom she taught astrology as Moronoe, Mazoe, Gliten, Glitonea, Gliton, Tyronoe and Thiten.

32 Bromwich, 1978, p.459.

33 Ibid., pp.185–6 and pp.458–63.

34 Jones and Jones, 1993, p.ix.

35 Davies, 1959, pp.110–11.

36 Rhys, John, ed., *Pennant's Tours in Wales*, 1883, Vol.II, p.36.

37 On the hill known today as Moel y Parc. *Wrach* means 'hag' or 'crone' and in later Welsh came to mean 'witch'.

38 Blake, 1990. Bannon/Manon can mean 'queen', 'maiden consort' and, very rarely, as in *The Black Book of Carmarthen*, a personal name, e.g. Banon tad Kysceint.

39 Loomis, 1956, p.122.

40 For the development of the character Morgan Le Fay see Loomis, 1956, pp.105–30. Loomis takes her origins back further, through Modron to the Irish goddess known as Morrigan, but this final step is unlikely.

41 Chrétien de Troyes, *Arthurian Romances*, translated by Owen, D.D.R., Everyman, 1987, p.26.

42 Loomis, 1956, p.114.

43 Lapidge, 1981, p.79. *Denique rex, parumper melioracioni restitutus, iubet se transuehi ad Venodociam, quia Auallonis insula delectabili propter loci amenitatem perendinari proposeurat (et quietis gracia causaque uulnerum suorum mitigandi dolorem).* An English translation is also available in *The Arthurian Legends, An Illustrated Anthology*, selected and introduced by Barber, Richard, Boydell, 1979, pp.31–2.

44 For a discussion of this text see Lapidge, 1981.

45 Ibid., p.71.

46 Ibid., p.80.

47 Lapidge, Michael, 'Additional Manuscript Evidence for the *Vera Historia de Morte Arthuri*', *Arthurian Literature II*, Boydell and Brewer, 1982, pp. 163–8 and notes therein. See also Barber, Richard, 'The Manuscripts of the *Vera Historia de Morte Arthuri*', *Arthurian Literature VI*, 1986, pp. 163–4, which describes the discovery in Paris of two versions of the *Vera Historia* contained within manuscripts of Geoffrey's *Historia*. There is still the possibility that the excellent research being done on these medieval texts will reveal further copies of the *Vera Historia* that will then enable us to gain a clearer understanding of the events surrounding the death of Arthur.

48 Jones, 1967, pp.126–7, #44.

9 AVALON, ANNWN AND THE CELTIC OTHERWORLD

1 Loomis, 1956, p.51.

2 Sikes, Wirt, *British Goblins*, Sampson Low, 1880, p.5.

3 Loomis, 1956, pp.137–41.

4 Rhys, 1886, p.179. Rhys's idea of portraying Gwyn ap Nudd as a Dark God is open to question.

5 Bartrum, 1993, p.353.

6 Loomis, 1956, pp.137–41.

7 Skene, W.F., *The Four Ancient Books of Wales*, Edmonston & Douglas, 1868, Vol.I, pp.202–3.

8 Jones, T. Gwynn, 1930, p.52.

9 Robinson, 1926, pp.30–31.

10 Ellis, 1959, p.51.

11 Rhys, 1901, p.441.

12 Thorpe, 1978, p.198.

13 Morfran was also known as Afaggdu (Utter Darkness).

14 The story can be found in an English translation in Ford, 1977, pp.162–4. For a detailed academic edition of the oldest Welsh text with English notes, see Ford, Patrick K., *Ystoria Taliesin*, University of Wales Press, 1992.

15 *The Myvyrian Archaiology*, 1870, p.364.

16 Bromwich, 1972, p.3. Current thinking dates the composition of the 200-line-long *Armes Prydein* found with *The Book of Taliesin* to about 930. The prophecy asks the Britons to remember their past and draw upon this history to give them strength to get through their current troubles. The influential *Prophecy of Myrddin* found within the *Brut* shares some of the place names and possibly a common origin.

17 Ibid., p.xxxv.

18 Jones, T. Gwynn, 1926, Vol.1, p.163.

19 Ibid., Vol.II, p.584. 'There is a Nant Beryddon not far from Llandderfel.' See also Bromwich, 1972, p.xxxviii, n.1 and references therein.

20 *Roman du Silence* is a Breton text within which there is reference to the *lai Mabon* being performed. See Thorpe, L., 'Roman du Silence', *Nottingham Medieval Studies*, Vol.V, 1961, lines 2761–5.

21 Bereton, Georgeine E., 'A Thirteenth-Century List of French Lays and other Narrative Poems', *Modern Language Review*, Vol.XLV, No.1, January 1950. Among the lays recorded in Shrewsbury School MS. vii are some well-known titles, others possibly identifiable with poems that exist today or that are known to have existed and also a large amount of previously unknown titles. Recorded within the list are possible versions of: the legend of the finding of the Cross by Helen, mother of Constantine; an

unknown lay entitled *Merlin le suuage*; *Glou degloucests*, a poem relating to either Gloius (son of Claudius) or Glovus (ancestor of Vortigern); *Laumaul* (Lanval), by Marie de France, interesting because of its Avalonion connection; and *Vygamer*, which is believed to be a poem relating to Guigomar, who is recorded as the Lord of Avalon by Chrétien de Troyes. This name is included within the list as part of a section of linked lays that include *Karleyn*, believed to be a poem regarding the history of Chester. It has been suggested that several of these poems and lays appear to be based on traditional Welsh material.

22 *Culhwch and Olwen* is the oldest story within *The Mabinogion* and the story involves a quest imposed on Culhwch by Olwen's father that he must complete in order to win her hand in marriage. The tale contains many early traditions, including a significant scene whereby Arthur is asked to cut the hair of Culhwch. Within Welsh tradition there is greater significance to the act of trimming hair; it was a recognition of ties of descent from a common ancestor and bound both parties together in an acceptance of their mutual kinship.

23 Culhwch's mother was Goleuddydd, a daughter of Amlawdd Wledig, as was Eigyr, Arthur's mother.

24 It has been suggested that Caer Glini and Caer Loyw are the same place and they are currently identified with Gloucester on the River Severn. As we have already shown, Caer Gloyw can be identified with Chester from the evidence given in the *Brut*. The reference to Caer Glini having ramparts and being situated on a crag in Culhwch and Olwen suggests a hillfort location and therefore a site quite different and separate from Caer Loyw.

25 The evidence put forward here is a simplified version of an unpublished paper by Steve Blake, 1990.

26 This name was recorded in *Britannia* by William Camden in 1587 as 'Killgury'.

27 In the absence of further evidence it has been concluded that the Wirral is most likely to be the Cilgwri referred to in *Culhwch and Olwen*. There is also a Cilgwri near Llangar on the River Dee near Corwen; see Richards, 1969, p.256. In a variant of the Oldest Animals, Dafydd ap Gwilym compares himself to the Stag of Cilgwri, thus changing blackbird for stag, but this may be in reference to the tradition that the church of Llangar was built on the site where a white stag appeared.

28 This independent version of the folk tale was recorded by Thomas Williams of Trefiw, see 'Pethau Nas Cyhoeddwyd', *National Library of Wales Journal*, Vol.VII, 1951, pp.62–6.

29 Halkyn Mountain's present name in Welsh is Helygain (willow tree, or place of willows); however no satisfactory explanation has yet been given for the earliest name recorded, Alchene. See Davies, 1959, pp.83–4. It seems obvious from the evidence that the Alchene of the 'Domesday Book' is a Norman rendering of the Welsh Mwyalchen; the dropping of the first element of the Welsh place name when recorded by a non-Welsh-speaking scribe is not unusual.

30 Richards, 1969, p.256.

31 Bartrum, 1993, p.113. Caw is also recorded as Caw of Prydyn and Caw of Twrcelyn. Prydin is simply a variant spelling of Prydein and the commonly held idea that it refers to 'Pictland' (wherever that may be) is not based upon any textual authority. Twrcelyn is an area of northern Anglesey that contains several church dedications to children of Caw.

32 For more on *Gwernabwy*, see Williams, Ifor, *Canu Aneirin*, University of Wales Press, 1938, pp.150–51.

33 Evans, 1922, see map at rear.

34 Before the building of the weir on the River Dee at Chester, the tidal bore is supposed to have extended as far upstream as Holt.

35 For the village of Trefor to the east of Llangollen, see *The History of the Family of Mostyn of Mostyn*, Rt Hon. Lord Mostyn and Glenn, T.A, privately published, 1925, p.1.

36 See Chapter 3.

37 Loomis, 1956, p.120 n. 71. See also Grufydd, W.J., *Math vab Mathonwy*, University of Wales Press, 1928, p.179, n.41.

38 Price, 1952, p.222 quoting from Orwell, Robert, *The Life and Works of the Cistercian Monks*, 1684.

10 THE POLITICS OF ARTHUR AND AVALON

1 For discussions of this event see Chambers, 1927, pp.112–27 and Robinson, 1926, pp.1–27.

2 Giraldus tells us that Henry ordered the monks to dig up the grave situated sixteen feet down. Thorpe, 1978, pp. 282–3.

3 See Appendix 2.

4 Jones, T. Gwynn, 'Some Arthurian Material in Keltic', *Aberystwyth Studies*, Vol.VIII, 1927, pp.42–3.

5 MacDougall, 1982, p.13.

6 Jones, T., 1966, pp.175–85. One cannot help but think that the Norman monarchy eventually became a victim of its own propaganda with the rise to throne of the Welsh Tudor dynasty in 1485.

7 Giraldus mentions the exhumation on two occasions. The first gives no date but the second tells us that it took place in the lifetime of Henry II, who died in July 1189. The second account also mentions Abbot Henry, who was Henry de Sully and was not appointed until September 1189. Ralph of Coggeshall records the date as 1191 and Adam of Domerham records that the event took place 648 years after the death of Arthur, given by Geoffrey of Monmouth as 542, thus 1190. Is it perhaps possible that the sources are talking of two different events? For a discussion and English translations of the two sources see Thorpe, 1978, pp.280–88.

8 Wood, C.T., 'Fraud and its Consequences: Savaric of Bath and the Reform of Glastonbury', in *The Archaeology and History of Glastonbury Abbey*, Woodbridge, 1991, pp.273–83.

9 Latin text in Chambers, 1927, p.269.

10 Ibid., p.268.

11 In the 16th century Leland gives, '*Hic iacet sepultus inclitus rex Arturius in insula Avalonia*' and also quotes from the supposed eyewitness account of Simon of Abingdon, '*Hic iacet gloriosissimus rex Britonum Arturus*'. Camden in his *Britannia* of 1587 gives, '*Hic iacet sepultus inclitus rex Arturius in insula Avalonia*'.

12 For further discussion on the inscriptions see Barber, 1972, pp.126–31.

13 Chambers, 1927, pp.112–27 and Robinson, 1926, pp.1–27.

14 There is no reason to doubt William of Malmesbury's original statement that King Ine of Wessex founded Glastonbury. William later elaborated upon the foundation of Glastonbury in his *Vita Sancti Dunstan* (Life of St Dunstan, of unknown date but definitely after 1125) by adding that Glastonbury was probably much older than he originally thought. This conflicts with an earlier biographer of Dunstan, named Osbern, who stated that Dunstan was the first Abbot of Glastonbury. This suggests that at some point between 1125 and his completion of the Life of St Dunstan, William altered his opinion of Glastonbury's origins. He stated in Book I of his *Life of St Dunstan* that he had decided to write a separate history of Glastonbury. On his completion of Book II he stated that this history was now complete and referred readers to it for a fuller account. William later stated that the charter granted by King Ine was for the refoundation of Glastonbury Abbey, adding that the Abbey was the first church in the Kingdom of Britain and the source and foundation of all religion. It is worth noting that William dedicated his *De Antiquitate* to the Abbot of Glastonbury, a certain Henry de

Blois, who was none other than the grandson of William I and nephew of Henry I, who had appointed him to the abbacy of Glastonbury.

15 See Gerould, 1927, passim.

16 Haddan and Stubbs, *Councils and Ecclesiastical Documents Relating to Great Britain*, Clarendon Press, 1869, Vol.II, p.484–5.

17 MacDougall, 1982, p.12.

18 Gerould, 1927, passim.

19 Ibid.

20 Loomis, 1953, pp.114–27.

21 For the political connotations of this act see Parsons, 1987, pp.173–7.

22 Ibid.

23 Ibid.

24 Davies, R.R., 1990, p.109.

25 Jones, Thomas, 1955, p.79.

26 Within a document dated 25 June 1283 and signed at Rhuddlan in North Wales, the seven Welsh officials that presented Edward I with the relics of the house of Gwynedd at Aberconwy are named as Einion ap Ynor, Llewelyn, Dafydd, Meilir, Gronow, Dayoc and Tegwared. As their reward these officials were granted 'privileges'.

27 Chambers, 1927, p.124.

28 The Cross has been known by various names during history, amongst which are: Croizneth, Croes Naidd, Nawddm, Gneyth and Niet. These forms variously mean the Cross of Refuge, or Protection or the True Cross. For a detailed history of the relic see Tennant, Winifred Coombe, 'Croes Naid', *National Library of Wales Journal*, Vol.VII, 1951, pp.102–15.

29 For further discussion on Arthur's Crown see *Révue Celtique*, Vol.XII, 1891, p.281. On the Welsh royal regalia. See Prestwich, M., *Edward I*, Berkeley, 1988, pp.203–4, Gwilym ap Iorwerth, 'The Cross and the Crown', *Journal of the Pendragon Society*, Vol.XXVI, no.4, 1997 and Loomis, 1953, p.117.

30 Tennant, op. cit.

31 'The Books of the Cymry and their murderer,/Went to the White Tower in secret/It was cruel for Yscolan to throw the pile of books into the fire.' Attributed to Gutor Glyn (c.1450).

32 Chambers, 1927, p.118.

33 *Arthurian Literature Vol.I*, Boydell, 1981, p.73.

34 Treharne, 1967, p.106.

11 IN SEARCH OF GLAESTINGABURH

1 Bartrum, 1993, p.644.

2 This charter is mentioned by William of Malmesbury in both *De Antiquitate Glastoniensis Ecclesiae* and his *Gesta Regum*.

3 Nicholson, E.W.B., *Y Cymmrodor*, Vol.XXI, 1908, p.98.

4 Thorpe, 1978, p.283.

5 Bartrum, 1993, p.285.

6 For further discussion on this matter see Gray, Louis H., *A Note on the Names of Glastonbury*, Speculum, Vol.X, 1935, pp.46–53, and the excellent reply by Slover, Clark H., *A Note on the Names of Glastonbury*, Speculum, Vol.XI 1936, pp.129–132. Also of note is Wade-Evans, A.W., 'The Origin of Glastonbury', *Notes and Queries*, 3 April, 1948, pp.134–5.

7 Bartrum, 1966, p.12, §25.

8 Wade-Evans, 1938, p.80.

9   Ibid. Maelgwyn Gwynedd, called by Gildas (his contemporary) Maglocunus. He is the last of the five kings mentioned in Gildas's *Epistola*. See Williams, 1899, p.76–87, §33–6.

10 Bartrum, 1966, p.13, §32–3.

11 Originally Dogfeiling was the name of the whole cantref, but now it only constitutes a part of Dyffryn Clwyd, the name that replaced Dogfeiling as the name of the cantref. Its main stronghold appears to have been Ruthin. Wade-Evans, 1934, p.38.

12 Wade-Evans, 1934, p.38. Edeirnion was later incorporated into Powys Fadog.

13 The area over which he ruled did not receive his name, but was known as Rhos. His grandson was Cynlas, one of the five kings mentioned in the *Epistola* of Gildas, who held the stronghold of Dinerth. Williams, 1899, p.73.

14 Wade-Evans, 1934, p.38. Llanfaes, or Llanfaes Ysfeilion, 'the Monastery of the Ysfeilion Plain'.

15 See the genealogical chart in Appendix 1, p.228

16 Tegeingl is an early name for an area covered by the modern county of Flintshire, although it is more likely that this area is named after the Decaengli tribe who occupied it during the Roman invasion.

17 These later sons appear in some genealogies, see Bartrum, 1966, p.92.

18 Bromwich, 1978, p.201.

19 Cynlas Goch was a son of Owain Danwyn, the ruler of the Kingdom of Rhos in what later became Gwynedd. He is the Cuneglasus talked of by Gildas in his epistle. Gildas names him as 'the driver of a chariot belonging to a bear's den'. The bear's den referred to is Dinarth, a township near Llandrillo-y-Rhos, which translates as 'the Bear's Fortress' or 'the Bear's Stronghold'; 'Bear' in the early Welsh/British language is *Arth*.

20 One of the five kings whom Gildas mentions in his *Epistola*, 'superior to almost all the kings of Britannia'. His stronghold was on the River Conwy above the town of Deganwy and he is mentioned on many occasions in Welsh history and folklore.

21 Caradog Freichfras is thoroughly interwoven into the Matter of Britain. We are told that his kingdom extended even across the boundaries of Britannia, again enforcing our argument that Britannia is only an area within the greater Britain, and that he took Letavia (Llydaw) under his rule. He is mentioned in the tale known as *Rhonabwy's Dream*, where he is described as 'a man who had a right to speak to him [Arthur] as bluntly as he wished' as he was Arthur's chief councillor and his first cousin. (Jones and Jones, 1993, p.119.) Caradog is also mentioned in the *Triads*, where he is recorded as the 'Chief elder in Celliwig in Cernyw', one of the main courts of Arthur, and in another *Triad* he is named as one of 'the three favourites of Arthur'. He also survived into the French Grail romances, where he is called Karadues Briebraz.

22 Bartrum, 1966, p.12, §25.

23 Ibid.

24 Peniarth MS. 177, p.217, see Bartrum, 1993, p.284.

25 Caer means 'fortress' or 'stronghold'. Caer Loytcoyt is also mentioned as a battlesite of Athur in the *Brut* and the *Historia Gruffudd ap Cynan* (Evans, D.S., 1990). See Chapter 6.

26 The town called Aldud is unusual and as far as we are aware there have been no suggestions as to the meaning of this, although Aldud does appear as a personal name within the Welsh genealogies. The importance of Aldud is that it is used in the context of 'the town called Aldud today', which would appear to mean at the time of writing. The name Aldud is found in Welsh genealogies as the son of Edwin of Tegeingl (the Welsh name for Flintshire) and the descendants of Aldud formed a small enclave of the tribe of Edwin of Tegeingl; therefore it would seem possible that what is meant by 'Aldud today' is a place possibly owned by the descendants of Aldud. Aldud would appear to be a distinctly Welsh name, at present appearing to be localized only in northeast Wales. Research on this point continues.

27 'Twry *Berved y Wlat* en y daeth y Gaer', *Historia Gruffudd ap Cynan*, op. cit., p.140.

28 There has been a lot of confusion over the name of Llwydcoed and its various spellings; the usual identification of Lichfield is obviously not meant in most cases and several places of this name exist in Wales, any one of which is more likely than a cathedral town in the Midlands.

29 Jones and Jones, 1993, pp.58–9.

30 Palmer, A.N., *The History of The Parish of Ruabon*, Bridge Books, 1992, pp.82–3.

31 Baring-Gould and Fisher, 1907–13, Vol.IV, pp.375–8.

32 Jones, T. Gwynn, 1930, p.52.

33 Ibid.

34 Sikes, Wirt, *British Goblins*, 1880, pp.7–8.

35 Spelt as 'Rhyfsa Cadfarch' in the edition of the *Life of St Collen* published in *Greal*, London, 1805, p.337.

36 Rhys, John, ed., *Pennant's Tour Through Wales*, 1883, Vol.I., p.296.

37 Bowen, E.G., *Settlements of the Celtic Saints in Wales*, University of Wales Press, 1954, p.9.

38 *Royal Commission for Ancient Monuments: Denbighshire*, p.119, #424.

39 Baring-Gould and Fisher, 1907–13, Vol.II, p.160 and references therein.

12 AVALON: THE WORLD'S END

1 Lomax, 1992, p.65.

2 Ider appears on the early 12th-century sculpture at Modena, in Italy, as Isdernus. Within Welsh texts he is referred to as Edern ap Nudd and in French as Yder fis Nu.

3 For more on Arthur slaying giants, see Jones, T. Gwynn, 1930, pp.77–9.

4 Aravius Mons is usually translated as Snowdon, but it is probably a Latinization of the Welsh word Eryri, which denotes the area in which Snowdon is situated (Snowdonia), rather than the summit itself.

5 Williams, 1901, p.411.

6 Ibid., p.409.

7 Chrétien de Troyes, *Arthurian Romances*, translated by Owen, D.D.R., Everyman, revised edition, 1993, p.193, lines 643–7.

8 Ibid., p.26, lines 1939–40.

9 Tudur Aled was not a Black Friar as sometimes suggested, but a Franciscan. See Price, 1952, p.170.

10 *Dwy Faelor, deau Felwas:/Deheulaw wyt draw hyd tren./A deheufraich hyd Hafren*, Jones, T. Gwynn, 1926, p.164.

11 By this time the Hafren was the name applied to the Severn, as described in Chapter 3.

12 Williams and Williams, 1939, p.169.

13 Davies, 1959, pp.102–3.

14 Jones, T. Gwynn, 1926, Vol.II, pp.586–7.

15 The two texts in question are Llanstephan MS. 122 and Wynnstay MS. 1. Many of the books and documents taken from and pertaining to Valle Crucis Abbey were destroyed by a fire at the library of the nearby Wynnstay Hall in 1857.

16 Williams, Mary, 'An Early Ritual Poem in Welsh', *Speculum*, Vol.13, 1938, pp.38–51.

17 Geraint ap Erbin is mentioned in the tale of *Culhwch and Olwen* as the father of Cadwy and he appears in some of the earliest Welsh poetry contained within *The Red Book of Hergest* and *The Black Book of Carmarthen*. The latter contains a poem titled *Gereint fil' Erbin*, which contains one of the ealiest references to Arthur: 'At Llongborth I saw Arthur,/brave men hewed with steel;/emperor, ruler of battle' (Jarman, 1982, p.48).

18 Bromwich, 1978, p.382.

19 Bartrum, 1993, p.512 and references therein.

20 *Royal Commission Report on Ancient Monuments in Denbighshire*, p.124, §432.

21 Bartrum, 1993, p.470.

22 Bromwich, 1978, p.383.

23 Bartrum, 1993, p.469.

24 Morris, Lewis, *Celtic Remains*, The Cambrian Archaeological Association, 1870, p.220.

25 When threatened by an invading force it was an easy and well-practised manoeuvre for the Welsh to remove themselves and their property into the high summer lands, beyond the reach of all but the most foolhardy of foes.

26 William of Malmesbury was reluctant to comply with the tradition that Gildas was buried at Glastonbury; see Scott, John, ed., *The Early History of Glastonbury: An Edition, Translation and Study of William of Malmesbury's De Antiquitate Glastonia Ecclesiae*, Boydell, 1981.

27 Williams, 1901, pp.394–413.

28 The identification of this text is uncertain, although it might be a version of the *Historia Brittonum*. Many of the surviving manuscripts of this text claim that Gildas was the author.

29 Williams, 1901, pp.322–89.

30 Ibid., pp.394–413.

31 Wade-Evans, 1934, p.196.

32 Ibid., p.237.

33 Bartrum, 1993, pp.112–13.

34 Wade-Evans, 1934, p.181.

35 Possibly the oldest reference is in the 'Gododdin': *'Vn maban e gian o dra bannauc'* (Cian's son, from beyond Mount Bannawg). *Canu Aneirin*, Williams, Ifor, University of Wales Press, 1938, p.10, line 255. Bannog is also mentioned on several occasions by the later bards, see Bromwich, 1978, pp.278–9 and references therein.

36 These magical oxen are also mentioned in the tale *Culhwch and Olwen*, Jones and Jones, p.96.

37 Williams, Ifor, *Canu Llywarch Hen*, University of Wales Press, 1935, p.22 and consult notes on pp.156–8. *'Ysydd Lanfawr tra Bannawg./Ydd aa Clwyd yng Nghlywedawg./Ac ni wn ai hi, laallawg.'*

38 Also in the area are Cefn Bannog, Waen Bannog and Llyn Dau Ychain where the two oxen are said to have disappeared. Another tradition linked to this locality concerns the Fuwch Frech (Speckled Cow), who is said to be the mother of the Ychain Bannog. Place names linked to her are Preseb y Fuwch Frech, Ffynnon y Fuwch Frech at Cefn Bannog, another well of the same name in the nearby parish of Nantglyn, and finally Gwal Erw y Fruwch Frech. The Ychain Bannog are also mentioned in other parts of Wales in the parishes of Llandewibrefi in Ceredigion, Llandecwyn in Ardudwy and often in connection with the legend of Hu Gadarn, who drew the Afanc out of Lyn Llyw (Lake Bala?) with the help of the Ychain Bannog.

39 See Appendix 3.

40 Wade-Evans, 1934, pp.237–9.

13 THE GRAIL LAND

1 All other traditions that give Joseph of Arimathea a burial place state that he is buried in Avalon, Glastonbury or simply Britain – namely Britannia (Wales).

2 Skeat, 1871, p.41.

3   Loomis, 1963, p. 252.

4   Evans, 1910.

5   Robinson, 1926, p.36. Treharne, 1967, p.40.

6   Juvenal, *The Sixteen Satires*, trans. Green, Peter, revised edition, Penguin, 1974, p.109.

7   The names Arviragus and Gweirydd appear to be linguistically unrelated, although which is the original attached to the story of the founding of Caer Loyw it is impossible to say. Why would the Welsh gloss Arviragus to Gweirydd in the *Brut* without some prior tradition attached to this name?

8   Bartrum, 1993, p.456 and notes therein.

9   Oman, 1921, p. 104.

10 For the evolution of St Joseph's legend at Glastonbury, see Lagorio, 1971, pp.216–17. Also Carley and Townsend, 1985, pp.xlviii–lx and Robinson, 1926.

11 This is believed to be based on a Latin form of *Transitus Mariae* (The Passing of Mary), claimed to have been written by St Joseph of Arimathea himself.

12 John Capgrave also professes to quote from this same source in his *Life of Joseph, Nova Legenda Angliae.*

13 As shown earlier, at the time this text was written Britannia was used to define Wales.

14 In translation *nepos* can mean either 'nephew' or 'grandson'. The Helaius referred to is believed to be Bron/Hebron, brother-in-law of St Joseph.

15 The genealogy gives the order as follows: 'Petrus, cousin of Joseph of Arimathea begat Erlan who begat Melian(um) who begat Arguth who begat Edor who begat Loth who took as his wife Arthur's sister on whom he begat Walwanum (Gawain), Agraueyns (Agravains), Gwerehes (Guerrehes) and Geheries (Gaheriet).'

16 Robinson, 1926, pp.30–31.

17 Ashe, 1960, pp.227–8.

18 Carley and Townsend, 1985, p.279 n.76.

19 Robinson, 1926, pp. 30–31. For a new translation of this prophecy and an excellent discussion of Melkin, see Carley and Townsend, 1985, pp.27–31.

20 Bartrum, 1993, p.467.

21 For the political background of Hardyng's *Chronicle*, see Kennedy, 1989, pp.185–206.

22 Skeat, 1871, p.xli.

23 Riddy, 1991, p.325.

24 For a discussion of John Hardyng's *Chronicle* in relation to Joseph of Arimathea and Glastonbury, see Riddy, 1991, pp. 317–31.

25 Melkin is variously cited as Maryan, Nennius, Mewinus and Mewyn, although the general context makes it clear that Melkin is intended.

26 *Relationum Historicarum de Rebus Anglicis tomus primus quatuor partes complectens,* which basically synopsized Bale's discussion while adding several significant elaborations.

27 Carley and Townsend, 1985, p.lvi.

28 Ibid., p. lvi and n. 32.

29 Rhys, 1886, p.122, Wade-Evans, 1956, p.31, n.4.

30 Ellis, 1959, p.107, 'In Pichetone et Melchanstone.'

31 Treharne, 1967, p.5.

32 Ibid., p.121. Also Loomis, 1963, p.266. The first mention of a link between the Holy Thorn and St Joseph was made by a Dr Plot in 1677: 'some take it for a miraculous remembrance of the birth of Christ, first planted by Joseph of Arimathea'.

33 Robinson, 1926, p.20.

34 The confusion of Caerlleon and Carlisle can be traced to Geoffrey of Monmouth's Latin *Historia*, according to which Leil was a son of Brutus Viride Scutum, who built a city in

North Britain named Kaerleil, which has been interpreted as Carlisle. The Welsh *Brut* clarifies the Welsh tradition, for in place of Geoffrey's Leil and Kaerleil it gives the names Lleon and Caerlleon (Chester). The *Brut* records that Caerlleon was founded by the British king Lleon ap Brutus Darianlas, also known as Lleon Gawr. Again, most of the conflicting evidence presented by sources can actually be complementary once the misunderstandings regarding the geographical context of compatible material are clarified.

35 There are other examples of ancient towns being known under a variety of names. For instance, the town of Caernarfon has been known variously as Caereudaf', Caercystenydd, Caer Sain, Caer Sallwg, Caer Seiont, Aber Seiont, and Aber Sain among others. Some of these are geographical descriptions, but in the case of Caereudaf' and Caercystenydd the names refer to the figures of Eudaf Hen and Custennin (Constantine), who at different times held Caernarfon.

36 Budden, 1922. As previously mentioned, we were also aware of another ancient chapel dedicated to St Peter within Ynys Afallach, namely the remains of the chapel that stood near Manachlog, the monastic site beneath Caerfallach, opposite Wirral.

37 It is possible that the ancient church of St Mary on Hilbre Island is a candidate for the chapel in John of Glastonbury's version.

38 The Ford of the Holyhead is in reference to the legend of St Winefrid.

39 Also known as *Catalogus Felicianus*. See Baring-Gould and Fisher, 1907–13, Vol.III, p.353.

40 According to a theory put forward by Dr Harnach in 1904, Britannio is supposedly a mistake for Britum and he makes Lucius rule from Birtha in Edessa, although this particular king's full name was Lucius Aelius Septimius Megas Abgarus IX (AD 174–179). Yet the text specifically states *Lucio Britannio rege*, Lucius, King of Britannia. It is also worth noting that Bede fails to mention the event in his *De temporibus* of 702 but does record it in his Chronicle of 725. The simple fact that Bede was known as the father of English history, not British, is more than enough to account for this. Bede obviously accepted the event for him to have recorded it within his chronicle. Furthermore, within the British tradition Lucius is a great-grandson of Arviragus, who granted Ynys Witrin to St Joseph of Arimathea.

41 See also Baring-Gould and Fisher, 1907–13, Vol.III, p.352 and notes therein. Also Bartrum, 1993, pp.427–8.

42 Baronius, *Annales Ecclesiatici*, 12 vols., 1588–1607, Vol.II, under AD 183.

43 Or 'wrestler's hold'.

44 According to others or otherwise Damianus.

45 See *Acta Sanctorum*, Vol.I, p.10.

46 See Davies, W. S., *Cymmrodor*, 30, 1920, pp.143–6.

47 Fagan and Duvian are the Welsh forms of Phagan and Deruvian.

48 Flamens and Archflamens are omitted from *Brut Y Brenhinedd*, though most other details remain parallel to Geoffrey's Latin *Historia*.

49 Budden, 1922, p.90.

APPENDIX 2: THE UNKNOWN ARTHUR

1 Translated by Scott Lloyd and Sandra Thomas from the extract edited from the manuscript by Thomas Jones and published in his study of the story, *Chwedl Huail ap Caw ac Arthur*, Astudiaethau Amrywiol, University of Wales Press, 1968, pp.48ff.

2 *Polychronicon*, Rolls edition, 1875, Vol.V, pp.328–30.

3 Vinaver, 1947, pp.649–70, Book IX, *The Tournament at Surluse*. Surluse is also mentioned in *The Vulgate Cycle*, see Sommer, 1908–16, Index Volume.

4 Jones and Jones, 1993, p.85.

5 Williams, 1901, pp.400–403.

6 Loomis, Roger, *Chrétien de Troyes and the Arthurian Tradition*, Columbia University Press, 1949, p.76.

7 Bromwich, 1978, p.1. This translation differs slightly from that of the text on p.1 as we have used the place names given in a variation of the same *Triad*, contained in Peniarth MS. 77.

8 Jones, T. Gwynn, 1927, p.41. Welsh text in Anwyl, 1909, p.217.

9 Bachellery, 1950, p.251, line 18.

10 This site has also been identified with the Bears' Den mentioned in the *Epistola* of Gildas, Williams, H., 1899, p.73, §32.

11 Bishop Alexander Penrose Forbes, 'The Lives of St. Ninian and St. Kentigern', *The Historians of Scotland*, Vol.5, Edinburgh, 1874.

12 Bartrum, 1966, p.66, n.85.

13 Jones, T. Gwynn, 1927, p.42. Welsh text in Morris-Jones and Parry-Williams,1971, p.301.

14 Jones, T. Gwynn, ibid.

15 Jones, Thomas, 'A Sixteenth-Century Version of the Arthurian Cave Legend', in *Studies in Language and Literature in Honour of Margaret Schlauch*, Warsaw, 1966, p.179.

16 Bartrum, 1993, pp.80–81.

APPENDIX 3: THE 'LOST' KINGDOMS OF NORTHERN BRITAIN

1 Evans, 1910, p.xii.

2 Anwyl, 1909, p.86. Translation in Conran, 1967, p.109.

3 Evans, 1910, pp.xiii–xiv.

4 Morris-Jones and Parry-Williams, 1971, p.64, line 4. See also the index to Evans, 1926, p.422.

5 Evans, 1922, p.xviii, n. 12.

6 Anwyl, 1909, p.130.

7 Williams, Ifor, *Canu Anerin*, University of Wales Press, 1937, p.75.

8 Evans, 1922, p.xviii, note 12.

9 Evans, 1911, p.2, line 40. Translation in *Merlin Through the Ages*, Stewart, R.J., and Matthews, John, eds., Blandford, 1995, p.37.

10 Evans, 1926, see references to Manaw in index p.415.

11 Williams, 1901, p.403.

GLOSSARY OF PERSONAL NAMES

Welsh name	Latin name	Welsh name	Latin name
Aldwr	Aldroenus	Emyr Llydaw	Budicius
Arawn	Auguselus	Eppa	Eopa
Awstin	Augustine	Garmon	Germanus
Bedwyr	Bedivere	Gillamuri	Gillomurius
Bleid	Lupus	Gormwnt	Gormundus
Braint Hir	Brianus	Gwalchmai	Gawain
Brochvael	Brochmail	Gwenwyfar	Guinevere
Cadwaladr	Cadwallader	Gwerthefyr	Vortimer
Cadwallon	Cadwallo	Gwrgant	Gorangonus
Cadwr	Cador	Gwrlois	Gorlois
Caledfwlch	Caliburn/ Excalibur	Gwrtheyrn Gwrtheneu	Vortigern
Cai	Kay	Hywel	Hoel
Constans	Constans	Llew	Loth
Cuhelyn	Guitelinus	Macsen Wledig	Maximianus
Custennyn	Constantine	Maelgwn Gwynedd	Malgo
Custennyn ap Cadwr	Constantine son of Cador	Medrawd	Medrod
Cynderyn	Kentigern	Myrddin	Merlin
Cynan Wledig	Aurelius Conanus	Pasgen	Paschent
		Rhita	Ritho
Dewi	David	Ronwen	Renwein
Dunod	Dinoot	Selyf	Salomon
Dyfrig	Dubricius	Urien	Urian
Eidol	Eldol	Uthyr Pendragon	Uther Pendragon
Eigyr	Igerna		
Emrys Wledig	Aurelius Ambrosius		

Gazetteer of Comparative Place Names

Welsh name	Latin name	Present location	Actual location
Alban	Albania	Scotland	Powys
Caer Alclut	Alclud	Dumbarton	Hillfort at Melin Y Wig
Caer Caradoc	Salesburiensis	Salisbury	Hillfort near Cerrigydrudion
Caer Ceint	Cantuaria	Canterbury	Kentchester, near Hereford
Caer Cynan	Cunungeburg	Conisbrough	Cefn Meiriadog, near St Asaph?
Caer Dunod	Dimlot	Tregare Rounds	Caer Dunod, near Llanfihangel?
Caer Efrog	Eboracum	York	Wroxeter
Caer Faddon	Mons Badonis	Bath	Breiddin Hills
Caer Fuddai	Silcestria	Silchester	Machynlleth
Caer Llwytcoet	Lincolniensis	Lincoln	Hope
Caer Loyw	Glouecestrensis	Gloucester	Chester
Caer Vyrddyn	Kaermerdin	Carmarthen	Carmarthen
Caer Wrangon	Wigornia	Worcester	Worcester
Caer Wynt	Wintonia	Winchester	Corwen
Caerlleon	Urbs Legionum	Chester	Chester
Caerlion ar Wysg	Urbs Legionum	Caerleon on Usk	Chester
Camlan, Afon	Camblanum	Camelford, Cornwall	Afon Gamlan, near Dolgellau
Coed Celyddon	Silva Colidon	Southern Scotland	Clocaenog Forest Area
Cor Y Cewri	Corea Gigantum	Stonehenge	Cerrigydrudion
Cymru	Cambria	Wales	Gwynedd/North Wales
Deifyr	Deira	Northeast England	Cheshire
Denmark	Denmark	Denmark	Northeast England?
Derwenydd, Afon	Derewend	Derwent	Uncertain
Dinas Verolam	Verolamium	St Albans	Beeston Hill?
Dinas y Garrei	Thanceaster	Caistor, Lincolnshire	Tong, Shropshire
Dindagol	Tintagol	Tintagel	Castellmarch, Lleyn Peninsula
Frainc	Francia	France	Southern England?
Gogledd	Northanimbria	Scotland/ Strathclyde	North Wales
Gwynedd	Venedotia	Gwynedd	Gwynedd
Hafren	Sabrina	Severn	Dee (later ascribed to the Severn)

Welsh name	Latin name	Present location	Actual location
Hwmr	Humbrum	Humber	Severn
Iwerddon	Hibernia	Ireland	Ireland
Keint	Cantia	Kent	Gwent
Kernyw	Cornubia	Cornwall	Lleyn and Gwynedd coast
Lloegyr	Logres	England	Deheubarth/South Wales
Llundein	Lundonia	London	Ludlow
Llychlyn	Norguegensis	Norway	Southwest Scotland?
Llydaw	Armorica	Brittany	Cornwall
Lyndesei	Lindiseiensis	Lincolnshire	Part of Shropshire
Maes Beli	Maisbelum	Uncertain	Nercwys Mountain
Mynwy	Menevia	St Davids	Henfynyw
Orc	Orcades	Orkneys	Anglesey?
Penrhyn Blathaon	Catanensia	Dunnet Head	Wirral peninsula
Rheged	Murefensium	Moray	Dee Valley and Oswestry
Ynys Afallach	Insula Avallonia	Isle of Avalon	Northeast Wales/ Flintshire
Ynys Danet	Insula Thaneth	Isle of Thanet	Forest of Dean
Ynys Prydein	Insula Britannia	Great Britain	Wales and the Marches
Ysgotland	Scotia	Scotland	Cheshire (part of Alban/Powys)

GLOSSARY OF ELEMENTS
OF WELSH PLACE NAMES

Aber estuary, confluence of two rivers
Afon river
Allt hillside, slope, height
Ar on, upon, by

Bach small, little, lesser
Ban, *pl.* **bannau** peak, crest
Banc bank, hill, slope
Bangor consecrated land or monastery within a wattle fence
Bedd *pl.* **beddau** grave
Bod abode, dwelling
Bont bridge
Bro region, vale, lowland
Bron hillbreast, hillside
Bryn, *pl.* **bryniau** hill
Bwlch pass, gap
Bychan little, lesser

Cadair, cader seat, stronghold
Cae, *pl.* **caeau** field, enclosure
Caer, *pl.* **caerau** fort, stronghold, hillfort
Canol middle
Capel chapel
Carn, *pl.* **carnau** cairn, mountain, rock
Carnedd, *pl.* **carneddau** cairn, tumulus, mountain
Carreg, pl. **cerrig** stone, rock
Castell castle
Cefn ridge
Celli grove, copse
Cerrig, *see* **carreg**
Cil, *pl.* **cilau** corner, retreat, nook
Clawdd dyke, hedge, ditch
Clogwyn crag, clifff
Coch red
Coed trees, wood, forest
Craig, *pl.* **creigiau** rock
Croes cross
Crug, *pl.* **crugiau** knoll, tump
Cwm valley
Cwrt court
Cymer confluence

Dan under, below
Dau, *f.* **dwy** two
Derwen, *pl.* **derw** oak
Din hill fortress
Dinas fortress, walled town
Diserth hermitage
Dol water meadow
Dre, *see* **tre**
Du, *f.* **ddu** black
Dwfr, dwr water
Dwy, *see* **dau**
Dyffryn valley

Eglwys church
Erw acre
Esgair long ridge

Fach, fechan, *see* **bach**
Fan, *see* **ban**
Fawr, *see* **mawr**
Felin, *see* **melin**
Fron, *see* **bron**

Ffordd road, way
Ffos ditch, trench
Ffynnon, *pl.* **ffynhonnau** well, source

Gaer, *see* **caer**
Gallt hill, slope, wood
Garn, *see* **carn**
Garnedd, *see* **carnedd**
Ganol, *see* **canol**
Garreg, *see* **carreg**
Gelli, *see* **celli**
Glan riverbank, bank
Glas green, blue
Glyn deep valley, glen
Graig, *see* **craig**
Groes, *see* **croes**
Gwaun moor, mountain pasture
Gwern place where alders grow, swamp
Gwlad land
Gwyn, *f.* **gwen** white, blessed, holy, sacred

Hafod, hafoty summer dwelling
Hen old
Hir long

Is below, under
Isaf lower, lowest

Las, *see* **glas**
Lwyd, *see* **llwyd**

Llan church, sacred enclosure
Llech slab, stone, rock
Llechwedd hillside
Llethr slope
Llwyd grey, brown, gate
Llwyn grove, bush
Llyn lake
Llys court, hall

Maen, *pl.* **meini** (sacred) stone
Maes field, plain
Mawr great, big
Meini, *see* **maen**
Melin mill
Moel bare hill, bald
Morfa marsh, sea strand
Mur wall
Mynachlog monastery
Mynydd mountain

Nant brook
Newydd new

Onnen, *pl.* **onn, ynn** ash tree

Pant hollow, valley
Pen head, top, end
Penrhyn promontory, headland

Pentre, pentref village
Plas hall, mansion, palace
Pont bridge
Porth gateway, harbour
Pwll pool

Rhaedr waterfall
Rhiw hill, slope
Rhos moorland
Rhyd ford

Sain, saint
Sarn paved way
Sych dry

Tair, *see* **Tri**
Tal end
Teg fair
Tir land, territory
Traeth shore, beach, strand
Tre, tref town, homestead
Tri, three
Tros over
Trwyn point, cape, nose
Ty house

Uchaf upper, higher, highest
Uwch above

Waun, *see* **Gwaun**
Wen, *see* **Gwen**
Wern, *see* **Gwern**

Y, yr, 'r the (*definite article*)
Ych, *pl.* **ychain** ox
Yn in
Ynys island, realm, kingdom
Ystrad valley floor, strath

ABOUT THE AUTHORS

Between them, **Steve Blake** and **Scott Lloyd** have devoted decades of research to the subject of Arthur and Ancient Britain. They have close links with the specialist Mold Library in Wales and are involved in the development of an Arthurian Centre planned for North Wales. They also work as historical consultants for the North Wales Tourist Board and make many media appearances. They are both based in North Wales.

John Baldock is a teacher, art historian and published author. He lives in rural Dorset.

USEFUL ADDRESSES

The Keys To Avalon is only an introduction to our researches into British history. Proposed future works will look closely at the Pre-Roman history of Britain, early Christianity in Britain, the Knights Templar and the Grail romances. If you feel you can add to our understanding of these subjects or wish to contact us, please either write to us care of the publishers, or contact us through our web-site which contains more detailed articles on various points raised in *The Keys To Avalon*:
www.grailand.co.uk

SOURCE PUBLISHERS

Anybody wishing to obtain copies of the source texts used in this book should start by contacting the publishers given below.

Boydell & Brewer
PO Box 9
Woodbridge
Suffolk
IP12 3DF
Britain
Tel: 01394 411320
Fax: 01394 411477
www.boydell.co.uk

The National Library of Wales
Aberystwyth
Cardiganshire
Wales, UK
www.llgc.org.uk

Dublin Institute of Advanced Studies
School of Celtic Studies
10 Burlington Road
Dublin 2
Ireland
www.cp.dias.ie/celtic.html

University of Wales Press
6 Gwynnyth Street
Cathays
Cardiff CF2 4YD
Wales, UK
Tel: 01222 231919
Fax: 01222 230908
www.swan.ac.uk/uwp/home.htm

OTHER RESOURCES

Flintshire Library Headquarters
Mold
North Wales
Tel 01352 704400

One of the leading Arthurian collections in the world is kept at the Flintshire Library Headquarters in Mold. The collection includes over 2,500 items, in eleven different languages, dealing with the subjects of Arthur, the Holy Grail, Celtic Mythology and Dark Age British History. This collection together with another extensive collection of academic journals and history books regarding Wales, and the friendly and helpful staff, make the Mold Library a wonderful resource which is available to the general public. The Arthurian collection catalogue is now available online at: http://seren.newi.ac.uk/arthur/

The Journal of the Pendragon Society
c/o John and Linda Ford,
41 Ridge Street
Watford
Herts, WD2 5BL
England

The Journal of the Pendragon Society (established 1959) is published three times a year and contains many useful articles, including book reviews and a letters column which creates a great deal of discussion on all matters of Arthurian interest.

INDEX

Aber Conway Abbey 135, 136, 161, 162, 164
Aber Seint *see* Caernarfon
Abererch 171, 219
Abergele 114
Abersoch 171
Aberystwyth 84
Acts of Union 10
Aerfen (goddess) *see* Ceridwen
Aerfen (village) 145
Afallach (Aballach, Avalloc, Evelach), King
    of Annwn 124, 125–7, 132, 133, 134,
    138, 147, 151, 152, 153, 169, 200, 238
Afloeg ap/son of Cunedda 171
Afloegion 171
Afon Christionydd 216
Afon Eitha 190
Afon Gamlan *see* Camlan
Afon Lliw (Llyw), 151
Afon Meirchion 101, 222
Afon Twrch 151, 152
Agned Mountain 99, 102
Agrestes, King of Kamaalot 206
Alain, son of Bron 199, 200
Alanus de Insulis *Prophetiae Merlini*
    (Prophecies of Merlin) 124
Alban (Albania, Powys, Scocia) 29, 33, 63,
    64, 78, 80, 93, 94, 97, 108, 146, 187,
    194, 197, 198
    confusion with Scotland 24–6, 98, 191, 196
    identified as Chesire and northern Powys
    24–6, 42, 189, 191, 195
    Picts of 53–4
Alban, St 50, 94
Alclud (Caer Alclud) *see* Caer Alclud
Alclud, Clydeside
    confusion with Arecluta (Vale of Clwyd)
    196
Alderley Edge 115
Aldud 173
Aldwr ap/son of Cynfor 49–50, 219
Aled, River 241
Alfonso, son of Edward I 163
Alleccus ap/son of Caw 194
Alun, River 98, 132, 146
Alun valley 79, 154
Amaethon ap/son of Don 125
Ambri (Ambrius), monastery of 81, 82, 83,
    84, 85, 127, 217
Ambrosius Aurelianus *see* Emrys Wledig
    ap/son of Custennin
Amhar/Amr ap/son of Arthur 232
Aminadab 204
Amlawdd Wledig 91, 172, 219, 220, 221
Amphilabus, St 50, 94
Amphibalus, monastery of 85, 94
An ap y lleian *see* Merlin/Myrddin

Anarawn ap/son of Cynfarch 219
Angevin dynasty 160
Angles 55, 56, 58–9
Anglesey (Ynys Mon, Surloes) 46, 171,
    172, 194, 195, 196, 219, 220, 222,
    223, 225–6, 227, 240, 241
Anglia *see* England
Anglo–Norman monarchy 156, 158–9
Anglo–Saxon Chronicle 27, 52, 56, 67,
    245–6
Anguselus 161 *see also* Arawn
Anna, daughter of Joseph of Arimathea
    125
Anna ferch/daughter of Uther 91, 116,
    126, 134, 219, 222
    welded with Gwyar 91, 219
Annales Cambriae (Annals of Wales) 103,
    113, 223, 245
Annals of Waverly 160
Annwn (Annfwyn), Celtic Otherworld 123,
    130, 134, 139–41, 217
    geographical location 141–4, 153–4, 167
    Joseph of Arimathea's burial 215
    links with Ynys Afallach/Avalon 131,
    133, 137–8, 140–1, 146, 166
Antonine Itinerary 144
Antonine Wall 60, 62, 63, 142
Antoninus, Emperor 61, 62, 63
Apocryphal Gospels 199
Aran Mountains (Aran Penllyn,
    Brentecnol, Mynydd Aran Mawr) 39,
    91, 92, 104, 184–5, 186
Arawn ap/son of Cynfarch, King of
    Alban (possibly identified with
    Anguselus) 108, 111, 219
Archenfield *see* Erging
Archfedd ferch/ daughter of Arthur 232
Arderydd, Battle of 101, 221, 223
Arecluta (Vale of Clwyd) 194
    confusion with Alclud, Clydeside, 196
Arfon 46, 47, 172
Argante (Margante) *see* Morgan le Fay
Arianrhod ferch/daughter of Don 125, 174
Arllechwedd 172
Armes Prydein 77, 146, 215
Arthur 1–2, 8–11, 27, 72, 87, 146, 176, 177
    adoption by Normans and Plantagenets
    2, 156–7, 158–61, 234–5
    alleged exhumations 155–6, 157–8,
    160–1, 164, 200
    alleged links with England and
    Scotland 2–3, 24
    alleged links with Glastonbury 165–6,
    167, 183–4, 186
    battles 98–104
    children 232

Chronica genealogy 204
conception 88, 89, 90, 104
continental campaigns 107
coronation 107–8
courts 228–31 *see also* Camelot
as Culhwch's companion 17, 147, 148
death 121, 135–8
Dux Bellorum 97–8
early life 92–3
final battle 113–16
final days 51, 110–13
links to Eglwyseg valley 179
and Glaestingaburh Abbey 183–6
and Guinevere/Gwenhwyfar 106
and the head of Bran 233–4
and Huail/Hueil 194, 195, 196, 225–8,
    241–2
identity 117
and Melwas 186–7, 193, 197
mistresses 231
and Morgan le Fay 130, 131, 134
the once and future king 156–7, 234–5
relatives 46–7, 91–2, 125–6, 172–3,
    218–24
and Rhita Gawr 39, 91
search for the historical 10, 16–19
and the sword in the stone 95–7
theft of cauldron from Annwn 140
and the Wirral 209–11
Arthur, grandson of Henry II 156
Arthur, son of Henry VII 10, 30, 235
Arviragus (Gweirydd), King of Gwynedd
    30, 53, 168, 202, 203, 206, 212, 214,
    215
Arwystl ap/son of Cunedda 172
Arwystli 174
Asaph, St 128
Ashe, Geoffrey *King Arthur's Avalon* 126,
    205
Asser *The Life of King Alfred* 14–15, 21, 65
Augustine, St 127
Avalon *see* Ynys Afallach

Badbury Rings, Dorset
    confusion with Caer Faddon 103
Badon *see* Caer Faddon
Bala 92, 137
Bala, Lake (Llyn Aerfen, Llyn Llyw, Llyn
    Tegid) 39, 92, 104, 114, 145, 151–2,
    185, 186, 189, 193, 196
Baldulf 97, 103
Bale, John 206, 207
Bangor–Is–y–Coed 127
Bangor–Is–y–Coed, Archdeacon of 22
Bangor–Is–y–Coed, Battle of 31
Bannog Mountain (Mons Bannauc,
    Mynydd Bannog) 195–6
bards 5, 15, 16, 17, 22, 33, 34, 36, 73, 74,
    114, 115, 131, 136, 146, 155, 163–4,

165, 176, 187, 188, 189, 190, 193,
    240, 241, 249
    see also Gogynfeirdd
Bartrum, Professor P. C.
    Welsh Classical Dictionary 18, 168
Baschurch 101
Basingwerk Abbey 64, 101
Bassaleg 101
Bassas, River 99, 101
Bath
    confusion with Caer Faddon 103
Beardsley, Aubrey 10
Bedd Gawr Benlli 79
Bedd Gwrtheryn 77
Bedd Rhita Gawr 185
Beddgelert 71, 223
Bede 11, 27, 36, 52, 60, 62, 103, 221, 222,
    244
    Chronicle 212
    *A History of the English Church and
    People* (*Ecclesiastical History*) 55, 63,
    212
Bedivere/Bedwyr 72, 149
Beeston Tor 94
Belgae 68
Beli, brother of Bran 111
Beli ap/son of Benlli Gawr 32, 40, 78–9
Beli Mawr ap/son of Mynogan, King of
    Ynys Prydein (Beli ap Mynogan) 125
Benedict, St 127
Benlli Gawr 79, 154
Bernica *see* Bryneich
Béroul
    Le Roman de Tristan et Iseut 89
Berwyn (Bre–wyn) Mountains 102–3, 142,
    171, 177, 195, 239
Bicanus 219, 223
Black Book of Carmarthen, The 102, 232
    Afallennau 113
Blasius, Bishop 95
Bodfari 171, 220
Bon y Don 226, 227
Bonedd Gwyr y Gogledd (Lineage of the
    Men of the North) 237
Bonedd Y Saint (Lineage of the Saints) 232
Boniface VIII, Pope 161
Book of Aneirin, The 240, 241
Book of Llandaff, The 11, 14, 67
Botwnnog 230
Brad y Cyllill Hirion *see* Treachery of the
    Long Knives
Bran Fendigaid 111, 126, 154, 233–4
Branwen the Daughter of Llyr 125, 233
Bravonium 103
Brecon (Brycheiniog) 72, 219
Breiddin 104
Brent 184
Brent Knoll 184
Brentmareis 184

Bretons 158
Bridgit, St 158
Bristol Channel *see* Mor Freinc; Mor Ud
Britain 27
   confusion with Ynys Prydein/ Britannia
      8, 15–16, 58, 60, 159, 160
   creation of Great Britain 10
Britannia *see* Ynys Prydein
Brithael 88
Britons 49–50, 53, 58, 60, 62, 68–9, 75,
   76, 81, 93, 97–8, 102, 103, 105–6, 127,
   141, 144, 159, 161, 163, 169, 190,
   193, 212, 226
Brittany 12, 123, 160, 194
   confusion with Llydaw 47–9
Brochwel 31
Bron (Hebron) 199
Bronze Age 142, 150
Broxton hundred 186
Brut (Y Brenhinedd) (Chronicle of the
      Kings) 12–14, 15, 19, 24, 26, 27, 28–9,
      30, 31, 33, 38, 39, 40, 43, 45, 46, 49,
      51, 52, 53, 56, 58, 63, 67, 68, 69, 71,
      72, 73, 76–7, 78, 80, 81, 82, 83, 87, 88,
      89, 90, 91, 94, 95, 96, 97, 98, 99, 100,
      102, 103, 105, 106, 107–8, 109, 113,
      115, 122, 131, 134, 136, 202, 214, 219,
      220, 231, 247
Brut y Tywysogion (Chronicle of the
      Princes) 11, 24, 32, 57
Brutus the Trojan 7, 12, 24, 29
Brychan 72, 219
Brycheiniog *see* Brecon
Bryn Afallen 175
Bryn Bannon 133
Bryneich (Bernica) 240, 242
   identified as Shropshire 34–8, 43, 64, 66
Brynglas, Caer Afallach 128
Buchedd Collen (The Life of Collen) 176–8
Bugi ap/son of Gwynllyw 219
Builth 162, 232
Buttington 104
Bwlch Rhiwfelen (Horseshoe Pass) 179
Bwlch Y Groes 39, 185
Bwlch Y Saethaeu 115
Bytwini, Bishop 229

Cadair (Cader) Dinmael 73, 75, 82, 86
Cadbury Castle, Somerset
   alleged site of Camelot 2
Cadell Ddyrnllug, Prince of Powys 152
Cader Dinmael 86
Cadog (Cadoc), St 195, 196, 208, 219, 220,
   222
Cador *see* Cadwr
Cadwaladr 12, 146, 156, 234, 235
Cadwallon 64
Cadwr (Cador) ap/son of Gorlois, Earl of
   Kernyw 91, 97, 106, 116, 105, 108, 137

Cadwy ap/son of Geraint 219
Caeaugwynion Mawr (Kayegunnion)
   101–2
Caer Afallach (Caerfallch, Caerfallach,
   Caerfallwch, Caerfllwch, Moel y Gaer)
   127–8, 132, 133, 137, 138, 142, 150,
   151, 154, 208
   located at Rhosesmor 126–7, 138
Caer Alclud 86, 102, 103, 105
   confusion with Rock of Dumbarton 80
   located at Melin Y Wig 80–1
Caer Cai (Caer Cynyr) 92–3, 186, 189, 217
Caer Caradog (Caer Garadawg) 81, 82, 127
Caer Ceint (Keynt)
   confusion with Canterbury 13, 57
   identified as Kenchester 57–8
Caer Cynan (Cunungeburg) 79–80, 81, 88
   confusion with Conisbrough 79
   located at Cefn Meiriadog 80
Caer Cynyr *see* Caer Cai
Caer Digoll 104
Caer Dunod (Dimilot, Dimilioc) 88, 90
   confusion with Tregare Rounds 90
Caer Drewyn 51, 142
Caer Efrog (Eboracum, Viroconium)
   28–9, 81, 85, 97, 100, 102, 106, 112,
   188, 214
   confusion with York 29, 33
   identified as Wroxeter 33, 37, 42–3
Caer Estyn 98
Caer Faddon (Badon, Monte Badonis) 8,
   17, 98, 99, 102,105, 228
   confusion with Bath and Badbury Rings
   103
   possible location at Breiddin 103–4
Caer Fuddai 50, 95–6, 100, 104
   confusion with Silchester 50
   identified as Machynlleth 50
Caer Fyrddein *see* Carmarthen
Caer Garadawg *see* Caer Caradoc
Caer Glini 148
Caer Gloyw *see* Caer Loyw
Caer Gwrtheryn 76
Caer Lingkoll *see* Caer Llwytcoed
Caer Llwytcoed (Caer Lingkoll, Caer
   Lyncoll, Lindsey)
   confusion with Lincoln 69, 98
   located in Hopedale 97–8
Caer Loyw (Caer Gloyw) 149, 202
   confusion with Gloucester 30–1, 152
   identified as Chester 30–1, 152
Caer Lyncoll *see* Caer Llwytcoed
Caer Ogrfan (Knucklas Castle, Castell
   Pendragon) 189
Caer Ogrfan (Old Oswestry) 106, 189,
   222
Caer Wrangon *see* Worcester
Caer Wynt 50, 53, 69, 73, 81, 84, 85, 94,
   112, 137, 142, 151

confusion with Winchester 13, 51, 113
identified as Corwen 51
Caerfallach/ Caerfallch/ Caerfallwch/
    Caerfllwch see Caer Afallach
Caerfyrddyn see Carmarthen
Caergwrle Castle 98
Caergybi see Holyhead
Caerlleon (Caerleon, Caerleon ar Wysg,
    Cardueil, Urbes Legionum) 28–9, 47,
    107, 112, 116, 126, 153, 184, 185,
    189, 206, 210, 214, 222, 229
  confusion with Caerleon on the Usk 31
  Cardueil/Carlisle confusion 210
  identified as Chester 31–3, 42–3
  identified as site of Battle of Urbes
    Legiones 102
Caernarfon (Aber Seint, Segontium) 46,
    47, 48, 65, 220, 221, 222, 223
Caerpenhuelgoit 13
Caersws 100
Caerwys (Caerhaas, Caerhass, Cairos,
    Quarrois) 226, 241
  identified as site of Arthur's court 228
Cafall (Caball), Arthur's dog 232
Cai see Kay, Sir
Caledfwlch see Excalibur
Caledonia
  confusion with Coedd Celyddon 101
Camborne 49
Camden 157
Camelot 2–3, 108–10
  modelled on Montgomery 110, 117, 217
Camlad, River 109–10
Camlan, Battle of 9, 38, 87, 91, 102, 106,
    113–16, 121, 122, 130, 131, 135, 137,
    145, 167, 222
  identified with Afon Gamlan 113, 115,
    137
  located at Rhinog Mountains 115, 117
Campus Elleti 72
Canhastyr Canllaw 148
Canterbury
  confusion with Caer Ceint 13, 57
Canu Llywarch 196
Capel Collen, Ruabon 179
Capel Marchell, Llanrwst 222
Capel y Gwial, Nannerch 229
Capetians 160
Capgrave Nova Legenda Angliae 206, 207,
    208
Caradoc of Llancarfan Vita Gildae (Life of
    St Gildas) 159, 165, 168, 186, 192,
    193, 194–5, 228, 242
Caradog Freichfras ap/son of Tywanedd
    173, 178, 219, 220, 223, 229
Cardigan Bay 171
Cardueil see Caerleon
Carley, Professor J. P. 208
Carlisle 63

confusion with Cardueil 210
Carlovingians 160
Carmarthen (Caer Fyrddein, Caerfyrddyn)
    47, 72, 73, 222
Carmarthenshire 76
Carnarvonshire 163
Carnedd Arthur, Snowdonia 115
Carreg Gwynion 102
Castell Dinas Bran (Castle of the Grail)
    153–4, 176, 216–17, 231
Castell Gawr 114
Castell Goronw 77
Castell Mynydd Agned (Castell Morynyon,
    Castle of the Maidens) 102
Castellmarch 222
    see also Dindagol
Castellors 204
Castellum Guinnion (Castello
    Guinnion/Gwynion) 99, 101–2
Castle Aber Lleiniog 241
Castle Galafort 200
Castle of Corbenic 200
Castle of the Grail see Castell Dinas Bran
Caswallan Llaw Hir, King of Gwynedd 108
Catraeth 240–1
  confusion with Catterick 240
Catterick
  confusion with Catraeth 240
Caw of Prydein (Cau Pritdin, Caunus,
    Cawr), Lord of Cwm Cowlwyd 151,
    194, 195, 196, 219, 226
Cawdraf ap/son of Caradog Freichfras
    178, 219
Cawr see Caw of Prydein
Cawres y Bwlch 179
Caxton, William 2, 109
Cedwyn, St 114
Cefn Digoll 104
Cefn Eurgain 128
Cefn Gwynnys 76
Cefn Meiriadog 80
Cefn Ucha 179
Celdric 103, 105
Celidon see Coed Celyddon
Celtic Church 127
Celtic Mother Goddess see Modron
Celtic Otherworld see Annwn
Celtic religion and mythology 2, 10,
    125–6, 129, 180
Ceneu ap/son of Coel 219
Cerdic, King of the West Saxons 225, 227
Ceredig ap/son of Cunedda 171
Ceredigion (Ceredigiawn) 171, 174
Ceri 174
Ceridwen (Aerfen, Y Wrach) 145, 146
Cerrigydrudion (Llancerrigydrudion) 73,
    101, 127
  identified as site of Giants' Dance 82–4,
    86

Chad, St 36
Chambers, E. K. *Arthur of Britain* 10, 12, 166
Chapter of St Andrew's and St David's
    213–14
Charlemagne 159
Charles, Prince 46
Cheldric 97
Chepstow 64
Chesire 21, 22–3, 94, 102
    see also Alban; Deifr
Chesire plain 126
Chester 35, 57, 65, 102, 135, 147, 188, 189,
    190, 196, 209, 227
    see also Caer Loyw; Caerlleon; Deva
Chester, Battle of 102, 127, 146
Chester, Robert 30, 202
Chester Apprentice Rolls for Ironmongers
    101
Chirk 105
Cholcrin *see* Colcrin
Chrétien de Troyes 17
    Erec et Enide 131, 134, 187, 228, 232
    Lancelot 109, 187
    Perceval 9
    Yvain (Owein ap Urien Rheged) 131, 210
Christianity 28, 140, 145, 166, 180, 206,
    212–14, 217
Church 75, 204
Cilgwri of *Culhwch and Olwen* 150–1
    see also Wirral peninsula
Cilydd ap/son of Cyleddon Wledig 219,
    221
Cistercians 9, 131, 135, 136, 164, 199–200
Claudius (Gloyw), Emperor 30–1, 202, 214
Clawdd Collen 179
Clemens, Prince of Kernyw 114
Clocaenog Forest 101
Clovis 159
Clud, River
    confusion with Clyde 80
    identified as Clwyd 80
Clwyd 142–3 *see also* Vale of Clwyd
Clwyd, River 171, 172
    confusion with Clyde 196
    see also Clud, River
Clwydian hills 79, 137
Clyde, River
    confusion with Clud 80
    confusion with Clwyd 196
Clywedog, (Clwedawg) River 171, 196
Coed Celyddon (Celidon) 98, 99
    confusion with Caledonia 101
    located at Clocaenog Forest 101
Coed Glas 190
Coel ap/son of Cunedda 172
Coel (Coillus) son of Marius, King of
    Britain 127, 202, 204, 214
Coel Hen (Coel Godebog) 126, 220, 221,
    223

Coillus *see* Coel
Colcrin (Cholcrin) 95, 97, 103
Coleddog ap/son of Cawdraf 178, 220
Collen, St ap/son of Pedrwn 176–81, 220,
    221
Concenn 52
Conisbrough
    confusion with Caer Cynan 79
Constantine, Emperor 33
Constans ap/son of Custennin Fendigaid
    50, 52–3, 54, 76–7, 85, 220
*Conversation Between Merlin and his Sister
    Gwenddydd, A* 22
Conway Abbey *see* Aber Conway Abbey
Conway (Conwy), River 75, 171, 174, 240
Cor Saeson 82–3
Cor y Cewri *see* Giants' Dance
Cornwall 27, 40, 97
    confusion with Kernyw 38, 49, 115, 229
    Tintagel/Dindagol confusion 89
    Tregare Rounds/Caer Dunod confusion
    90
    see also Llydaw
Corwen 101, 105, 171, 189, 195
    see also Caer Wynt
Council of Trent (1543) 75
Cowper Powys, J. 215
Craig Arthur (Cadair Arthur), Eglwyseg 179
Craig Bron Bannog 196
Craig Gwrtheryn 76
Craig y Forwyn 190
Crayford/ Creganford confusion 67
Creirwy ferch/daughter of Ceridwen and
    Tegid Foel 145
Croes Gwenhwyfar 190, 221
Croes Naidd 162, 163
Cross of Refuge 162
Crown of Arthur 162, 163
Crudel, King of North Wales 200, 206, 214
Crusades 9
Cuhelyn, Archbishop of Llundain 49, 50,
    53, 54
Cuillus *see* Huail ap/son of Caw
Culhwch ap/son of Cilydd 17, 91, 147,
    148, 219, 220, 221, 222
Culhwch and Olwen 17, 30, 38–9, 49, 91,
    106, 114, 140, 150, 151, 219, 220,
    221, 222, 228, 229, 231, 232
    see also Search for the Mabon, The
Cunedda Wledig (Cunedag) 126, 169, 170,
    172–3, 178, 187, 191, 208, 220, 221,
    241,
Cuno Bellinus 125
Cunungeburg *see* Caer Cynan
Custennin ap/son of Cadwr
    (Constantine) 91, 116, 131, 137
Custennin ap/son of Macsen Wledig 220
Custennin Fendigaid (Gorneu) ap/son of
    Cynfor 46, 50, 52, 59, 69, 219, 220

possible identification with
St Custennin 220
Cwmllan 115
Cwn Annwn (Cwn Bendith y Mamau,
Hounds of the Otherworld) 132, 140
Cwrs Cant Ewin 148
Cybi, St ap/son of Selyf 220, 221, 223
Cydfan ap/son of Arthur 232
Cyfeiliog 223
Cymry (Cambria, Cymru), realm of Ynys
Prydein, 29, 32, 71, 108, 187
confusion with whole of Wales 24–6
identified as Gwynedd/North Wales
24–6, 42
Cymry, Welsh word for Wales 14
Cynan Meiriadog ap/son of Eudaf Hen 47,
49, 80, 90, 146, 156, 219, 220
Cynderyn Garthwys 229
Cynfarch Oer ap/son of Meirchion Gul
220, 222
Cynfor ap/son of Tudwal 220, 223
Cyngar ap/son of Geraint 220
Cyngen, King of Powys 129, 215
Cynlas Goch 173
Cynvarch 91
Cynwal ap/son of Ffrwdwr 220, 221
Cynwyd 101
Cynwyl, St 114
Cynyr of Caer Gawch 220
Cynyr Farfog see Hector, Sir
Cyrn-y-Brain 179
Cywryd Ceint 57
Cywyllog (Cwyllog ferch/daughter of
Caw) 219, 220, 222

Dafydd, brother of Llewelyn 162
Dafydd ap/son of Edmund 190
Dafydd ap/son of Gwilym 189
Dafydd ap/son of Owain Gwynedd 240
Dafydd Nanmor 114
Danet see Ynys Danet
Dark Ages 3–4, 26, 45, 66, 80, 129, 152,
173, 237, 242
Darowen 223
David (Dewi), St 108, 220, 221, 222, 229
Dee, River (Dyfyrdwy, Peryddon) 36, 39,
93, 101, 111, 112, 114, 127, 137, 142,
151, 152, 153, 171, 174, 175, 176,
187, 188, 189, 190, 193, 195, 196,
197, 211, 215, 217, 221
called Deva 144
and the Goddess 144–6
see also Hafren
Dee estuary (Aber Peryddon) 15, 36, 64,
112, 126, 137, 146, 150, 151, 209
Dee valley 51, 137, 175, 239
Deganwy 231
Deheubarth see Lloegyr
Deifyr (Deira) 63, 144, 240, 242

identified as Chesire 34–8, 43, 64, 66
Denbigh 101, 102, 222, 241
Denbighshire (Powys Fadog) 73, 82, 86,
102, 132, 139, 142, 181, 197, 220, 238
Denw ferch/daughter of Lleuddun
Lwyddog 220
Derfel Gadarn 114–15, 137
Deruvian (Duvian, Duvianus, Donatianus,
Dwywan, Dyfan) 28, 212, 214
Derwen 171
Deva
ancient name for River Dee 144
Roman name for Chester 36, 144
Devon 27, 40
confusion with Dyfnaint 189
Dewi, St see David, St
Digain, St ap/son of Custennin 220
Diheufyr ap/son of Hawystyl Gloff 220
Dimilot see Caer Dunod
Dinarth 231
Dinas Bran see Castell Dinas Bran
Dinas Emrys 71, 73, 75, 77, 85, 221, 234
Dinas Verlorum (Verolamium) 93–4, 104
confusion with St Albans 94
Dinas y Garrei (Dwong chestyr,
Thongchester) 56, 59
located at Tong/Tong Sutton 58
Dindagol 38, 88, 92
confusion with Tintagel, Cornwall 89
identified as Castellmarch 89–90, 104
Dinhengroen 114
Dinhinlle Isaf 179
Dioneta, ferch/daughter of Gwyar 91
Dioneta, ferch/daughter of Eigyr 91
Dissolution of the Monasteries 207
Dogfael ap/son of Cunedda 171, 173
Dogfeiling 171, 173, 174, 176, 181, 195
Dolgellau 40, 115, 137
Domitian, Emperor 202
Don (Celtic goddess) 125
'Domesday Book' 80, 94, 150, 186, 208,
228–9
Doré, Gustave 10
Dovey, River see Dyfi, River
Dream of Macsen Wledig, The 46, 47, 49,
73, 220, 221, 222
Dream of Rhonabwy, The 17, 103–4, 113,
219, 223, 228, 232
Drudwyn (hound of the Otherworld) 148
Druids 71
Dubglas, River see Dulas
Dubricius see Dyfrig
Dulas (Dubglas), River 99, 97, 100–1, 227
Dunod ap/son of Cunedda, Earl of
Kernyw 90, 171
Dunoding 90, 171
Dwong chestyr see Dinas y Garrei
Dwrcelyn see Twrcelyn
Dyfan see Deruvian

Dyfed 76, 78 *see also* Lloegyr
Dyffryn Clwyd *see* Vale of Clwyd
Dyfi (Dovey), River 50, 97, 171
Dyfnaint (Dibneria, Dyfneint) 186, 193
    confusion with Devon 189
Dyfrig (Dubricius), Archbishop of
        Caerlleon 95, 96, 103, 108
Dyfwn ferch/daughter of Glywys 220
Dyfyrdwy, River *see* Dee, River

Eagle of Gwernanbwy 148, 151
Eaton Constantine 33
Ebbsfleet
    possible confusion with Port
        Ysgewit/Portskewett 68
Ebraucus *see* Efrog 80
Edeirnion 146, 151, 171, 187, 189, 193,
        195, 196, 197, 215, 219, 221, 226, 239
Edern ap/son of Cunedda 171
Edinburgh 36
Ednyfed *see* Idnerth
Edward, King of the Saxons 32
Edward I 160–1, 161–4
Edward II 163
Edward III 2, 163
Edward the Confessor 158, 163
Edwards, Thomas 128–9
Edwin, King 58
Efadier 232
Efrog (Ebraucus), King 80, 102
Eglwys Dudur 223
Eglywseg valley 176, 179, 181, 190, 193, 216
Egreas (Eugrad) ap/son of Caw 194
Eidol (Eidiol), Earl of Caerloyw 69, 79, 81,
        148, 150
Eigyr *see* Igraine
Einion ap/son of Ynor 162
Einion Yrth ap/son of Cunedda 171, 178
Eisteddfod 176
Eitha' byd 190, 193
Eleanor of Castile 160, 163
Eleanor de Montfort 162
Eledenius, Bishop of Alclud 80
Elen ferch/daughter of Eudaf 47, 80, 111,
        126, 220, 221, 222, 223
Elenid 174
Elerich ferch/daughter of Iaen 232
Eleutherius, Pope 212, 213, 214
Elfael 194
Elgud ap/son of Glast 173
Elidanus, Bishop of Caer Alclud 108
Elidir Sais 240
Elidon Hills 115
Eliffer Gosgorddfawr 221
Eliseg's Pillar 52, 215, 216, 223
Elvanus 212
Elwy, River 171
Emrys Wledig ap/son of Custennin
        (Ambrosius Aurelianus) 50, 52–3, 54,

76–7, 80, 81, 82, 83, 84–5, 94, 220, 221
    and Uther 78–81
Emyr Llydaw 91
England 10, 66, 145, 167
    confusion with Lloegyr/South Wales
        24–6
    Saxon (Anglia, Germania) 7, 8, 14, 56,
        58–9, 60, 84, 85, 93, 97, 98, 107
Enygeus *see* Eurgain
Eppa 84
Erbin ap/son of Custennin 220, 221
Erbistock 221
Erch 171
Erging (Archenfield, Herefordshire) 52,
        54, 232
Eryri *see* Snowdonia
Essyllt 101, 221
Ethni Wyddeles 178
Eudaf Hen 46–7, 80, 126, 221
Euddolen, ap/son of Afallach 126
Eurgain (Enygeus), sister of Joseph of
        Arimathea 199
Eurgain, St ferch/daughter of Maelgwn
        Gwynedd 128, 129
Eusebius of Caesarea *Chronicle* 62–3
Evans, Dr John Gwenogfryn 27–8, 36, 95,
        151, 238, 239, 240, 241
Evans, Theophilus *Drych Y Prif Oesoedd*
        (Mirror of the Chief Ages) 32
Ewias (in Herefordshire) 52, 54, 81
Excalibur/Caledfwlch (Caliburnis) 97, 103
Exeter 13

Farndon (Rhedynfre), Chesire 151
Ffagan *see* Phagan
Ffraw, River 114
Ffridd Faldwyn 110
Ffrwdwr ap/son of Morfawr 221
Ffynnon Armon 76
Ffynnon Arthur, Eglwyseg 179
Ffynonn Fair 150
Ffynnon Gollen 179
Ffynnon pen y Capel, Caer Afallach 128
Ffynon Dudur 223
Flintshire 64, 150, 151
Flintshire plateau 142–3
Foel Fenlli 79
Foel Las Hall 83
Ford of the Barking *see* Rhyd y Gyfarthfa
Forest of Dean *see* Ynys Danet
Fortunate Island 123
Fouke le Fitz Waryn 110, 210
France (Freinc) 48–9, 85, 159, 160
    Brittany/Llydaw confusion 47–9

Gabriel, Archangel 201, 203
Gadeon ap/son of Eudaf Hen 47, 221
Galahad 200, 204
Ganerew 77

Gardden ford 110
Garmon, St *see* Germanus, St
Garwen, mistress of Arthur 231
Garwy Hir 231
Gawain/Gwalchmai ap/son of Gwyar
   (Walwanum, Walwen) 80, 91,
   111–12, 116, 126, 134, 146, 204, 209,
   211, 221
Gelliwig (Kelliwig) 38
   confusion with Kelly Rounds 229
   located on Lleyn Peninsula 229–30
Gelliwig Farm 230
Geneid Hir 115
Geoffrey, son of Henry II 160
Geoffrey of Gaimar *L'Estoire des Englies*
   (The History of the English) 12
Geoffrey of Monmouth 11, 14, 135, 191
   Historia Regum Britanniae (The History
   of the Kings of Britain) 1–2, 3, 7–9,
   11–14, 15–16, 24, 26, 28, 29, 30, 31,
   33, 38, 39, 40, 45, 50, 51, 52, 57, 69,
   78–9, 81, 82, 83, 89, 94, 97, 98–9, 103,
   105, 107, 115, 122–3, 130, 131, 136,
   146, 156, 158–60, 164, 165, 183,
   185, 191, 202, 214, 246–7
   Vita Merlin (Life of Merlin) 123, 130, 140
Geraint ap/son of *Erbin*, Prince of
   Dyfnaint 189, 193, 221, 223
Geraint son of Erbin 221
Germania *see* England
Germanus, St (St Garmon) 52, 76, 79
Germany 59
Gerthmwl Wledig 229
Gewissi *see* Saxons
Giants' Dance (Cor y Cewri) 81–4, 85, 90,
   94, 127, 217, 221
   alleged location at Stonehenge 82
   located at Cerrigydrudion 82–4, 86
Gildas, St ab/son of Caw 11, 15, 24, 27,
   49, 50, 52, 60, 62, 129, 158, 165, 186,
   193–8, 219, 221, 222, 225, 226, 243–4
   De Excidio et Conquesta Britanniae (The
   Ruin of Britannia) 18, 55, 103, 243
   Epistola 208, 243
   Historias de Regibus Britanniae
   (Histories of the Kings of Britain) 194
Gilfaethwy ap/son of Don 125
Gillamuri, King of Ireland 82, 84, 85, 106,
   107
Giraldus Cambrensis 24, 125, 131, 132,
   145, 156, 157, 168, 195
   De Instructione Principium 131
   De Invectionibus 213
   Description of Wales 18–19
   Speculum Ecclesiae 131, 140
Glaestingaburh (Glassymbyri) 153, 165,
   167–8
   and the abduction of
   Guinevere/Gwynhwyfar 186–93

Arthur and the Abbey 183–6
   founding 169–76
   land granted to Joseph of Arimathea
      168, 201, 203, 206, 212, 214, 215
   St Collen and 176–81
   St Gildas and 186, 193–8
   and Valle Crucis Abbey, 215–17
Glaestings 173, 217
Glamorganshire 31
Glasgow 63
Glast (Glas, Glasteing) 124, 169, 173, 174,
   175, 181
Glastonbury
   alleged exhumations of Arthur 155–6,
      157–8, 160–1, 164, 200
   alleged links with Arthur and Avalon 3,
      124, 131, 155–8, 165–6, 167–8, 183–4,
      186, 191, 209–11
   alleged links with Joseph of Arimathea
      3, 166, 197–8, 200–1, 201–4, 206,
      207, 209
   alleged links with St Collen 181
   alleged links with St Gildas 193–4
   late arrival of Melkin tradition, 208
Glastonbury Thorn 3, 211
Glastonbury Tor 181, 209, 213
Glastonia
   confusion with Glastonbury 165,
      193–5
   first written connection with Avalonia
      131
   mistakenly called Urbs Vitrea (Glassy
      City) 168, 186
Glein, River 99
   Confusion with Glen 100
   identified as Nant Y Gleiniant 100
Gleiniant 100
Glen, River
   confusion with Gleint 100
Glesynfre *see* Ynys Afallach
Gloucester (Caer Glovi)
   confusion with Caer Loyw 30–1, 152
Gloucestershire 135
Glovi 30
Glywys ab/son of Solor 72, 221, 223
Glywyssing (Gleguissing) 72
Gododdin 240–1
Gofannon ap/son of Don 125
Gogledd Cymru (modern North Wales)
   238
Gogynfeirdd (Poets of the Princes) 17–18,
   28, 36, 80, 156, 229, 234, 238, 251
Goirre 187
Goleuddydd ferch/daughter of Amlawdd
   Wledig 91, 219, 221
Gop cairn 142–3
Gorlois (Gwrlois, Hoel), Duke of Tintagel,
   Earl of Kernyw 8, 79, 85, 88–9, 90,
   91, 97, 116, 131

Gormant ap/son of Ricca 91
Gracia ferch/daughter of Gwyar 91
Graeria ferch/daughter of Gwyar 91
Grassholm (Gwales) 233
Gratian, King of the Romans 49
Greid, son of Eri 149
Griscom, Reverend Acton 13
Gruffudd ap/son of Maredudd *I'r Grog o Gaer* (To the Chester Cross) 34–6
Gruffydd, Elis *Chronicle* 74–5, 195, 225–7, 228, 234
Gruffydd, Professor W. J. 152
Grufudd Hiraethog 73, 173
Guanius/Gunvasius/Gwynias *see* Melwas
Guaul *see* Wall of Severus
Guest, Lady Charlotte 17
Guigomar, Lord of Avalon 131, 134
Guinevere/Gwenhwyfar ferch/daughter of Ogryfran Gawr 9, 87, 106, 111, 112, 113, 116, 157, 165, 194, 195, 200, 221, 222
    abduction 186–93
Guto'r Glyn 15, 33, 164, 188
Gutun Owain 15, 31, 229
Guunnessi 76
Gwalchmai *see* Gawain
Gwald y Madron 153
Gwaltwen ferch/daughter of Afallach 125, 129
Gwawl ferch/daughter of Coel Hen 220, 221
Gweirydd *see* Arviragus
Gwen ferch/daughter of Cunedda 172, 219, 221
Gwen ferch/daughter of Cynyr (Tonwen) 220, 221, 222, 223
Gwenabwy ferch/daughter of Caw 151
Gwenddydd, sister of Merlin 75
Gwenhwyfar *see* Guinevere
Gwenn (Arthur's shield) 103
Gwennog 178, 221
Gwent *see* Keint
Gwernabwy 151
Gwerthefyriwg 67
Gwrangon, ruler of Keint 59
Gwrgi ap/son of Eliffer Gosgorddfawr 221, 223
Gwrhei, brother of Gildas, 197
Gwrhyr 149
Gwrial 232
Gwrlois *see* Gorlois
Gwron ap/son of Cunedda 172
Gwrtheyrn Gwrtheneu *see* Vortigern
Gwrtheyrnion 76
Gwrwst Ledlwm ap/son of Ceneu 221
Gwyar, daughter of Eigyr and Gwrlois 91, 134
    welded with Anna ferch Uthyr 91, 219

Gwyddfa Rita 39
Gwyddyl Ffichti (Irish Picts) 53–4
Gwydion ap/son of Don 125, 174
Gwydre, ap/son of Arthur 232
Gwyl, mistress of Arthur 231
Gwyn ap/son of Nudd, Lord of Annwn 140, 142, 177–8, 180, 184
Gwyn's Land 142
Gwynedd (Guenedota, Venedocia) 30, 39, 77, 78, 80, 126, 128, 135, 136, 138, 139, 161, 164, 166, 167, 169, 172, 185, 202, 208, 214, 240
    see also Cymry; Kernyw
Gwynedd, House of 162
Gwynfryn 233
Gwynllyw ap/son of Glywys 220, 221, 222
Gwynnog ap/son of Gildas 197
Gwynnys 76
Gwynwas 50
Gyn (Gwyn), frater W. 135

Hades 140
Hadrian's Wall 34, 62, 63, 147
    confusion with Offa's Dyke/Wall of Severus 4, 36, 60, 66, 142, 242
Haethfeld 58
Hafgan, Lord of Annwn 140
Hafod 193
    hafod/Somerset confusion 192–3
Hafren, River 187
    confusion with Severn 28, 30
    identified as Dee 31, 32–3, 43
    later ascribed to Severn 33, 188
Hales, monastery of 135
Halkyn church 150
Halkyn (Alchene, Mwyalchen) Mountain 126, 142, 150, 151
Hampshire 225, 227
Hanes Taliesin (Book of Taliesin) 59, 103, 140, 145
Hanesyn Hen 173
Hanover, House of 10
Hardyng, John *Chronicle of English History* 206–7, 208
Harlech 233
Harleian manuscripts 126, 169, 171, 173, 175
Harold II of England 158
Hart Hill 151
Hawystyl Gloff ap/son of Owain Ddantgwyn 222, 223
Hebron *see* Bron
Hector, Sir/Cynyr Farfog 92, 95, 96, 104, 130–1, 189
    called Timon 93
Helaius nepos Joseph 204
Helsby 211
Hen Domen 110

Hen Voelas 94
Henfynyw 84, 85, 220
Hengist 56, 59, 61, 65, 67, 68, 69, 71, 78, 79, 81, 88, 98, 111
Hengroen (St Cynwyl's horse) 114
Henllan 222
Henry I 2, 7, 158, 159, 161
Henry II 155, 157, 158, 159, 160
Henry III 110
Henry IV 22
Henry VII 10, 235
Hereford 57
Herefordshire 21 see also Erging; Ewias
Hermitage of St Mary Magdelene of Bekery 209, 210
Hertfordshire 94
Heswall Hill 214
Hevyn Felt see Maes Nefawel
Hexham 64
Higden, Ranulph Polychronicon 107
High History of the Holy Grail, The 210
Hilary, St 127
Historia Meriadoci 134
Historical Atlas of Wales, An 22
Hoel see Gorlois; Hywel
Holt 152, 186
Holy Grail 3, 9, 10, 121, 198, 199, 200, 205, 214, 216
Holyhead (Caergybi) 83, 211, 220
Holywell 112, 211
Honorius II, Pope 213
Hope 220
Hopedale 97–8
Horsa (Hors) 56, 67
Horseshoe Pass see Bwlch Rhiwfelen
Huail ap/son of Caw (Hueil, Cuillus), Prince of Alban 194, 195, 196, 219, 222
death 225–8, 241–2
Humber, River
confusion with Hwmyr 28, 33
Hwmyr, River 95, 111
confusion with Humber 28, 33
identified as Severn 33–4, 43
Hywel (Hoel) ap/son of Emyr Llydaw 91, 97, 103, 106, 108, 111
Hywel ab/son of Einion Llygliw 231
Hywel ab/son of Owain Gwynedd 238–9

Iaen 232
Iddog Cordd Prydein 113
Ider ap/son of Nudd 184
Idnerth (Ednyfed) 173
Iestyn ap/son of Geraint 222
Ieuan Gwas Padrig 83
Igraine/ Eigyr ferch/daughter of Amlawdd Wledig (Ygernam) 8, 79, 86, 88–9, 91, 92, 93, 104, 116, 126, 134, 172, 204, 219, 221
Illtud, St 219, 222, 223

Indeg, mistress of Arthur 231
Ine, King of Wessex 157
Ireland (Iwerddon) 31, 53, 81–2, 84, 106, 140, 191, 233
Irish (Gwyddyl) 32, 106
Irish Sea (Mor Iwerddon) 23, 39–40
Isle of Senna 123, 130
Italy 186
Iwerddon see Ireland

James, St 202
Jerome, St 62–3
Jesus Christ 9, 36, 76, 99, 115, 145, 162, 199, 201, 203, 213, 216
John of Glastonbury Chronica 184, 194, 195, 202–4, 205, 203, 207, 208, 209–10, 211, 213
John of Tinmouth Life of St Patrick 202
John Pecham, Archbishop of Canterbury 163
Johns, David 190
Jones, John 79
Jones, Professor T. Gwynn 36, 103, 156, 234
Jones, Professor Thomas 16–17
Joseph of Arimathea, St 125, 126
alleged links with Glastonbury 3, 166, 197–8, 200–1, 201–4, 209
arrival in North Wales (Norgales) 199–200, 214–15
granted lands in Ynys Wytrin 168, 201, 203, 206, 212, 214
Melkin's prophecy, 205–8
possible location of chapel under Valle Crucis Abbey 216, 217
Josephes, son of Jospeh of Arimathea 200, 201, 203
Josue 204
Julian, St (St Sulien) 51, 108
Julius Caesar 111, 125
Jurdan of Dindagol 88
Juvenal satires 30, 202

Kau, King of Scocie 194
Kay, Sir/Cai (Cei) 72, 95, 96, 149, 187, 189, 193, 227
Kayegunnion see Caeaugwynion Mawr
Keint (Keynt, Ceint, Guent) 54, 59, 61, 111
confusion with Kent 55, 59–60, 67
identified as Gwent 56–8, 67, 69
Kelly Rounds
confusion with Gelliweg 229
Kemble, J. M. 55
Kenchester see Caer Ceint
Kent
confusion with Keint 55, 59–60, 67
Kentigern, St (Cyndeyrn Garthwys) 220, 222, 223, 231

Kernyw (Cornubia) 88, 89, 90, 91, 101,
    108, 113, 186, 189, 193, 217, 219,
    confusion with Cornwall 38, 49, 115, 229
    identified as coastal region of
    Gwynedd/Lleyn Peninsula 38–9, 43
Kilara Mountain 82
Kilydd Canhastyr 148
Knighton 189
Knucklas Castle (Caer Ogrfan, Castell
    Pendragon) 189
Koran 216

Lady of the Lake 87, 97, 134
Lambord 204
Lancelot 9, 87, 200
Lanfor see Llanfawr
Layamont 81, 131
Leabhar Breathnach 65
Leintwardine 29, 103
Leland (Leyland), John 2–3, 157, 206, 207,
    208
Levelinus 83
Lewis Glyn Gothi 74, 114
Lewys Mon 74
Lhwyd, Edward 73, 179
    Parochialia 229
Liber Pontificalis 212
Lichfield (Maes y Cryph)
    confusion with Loytcoyt 173–4
Life of Grufudd ap Cynan, The 98
Life of King Alfred 64
Life of St Cadoc, The 47, 72, 195, 208, 219,
    221sp, 223
Life of St Goeznovious, The 58–9
Life of St Oswald, The 64
Lincoln
    confusion with Caer Llwytcoed 69, 98
Lindes farona see Lyndesei
Lindsey see Caer Llwytcoed
Linnius 99
Little Doward hill 77
Lives of the British Saints 181
Lives of the Welsh Saints 18
Lollius Urbicus 62
London 29, 114, 162, 163
    confusion with Llundain 29, 233
Long Mountain 104
Longdendale 23
Loomis, Professor R. S. 132, 134, 139–40,
    152, 200, 201
Lot see Lleu ap/son of Cynfarch
Loth 204
Loytcoyt (Escebtiorne, Lwydcoed)
    confusion with Lichfield 173–4
    identified as Loydcoyd, Rhos 174, 175
Lucius, Emperor 108, 110
Lucius, King of Britannia (Lles, Lucio of
    Britannio) 202, 212–15
Ludlow 30 see also Llundain

Lydgate, John 50
Lyndesei (Lindes farona) 56, 59
    located in Shropshire 58

Llacheu (Loholt) ap/son of Arthur 232
Llanallgo 194
Llanarmon Dyfryn Ceiriog 102
Llanarmon yn Ial 79
Llanbeblig 223
Llanbedrog 114
Llanbister 239
Llancadog 194
Llancerrigydrudion see Cerrigydrudion
Llandaf Cathedral 11
Llanderfel 114, 137
Llandrindod Wells 239
Llandudno 231
Llandyfrydog 223
Llandyrnog 223
Llanelidan 80, 223
Llanelwy see St Asaph
Llaneugrad 194
Llaneurgain 128
Llanfawr (Lanfor) 196
Llanferres 132, 238
Llanfihangel-ar-Arth 76
Llanfihangel Dinsylwy 223
Llanfihangel Glyn Myfyr 73, 90
Llangedwen chapel 114
Llangefni 220
Llangernyw 220
Llangoed 219
Llangollen 51, 52, 110, 137, 142, 143, 152,
    176, 179, 180, 181, 187, 188, 189,
    190, 193, 196, 216, 220, 221, 231
    see also Vale of Llangollen
Llangollen Church 178
Llangwm 222
Llangwn Dinmael 197
Llangwyllog 220
Llangybi 220
Llangynwyl see Penrhos
Llangystennin 220
Llanidloes 100
Llaniestyn, Anglesey 222
Llaniestyn, Lleyn 222
Llanrhaeader–ym–Mochnant 114
Llanrwst 222
Llanstephan manuscripts 151, 189, 195
Llanuwchllyn 92, 137, 223
Llanwnnog 197
Llawfrodedd Farchog 232
Lledin 231
Lleon Gawr 32
Lles see Lucius
Lleu (Llew) ap/son of Cynfarch (Lot) 91,
    93, 219, 222
Llevyn Sea 106
Llewelyn, Prince of Wales 160, 162, 163

Llewelyn the Great of Gwynedd 135, 164
Lleyn (Llyn) Peninsula 39, 43, 76, 77, 89,
    104, 172, 219, 222, 229–30 see also
    Kernyw
Lliwedd 115
Lloegyr (Deheubarth, Logres, Sudwallia)
    29, 39, 69, 108, 109, 187
  confusion with England 24–6
  identified as Dyfed/South Wales 24–5,
    42
Llongborth 232
Llowes 194
Lloyd, Professor 196
Lloyd, Reverend John 73
Lludd Silver–Hand 149
Llundain 28–9, 53, 54, 68, 69, 81, 86, 88,
    93, 97, 214, 233
  confusion with London 29, 233
  identified as Ludlow 29–30, 43
Lluyd, Edward 52
Llwyd, Angharad 229
Llwyn Danet see Tanet
Llwyn Huwcyn 128, 150
Llwytgoed 98
Llydaw (Amorica, Lettau, Letavia) 54, 76,
    78, 80, 90, 220
  confusion with Brittany 47–9
  identified as Cornwall 47–9, 69
Llygad Amr 232
Llygad Gwr 239
Llyn Aerfen see Lake Bala
Llyn Lliwbran 151, 152
Llyn Llumonwy 106
Llyn Tegid see Lake Bala
Llyr (Celtic god) 126, 233
Llyr Marini 178
Llys Meirchion 101, 222
Llywarch Hen 114, 196, 238
Llywelyn ap/son of Grufudd 36

Mabinogion, The 17, 31, 92, 139, 140, 174,
    221, 248
  see also Branwen the Daughter of Llyr;
    Culhwch and Olwen; The Dream of
    Macsen Wledig; The Dream of
    Rhonabwy
Mabon ap/son of Modron (Maponus)
    133, 146, 150, 152–3
  as name for Christ 216
  the search for 147–9, 150–4
Machynlleth 24, 39, 97, 101
  see also Caer Fuddai
Macsen Wledig see Maximus
Mael, brother of St Julian 51
Mael ap/son of Cunedda 172
Maelgwn Gwynedd (Maglocunus,
    Mailcunus) King of Gwynedd 125,
    126, 128, 129, 143, 169–70, 173, 229,
    230, 231

  identified with Melkin 208, 214
Maelienydd 239
Maelog (Mailocus, Meilig) see Melwas
Maelor 127, 152, 187–8, 190, 193, 197, 239
Maelor Gymraeg 152, 187–8
Maelor Saesneg 152, 187–8
Maen Huail, Ruthin 222, 227, 228
Maen y Bardd 73
Maes Beli
  located on Nercwys Mountain 78–9
Maes Glas 211
Maes Mawr 69, 71, 82
  identified with Maes Beli 79
Maes Nefawel (Hefenfelth, Hevyn Felt) 36,
    64
Maes Urien 51
Maes y Cryph see Lichfield
Maesbury 64
Magi 71
Magnus Maximus see Maximus
Magos 71
Maidens' Castle (Maidens' Tower) 102
Malory, Sir Thomas Morte D'Arthur 2, 10,
    109, 113, 134, 206, 227
Manael 204
Manaw Gododdin 170, 171
  alleged location in Scotland 241–2
  located in North Wales 241–2
March ap/son of Meirchion (Mark, King
    of Cornwall) 89, 101, 221, 222
Marchell ferch/daughter of Hawystyl
    Gloff 222
Marches 21, 109, 110, 117, 136, 147, 159,
    183, 210, 238
Marchia 105, 239
Marchwiel 175
Marcus Aurelius, Emperor 212
Marie de France Lanval 210
Marius (Meurig), son of Arviragus 30, 53,
    202, 204, 214
Mark, King of Cornwall see March ap/son
    of Meirchion
Marne, River 133
Martianus 56
Mary, St see Virgin Mary
Mary Magdalene 83
Mathilda 7, 8
Matrona see Modron
Mawddach 171
Mawddwy 185
Maximus (Macsen Wledig, Magnus
    Maximus) 46–7, 49, 52, 80, 111, 126,
    221, 222, 223
Medrad, River 222
Medrawd see Mordred
Medrod ap/son of Llew see Mordred
Medwin 212
Meirchion ap/son of Custennin 101, 220,
    222

Meirchion Gul ap/son of Gwrwst Ledlwm 221, 222
Meirion ap/son of Tybion 79, 171
Meirionydd 171, 185
Melchanstone 208
Melin Y Wig 80
Melkin of Avalon (Melchinus, Mewynus) 143, 204, 205–8, 214
Melwas (Guanius, Maelog, Mailocus), Prince of Alban 50, 165, 186–93, 195, 197
Men of the North 219, 220, 222, 223, 237
Menai Straits 240, 241, 226
Mercia 15, 23, 58, 64, 95, 98
Merfyn Frych, Prince of Gwynedd 241
Merlin/Myrddyn 8, 9, 10, 72, 76, 81, 82, 85, 86, 88, 92, 95, 101, 108, 113, 116, 146, 207
    called An ap y lleian 73–4
    early life 72–5
    and the Red Dragon 75
Merovingians 160
Merrick, King of Dyfed 108
Mersete hundred 239
Mersey 22, 23
Meurig see Marius 202
Michael, St 213
Midlands
    confusion with Y Berfeddwlad/Middle Lands 173–4
Mochdre (Mochdref), Rhos 174, 175
Mochdref, between Ceri and Arwystli 174
Mochdref, Ceredigion 174
Mochnant, Powys 174
Modena Cathedral 186
Modron (Matrona, Celtic Mother Goddess) 125, 129–30, 132–5, 138, 147, 154, 238
    association with the Dee 146, 152–3
    triple form 133–4, 154
Moel Famau (Moel Fammau, Mothers' Mountain) 132, 133, 146, 152, 154
Moel Gwynnys 76
Moel y Gaer see Caer Afallach
Monachlog 128–9, 150
Monmouth 11, 77
Mons Breguion 99, 102–3
Montgomery 110, 117, 217
Montgomery Castle 110
Montgomeryshire 197
Mor Caitness (Kaitness) 39–40, 95
Mor Freinc (Bristol Channel) 67–8
Mor Iwerddon see Irish Sea
Mor Ud (Severn estuary and Bristol Channel) 39–40
Moray Firth
    confusion with Rheged 105, 238, 240
Mordei 240
Mordrain, King of Saraz 203

Mordred/Medrod ap/son of Llew/ Medrawd 9, 51, 87, 91, 111, 112–13. 113–14, 115, 116, 117, 121, 134, 219, 220, 222
Morfa Rhianedd 230–1
Morfael ap/son of Glast 173
Morfawr (Gwrfawr) ap/son of Gadeon 222, 223
Morfran ab/son of Tegid 114, 145
Morfudd, ferch/daughter of Urien 132–3, 134
Morgan le Fay (Morgain la Fee, Morganis, Morgen) 121, 123, 130–2, 134, 135, 140
    called Argante 131
    called Oruen 134
    correlation with Modron 134–5, 138
Morgant, Bishop of Caer Fuddai 108
Morris, Lewis 190–1
Mortimer, Lord Edmund 22
Mound of Emrys 94
Mount Damen 85
Mwrieff see Rheged
Mwyalchen see Halkyn Mountain
Myfanwy Fychan 231
Mynydd Aran Mawr see Aran Mountains
Mynydd Bannog see Bannog Mountain
Mynydd Dolorus 102
Mynydd Kilara see Kilara Mountain
Mynydd Main/Maen 83
Mynyw (Henfynyw) see Henfynyw
Mynyw (St Davids) see St Davids
Myvyrian Archaiology 188

Nanheudwy 181, 187
Nannerch 227, 229
Nant Beryddon 146
Nant Craig y Moch 176
Nant Gwrtheyrn 76, 77
Nant Gwyn 142
Nant Y Gleiniant see Glein, River
Nant Y Meini 79
Nant y Wrach 133
Nantconwy 75
Nasciens 203
Native Americans 16
Nau, King of Scotia 195
Nennius 244
    Historia Brittonum 18, 24, 27, 30, 36–7, 49, 52, 56, 59, 60–2, 65, 67, 68, 69, 71, 72, 73, 76, 77, 79, 87, 99, 102, 113, 169–70, 222, 227, 232, 234, 244–5
Neolithic period 143
Nercwys Mountain 79
Nevyn 163
New Age movement 3, 121
Newcastle 63
Newport 222
Nitze, Professor 109

Noethon ap/son of Gildas 197
Non ferch/daughter of Cynyr 220, 221, 222
Nor ab/son of Owain Finddu 222
Normans 3, 11, 131, 234–5 see also
    Anglo–Norman monarchy
North Wales see Cymry; Gogledd Cymru
Northumbria
    confusion with Y Gogledd 33
    location of Deira and Bernica in Chesire
        and Shropshire 34–8, 63–4
Norwich Taxatio 179
Nudd (Nuth), King 184
Nyfain ferch/daughter of Bruchan 220, 222

Oakenholt 112
Octa 61, 65, 81, 85–6, 93
Offa 15, 64, 65
Offa's Dyke 15, 21, 36
    see also Wall of Severus
Ogof Llanciau Eryi 115
Ogrfan (Ogryfan) Gawr 106, 189–90, 222
Old Oswestry (Caer Ogrfan) 106, 189, 222
Oldest Animals motif 150
Olwen ferch/daughter of Ysbadden
    Pencawr 17, 147, 222
Onennau Meigion 22
Order (Knights) of the Garter 2, 163
Ordericus Vitalis 60
Oruen see Morgan le Fay
Ossa 61, 65, 80, 81, 85–6, 93
Oswald, St 36, 63–4
Oswestry 36, 64, 105, 106, 110, 189, 222
Otadini 241
Ouzel of Cilgwri 148, 150
Owain, Prince of Gwynedd 36, 80
Owain ap/son of Afallach 126
Owain (Owein) ab/son of Urien 132–3,
    134, 220, 223
Owain Ddantgwyn 117
Owain Finddu ap/son of Macsen Wledig
    223
Owain (Owen) Glyndwr 22, 24, 50, 164
Owen, Reverend H. T. 216
Owl of Cwm Cawlwyd 148, 151
Oxford 7, 8, 11

Palug's Cat 227
Pasgen 84, 85
Patrick, St 158, 213
Paul, St 213
Peblig ap/son of Macsen Wledig 223
Peckforton Hill 94
Pedrog, St 114
Peithien (Peteova) ferch/daughter of Caw
    194
Pembrokeshire (Penfro) 108, 233
Penaran 151, 186
Penarddun ferch/daughter of Beli Mawr
    125, 126

Penda, King of Mercia 63–4
Pengwern 179
Penllyn 92, 114, 185, 196
Penmon 223
Pennal 40, 100
Pennant, Thomas 77, 106, 178, 189
Penrhos (Llangynwyl)114
Penrhyn Bay 231
Penrhyn Blathaon
    identified as head of Wirral peninsula 95
Penrhyn Rhianedd 222, 229, 230–1
Penstrowed 197
Pentrefoelas 82, 83, 85, 94
Penycloddiau 102
Percy, Henry 22
Peredur ab/son of Cadwy 219, 223
Peredur ap/son of Eliffer 221, 223
Perferren 219
Perlesvaus 109–10, 201, 209, 210, 232
Pertinax 212
Peryddon see Dee, River
Peter the Apostle, St 128, 209, 211, 213,
    214
Petrus (Peter), cousin of Joseph of
    Arimathea 204
Phagan (Fagan, Faganus, Ffagan,
    Fugatius) 212, 214
Philip, St 202, 203, 213
Picton 208
Picts (Cruithnians) 8, 49, 50, 52, 59, 61,
    65, 77, 97, 98, 105, 106, 108, 111, 191
    of Powys 53–4
Pits, John 207, 208
Plant Annwn (Fairies) 140
Plantagenets 158–60, 164
Plas Gelliwig 230
Polden (Poldone, Poulden) 184
    identified as Poulton, Llangollen 186
Pomponius Mela 123
Pont y Brenhin 115
Port Ysgewit see Portskewett
Porth Hamo 111, 219
    confusion with Southampton 113
    located on Dee estuary 112
Porth Neigwl 230
Portskewett (Port Ysgewit)
    possible location of Ypwnesfloet 68
Poulton see Polden
Powys 52, 76, 104, 114, 139, 174, 185,
    194, 238
    see also Alban
Powys Fadog see Denbighshire
Preseleu (Preseli) mountains 232
Prestatyn 112
Princes of Glaestingaburh 173
Princes of Powys 152
Privilege of St Teilio, The 14
Procopius 141–2
Pryderi 174

Ptolemy 144, 241
  Geographia 36
Pulford 146
Pwyll, Prince of Dyfed 140
Pynson, Richard *Lyfe of Joseph of Armathia* 200

Quaraduel *see* Rhuddlan
Quarrois *see* Caerwys

Radnorshire 194
Ralph Fitz–Stephen 158
Ralph of Coggeshall 157
Ranulph Higden *Polychronicon* 225, 227
Red Book of Hergest, The 105, 241–2
Red Dragon 75
Reginald, Earl of Cornwall 2
Reinecke, George 50
Rey Mabon (lay) 147
Rhayader 76
Rhedynfre *see* Farndon
Rheged (Mwrieff, Murefensium)
  confusion with Moray Firth 105, 238, 240
  located in Dee valley 105, 238–40
Rhieinwylydd ferch/daughter of Amlawdd
  Wledig 219, 223
Rhinog Mountains 115, 117
Rhita Gawr (Ricca) 39, 91, 185
Rhiw Lledin 231
Rhiw Vabon *see* Ruabon
Rhodri ap/son of Owain Gwynedd 240
Rhodri Mawr 24
Rhos 111, 171, 174, 175
Rhosesmor 112
  identified as site of Caer Afallach 126–7, 138
Rhuddlan (Quaraduel, Rotelan, Rodelen)
  identified as site of Arthur's court 228
Rhufon ap/son of Cunedda 171
Rhufoniog 171, 174, 241
Rhun ap/son of Maelgwyn Gwynedd 129, 231
Rhyd Ben Clwyd 241
Rhyd Y Groes 103–4
Rhyd y Gyfarthfa (Ford of the Barking,
  Modron's Ford) 79, 132, 133, 142, 146, 152, 154
Rhys, Professor J. 133, 208, 240
Rhysfa Maes Cadfarch 178
Ricca *see* Rhita Gawr
Richard, Earl of Cornwall 89
Richards, Melville 151
Riothamus 117
Robert, Earl of Gloucester 2, 7, 8, 12, 159, 165
Robert de Boron *Joseph d'Arimathie* 199, 200
Robert de Torigny 12
Roberts, Brynley F. 124

Rock of Dumbarton
  confusion with Caer Alclud 80
  presumed region of Y Gogledd 237
Roden, River 188
Rodric, King of the Picts 53
Roger de Montgomery 110
Roman artifacts 65
Roman de Troie 130
Roman Empire 46
Roman Ravenna 147
Romans 3, 31, 49, 62, 144, 202
Rome 8–9, 10, 28, 46, 47, 49, 108, 110–11, 161, 202, 213
Ron Gymhynieit (Arthur's lance) 103
Ronwen, wife of Vortigern 59, 68
Ros *see* Rhos
Round Table 9
  held by Edward I at Caerleon 107
  held by Edward I at Nevyn 163
  'relic' at Winchester 2, 51
Ruabon (Rhiw Vabon) 65, 152, 175
Ruabon Church 178–9
Ruabon Mountain (Glasfre, Glesynfre,
  Mountain of Mabon) 142, 143, 153, 176, 180, 184, 188–9, 193, 216
Ruthin (Rhuthun) 195, 222, 226–7, 228, 242

Salisbury Plain
  alleged site of battle between Arthur
    and Mordred 113–14
  see also Stonehenge
Salmon of Llyn Llyw 149, 151–2
Samson, Archbishop of Caer Efrog 108
Sanan, wife of Maelgwyn Gwynedd 129
Sandde ap/son of Llywarch Hen 114
Sandde Bryd Angel, confused with
  Sandde ap/son of Llywarch Hen 114
Sangreal 226, 227, 228
Sarn Elen 40, 47, 221
Saxons 4, 18, 31, 54, 59, 61, 71, 75, 78,
  79, 81, 84, 85–6, 88, 93–4, 95, 97, 98,
  102, 103, 105, 106, 108, 111, 117,
  127, 152, 158, 159, 165, 184, 191,
  207, 225, 227
  called Gewissi 52
  invasion located in Gwent, not Kent
    55–60
  murder of the nobles 68–9
  Vortimer and 67–8
Scilly Isles 24
Scocia *see* Alban
Scotland 5, 115, 190
  Act of Union (1707)
  alleged location of Manaw Gododdin
    241–2
  alleged location of Rheged 238–40
  confusion with Alban 24–6, 98, 191, 196
  confusion of Celyddon/Caledonia 101
  confusion of Clud/Clyde 80

confusion of Hadrian's Wall with Offa's Dyke/Wall of Severus 4, 36, 60, 66, 142, 242
confusion with Y Gogledd 81, 230, 237–8
Edward I's claim to rule 161
Ysgotland (Wales in the hands of the Scotti) 191
Scots 8, 49, 97, 105, 106, 108, 111, 191
Scotti 61, 170, 191, 193
Scriptores Historia Augustae 62
Search for the Mabon, The 133, 147–9
Seint, River 46
Selfan ap/son of Geraint 223
Selyf ap/son of Erbin 221, 223
Severa 52, 223
Severn, River 23, 29, 54, 58, 59, 68, 103, 104, 103, 109, 110, 228
confusion with Hafren/Dee 28, 30
later identification with Hafren 33, 188
see also Hwmyr, River
Severn estuary 15, 22, 36, 40, 64, 65
Severus (Septimus Severus), Emperor 61–2, 63, 65, 69
Shrewsbury 64
Shropshire 21, 58, 101, 105, 189
see also Bryneich
Silbury Hill 143
Silchester
confusion with Caer Fuddai 50
Sir Gawain and the Green Knight 211
Skene, William F. The Four Ancient Books of Wales 141
Snowdon 39, 115
Snowdonia (Eryri) 46, 71, 75, 85, 115, 117
Solomon, King 203
Solor ap Nor 222, 223
Somerset 225, 227
confusion with hafod 192–3
see also Cadbury Castle; Glastonbury
South Wales see Lloegyr
Southampton
confusion with Porth Hamo 113
Sows Way 174–5
Spenser, Edward The Fairie Queen 93, 206
Spoils of Annwn, The 140
Spring of Galabes 81
St Albans
confusion with Dinas Verloram 94
St Asaph (Llanelwy) 80, 222, 231, 239
St Augustine's in the White Forest 210
St Davids (Mynyw) 84, 108, 220
St Fagan's 214
St George's Chapel, Windsor Castle 163
St Paul's, London 210
St Werburg Abbey 147
Stadtbibliothek, Bern 13
Staffordshire 22
Stag of Rhedynfre 148, 151
Stanzas of the Graves 73, 77, 111, 137, 146, 231

Stenton, Sir Frank 67
Stephen, King 7, 8
Stirling 63
Stonehenge
alleged site of Giants' Dance 82
Story of Myrddin Wyllt (Merlin the Wild) 74–5
Strata Marcella (Sdrettmares, Ystrad March) 227, 228
Strathclyde
Clud/Clyde confusion 80
Stryt y Hwch 175
Suite de Merlin 134
Sulien, St see Julian, St
Survey of Denbigh, The 174
Sylwein ferch/daughter of Geraint 223

Taliesin 145, 146
Tanet see Ynys Danet
Tattenhall 94
Tegeingl ferch/daughter of Cunedda (Tegid) 172
Tegeingl (place) 150, 172, 174
Tegid Foel 114, 145
Teifi (Teify), River 76, 171, 172
Teilio, Archbishop of Caer Efrog 108
Teme, River 29–30, 43
Temys, River
confusion with Thames 28, 29–30
identified as Teme 29–30, 43
Tennyson, Alfred Idylls of the King 10
Terre Foraine 200
Thames
confusion with Temys 28, 29–30
Theodosius, Emperor De Sancto Joseph ab Arimathea 203
Thomas, Earl of Arundel 110
Thongchester see Dinas y Garrei
Three Perpetual Harmonies 127–30, 153
Tintagel 2
Confusion with Dindagol 89
Tong 58
Tong Sutton 58
Tour of Wales, The 106
Tower of London 162, 163, 164, 233
Tract of the Twenty-Four Mightiest Kings, The 31–2, 59, 107
Trannon, River 100
Tre Beddau 83
Tre'r Ceiri 39
Treachery of the Long Knives (Brad y Cyllill Hirion) 68–9, 71, 77, 79, 81, 83, 127, 148
Trebellius 212
Trefeglwys 100
Tregare Rounds
confusion with Caer Dunod 90
Treharne, R. F. The Glastonbury Legends 166, 209

Tremeirchion 101, 222
Tren 187, 188
Trent, River 22, 23
Treuddyn 64
Trevor Hall 216
Triads 17, 57, 68, 106, 113, 115, 127, 133,
    150, 219, 221, 222, 223, 229, 231,
    234, 248
Tribal Hidage, The 58
Tribruit, River 99
    identified as Tyrfrwyd 102
Tripartite Indenture, The 22
Tristan 89
Trystan 101, 221
Tryston, River 101
Tudor Dynasty 10, 152, 235
Tudur 223
Tudur Aled 114, 146, 187 *Edeirnion* 187
Tudur Trefor, King of Caer Loyw 152
Tudwal ap/son of Morfawr/Gwrfawr
    222, 223
Twrcelyn (Dwrcelyn) 194, 195, 196, 219
Twrch Trwyth (boar) 232
Tybion ap/son of Cunedda 171
Tyfrydog 223
Tylwyth Teg (Bendith y Mamau, Y
    Mamau) 133–4
Tyrfrwyd, River *see* Tribuit, River
Tyrnog 223
Tywenedd ferch/daughter of Amlawdd
    Wledig 222, 223

Uffren (hell) 140
Ulfin of Rhyd y Caradog 88
Urbes Legiones 99
    identified as Chester 102
Urien Rheged 51, 103, 125, 129, 132–3, 134,
    154, 196, 219, 220, 222, 223, 238, 239
Urlard 204
Ursula, St 191
Usk, River
    confusion with Wysg 31–2
Uther Pendragon 8, 50, 52–3, 54, 76–7,
    82, 91, 95, 96, 104, 116, 117, 126,
    134, 172, 204, 220, 221, 223
    death 93–4
    and Eigyr 88–9
    and Emrys 78–81
    naming of 84–6

Vale of Clwyd (Dyffryn Clwyd) 80, 102,
    132, 154, 171, 173, 220, 222, 223
    Gildas' birthplace (Arecluta) 194, 196
Vale of Llangollen 175–6, 178–9, 181,
    184, 186, 187, 194, 216–17
Valentinian 56
Valle Crucis Abbey 52, 153, 164, 176,
    178, 179, 180, 181, 187, 188, 190,
    193, 215–17

Venedotia/Venedocia *see* Gwynedd
Vera Historia De Morte Arthuri 115, 135–7,
    164, 202, 208
Virgin Mary (St Mary) 99, 115, 125, 136,
    145, 150, 178, 179, 187, 201, 203, 204
Visigoths 46
von Eschenbach, Wolfram Parzifal 9
Vortigern (Guorthigern, Gwrtheyrn
    Gwrtheneu) 27, 30, 52–3, 61, 65, 67,
    68, 69, 71–2, 75, 77, 84, 85, 98, 111,
    126, 215, 223
    death 76–8
    and the Picts of Powys 53–4
    and the Saxon invasion 55–60
Vortimer 59, 67, 69
    and the Saxons 67–8
Vulgate Cycle 9, 91, 131, 136
    L'Estoire del Saint Graal 199–200, 201,
    203, 204
Vyrnwy Lake 189

Wace, Robert *Roman de Brut* 9
Wade–Evans, Reverend A. E. 4, 99, 208
    The Emergence of England and Wales 27
Wales 5, 7, 17, 26, 145, 159, 207
    Act of Union (1536) 10
    Edward I's annexation 161
    Edward I's plunder of sacred relics
        161–4
    Henry II's dislike 155
    Wellis/Wells confusion 174
    see also Cymry; Ynys Prydein
Wall of Severus (Guaul) 60–7, 95, 110,
    128, 141–2, 176, 242
    confusion with Hadrian's Wall 4, 36, 60,
        66, 142, 242
    as true identity of Offa's Dyke and
        Wat's Dyke 64–5
Walter, Archdeacon of Oxford 7, 8, 11,
    159
Walwen (person) *see* Gawain
Walwen (place) 112, 221
Wat's Dyke *see* Wall of Severus
Wearyall Hill 3
    confusion with Wirral peninsula 209,
        211
Wells
    confusion with Wellis 174
Welsh Birth of Arthur, The 91, 95, 134
Welsh Life of Arthur, The 94
Welshpool 58, 104, 228
Wenlock Abbey 64
Westminster Abbey 163, 209
Wheeler valley 142, 229
Whitchurch (Llanfarchell) 222
White Dragon 75
Whittington 210
Wigan 227
William I 111, 158

William of Malmesbury 111–12, 132, 158, 165, 168
De Antiquitate Glastoniensis Ecclesiae 124, 166, 168, 169, 173–4, 175, 183–4, 193, 201–2, 212–13
William of Newburgh 107
William Salesbury 164
Williams, Hugh 15
Wiltshire 68, 143
Winchester 2
confusion with Caer Wynt 13, 51, 113
Wirral peninsula (Cilgwri) 150, 151, 209–11, 214
confusion with Wearyall Hill 209, 211
see also Penrhyn Blathaon
Wonastow 67
Worcester (Caer Wrangon) 22, 29, 59
Worcester Cathedral 30
Worgret, Abbot 168
World's End 190, 193
Wrexham 98
Wright, Neil 13
Wroxeter see Caer Efrog
Wye, River 57, 77
Wynnstay Hall 188

Y Berfeddwlad (the Middle Lands) 175, 195–6
confusion with the Midlands 173–4
Y Croes, Caer Afallach 128
Y Gogledd (the North)
confusion with Northumbria 33
confusion with Scotland 81, 230, 237–8
Y Groes, Halkyn 150
Y Llysdir 73
Y Seint Greal (The Holy Grail) 126
Y Wrach see Aerfen
Ychain Bannog (magical oxen) 196
Ygernam see Igraine
ynys (island/realm confusion) 15–16, 123, 168, 238
Ynys Afallach (Isle of Avalon, Insula Avallonia) 9, 91, 116, 121–2
bounded by the Dee 143–4, 146
called Glesynfre 180
Glastonbury's claims 3, 131, 164, 165–6, 167–8, 203
the goddess of 132–5
the Isle of Apples (Insula pomorum) 122–3, 124, 130
Joseph of Arimathea's burial place (Melkin's prophecy) 205–6
landscape 133, 153–4, 216–17
links with Annwn 131, 133, 137–8, 140–1, 146, 166
located in Gwynedd/North Wales 126, 135, 137, 138, 164
merged with Fortunate Island 123
Morgan le Fay and 131, 134, 135

the realm of Afallach 124, 125, 132, 138
and the Three Perpetual Harmonies 127–30
visited by Phagan and Deruvian 213
and the Wirral 209–11
Ynys Danet (Tanet, Ruoihm) 56, 105
identified as Forest of Dean 57, 67
Ynys Mon see Anglesey
Ynys Prydein (Britannia) 11–12, 62, 137, 194, 196, 203, 208
arrival of Arthur's family 49–51
Arthur's right to kingship 92, 116, 117
chief ports 68
confusion with Britain 8, 15–16, 58, 60, 159, 160
connection with St Alban 94
Eastern boundaries 21–4
identified as Wales and the Marches 14–15, 16, 27, 42, 66–7
Maximus' dream 46–7
murder of the nobles 68–9
Procopius' visit 141
realms of 24–6, 108, 187
rivers and towns 28–39
Saxon invasions 52, 55–60, 84–6, 93, 95, 103
Three Perpetual Harmonies 127
Three Saintly Lineages 172–3
three seas 39–42
Three Tribal Thrones 229
Three Unfortunate Concealments and Disclosures 68, 233, 234
Three Womb Burdens 133
Uthyr crowned king 85
Ynys Wydrin (Mewetryne, Ynys Witrin, Ynys Wytherin, Ynysgutrin, Ynyswytryn)
associated with Avalon 168, 214
confused with city of glass 168, 186
granted to Jospeh of Arimathea 168, 201, 203, 206, 212, 214
oringinal name of Glaestingaburh 168
true meaning realm of Gwytherin/Vortigern 168
York 34, 61
confusion with Caer Efrog 29, 33
Ypwinesfleot 56
possible identification with Port Ysgewit/Portskewitt 68
Ysfael ap/son of Cunedda 171
Ysfeilion 171
Ysgotland 191
Yspadden 147
Ystrad Alun 79
Ystradwel ferch/daughter of Gadeon 220, 221, 223
Ystyfachau 77

STOP PRESS!

As this book was nearing completion we discovered an article about Wat's Dyke, the 40-mile-long earthwork in North Wales. The article in question, 'New Dating for Wat's Dyke', by Keith Nurse in *History Today* (August 1999, pp.3-4), reported the findings of an archaeological dig on a section of Wat's Dyke just south of the town of Oswestry.

Current opinion about the dyke would have us believe that it was constructed in the first half of the eighth century by Aethelbald, predecessor to the better-known King of Mercia, Offa. However, Keith Nurse's article reports that the remains of a hearth were found on the original ground level beneath the dyke, and that carbon-dated samples from it suggest that the date of the dyke's construction was about ad 446, 300 years earlier than previously thought. During the research for this book we had looked closely into all references in the source materials of walls or earthworks being constructed in Britain and this new carbon date finally proved a point we had long wondered about.

In the *De Excido Brittaniae* written by Gildas in around 540 we find a reference to the Romans building a wall in Britannia in the early part of the fifth century to protect the Britons from their enemies (Williams, 1899, p.37, n.18). This unusual reference has led many to dismiss Gildas as a corrupt source, as traditionally the only two walls built by Romans are those of Antonine and Hadrian in the second century. We propose that Gildas is entirely correct in what he says and that Wat's Dyke is the wall built by the Romans around 446. This leads us to consider whether the wall built by Severus around 200 incorporated the northern half of Wat's Dyke or the northern reaches of the earthwork known as Offa's Dyke from Ruabon to the village of Treuddyn.

The above serves as a prime example of why we should read what our source texts actually say, not what we want them to say. All too often it is only our modern, limited understanding of these sources that is corrupt, not the texts themselves.

Obviously this information regarding the dating of Wat's Dyke provides archaeological evidence that further supports the identification of the wall spoken of by Procopius related in Chapter 10 and establishes that there was indeed a wall running north and south in Britannia in the sixth century. It is no longer necessary to continue to presume that every reference to a wall means Hadrian's; furthermore, the geography based upon this presumption can now be returned to its correct context and our history returned to its origins. Of course this evidence also establishes beyond doubt that the location of the Otherworld was to the west of the wall – and so Avalon and the Land of the dead return home.